Annals of Anthropo

M000267026

Syndemics and Global Health: Implications for Prevention, Intervention, and Training

Merrill Singer, Nicola Bulled and Bayla Ostrach

Volume Coeditors

Satish Kedia and David Himmelgreen

General Editors

NATIONAL ASSOCIATION FOR THE PRACTICE OF ANTHROPOLOGY
A SECTION OF THE AMERICAN ANTHROPOLOGICAL ASSOCIATION

Annals of Anthropological
Practice 36.2

Annals of Anthropological Practice (2153-957X) is published in May and November on behalf of the American Anthropological Association by Wiley Subscription Services, Inc., a Wiley Company, 111 River St., Hoboken, NJ 07030-5774.

Mailing: Journal is mailed Standard Rate. Mailing to rest of world by IMEX (International Mail Express). Canadian mail is sent by Canadian publications mail agreement number 40573520. POSTMASTER: Send all address changes to Annals of Anthropological Practice, Journal Customer Services, John Wiley & Sons Inc., 350 Main St., Malden, MA 02148-5020.

Publisher: Annals of Anthropological Practice is published by Wiley Periodicals, Inc., Commerce Place, 350 Main Street, Malden, MA 02148; Telephone: 781 388 8200; Fax: 781 388 8210. Wiley Periodicals, Inc. is now part of John Wiley & Sons.

Information for Subscribers: Annals of Anthropological Practice is published in two one-issue volumes per year. Institutional subscription prices for 2013 are: Print & Online: US$67 (US), US$65 (Rest of World), €42 (Europe), £34 (UK). Prices are exclusive of tax. Australian GST, Canadian GST and European VAT will be applied at the appropriate rates. For more information on current tax rates, please go to www.wileyonlinelibrary.com/tax-vat. The institutional price includes online access to the current and all online back files to January 1st 2008, where available. For other pricing options, including access information and terms and conditions, please visit www.wileyonlinelibrary.com/access.

Delivery Terms and Legal Title: Where the subscription price includes print issues and delivery is to the recipient's address, delivery terms are Delivered Duty Unpaid (DDU); the recipient is responsible for paying any import duty or taxes. Title to all issues transfers FOB our shipping point, freight prepaid. We will endeavour to fulfil claims for missing or damaged copies within six months of publication, within our reasonable discretion and subject to availability.

Back Issues: Single issues from current and recent volumes are available at the current single issue price from cs-journals@wiley.com. Earlier issues may be obtained from Periodicals Service Company, 11 Main Street, Germantown, NY 12526, USA. Tel: +1 (518) 537-4700, Fax: +1 (518) 537-5899, Email: psc@periodicals.com.

Journal Customer Services: For ordering information, claims and any inquiry concerning your journal subscription please go to www.wileycustomerhelp.com/ask or contact your nearest office.

Americas: Email: cs-journals@wiley.com; Tel: +1 781 388 8598 or +1 800 835 6770 (toll free in the USA & Canada).

Europe, Middle East and Africa: Email: cs-journals@wiley.com; Tel: +44 (0) 1865 778315.

Asia Pacific: Email: cs-journals@wiley.com; Tel: +65 6511 8000.

Japan: For Japanese speaking support, Email: cs-japan@wiley.com; Tel: +65 6511 8010 or Tel (toll-free): 005 316 50 480.

Visit our Online Customer Get-Help available in 6 languages at www.wileycustomerhelp.com

Associate Editor: Shannon Canney
Production Editor: Sarah J. McKay, Email: napa@wiley.com
Advertising: Kristin McCarthy, Email: kmccarthy@wiley.com

Print Information: Printed in the United States of America by The Sheridan Press.

Online Information: This journal is available online at *Wiley Online Library*. Visit www.wileyonlinelibrary.com to search the articles and register for table of contents e-mail alerts.
Access to this journal is available free online within institutions in the developing world through the AGORA initiative with the FAO, the HINARI initiative with the WHO and the OARE initiative with UNEP. For information, visit www.aginternetwork.org, www.healthinternetwork.org, and www.oarescience.org.

Aims and Scope: The Annals of Anthropological Practice (AAP) is dedicated to the practical problem-solving and policy applications of anthropological knowledge and methods. AAP is peer reviewed and is distributed free of charge as a benefit of NAPA (National Association for the Practice of Anthropology) membership. Through AAP, NAPA seeks to facilitate the sharing of information among practitioners, academics, and students, contribute to the professional development of anthropologists seeking practitioner positions, and support the general interests of practitioners both within and outside the academy. AAP is a publication of NAPA produced by the American Anthropological Association and Wiley-Blackwell. Through the publication of AAP, the AAA and Wiley-Blackwell furthers the professional interests of anthropologists while disseminating anthropological knowledge and its applications in addressing human problems.

Author Guidelines: For submission instructions, subscription and all other information visit: www.wileyonlinelibrary.com

ISSN 2153-957X (Print)

ISSN 2153-9588 (Online)

Contents

SYNDEMICS AND HUMAN HEALTH: IMPLICATIONS FOR PREVENTION AND INTERVENTION

MERRILL SINGER
University of Connecticut

NICOLA BULLED
University of Connecticut

BAYLA OSTRACH
University of Connecticut

Use of the syndemics concept has diffused from medical anthropology to an array of health-related disciplines. This development reflects a growing awareness that diseases and disease sufferers do not exist in a vacuum and that many of the most damaging human epidemics are the possible or probable consequence, not of a single disease acting alone but of several diseases acting in tandem. Syndemics offer a useful conceptual framework for the study of global health inequality. As work guided by a syndemics perspective is conducted on a range of diseases and in diverse regions of the world, the practical health implications of this approach are beginning to unfold. [syndemics, practical applications, funding for syndemics research]

Over the last 20 years, the biocultural and political economic concept of syndemics—which draws attention to the role of adverse and unjust social conditions in the deleterious clustering and interaction of diseases—has emerged from several initial publications in medical anthropology into an increasingly widely used multidisciplinary disease model (Herring and Sattenspiel 2007; Himmelgreen et al. 2009; Littleton and Park 2009; Marshall 2005; Mendenhal 2012; Rock et al. 2009; Singer 2009; Singer et al. 2011; a continually updated syndemics bibliography is available at http://en.wikipedia.org/wiki/Syndemic). The growth in the recognized utility of the syndemics approach is evident in its diffusion across health-related disciplines and the ever-increasing pace of syndemics-related publications in the journals and edited books of various health-related disciplines. It has come to be recognized that health care must "increasingly address the management of individuals with multiple coexisting diseases" (Valderas et al. 2009:357). Because individual diseases do not exist in a vacuum, the same is true in terms of sufferer experience and management of disease and the burden of diseases on community well being. Additionally, there is growing awareness that many of the most damaging human epidemics across time and location—from the lethal influenza epidemic of 1918/19 to the contemporary global AIDS pandemic, and from Black Plague to the European diseases that devastated New World Native American populations—are the possible or probable consequence not of a single disease acting alone but of several diseases acting in tandem. Moreover, these

ANNALS OF ANTHROPOLOGICAL PRACTICE 36.2, pp. 205–211. ISSN: 2153-957X. © 2013 by the American Anthropological Association. DOI:10.1111/napa.12000

adverse synergies are promoted by social conditions and unjust structural relationships. As Mark Nichter observes, the syndemic idea, "is a useful conceptual framework for social science investigations into global health inequality that are sensitive to environments of risk and agents promoting risk, [and that take us beyond a narrow conception of] groups at risk and risky behaviors." (Nichter 2008:57). From an applied standpoint, an issue of critical importance is the prevention/intervention implications of syndemics understanding and action.

Syndemics involve the adverse interaction of diseases of all types (e.g., infections, chronic noncommunicable diseases, mental health problems, behavioral conditions, toxic exposure, and malnutrition) and as a result of such interaction produce an increased burden of disease in a population. For example, the WHO World Health Survey (Moussavi et al. 2007), which studied a sample of almost 250,000 adults from 60 countries to understand health-related outcomes and their determinants, used four chronic diseases (angina, arthritis, asthma, and diabetes) to determine mean health scores. The study found that an average of between 9.3 percent and 23 percent of study participants with one or more of these chronic diseases also suffered from comorbid depression. Notably, the researcher who conducted this study concluded that

> Depression produces the greatest decrement in health compared with the chronic diseases angina, arthritis, asthma, and diabetes. The comorbid state of depression incrementally worsens health compared with depression alone, with any of the chronic diseases alone, and with any combination of chronic diseases without depression. [Moussavi et al. 2007:851]

Similarly, SARS (severe acute respiratory syndrome), which the World Health Organization (2003) has labeled the first severe and readily transmissible new disease to emerge in the 21st century, was consistently found to produce the worst outcomes, including death, when it was syndemically linked with chronic ailments like diabetes and heart disease (Chan et al. 2003; Chen et al. 2005). In Hong Kong, for example, an analysis of over 1,700 SARS patients found that the case fatality rate for patients diagnosed with comorbid chronic conditions was 46 percent, compared to 10 percent for patients without such conditions (Leung et al. 2004). Likewise, in a case of pathogen–pathogen interaction, women with human papillomavirus (HPV) cervical infection who also are infected with HIV have 1.8 to 8.2 times higher rates of viral shedding (i.e., latent HPV reactivation and recurrence) compared with women not infected with HIV (Theiler et al. 2010). Some syndemics involve multiple diseases and health conditions that can be shown to have an additive effect, with the addition of each new condition into the mix contributing to an ever greater overall health burden (Brennan et al. 2012; Stall et al. 2007). The mechanics and significance of syndemics as well as the utility of a syndemics perspective can be illustrated by examining the interaction of chronic alcoholism and HIV infection. Both of these conditions are known to have damaging effects on brain function, including cognitive and motor impairments expressed as diminished executive functions, memory, visuospatial comprehension, and speed of cognitive processing (Fein et al. 2006; Pitel et al. 2007). Moreover, a growing body of clinical research indicates that in dually diagnosed individuals there is "adverse synergism of HIV infection and alcoholism on brain function [which] is consistent with neuroimaging reports of compromised hippocampal and associated member structures . . . " (Fama et al. 2009:1815). Neuropsychological studies of cognitive functioning have shown that comorbid individuals perform worse on established assessment batteries than do single diagnosis chronic alcoholic or HIV infected groups (Fama et al. 2009; Green et al. 2004; Rothlind et al. 2005). Notes Edith Sullivan (quoted in ScienceDaily 2009), who has directed some of the key studies on this syndemic, "Chronic heavy drinking co-occurring with HIV infection is highly prevalent, and the separate and combined untoward effects on the brain and its processes can be significant and disruptive of activities of daily living." While the precise pathways of disease interaction remain to be fully defined, it is evident that they involve both behavioral (e.g., drinking to self-medicate emotional costs of HIV infection, contributions of chronic drinking to HIV risk behavior) and biological (e.g., accelerated hippocampal damage, alcohol-accelerated HIV disease progression through reduced immunocapacity) factors (Samet et al. 2007; Stall et al. 2003).

While the intersection of chronic alcoholism and HIV infection can occur in any sector of the society, social and economic marginalization appears to play a significant role in this syndemic. In a study of three urban communities in Cape Town, South Africa, for example, Kalichman et al. (2006:147) report that significant factors in the relationship between drinking and sexual risk for HIV are the "pressures of living in poverty." These researchers found that "[i]ndividuals who perceived greater stress resulting from violence, crime, and discrimination reported greater risks for HIV infection" and that "alcohol use was related to both perceived stress and HIV risk behavior." (Kalichman et al. 2006:147). In a systematic review of the literature on alcohol use and sexual risk for HIV infection in sub-Saharan Africa, Kalichman et al. (2007) found that one of the factors linking poverty, drinking, and HIV risk is transactional sex. Additional factors include sexual coercion and assault of women. For the sufferers of the chronic alcoholism/HIV infection syndemic, consequences include facing challenges in maintaining prescribed medication regimes for HIV infection, keeping medical and other appointments, management of routine daily tasks, and fulfilling emotionally important interpersonal and kinship responsibilities. Immediate intervention implications of this syndemic include the simultaneous targeting of drinking patterns among individuals living with HIV infection, focusing on drinking establishments as sites of prevention education, the close monitoring of dually diagnosed individuals to ensure appropriate treatment, and the provision of training that assists individuals in handling cognitive and motor impairments. In addition, there is a critical need for broader interventions that address the social origins of this syndemic (including factors like poverty and discrimination) as a health disparity. As indicated by the Center for Excellence for Health Disparities Research at Georgia State University, differences in health experiences caused by racial, gender, and socioeconomic inequality that contribute to differing outcomes constitute "syndemics of disparity" (George State University 2011).

In another application of syndemics theory, several projects initiated by Jason Farley of Johns Hopkins University School of Nursing (Newswise 2011) addressed the interaction of HIV and drug-resistant tuberculosis in South Africa. Based on a recognition that both of these significant health problems must be treated simultaneously in dually infected patients, Farley's Co-INFECT intervention model involves intensive nurse monitoring and case management. In the program, nurses perform a "bundle of interventions," including diagnosing dually infected patients, following identified patients through the care trajectory, monitoring adverse drug events iatrogenically produced by having two treatment regimens, and tracking patient treatment adherence. In these examples, we see the value of a syndemics approach in both understanding the social embeddedness of disease, its interactive nature, and the importance for intervention of not treating diseases as independent entities. As Gassman et al. (2012:90) indicate, the traditional "'silo' approach is unfortunate because it leads to inefficiencies and less effective approaches to prevention" and treatment. Growing recognition of the importance of a syndemics approach to intervention is seen in the creation by the CDC of a grant opportunity entitled "Addressing Syndemics through Program Collaboration and Service Integration" (PCSI) (CDC-RFA-PS10–10175). PCSI is an approach to public health intervention that

> provides a way of thinking about public health work that focuses on connections among health-related problems, considers those connections when developing health policies and aligns public health activities with other avenues of social change to foster conditions in which all people can be healthy. [While the] usual public health approach to disease prevention often begins by defining the disease in question; a syndemic-oriented approach first defines the population in question, identifies the conditions that create and sustain health in that population, examines why those conditions might differ among groups and determines how those conditions might be addressed in a comprehensive manner. (CDC 2009)

As a result of grant announcements of this sort, a number of researchers, including contributors to this set of articles, have been funded to study syndemics and their public health implications.

This issue of *Annals of Anthropological Practice* examines the practical health implications of syndemic theory and perspectives. The issue consists of a set of articles by anthropologists, public health researchers, nurses, and others who are actively working on the study of syndemics. It addresses the global and local health impacts of syndemics and the implications of syndemics knowledge for medical, public health, and health social science practice. Focusing on syndemics in vulnerable groups across time and place, these articles investigate the intricacies of biosocial relationships and processes, reflecting both a new level of understanding of the nature of health and disease and the unique perspective of anthropology on human/environmental intersection, bioculturalism, and the political economy of health. A critical question uniting the papers in this issue is how does recognition of syndemics affect the work of applied medical anthropologists and colleagues from other disciplines involved in public health education, disease prevention, and treatment? Corollary issues that are addressed include specification of the biocultural pathways, linkage mechanisms, and patterns of disease interaction operating in various syndemics; how social conditions facilitate disease clustering and interaction; and the value of incorporating a syndemics approach in health training and education.

REFERENCES CITED

Brennan, Julia, Lisa M. Kuhns, Amy K. Johnson, Marvin Belzer, Erin C. Wilson, and Robert Garofalo
    2012 Syndemic Theory and HIV-Related Risk Among Young Transgender Women: The Role of Multiple, Co-Occurring Health Problems and Social Marginalization. American Journal of Public Health 102(9):1751–1757.

Centers for Disease Control and Prevention (CDC)
    2009 Program Collaboration and Service Integration: Enhancing the Prevention and Control of HIV/AIDS, Viral Hepatitis, Sexually Transmitted Diseases, and Tuberculosis in the United States. NCHHSTP White Paper. Washington, D.C.: U.S. Department of Health and Human Services. http://www.cdc.gov/nchhstp/programintegration/docs/207181-C_NCHHSTP_PCSI%20WhitePaper-508c.pdf, accessed May 16, 2012.

Chan, Johnny, Chun Ng, Yiu, Chan, T. Mok, S. Lee, S. Chu, W. Law, M. Lee, and P. Li
    2003 Short Term Outcome and Risk Factors for Adverse Clinical Outcomes in Adults with Severe Acute Respiratory Syndrome (SARS). Thorax 58(8):686–689.

Chen, Cheng-Yu, Chen-Hsen Lee, Cheng-Yi Liu, Jia-Horng Wang, Lee-Min Wang, and Perng Reury-Perng
    2005 Clinical Features and Outcomes of Severe Acute Respiratory Syndrome and Predictive Factors for Acute Respiratory Distress Syndrome. Journal of the Chinese Medical Association 68(1):4–10.

Fama, Rosemary, Margaret J. Rosenbloom, Margaret B. Nolan Nichols, Adolf Pfefferbaum, and Edith V. Sullivan
    2009 Working and Episodic Memory in HIV Infection, Alcoholism, and Their Comorbidity: Baseline and 1-Year Follow-Up Examinations. Alcoholism: Clinical and Experimental Research 33(10):1815–1824.

Fein, George, Jennifer Torres, Leonard J. Price, and Victoria Di Sclafani
    2006 Cognitive Performance in Long-Term Abstinent Alcoholic Individuals. Alcoholism: Clinical and Experimental Research 30(9):1538–1544.

George State University
    2011 Center of Excellence for Health Disparities Research (CoEX). http://coex.gsu.edu/, accessed March 9, 2012.

Gassman, Ruth A., Jon Agley, Jeanne D. Johnston, Susan E. Middlestadt, Marieke van Puymbroeck, and Ahmed H. YoussefAgha
    2012 Catalyzing Transdisciplinary Studies in Public Health: A College Health Survey and Data Platform. Health Promotion Practice 13(1):90–97.

Green, Jill E., Radu V. Saveanu, and Robert A. Bornstein
    2004 The Effect of Previous Alcohol Abuse on Cognitive Function in HIV Infection. American Journal of Psychiatry 161(2):249–254.

Herring, D. Ann, and Lisa Sattenspiel
    2007 Social Contexts, Syndemics, and Infectious Disease in Northern Aboriginal Populations. American Journal of Human Biology 19(2):190–202.

Himmelgreen, David A., Nancy Romero-Daza, David Turkon, Sharon Watson, Ipolto Okello- Uma, and Daniel Sellen
    2009 Addressing the HIV/AIDS-food Insecurity Syndemic in Sub-Saharan Africa. African Journal of AIDS Research 8(4):401–412.

Kalichman, Seth C., Leickness C. Simbayi, Ashraf Kagee, Yoesrie Toefy, Sean Jooste, Demetria Cain, and Chauncey Cherry
    2006 Association of Poverty, Substance Use, and HIV Transmission Risk Behaviors in Three South African Communities. Social Science & Medicine 62(7):1641–1649.

Kalichman, Seth C., Leickness C. Simbayi, Michelle Kaufman, Demetria Cain, and Sean Jooste
    2007 Alcohol Use and Sexual Risks for HIV/AIDS in Sub- Saharan Africa: Systematic Review of Empirical Findings. Prevention Science 8(2):141–151.

Leung, Gabriel M., Anthony J. Hedley, Lai-Ming Ho, Patsy Chau, Irene O.L. Wong, Thuan Q. Thach, Azra C. Ghani, Christi A. Donnelly, Christophe Fraser, Steven Riley, Neil M. Ferguson, Roy M. Anderson, Thomas Tsang, Pak-Yin Leung, Vivian Wong, Jane C.K. Chan, Eva Tsui, Su-Vui Lo, and Tai-Hing Lam

2004 The Epidemiology of Severe Acute Respiratory Syndrome in the 2003 Hong Kong Epidemic: An Analysis of All 1755 Patients. Annals of Internal Medicine 141(9):662–673.

Littleton, Judith, and Julia Park
2009 Tuberculosis and Syndemics: Implications for Pacific Health in New Zealand. Social Science & Medicine 69(11):1674–1680.

Marshall, Mac
2005 Carolina in the Carolines: A Survey of Patterns and Meanings of Smoking on a Micronesian Island. Medical Anthropology Quarterly 19(4):354–382.

Mendenhal, Emily
2012 Syndemic Suffering: Distress, Depression, and Diabetes Among Mexican Women in Chicago. Walnut Creek, CA: Left Coast Press.

Moussavi, Saba, Somnath Chatterji, Emese Verdes, Ajay Tandon, Vikram Patel, and Bedirhan Ustun
2007 Depression, Chronic Diseases, and Decrements in Health: Results From the World Health Surveys. The Lancet 370(9590):851–858.

Newswise
2011 Nurses to Play in Central Role of Managing South African Syndemic. http://www.newswise.com/articles/nurses-to-play-in-central-role-of-managing-southafrican-syndemic, accessed May 16, 2012.

Nichter, Mark
2008 Global Health: What Cultural Perceptions, Social Representations and Biopolitics Matter. Tucson: University of Arizona Press.

Pitel, Anne L., Thomas Witkowski, François Vabret, Bérengère Guillery-Girard, Béatrice Desgranges, Francis Eustache, and Hélène Beaunieux
2007 Effect of Episodic and Working Memory Impairments on Semantic and Cognitive Procedural Learning at Alcohol Treatment Entry. Alcoholism: Clinical and Experimental Research 31(2): 238–248.

Rock, Melanie, Bonnie J. Buntain, Jennifer M. Hatfield, and Benedikt Hallgríimsson
2009 Animal-Human Connections, 'One Health,' and the Syndemic Approach to Prevention. Social Science & Medicine 68(6):991–995.

Rothlind, Johannes C., Tanya M. Greenfield, Anne V. Bruce, Dieter J. Meyerhoff, Derek L. Flenniken, Joselyn A. Lindgren, and Michael W. Weiner
2005 Heavy Alcohol Consumption in Individuals with HIV Infection: Effects on Neuropsychological Performance. Journal of the International Neuropsychological Society 11(1):70–83.

Samet, Jeffrey H., Debbie M. Cheng, Howard Libman, David P. Nunes, Julie K. Alperen, and Richard Saitz
2007 Alcohol Consumption and HIV Disease Progression. Journal of Acquired Immune Deficiency Syndrome 46(2):194–199.

ScienceDaily
2009 HIV Infection and Chronic Drinking Have a Synergistic, Damaging Effect on the Brain. http://www.sciencedaily.com/releases/2009/07/090723175425.htm., accessed February 25, 2012.

Singer, Merrill
2009 Syndemics in Public Health. Introduction to Syndemics: A Critical Systems Approach to Public and Community Health. San Francisco, CA: Jossey-Bass.

Singer, Merrill, Ann Herring, Judith Littleton, and Melanie Rock
2011 In Syndemics in Public Health, In a Companion to Medical Anthropology. Merrill Singer and Pamela Erickson, eds, Pp 159–180. San Francisco: Wiley.

Stall, Ron, Thomas C. Mills, John Williamson, Trevor Hart, Greg Greenwood, Jay Paul, Lance Pollack, Diane Binson, Dennis Osmond, and Joseph A. Catania
2003 Association of Co-occurring Psychosocial Health Problems and Increased Vulnerability to HIV/AIDS Among Urban Men Who Have Sex with Men. American Journal of Public Health 93(6):939–942.

Stall, Ron, Mark Friedman, and Joseph A. Catania
2007 Interacting Epidemics and Gay Men's Health: A Theory of Syndemic Production among Urban Gay Men. In Unequal Opportunity: Health Disparities Affecting Gay and Bisexual Men in the United States. Richard J. Wolitski, Ron Stall, and Ronald O. Valdiserri, eds. Pp. 251–274. Oxford: Oxford University Press.

Theiler, Regan, Sherry L. Farr, John M. Karon, Pangaja Paramsothy, Raphael Viscidi, Ann Duerr, Susan Cu-Uvin, Jack Sobel, Keerti Shah, Robert S. Klein, and Denise J. Jamieson

  2010 High-Risk Human Papillomavirus Reactivation in Human Immunodeficiency Virus—Infected Women: Risk Factors for Cervical Viral Shedding. Obstetrics & Gynecology 115(6): 1150–1158.

Valderas, Jose M., Barbara Starfield, Bonnie Sibbald, Chris Salisbury, and Martin Roland

  2009 Defining Comorbidity: Implications for Understanding Health and Health Services. Annals of Family Medicine 7(4):357–363.

World Health Organization

  2003 Severe Acute Respiratory Syndrome (SARS): Status of the Outbreak and Lessons for the Immediate Future. Geneva: World Health Organization, CDS Information Resource Centre. http://www.who.int/csr/media/sars_wha.pdf, accessed May 16, 2012.

CULTURAL PHENOMENA AND THE SYNDEMIC FACTOR: SUBSTANCE ABUSE, VIOLENCE, HIV, AND DEPRESSION AMONG HISPANIC WOMEN

Rosa M. Gonzalez-Guarda
University of Miami School of Nursing and Health Studies

Brian E. McCabe
University of Miami School of Nursing and Health Studies

Amber L. Vermeesch
Michigan State University College of Nursing

Rosina Cianelli
University of Miami School of Nursing and Health Studies

Aubrey L. Florom-Smith
University of Miami School of Nursing and Health Studies

Nilda Peragallo
University of Miami School of Nursing and Health Studies

Researchers exploring the health of Hispanics in South Florida utilizing a combination of qualitative and quantitative research methods have identified that substance abuse, violence, risky sexual behavior, and depression are not only conceptualized as tightly interrelated health and social problems, but also hold together in a measurement model to represent an underlying phenomenon (i.e., the Syndemic Factor). The purpose of this study is to test hypothesized relationships between cultural phenomena and the Syndemic Factor among community-dwelling Hispanic women. Standardized questionnaires assessing Acculturation, Hispanic Stress, Familism, and the Syndemic Factor were administered to a cross-sectional sample of 548 Hispanic women from South Florida. Structural equation modeling was used to analyze relationships. The model explained 61 percent of the variance in the Syndemic Factor. There was a large positive relationship between the Syndemic Factor and Hispanic Stress, and a small inverse relationship between the Syndemic Factor and Familism. Women with high Hispanic Acculturation and low U.S. Acculturation scored lower on the Syndemic Factor than Integrated/Bicultural women. Familism buffered the relationship between Hispanic Stress and the Syndemic Factor. Structural, community, family, and individual prevention strategies that address underlying conditions associated with the Syndemic Factor must be developed and formally evaluated. [Hispanic women, syndemic, culture, HIV, depression, substance abuse, violence]

ANNALS OF ANTHROPOLOGICAL PRACTICE 36.2, pp. 212–231. ISSN: 2153-957X. © 2013 by the American Anthropological Association. DOI:10.1111/napa.12001

Hispanics living in the United States experience health disparities related to substance abuse, violence, risky sexual behavior, and depression. For example, Hispanics have higher reported rates of binge drinking (SAMHSA 2006), intimate partner violence (IPV) (Caetano et al. 2005), and HIV when compared to non-Hispanic whites (Centers for Disease Control and Prevention [CDC] 2011). Although Hispanics have comparable rates of mental health disorders, such as depression, to non-Hispanics (SAMHSA 2006), Hispanics appear to suffer more negatively from mental health problems when affected by other problems such as IPV (Caetano and Cunradi 2003). It has been suggested that substance abuse, violence, risky sexual behavior, and depression do not occur in isolation among Hispanics, but rather cluster together to comprise a syndemic (Gonzalez-Guarda et al. 2011b). A syndemic is a complex web of interacting, mutually enhancing epidemics tied together by common risk and protective factors (Singer 1996, 2009). Researchers exploring the behavioral and mental health of Hispanics in South Florida utilizing a combination of qualitative and quantitative research methods have identified that substance abuse, violence, risky sexual behavior, and depression are conceptualized by community-dwelling women and men as tightly interrelated health and social problems with common causes (Gonzalez-Guarda et al. 2010, 2011c). These qualitative data have driven quantitative research documenting that substance abuse, violence, risky sexual behavior, and depression hold together in a measurement model to form a latent factor—the Syndemic Factor—thus suggesting that these conditions represent an underlying phenomenon (Gonzalez-Guarda et al., 2011c). The combination of these findings add support that a substance abuse, violence, risky sexual behavior, and depression syndemic exists from both an emic and etic perspective.

Exploring the role that culturally related phenomena may play in placing Hispanics at risk or protecting them from syndemics is paramount to understanding and addressing health disparities among this population (Gonzalez-Guarda 2009). Previous qualitative research with Hispanics in South Florida has identified various cultural phenomena such as the acculturation process, stressors relating to being Hispanic in the United States, and close-knit families as being related to various behavioral and mental health conditions (Gonzalez-Guarda et al. 2010, 2011c). For example, in a qualitative study of Hispanic adult women in South Florida, one participant explained, "Here, the young people are very liberated. Here, everything is liberal. Here, everything is normal, children leave their homes, they get pregnant, they have sex with other partners, they smoke or take drugs, Like, it is all so normal" (Gonzalez-Guarda et al. 2011c:48). The purpose of this study is to test hypothesized relationships between Acculturation, Hispanic Stress, and *Familism*, and substance abuse, violence, risky sexual behavior, and depression (i.e., the Syndemic Factor) among a community sample of Hispanic women.

SYNDEMIC FRAMEWORK

Merrill Singer coined the term "*syndemic*" (Singer 1996) as a way to describe multiple, simultaneous, interwoven health problems occurring in populations also experiencing less than optimal physical and social conditions that increase the burden of disease among that population (Singer 2009:14). Within the context of a syndemic, the adverse effects of multiple epidemics or conditions are exacerbated by their co-occurrence. Singer's seminal work identified the first syndemic, the Substance Abuse, Violence, and AIDS (SAVA) syndemic, among poor inner city Hartford, Connecticut residents, primarily Hispanics and African Americans. In this community he observed a collection of interrelated circumstances (e.g., poverty, loss of adequate housing, family instability, drug-related violence, inequitable health care) that were related to an increased risk for and acquisition of AIDS and a collection of other diseases (Singer 1996). A syndemic differs from traditional concepts of comorbidity in that two or more health issues interact with social and poor physical conditions to increase the burden of disease among vulnerable populations (Singer 2009). Singer maintains that health-care providers and public health workers cannot focus on only one of the components of a syndemic, but must address all factors if the syndemic is to be addressed effectively (Singer 2006). The CDC's establishment of the Syndemic Prevention Network, a group of researchers, citizens, and government officials committed to safeguarding public health, provides evidence that a syndemic orientation is viable and important to addressing health disparities (CDC 2008).

A recent review of the literature further elucidated the nature of the SAVA syndemic among women. SAVA's influence on several conditions was examined, including HIV-related risk behavior and mental health (Meyer et al. 2011). Overall, substance abusing women were more acculturated and educated, engaged in greater sexual risk behavior, and were significantly more likely to have experienced physical or sexual violence. The reciprocal nature of SAVA is exemplified by the findings that women who experienced violence were more likely to become substance abusers, and increased sexual risk behavior was correlated with substance abuse, IPV, and depression among women reporting those conditions concurrently. Socioeconomic factors were also impactful, as women who were in unstable housing and abusing substances were more likely to experience violence, regardless of HIV serostatus. Researchers argue that, among Hispanics, a syndemic orientation may provide an increased understanding of the relationships between the SAVA syndemic and mental health (Gonzalez-Guarda et al. 2008; Kurtz 2008). Recently scholars have developed conceptual models that describe and provide empirical support for syndemics, documenting that substance abuse, violence, risky sexual behavior, and depression represent an underlying phenomenon (i.e., the Syndemic Factor) among Hispanic women (Gonzalez-Guarda et al. 2011a, 2011c), and that these clustering epidemics disproportionately affect marginalized populations, such as men who have sex with men (MSM), by having a synergistic effect on increasing health risk (Stall et al. 2003). Although great progress have been made in understanding syndemics, more research is needed to uncover underlying phenomena that may give rise to these health and social disparities. This study aims to expand the conceptual basis for syndemics experienced by Hispanics by first testing whether cultural phenomena associated with being Hispanic in the United States are linked to the Syndemic Factor, and second, testing one possible avenue to mitigate the negative effects of these links. A sample of adult Hispanic women participating in a large HIV prevention trial that collected information regarding cultural phenomena and behavioral and mental health conditions was used to explore these relationships.

REVIEW OF THE LITERATURE

Acculturation

Acculturation is not a simple unidimensional process. Scholars have provided multiple conceptualizations of the acculturation process. These have ranged from descriptions of acculturation as a bipolar process (i.e., becoming more "American" and, therefore, less "Hispanic") to one that has multiple dimensions and allows for blending between cultures (Marin and Gamba 1996; Schwartz et al. 2010). Berry (1997) proposed a framework to understand the acculturation process as having four acculturation strategies or orientations. *Integrated* refers to preserving the culture of origin *and* embracing practices of the receiving culture. *Separated* refers to retaining values from the culture of origin, but not adopting practices from the receiving culture. *Assimilated*, the converse of separated, refers to adopting practices from the receiving culture, but not holding to values from the culture of origin. The fourth orientation, *marginalization*, refers to adhering to practices of either culture. Berry (1997) and other research groups (Gallo et al. 2009) have stated that in general, the Integrated/Bicultural strategy results in the most ideal equilibrium between integrating into the host culture and retaining practices of the culture of origin. Nevertheless, acculturation is often studied as a single dimension, heavily relying on language-based measures and failing to conceptualize the multidimensional process of cultural exchange between an individual's country of origin and her host country (Gallo et al. 2009).

Research investigating the relationship between acculturation and behavioral and mental health among Hispanics has documented mixed results. As Rogler et al. (1991) noted in their literature review, positive, negative, and curvilinear (i.e., bicultural levels being the most protective) relationships have been documented by researchers investigating the relationships between acculturation levels and the mental health of Hispanics. More than 20 years later, it still appears that the ambiguous nature of these relationships persists. For example, researchers have found that the higher the acculturation to the United States, the greater the sexual risk behaviors of the women (Moreno and El-Bassel 2007). Specifically, acculturation has been associated with an increase in sexual partners and in partners' HIV risk behaviors (Loue et al. 2003; Rojas-Guyler et al. 2005). Substance abuse and IPV have also been found to be positively associated with U.S. Acculturation among Hispanic women (Caetano et al. 2007).

Nevertheless, behavioral risk factors also have been documented among Hispanic women with low Acculturation to U.S. culture. Women with lower acculturation levels are less likely to be educated and less likely to use condoms than counterparts with higher acculturation (Moreno and El-Bassel 2007). Consequently, although less acculturated

Hispanic women may have fewer sexual partners (Loue et al. 2003; Rojas-Guyler et al. 2005), it appears that they are less likely to use condoms with the partners that they do have. Hispanic women with lower levels of acculturation also have been found to exhibit an unrealistic assessment of their own risks for HIV infection due to unawareness of their partners' extra-relational sexual activities and lower levels of HIV knowledge (Loue et al. 2003). They may also be at increased risk for HIV infection due to their lower levels of sexual communication and negotiation skills (Rojas-Guyler et al. 2005). They have also been found to score higher on depression scales when compared to more highly acculturated women (González et al. 2001).

Among Hispanic women, it appears that the relationship between acculturation and risk may vary according to the health behavior or condition being considered. It may also be possible that the inconclusive nature of these findings may be related to the fact that acculturation has often been studied in isolation from other phenomena (e.g., the climate toward Hispanics in geographical regions across the United States) that may also influence the behavior and mental health of Hispanics or the effects that acculturation has on these (Rogler et al. 1991). More research is needed to clarify the complex relationships between the acculturation process, other phenomena that influence experiences Hispanics have in the United States, and syndemic conditions.

Hispanic Stress

Hispanics in the United States represent a very heterogeneous group of individuals with origins in Spain or Spanish-speaking Latin America with varying countries of origin, ethnicity, acculturation levels, and cultural practices. Nevertheless, some scholars have found that this heterogeneous group experiences some common stressful events relating to being members of an ethnic minority group in the United States. Examples of these stressful events are problems with linguistic differences, changing personal and family values, changing gender role expectations, ability to meet daily needs, and immigrant status (Cervantes et al. 1991). There is a long tradition of research linking stress in general to a number of adverse outcomes. Dressler has quantified cultural consonance, the measure of agreement between individual behavior and cultural models, and has found that lower levels of cultural consonance are associated with higher perceived stress, in addition to depression and physical health indicators such as high blood pressure (Dressler 2004, 2012; Dressler et al. 2007). Among Hispanic women, Ickovics et al. (2002) found a positive association between higher stress, as measured by the community-based Inventory of Current Concerns (Nyamathi and Flaskerud 1992) and increased partner risk for sexually transmitted infections (STIs) (e.g., uncommitted relationships and unprotected intercourse). Acculturative stress, the stress associated with acculturating to the United States, has also been found to partially mediate the relationship between acculturation and risk for IPV among Hispanic women (Caetano et al. 2007). For example, among Hispanic women acculturation is inversely related to stress, which in turn is positively related to IPV. Nevertheless, research on the relationship between other types of stressors Hispanics may encounter and the behavioral and mental health of Hispanics is lacking.

Familism

Familism focuses on family unity among Hispanics and the belief that the family is interdependent, cooperative, and prioritized over an individual (Schwartz 2007). *Familism* is a multidimensional idea consisting of behavioral, structural, and attitudinal components and can directly influence health behaviors (Steidel and Contreras 2003). High levels of *Familism* mean that each member of the family has responsibilities and loyalties to the family unit and family members are consulted regarding health advice and important family decisions (Burk et al. 1995). The idea of *Familism* places the mother in the role of nurturer and protector of her children, which may lead her to put her children's needs above her own. In theory, Hispanic women with higher levels of *Familism* will have increased protection against sexual risk taking and consequently increased protection against HIV risk. Consistent with this perspective, Landau et al. (2000) found that increased knowledge and contact with family reduced the levels of sexual risk taking in their sample of Hispanic women.

Another way that *Familism* could benefit women is through a stress-buffering effect. The possibility of a buffering effect is similar to stress and coping theory (e.g., Cohen 2004). Support from the family, which could be conceptualized as a coping resource, may be particularly beneficial for women who experience high levels of stress. The direct relationships between reported levels of *Familism,* HIV risk, substance abuse, violence, and depression in addition to the role this cultural phenomenon may play in mitigating the effects of stress on behavioral and mental health outcomes need to be further addressed in the literature.

The current research was designed to address some of the aforementioned gaps in the literature concerning Hispanic women and substance abuse, HIV risk, violence, and depression (i.e., the Syndemic Factor). We tested the following research hypotheses: (1) Hispanic Stress will be positively related to the Syndemic Factor. (2) Family Support will be inversely related to the Syndemic Factor. (3) Acculturation will be related to the Syndemic Factor, such that (a) the Syndemic Factor will be greater for Separated women than Integrated/Bicultural women, and (b) greater for Assimilated women than Integrated/Bicultural women. (4) Family Support will moderate the relationship between Hispanic Stress and the Syndemic Factor.

METHODS

Design

Standardized, cross-sectional questionnaires were administered to participants of SEPA II (*Salud, Educación, Prevención y Autocuidado*—Health, Education, Prevention, and Self-Care), a randomized control trial of a group intervention designed for Hispanic women in the United States to reduce HIV risk, during their baseline assessments. These questionnaires were administered in English or Spanish to participants via face-to-face interviews conducted by bilingual, female study personnel between January 2008 and April 2009. All Spanish versions of measures used had been translated using a translation,

TABLE 1. Participant Characteristics and Syndemic Indicators ($N = 548$)

Variables	M	SD
Age	38.48	8.53
Years in United States	11.41	10.33
Depression	16.41	12.91
Partner violence	0.39	0.52
Lifetime abuse	1.07	1.49
Partner risk	0.15	0.36
Hispanic Stress	14.63	9.57
Family Support	4.01	0.74
	N	%
Employed	180	33
Family income < $2000/month	376	69
Community violence	140	26
STI history	37	7
Consistent condom use	84	15
Substance use	70	13

Note. Frequency (%) for positive answers shown for dichotomous variables.

back-translation, and verification process and found to be valid and reliable in previous studies (Peragallo et al. 2005; 2012). Although participants were followed for a 12-month period, only baseline assessments are used for this study because the SEPA intervention aimed to modify some of the variables of interests including HIV risk and IPV.

Sample and Setting

The sample consisted of 548 women from South Florida identifying as Hispanic or Latino, between the ages of 18 and 50, and reporting sexual activity in the past three months. A large proportion of the sample was recruited from a community-based organization (CBO) providing social services (e.g., English classes, childcare, tax assistance) to Hispanic, immigrants. Study personnel also recruited from other community-based settings (e.g., libraries, community clinics, churches) by posting flyers and making individual and group presentations about the study. Snowball sampling methods were also used (i.e., study participants were encouraged to tell family and friends). Assessments were conducted at the CBO and two study offices located in downtown Miami and Hollywood, FL. Table 1 summarizes characteristics of participants in this study.

Procedures

IRB approval was obtained for all study related activities. Candidates were screened for eligibility and scheduled over the phone for assessments. Upon meeting with candidates for their baseline assessments, assessors described study procedures, obtained informed consent, and completed the baseline assessment using a research management computer software system (Velos). These assessments took approximately three hours to complete. Participants were compensated $50 for their time and travel.

Measures and Variables

Control variables

Demographic information (e.g., country of origin, years living in the United States, income, health insurance status) was collected at the beginning of the assessment. The proportion of years lived in the United States and education was included as control variables based on findings from previous studies (Gonzalez-Guarda et al., 2011c). Education was dummy-coded (1 = at least a high school education, and 0 = less than a high school education).

Acculturation

The Bidimensional Acculturation Scale (BAS; Marín and Gamba 1996) was used to measure acculturation. This scale consists of 24 items that measure how acculturated Hispanics are to the U.S. culture (Americanism) and their culture of origin (Hispanicism). Examples of Americanism items are as follows: "how often do you speak English with your friends?" "How often do you watch television programs in English?" "How well do you write in English?" To score the BAS the 12 items that measure each cultural domain are averaged separately. Validity is supported by high correlation with criteria previously used for developing acculturation scales (Marín and Gamba 1996) in a sample of participants of Mexican and Central American heritage. In this study, the BAS demonstrated a high reliability for both the Hispanicism and Americanism subscales (Cronbach's α = .85 and .95, respectively). Scores for each domain can range from 1 to 4, with a score of 2.5 used as a cut-off point for low or high cultural activities. Berry's (1997) framework for understanding acculturation was used to assign women to three mutually exclusive categories: Separated (high Hispanicism, low Americanism), Assimilated (high Americanism, low Hispanicism), and Integrated/Bicultural (high Hispanicism, high Americanism). The marginalized (low Hispanicsim, low Americanism) was not used because no one fell under this category. For analysis, dummy variables were created for each group with Bicultural as the comparison group.

Hispanic stress

The Hispanic Stress Inventory (HSI; Cervantes et al. 1991) was used to assess Hispanic Stress. The immigrant version of this scale was used given the vast majority of the women in the study were immigrants (94 percent). The original version consists of 73 items divided into five subscales (Economic Stress, Parental Stress, Family/Cultural Stress, Marital Stress, and Immigration Stress). Examples of items on the Hispanic Stress Scale: "I have felt unaccepted by others due to my Latino culture." "Because of my poor English, people have treated me badly." "I have felt that I would never regain the status and respect that I had in my home country." The Parental Stress subscale was not used in this study because not all the participants were parents. These subscales demonstrated high reliability (Cronbach's α = .74, .80, .74, .83, respectively). The four subscales were summed to create a total Hispanic Stress Scale; this scale was log transformed for analyses to account for positive skew.

Familism

Familism was assessed through use of the *Familism* scale (Sabogal et al. 1987). This scale was created to assess the Hispanic cultural value that emphasizes the important role of family and loyalty and responsibility to family. The scale contains 15 items organized into three subscales: (1) Family Obligations (six items) indexes perceived obligation to assist the family (e.g., "A person should share her home with uncles, aunts or first cousins if they are in need"), (2) Family Support (three items) assesses beliefs that the family should be a source of social support (e.g., "One can count on help from her relatives to solve most problems"), and (3) Family as Referent (five items) assesses the belief that relatives should be used as behavioral and attitudinal referents (e.g., "One should be embarrassed by the bad things done by members of his family"). Reliability was not acceptable for two subscales, Familial Obligations (Cronbach's $\alpha = .61$) and Family as Referent (Cronbach's $\alpha = .57$), but was acceptable for Support from Family (Cronbach's $\alpha = .70$). Consequently, Support from Family was the only subscale used.

Substance abuse

An adapted form of the 9-item Substance Abuse Behavior Questionnaire (Kelly et al. 1994) was administered. For this study, a scale was created with three items: frequency of alcohol and illicit drug use (two questions) and being drunk or high before sex (one question) in the past three months. This subscale demonstrated good reliability (Cronbach's $\alpha = .77$). Due to extreme positive skew, this variable was coded as 0 (never on all items) and 1 (i.e., endorsing any item such as reporting being drunk before sex at least once in the past three months) for analysis.

Violence

Three variables were used to measure exposure to violence: lifetime exposure to abuse, community violence, and partner violence. Data on lifetime exposure to abuse and community violence were collected with the Violence Assessment, developed for a previous HIV risk reduction efficacy trial of SEPA (Peragallo et al. 2005) and adapted in a subsequent pilot study (Gonzalez-Guarda et al. 2008). The lifetime exposure to abuse scale summed six items of participant reports of ever having been physically, sexually, or psychologically abused during childhood (i.e., before age 18) and adulthood by someone other than a romantic partner. This subscale had good reliability (Cronbach's $\alpha = .74$). Community violence (one item) asked participants to report if they had ever lost a close friend or relative to a violent death, that is, suicide, homicide, or a substance abuse related accident (1 = yes, 0 = no). Although a fuller measurement of community violence that a woman might encounter was not feasible to administer in this study, this measure did provide information about the woman's environment. Partner violence was ascertained with the Partner-to-You (victimization) 10-item subscale of the Revised Conflict Tactics Scales, one of the most widely used instruments to measure IPV (CTS2; Straus and Douglas, 2004). The IPV subscale demonstrated strong reliability (Cronbach's $\alpha = .86$). To correct for positive skew, the square root of lifetime abuse and partner violence were used in analyses.

Risk for HIV

Two variables were used to measure risk for HIV: partner's risk for HIV and STI history. The Partner Table (Gonzalez-Guarda et al. 2008), which gathered information regarding the characteristics (e.g., demographics) and sexual behaviors of the participants' past five intimate relationships, was used to capture most recent partner's risk for HIV. Partner risk was assessed with six items, which asked participants to report whether their partner was ever drunk or high (during and not during sexual intercourse, four items), ever injected drugs (one item), and had sex with IV drug users, men, or commercial sex workers (three items). This scale had good reliability (Cronbach's $\alpha = .78$). The square root of partner risk was used for analysis due to positive skew. A health and sexual history was taken in which participants were asked their lifetime exposure to a list of STIs. Participants reporting diagnoses of one or more STIs in their lifetimes were coded as positive history of an STI ($1 = $ positive, $0 = $ negative).

Depression

The Center for Epidemiologic Studies Depression Scale (CES-D; Radloff 1977) was administered to assess depressive symptoms. This scale consists of a total of 20 questions asking participants to report the frequency (i.e., number of days in the past week) of experiencing depressive symptoms (e.g., not able to shake off the blues, having a hard time concentrating). Responses are added for a total score ranging from 0 to 60 points. Although this scale was used as a continuous measure, scores of 16 and above indicate a likelihood of clinical depression. This scale is widely used in population-based and community studies and has been translated and validated in Spanish (Roberts 1980). The CES-D demonstrated very good reliability (Cronbach's $\alpha = .94$).

Analysis Plan

Hypotheses were tested using SEM with Mplus 5.21 (Muthén and Muthén, 2007). Maximum-likelihood estimation was used to allow for the inclusion of all participants with missing data on endogenous variables. Previous analysis of SEPA II baseline data supported the proposition of a latent underlying variable composed of substance abuse, violence, risk for HIV, and depression representative of a syndemic (Gonzalez-Guarda et al. 2011b). Preliminary analyses used ANOVA and Bonferroni post-hoc tests for differences in Hispanicism, Americanism, percent years lived in the United States, and Hispanic Stress between women in the different acculturation orientations. Hypotheses were tested with a series of two models. A latent Syndemic Factor was used as the measurement model in both models. A measurement model was chosen as the analysis strategy because it allowed statistical modeling of the shared covariance between observed variables to test our proposition that the observed level of measured variables (depression, substance use, etc.) were the result of the level of an underlying, unobserved phenomenon (the Syndemic factor) plus measurement error. The path analysis part of the SEM model allowed us to test hypothesized relationships between hypothesized predictors (Acculturation, Hispanic Stress, and Family Support) and the unobserved Syndemic Factor. The path analysis tested relationships in a similar way to linear regression, for example, a positive coefficient indicated that as the level of the predictor variable increased, the level of the Syndemic Factor also increased. In Model 1, the first three hypotheses were tested simultaneously, with the Acculturation dummy variables, Hispanic Stress, and Family Support entered as exogenous variables, along with two control variables (percent years in the United States and education). Dummy-coded variables were used so that we could make comparisons between categorical variables. In Model 2, to test Hypothesis 4, one additional exogenous variable representing the interaction was added to Model 1. This exogenous variable was the product of Family Support and Hispanic Stress. To reduce possible collinearity between main effects and interaction variables, these variables were mean-centered (Garson 2011). In all analyses, model fit was evaluated with three fit indices: the relative χ^2 test, comparative fit index (CFI), and root mean square error of approximation (RMSEA). The relative χ^2 test (e.g., Kline 2009) adjusts for the effects of sample size on the χ^2 test and equals the χ^2 value divided by degrees of freedom, with values less than 3 indicating good fit. CFI (Bentler 1990) ranges from 0 and 1, with values $\geq$.90 indicating a good fit (Hu and Bentler 1999). RMSEA (Hu and Bentler 1999) values $\leq$.06 indicate good fit. Effect sizes for SEM coefficients were based on the suggestions of Kline (2009), with cutoffs of .10 as small, .30 as medium, and .50 as large.

RESULTS

The sample consisted of a diverse group of adult Hispanic women representing numerous countries in the Americas, with Columbia (34 percent), Cuba (13 percent), Peru (8 percent), and the United States (6 percent) being the most frequently reported countries of origin. Unlike other areas of the country where Mexican American and Puerto Ricans are the largest Hispanic subgroups, Hispanics in South Florida are more likely to be of Cuban origin or from South American countries such as Colombia, Nicaragua, and Peru (U.S. Census Bureau, 2011). Most of the women were white (53 percent), 42 percent did not report race (other than Hispanic), 4 percent were African American, and 1 percent were Asian or Native American. More detailed demographic characteristics of the sample are described in Table 1 and elsewhere (Peragallo et al. 2012).

Acculturation

The majority of women in this sample were in the Separated category (i.e., high Hispanic Acculturation and low U.S. Acculturation) ($n = 350$, 64 percent), with about a third in the Integrated/Bicultural group (i.e., high Hispanic and U.S. Acculturation) ($n = 175$, 32 percent), and a much smaller number in the Assimilated group (i.e., low Hispanic Acculturation and high U.S. Acculturation) ($n = 23$, 4 percent). No women had low scores on both dimensions, so none were coded as marginalized. Results of ANOVA showed significant differences in Hispanicism, $F(2,546) = 304.15$, $p < .001$, Americanism, $F(2,546) = 638.12$, $p < .001$, percent years in the United States, $F(2,546) = 127.67$, $p < .001$, and log Hispanic Stress, $F(2,546) = 9.56$, $p < .001$. With regard to Hispanicism, Bonferroni post-hoc analyses indicated significant differences between all three groups; Hispanicism was highest for Separated women ($M = 3.72$, $SD = 0.28$), followed by Integrated/Bicultural women ($M = 3.37$, $SD = 0.35$), and Assimilated women ($M = 2.23$, $SD = 0.33$). Post-hoc analyses also showed significant differences between all three groups in Americanism; Americanism was highest for Assimilated women ($M = 3.79$, $SD = 0.29$), followed by Integrated/Bicultural women ($M = 3.15$, $SD = 0.46$), and Separated women ($M = 1.87$, $SD = 0.43$). As with Americanism, post-hoc analyses also showed significant differences in percent years lived in the United States between all three groups, longest for Assimilated women ($M = 0.87$, $SD = 0.17$), followed by Integrated/Bicultural women ($M = 0.41$, $SD = 0.31$), and Separated women ($M = 0.21$, $SD = 0.17$). Post-hoc analyses indicated that Hispanic Stress was only significantly different between Separated women ($M = 16.05$, $SD = 9.81$) and Integrated/Bicultural women ($M = 12.20$, $SD = 8.78$), although Assimilated women were lower than both ($M = 11.48$, $SD = 7.27$). Although a log transformation was used in ANOVA to avoid violating assumptions of normality, the actual Hispanic Stress values are reported.

Hypotheses 1–3

Model fit was not satisfactory, χ^2 (49) = 114.61, $p < .001$, relative $\chi^2 = 2.34$, CFI = .88, RMSEA = .05, in the initial SEM model. One correlation between indicator errors in the measurement model (partner risk with partner violence) was added to the model after being suggested by a modification index. The modified model showed good fit, χ^2 (48) = 94.46, $p < .001$, relative $\chi^2 = 1.97$, CFI = .91, RMSEA = .04. Combined, all the exogenous variables accounted for a large amount (61 percent) of the variance in the Syndemic Factor. Standardized paths and loadings for this model are summarized in Figure 1. Both control variables were related to the Syndemic Factor: percent years in the United States, $\beta = .23$, $B = 1.36$, $SE = 0.32$, $p < .001$, and education, $\beta = -.12$, $B = -0.45$, $SE = 0.15$, $p = .002$. Consistent with Hypothesis 1, there was a large-sized relationship between the latent Syndemic Factor and Hispanic Stress, $\beta = .70$, $B = 1.48$, $SE = 0.15$, $p < .001$. Consistent with Hypothesis 2, there was a small-sized relationship between the Syndemic Factor and Family Support, $\beta = -.15$, $B = -0.33$, $SE = 0.09$, $p < .001$. With respect to Hypothesis 3, acculturation partially influenced the Syndemic Factor. Specifically, Assimilated women were not significantly different from Integrated/Bicultural women, $\beta = .01$, $B = 0.04$, $SE = 37$, $p = .91$, but Separated women were, $\beta = -.20$, $B = -0.68$, $SE = 0.17$, $p < .001$. That is, Separated women scored lower on the Syndemic Factor compared to Integrated/Bicultural women.

Hypothesis 4

This model showed good fit, χ^2 (55) = 101.20, $p < .001$, relative $\chi^2 = 1.84$, CFI = .90, RMSEA = .04. The addition of the interaction term to the model explains a significantly greater amount of variance in the Syndemic Factor, but the interaction itself was statistically significant. In this model, Hispanic Stress was positively related to the Syndemic Factor, $\beta = .70$, $B = 1.46$, $SE = 0.14$, $p < .001$, but Family Support was no longer significant, $\beta = .25$, $B = 0.54$, $SE = 0.40$, $p = .175$. Consistent with Hypothesis 4, the product (Hispanic Stress and Family Support) was significantly related to the Syndemic Factor, $\beta = -.40$, $B = -0.33$, $SE = 0.14$, $p = .021$. Figure 2 illustrates the

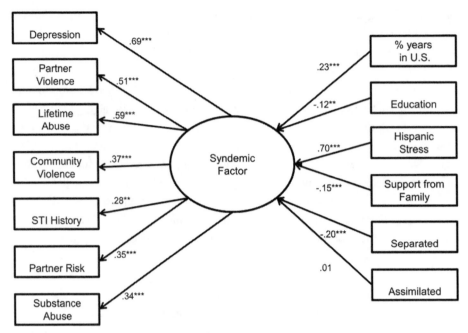

FIGURE 1. SEM of cultural variables predicting a latent Syndemic Factor.
Note. Standardized coefficients are shown. Error not shown. χ^2 (48) = 94.46, p < .001, relative χ^2 = 1.97, CFI = .91, RMSEA = .04. **p < .01, ***p < .001

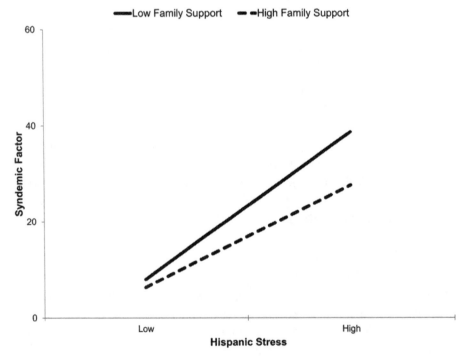

FIGURE 2. Estimated values of the Syndemic Factor for high and low Family Support and high and low Hispanic Stress.
Note. High = Mean + 1 SD; Low = Mean − 1 SD.

interaction with the Syndemic Factor, with estimated values at 1 SD above (high) and below (low) the mean of both Family Support and Hispanic Stress.

DISCUSSION

This study is the first, to our knowledge, to explore the relationship between intertwined behavioral and mental health conditions accounting for health disparities among Hispanic women (i.e., substance abuse, violence, HIV, and depression as a Syndemic Factor) and cultural phenomena that may place this population at risk for or protect them from this Syndemic Factor from a quantitative perspective. SEM results suggested that education, time in the United States, Acculturation, Hispanic Stress, and Family Support are related to, and account for a large amount of variance in, this Syndemic. This result supports the idea that for Hispanic women, cultural phenomena are an important influence on the interrelated conditions of substance abuse, violence, HIV risk, and depression. Further, the interaction between Hispanic Stress and Family Support adds information about an important mitigating relationship. Although it appears that Hispanic women with higher levels of stress are at an increased risk for the syndemic conditions under consideration in this study, strong Family Support can help buffer the effects of these stressors.

It is important to note that the effects of the proportion of the women's lifetime spent in the United States were controlled in these analyses, thus adding additional support to the importance of the acculturation process. Integrated/Bicultural individuals (high Hispanicism and Americanism) were used as the comparison group because integration and biculturalism has been associated with the best health outcomes (Berry 1997; Rojas-Guyler et al. 2005), but our results contrasted with these previous findings. Specifically, Separated women (low Americanism and high Hispanicism) had lower scores on the Syndemic Factor compared to Integrated/Bicultural women (high Americanism and High Hispanicism), and no differences were noted between Assimilated women (high Americanism and low Hispanicism) and Integrated/Bicultural women. One possibility is that because Separated women were more highly Hispanic than the Integrated/Bicultural women, these women ascribed to more traditional values associated with less sexual risk behaviors and substance abuse (Rojas-Guyler et al. 2005). It may be that women who ascribe to more traditional "Hispanic" values are more likely to be married, less likely to participate in risky behaviors, and be unaware of their partner's risk behaviors as has been documented in previous studies (Loue et al. 2003; Rojas-Guyler et al. 2005). Another possibility, consistent with the Separated women's much lower Americanism scores, is that U.S. culture is associated with greater health risks. This is consistent with qualitative findings describing the perception that substance abuse and sexual risk taking among Hispanic women is higher among women who are more assimilated to U.S. culture (Gonzalez-Guarda et al. 2011c). Lastly, Assimilated women did not score higher on the Syndemic Factor than Integrated/Bicultural women. This may be because Integrated or Bicultural women in this sample were struggling to negotiate between two cultures, a stressor that may have placed them at a comparable risk for the Syndemic Factor as the acculturated women. Future research with this population needs to be conducted to identify what aspects of the acculturating process are associated with health disparities among Hispanics. This research should take into account other potential phenomena that may be related to the acculturation process and confound these relationships (e.g., immigration status).

Hispanic Stress had a strong negative impact on the Hispanic women in this research study. In fact, Hispanic Stress had the largest relationship to the Syndemic Factor. This finding is consistent with previous research in which Hispanic Stress was associated with risk behaviors such as unprotected intercourse and increases in partner's sexual risk (Ickovics et al. 2002). It is possible that the psychological stress experienced by Hispanics that is related to immigration or discrimination processes and their lack of access to skills and resources to cope with these stressors may lead to maladaptive behaviors such as substance abuse, relationship conflict, risky sexual behaviors, and depression. These stressors appear to surface across several domains, including those related to economics, family, culture, marriage, and immigration, all subscales of the Hispanic Stress Inventory (Cervantes et al. 1991). However, because a total score was used to calculate Hispanic Stress, these results do not differentiate whether a subset of these stressors were responsible for an increase in risk for the Syndemic Factor. Future research needs to be conducted to identify which stressors are the most important predictors of the Syndemic Factor. This information could be useful in developing structural interventions aiming to prevent this syndemic among Hispanic women.

Family Support also appeared to have an important association with the Syndemic Factor. This result is consistent with past research showing that greater Family Support is associated with fewer sexual risk behaviors (Landau et al. 2000). More interestingly, the significant interaction with Hispanic Stress suggested that Family Support was particularly beneficial in the context of high Hispanic Stress. This effect is consistent with a social support buffering model from a stress-process perspective (e.g., Cohen 2004), with emphasis on the support women received from their families. This support is especially important for individuals or families experiencing higher levels of psychological stress associated with acculturation and discrimination.

Various study limitations need to be mentioned. First, the participants of this study included a convenience sample of Hispanic women from South Florida, an area in the United States where Hispanics represent the majority of the population (e.g., 65 percent in Miami-Dade County; U.S. Census Bureau 2011). Consequently, women from this study may have had more opportunities to maintain their Hispanic culture and navigate within their own language when compared to other Hispanic women living in areas with non-Hispanic majorities. Second, the *Familism* scale did not perform as intended. As a result, only one component of this phenomena, Family Support, could be examined. Further, this environmental context may have an impact on the amount of stress they experienced living as Hispanics in the United States. Results from this study do not rule out the possibility that alternative models may fit the data as well or better, and the cross-sectional nature of the data precludes strong causal inferences. Despite these limitations, this study provides an important contribution to the research literature by identifying important cultural phenomena that may link the substance abuse, violence, risk for HIV infection, and depression syndemic among Hispanics.

The findings from this study have important implications for the development of intervention strategies that aim to prevent or reduce the burden of syndemics among Hispanics. Hispanic Stress was found to be the most powerful predictor of the Syndemic Factor in this study. The measure used to capture stress encompassed a variety of phenomena (e.g., economics, immigration, discrimination) that could only be modified through structural interventions aimed at changing policies, opportunities, and norms that provide more support for this population. For example, in one of the qualitative studies informing the quantitative analysis presented in this article, Hispanic men identified structural unemployment (i.e., the unavailability of stable jobs, especially for undocumented individuals) as being a major stressor and "cause" of substance abuse and associated risk behaviors (Gonzalez-Guarda et al. 2010). In a similar study conducted with Hispanic women, participants described that although employment opportunities were scarce, that it was easier for women than men to find "under the table" service jobs as nannies or housekeepers. This created conflict in intimate relationships because women had to assume some of the traditional roles of men in regard to being the financial head of the household. This conflict was perceived as often resulting in violence (Gonzalez-Gaurda et al. 2011c). Policies limiting employment opportunities for Hispanics and other vulnerable populations that may face similar stressors must be critically analyzed and transformed to create more supportive environments where syndemics do not thrive.

In order to optimize the potential for prevention, structural interventions should be coupled with strategies targeting communities and families. Interventions must be developed to promote healthier norms around racial, ethnic and cultural diversity, gender-role expectations, and the maintenance of cultural and family ties. For example, this study found that women who are more "Hispanic" had lower scores on the Syndemic Factor. Community-level intervention strategies that promote *Hispanicism* (e.g., sponsoring cultural events) or support Hispanics (e.g., creating coalitions of culturally appropriate Hispanic service organizations) should be developed and formally evaluated for their potential to prevent or reduce syndemics. Family-level intervention that aims to preserve the strong ties that many Hispanics come with must also be developed. These interventions should address common stressors that Hispanics families may face in the United States (e.g., children and parents acculturating at different rates; less family support) and provide families with the skills (e.g., healthy communication) and strategies (e.g., work–family balance) to effectively cope with these stressful situations.

Lastly, the Transactional Model by Lazarus and Folkman (1984) suggests that in order to minimize the negative effects of stress and promote positive coping, one may alter an individual's appraisals of the threat of the stressor and her confidence of being able to cope effectively. This model supports the development of stress management interventions that provide Hispanics with the skills and resources to effectively cope with common stressors they may face, such as linguistic differences, changing personal and family values, changing gender role expectations, and ability to meet daily needs and immigrant status (Cervantes et al. 1991). Nevertheless, if these individually focused strategies are not combined with the structural, community and family level interventions previously discussed, it is likely that any improvements that are seen in regard to coping will not be sustained.

CONCLUSION

Substance abuse, violence, risk for HIV, and depression represent a Syndemic experienced by Hispanics. This Syndemic may represent an underlying phenomena shaped by health and social disparities. Acculturation, Hispanic Stress, and Family Support are cultural phenomena that explain a large amount of the variance in this Syndemic. While Hispanic Stress appears to be a risk factor for this Syndemic, high Hispanic Acculturation and Family Support protects Hispanic women from the Syndemic, especially those exposed to high levels of Hispanic Stress. Structural, community, family, and individually focused interventions that address common stressors Hispanic encounter, promote *Hispanicism*, provide access to community resources, and provide families and individuals with tools to effectively cope with a difficult environment are needed to prevent and reduce syndemics among this population.

NOTE

Acknowledgment. This research was funded by the National Center on Minority Health and Health Disparities (NCMHD) grant IP60 MD00266-Center of Excellence for Health Disparities Research: EL Centro (Nilda P. Peragallo, Principal Investigator).

REFERENCES CITED

Bentler, Peter M.
    1990 Comparative Fit Indexes in Structural Models. Psychological Bulletin 107(2):238–246.
Berry, John W.
    1997 Immigration, Acculturation, and Adaptation. Applied Psychology 46(1):5–34.
Burk, Martha E., Peggy C. Wieser, and Lynn Keegan
    1995 Cultural Beliefs and Health Behaviors of Pregnant Mexican-American Women: Implications for Primary Care. Advances in Nursing Science 17(4):37–52.
Caetano, Raul, and Carol Cunradi
    2003 Intimate Partner Violence and Depression Among Whites, Blacks, and Hispanics. Annals of Epidemiology 13(10):661–665. doi:10.1016/S1047-2797(03)00296-5
Caetano, Raul, Craig A. Field, Suhasini Ramisetty-Mikler, and Christine McGrath
    2005 The 5-Year Course of Intimate Partner Violence Among White, Black, and Hispanic Couples in the United States. Journal of Interpersonal Violence 20(9):1039–1057. doi:10.1177/0886260505277783
Caetano, Raul, Suhasini Ramisetty-Mikler, Patrice A. Caetano Vaeth, and T. Robert Harris
    2007 Acculturation Stress, Drinking, and Intimate Partner Violence Among Hispanic Couples in the U.S. Journal of Interpersonal Violence 22(11):1431–1447. doi:10.1177/0886260507305568
Centers for Disease Control and Prevention (CDC)
    2008 Syndemics Prevention Network. http://apps.nccd.cdc.gov/syndemics/network.asp, accessed January 3, 2012.
    2011 HIV Among Latinos. http://www.cdc.gov/hiv/latinos/index.htm, accessed January 7, 2013.

Cervantes, Richard C., Amado M. Padilla, and Nelly Salgado de Snyder
  1991 The Hispanic Stress Inventory: A Culturally Relevant Approach to Psychosocial Assessment. Psychological Assessment 3(3):438–447. doi:10.1037/1040–3590.3.3.438

Cohen, Sheldon
  2004 Social Relationships and Health. American Psychologist 59(8):676–684.

Dressler, William W.
  2004 Culture and the Risk of Disease. British Medical Bulletin 69:21–31.
  2012 Cultural Consonance: Linking Culture, the Individual and Health. Preventive Medicine 55(5):390–393. Accessed April 19, 2012, doi:10.1016/j.ypmed.2011.12.022

Dressler, William W., Mauro C. Balieiro, Rosane P. Ribeiro, and José Ernesto Dos Santos
  2007 Cultural Consonance and Psychological Distress: Examining the Associations in Multiple Cultural Domains. Culture, Medicine and Psychiatry 31(2):195–224.

Gallo, Linda C., Frank J. Penedo, Karla Espinosa de los Monteros, and William Arguelles
  2009 Resiliency in the Face of Disadvantage: Do Hispanic Cultural Characteristics Protect Health Outcomes? Journal of Personality 77(6):1707–1746.

Garson, G. David
  2011 Structural Equation Modeling. http://faculty.chass.ncsu.edu/garson/PA765/statnote.htm, accessed January 5, 2012.

González, Hector M., Mary N. Haan, and Ladson Hinton
  2001 Acculturation and the Prevalence of Depression in Older Mexican Americans: Baseline Results of the Sacramento Area Latino Study on Aging. Journal of the American Geriatrics Society 49(7):948–953. doi:10.1046/j.1532–5415.2001.49186.x

Gonzalez-Guarda, Rosa M.
  2009 The Syndemic Orientation: Implications for Eliminating Hispanic Health Disparities. Hispanic Health Care International 7(3):114–115. doi:10.1891/1540–4153.7.3.114

Gonzalez-Guarda, Rosa M., Aubrey L. Florom-Smith, and Tainayah Thomas
  2011a A Syndemic Model of Substance Abuse, Intimate Partner Violence, HIV Infection, and Mental Health Among Hispanics. Public Health Nursing 28(4):366–378. doi:10.1111/j.1525–1446.2010.00928.x

Gonzalez-Guarda, Rosa M., Brian McCabe, Aubrey Florom-Smith, Rosina Cianelli, and Nilda Peragallo
  2011b Substance Abuse, Violence, HIV and Depression: An Underlying Syndemic Factor Among Latinas. Nursing Research 60(3):182–189. doi:10.1097/NNR.0b013e318216d5f4

Gonzalez-Guarda, Rosa M., Johis Orlega, Elias P. Vasquez, and Joseph De Santis
  2010 La Mancha Negra: Substance Abuse, Violence, and Sexual Risks Among Hispanic Males. Western Journal of Nursing Research, 32 (1): 128–148, doi: 10.1177/0193945909343594.

Gonzalez-Guarda, Rosa. M., Nilda Peragallo, Maria T. Urrutia, Elias P. Vasquez, and Victoria B. Mitrani
  2008 HIV Risks, Substance Abuse, and Intimate Partner Violence Among Hispanic Women and Their Intimate Partners. Journal of the Association of Nurses in AIDS Care 19(4):252–266. doi:10.1016/j.jana.2008.04.001

Gonzalez-Guarda, Rosa M., Elias P. Vasquez, Maria T. Urrutia, Antonia M. Villarruel, and Nilda Peragallo
  2011c Hispanic Women's Experiences with Substance Abuse, Intimate Partner Violence, and Risk for HIV. Journal of Transcultural Nursing 22(1):46–54. doi:10.1177/1043659610387079

Hu, Li-tze, and Peter M. Bentler
  1999 Cutoff Criteria for Fit Indexes in Covariance Structure Analysis: Conventional Criteria Versus New Alternatives. Structural Equation Modeling 6(1):1–55. doi:10.1080/10705519909540118

Ickovics, Jeannette R., Susan E. Beren, Elena L. Grigorenko, Allison C. Morrill, Jennifer A. Druley, and Judith Rodin
  2002 Pathways of Risk: Race, Social Class, Stress, and Coping as Factors Predicting Heterosexual Risk Behaviors for HIV Among Women. AIDS and Behavior 6(4):339–350. doi:10.1023/A:1021100829704

Kelly, Jeffrey A., Debra A. Murphy, Carla D. Washington, Tracey S. Wilson, Jeffrey J. Koob, Debra R. Davis, Guadalupe Ledezma, and Bernadette Davantes
  1994 The Effects of HIV/AIDS Intervention Groups for High-Risk Women in Urban Clinics. American Journal of Public Health 84(12):1918–1922.

Kline, Rex B
  2009 Principles and Practice of Structural Equation Modeling. New York: Guilford Press.

Kurtz, Steven P.

    2008 Arrest Histories of High-Risk Gay and Bisexual Men in Miami: Unexpected Additional Evidence for Syndemic Theory. Journal of Psychoactive Drugs 40(4):513–521.

Landau, Judith, Robert E. Cole, Jane Tuttle, Colleen D. Clements, and M. Duncan Stanton

    2000 Family Connectedness and Women's Sexual Risk Behaviors: Implications for the Prevention/Intervention of STD/HIV Infection. Family Process 39(4):461–475. doi:10.1111/j.1545-5300.2000.39406.x

Lazarus, Richard S., and Susan Folkman

    1984 Stress, Appraisal and Coping. New York: Springer.

Loue, Sana, Marlene Cooper, and Jay Fiedler

    2003 HIV Risk Among a Sample of Mexican and Puerto Rican Men and Women. Journal of Health Care for the Poor and Underserved 14(4):550–565.

Marín, Gerardo, and Raymond J. Gamba

    1996 A New Measurement of Acculturation for Hispanics: The Bidimensional Acculturation Scale for Hispanics (BAS). Hispanic Journal of Behavioral Sciences 18(3):297–316. doi:10.1177/07399863960183002

Meyer, Jaimie P., Sandra A. Springer, and Frederick L. Altice

    2011 Substance Abuse, Violence, and HIV in Women: A Literature Review of the Syndemic. Journal of Women's Health 20(7):991–1006. doi:10.1089/jwh.2010.2328

Moreno, Claudia L., and Nabila El-Bassel

    2007 Dominican and Puerto Rican Women in Partnerships and Their Sexual Risk Behaviors. Hispanic Journal of Behavioral Sciences 29(3):336–347. doi:10.1177/0739986307303756

Muthen, Linda K., and Bengt O. Muthen

    2007 Mplus User's Guide (5th edition). Los Angeles: Muthen & Muthen.

Nyamathi, Adeline M., and Flaskerud, Jacquelyn

    1992 A Community-Based Inventory of Current Concerns of Impoverished Homeless and Drug-Addicted Minority Women. Research in Nursing and Health 15:121–129.

Peragallo, Nilda P., Deforge Bruce, O'Campo Patricia, Lee Sun, M. Kim, J. Young, Cianelli Rosina, and Ferrer Lilian

    2005 A Randomized Clinical Trial of an HIV-Risk-Reduction Intervention Among Low-Income Latina Women. Nursing Research 54(2):108–118.

Peragallo, Nilda P., Rosa M. Gonzalez-Guarda, McCabe Brian, and Cianelli Rosina

    2012 The Efficacy of an HIV Risk Reduction Intervention for Hispanic Women. AIDS and Behavior, 16(5):1316–1326. doi:10.1007/s10461-011-0052-6

Radloff, Lenore S.

    1977 The CES-D Scale: A Self-Report Depression Scale for Research in the General Population. Applied Psychological Measurement 1(3):385–401. doi:10.1177/014662167700100306

Roberts, Robert E.

    1980 Reliability of the CES-D Scale in Different Ethnic Contexts. Psychiatry Research 2(2):125–134. doi:10.1016/0165-1781(80)90069-4

Rogler, Lloyd H., Dharma E. Cortes, and Robert G. Malgady

    1991 Acculturation and Mental Health Status Among Hispanics: Convergence and New Directions for Research. American Psychologist 46(6):585–597.

Rojas-Guyler, Liliana, Nancy Ellis, and Stephanie Sanders

    2005 Acculturation, Health Protective Sexual Communication, and HIV/AIDS Risk Behavior Among Hispanic Women in a Large Midwestern City. Health Education & Behavior 32(6):767–779. doi:10.1177/1090198105277330

Sabogal, Fabio, Gerardo Marín, Regina Otero-Sabogal, Barbara V. Marín, and Eliseo Pérez-Stable

    1987 Hispanic Familism and Acculturation: What Changes and What Doesn't? Hispanic Journal of Behavioral Sciences 9(4):397–412. doi:10.1177/07399863870094003

Schwartz, Seth J., Jennifer B. Unger, Byron L Zamboanga, and Jose Szapocznik

    2010 Rethinking the Concept of Acculturation: Implications for Theory and Research. American Psychologist 65(4):237–251. doi:10.1037/a0019330

Schwartz, Seth J., Byron L. Zamboanga, Liliana Rodriguez, and Sherry C. Wang
  2007 The Structure of Cultural Identity in an Ethnically Diverse Sample of Emerging Adults. Basic and Applied Social Psychology 29(2):159–173. doi:10.1080/01973530701332229

Singer, Merrill
  1996 A Dose of Drugs, a Touch of Violence, A Case of AIDS: Conceptualizing the SAVA Syndemic. Free Inquiry in Creative Sociology 24(2):99–110.
  2006 A Dose of Drugs, a Touch of Violence, a Case of AIDS, Part 2: Further Conceptualizing the SAVA Syndemic. Free Inquiry in Creative Sociology 34(1):39–53.
  2009 Introduction to Syndemics. San Francisco: Jossey-Bass.

Stall, Ron, Thomas C. Mills, John Williamson, Trevor Hart, Greg Greenwood, Jay Paul, Lance Pollack, Diane Binson, Dennis Osmond, and Joseph A. Catania
  2003 Association of Co-occurring Psychosocial Health Problems and Increased Vulnerability to HIV/AIDS Among Urban Men Who Have Sex With Men. American Journal of Public Health 93(6):939–942. doi:10.2105/AJPH.93.6.939

Steidel, Angel, G. Lugo, and Josefina M. Contreras
  2003 A New Familism Scale for Use With Latino Populations. Hispanic Journal of Behavioral Sciences 25(3):312–330. doi:10.1177/0739986303256912

Straus, Murray A., and Emily M. Douglas
  2004 A Short Form of the Revised Conflict Tactics Scales, and Typologies for Severity and Mutuality. Violence and Victims 19(5):507–520.

U.S. Census Bureau.
  2011 State and County Quickfacts Miami-Dade County, Florida. http://quickfacts.census.gov/qfd/states/12/12086.html, accessed January 5, 2011.

U.S. Department of Health and Human Services, Substance Abuse and Mental Health Services Administration, Office of Applied Studies [SAMHSA].
  2006 Results From the 2005 National Survey on Drug Use and Health: National Findings. http://oas.samhsa.gov/nsduh/2k5nsduh/2k5results.htm, accessed January 5, 2012.

SYNDEMIC THEORY AS A MODEL FOR TRAINING AND MENTORSHIP TO ADDRESS HIV/AIDS AMONG LATINOS IN THE UNITED STATES

NANCY ROMERO-DAZA
USF Department of Anthropology

JULIE A. BALDWIN
USF Department of Community and Family Health

CELIA LESCANO
USF Department of Mental Health Law and Policy

HEATHER J. WILLIAMSON
USF Department of Community and Family Health

DAVID L. TILLEY
USF Department of Community and Family Health

ISABELLA CHAN
USF Department of Anthropology

MACKENZIE TEWELL
USF Department of Anthropology

WILSON R. PALACIOS
USF Department of Criminology

Syndemic Theory posits that an understanding of the HIV/AIDS pandemic can only be gained by examining the dynamic interaction of the disease with other health problems (e.g., tuberculosis, sexually transmitted infections, malnutrition, substance abuse), in the context of social and structural conditions such as poverty, unequal access to resources, violence, stigma, etc. While the theory has been extensively used to guide research, it has not been widely utilized as a training tool. This article presents a model for the use of Syndemic Theory as a framework for the training and mentorship of researchers and practitioners, particularly from underrepresented groups interested in HIV/AIDS prevention and treatment among ethnic minorities. [Syndemic Theory, Training and Mentorship, Minority Groups]

The usefulness of syndemic theory as a framework for understanding the complex nature of HIV/AIDS has been amply documented in the social science literature (Himmelgreen et al. 2009; Klein 2011; Kwan and Ernst 2011; Singer 1996, 2009b; Stall et al. 2008). However, the application of this theory for the training of researchers and practitioners, particularly from underrepresented groups interested in HIV/AIDS prevention and

ANNALS OF ANTHROPOLOGICAL PRACTICE 36.2, pp. 232–256. ISSN: 2153-957X. © 2013 by the American Anthropological Association. DOI:10.1111/napa.12002

treatment among ethnic minorities has been less discussed. This article addresses this important issue and presents a model for professional training and mentorship that would allow for interdisciplinary learning and practice, with the aim of providing trainees the needed tools to address the HIV/AIDS syndemic in a meaningful and applicable way. This article first provides an overview of the way in which syndemic theory has been used for the study of HIV/AIDS and then moves to the examination of existing models for the training of researchers and practitioners. It then presents the proposed model for the training of individuals particularly interested in conducting social science and clinical interdisciplinary research among Latinos in the United States using a syndemic approach.

INTRODUCTION TO SYNDEMIC THEORY AND HIV/AIDS AMONG RACIAL ETHNIC MINORITIES

Latinos are the fastest growing minority group in the United States, currently comprising 16.3 percent of the total population (Pew Hispanic Center 2011). Since 2000, the Latino population has grown to 43 percent, and is expected to account for 24.4 percent of the American population by 2050. Unfortunately, this rapidly growing minority group continues to be medically underserved and faces a disproportionately higher amount of health problems and health-care challenges as compared to white Americans and other minority groups. Health disparities including lower rates of adult immunizations and higher rates of diabetes, asthma, tuberculosis (TB), and HIV/AIDS disproportionately affect Latinos (Centers for Disease Control and Prevention n.d.a). According to the Pew Hispanic Center (2010), 24.7 percent of Hispanics lived in poverty as of 2010, making them the second largest minority group living in poverty after blacks at 26.7 percent. Moreover, Latinos experience societal, economic, and cultural differences that increase their vulnerability to HIV/AIDS, TB, and other health issues. Institutional discrimination creates emotional distress that can lead to risk-taking behaviors and which is exacerbated by the fact that undocumented individuals (a considerable number of whom are Latinos) are less likely to seek medical care (Castañeda 2010). In addition to the social and economic barriers, access to HIV/AIDS prevention information is hindered due to linguistic and cultural differences in messaging not relatable to Latinos.

In the United States, HIV/AIDS is one of the leading causes of death among Latinos between the ages of 25 and 44 years. In 2002, AIDS accounted for 10.4 percent of deaths among Latino men, and for 6.5 percent of deaths among Latino women (Anderson and Smith 2005). By 2007, HIV/AIDS was the third leading cause of death among Latinos aged 35–44 years (Centers for Disease Control and Prevention 2011b). Furthermore, by 2009, Latinos accounted for 20 percent of new HIV cases, and comparatively, the HIV infection rate among Latinos was almost three times that of white Americans (Centers for Disease Control and Prevention 2011b). The most common mode of HIV transmission among Latino men is male-to-male sexual contact, followed by injection drug use, which is also the second leading pathway of HIV transmission among women, behind heterosexual intercourse (Gonzalez et al. 2009). Latinos also face a faster rate of progression of HIV to AIDS and a greater number of HIV/AIDS-related deaths than white Americans (Gonzalez et al. 2009).

While HIV/AIDS has had a significant impact on morbidity and mortality among Latinos, the effects are magnified by the fact that the disease rarely occurs in isolation. HIV/AIDS is frequently linked with communicable diseases such as TB and a variety of sexually transmitted infections (STIs) (Centers for Disease Control and Prevention 2010; Singer et al. 2006). Moreover, a growing body of literature indicates that HIV/AIDS among Latinos often occurs alongside other co-occurring disorders such as depression, violence, and substance use, and that these issues are also linked with sociocultural and economic challenges, including discrimination, poverty, malnutrition, unemployment, and lack of access to healthcare (Gonzalez et al. 2009; Gonzalez-Guarda et al. 2011a, 2011b; Himmelgreen et al. 2009; Himmelgreen and Romero-Daza 2010). Therefore, it is evident that in order to gain a comprehensive understanding of the mechanisms that increase HIV/AIDS risk and result in disparities across ethnic groups, it is necessary to examine HIV/AIDS in relation to other health conditions with which it tends to co-occur and possibly interact.

As previously mentioned, nearly a quarter of Latinos in the United States live in poverty (Pew Hispanic Center 2011). They have been particularly hard hit by the recent U.S. recession, with their poverty rates increasing by six percentage points between 2006 and 2010—from 20.6–26.6 percent—the greatest increase of any ethnic group (Pew Hispanic Center 2012). Household income dropped significantly as well in the United States during this time, but most significantly among Latinos (66 percent) compared to blacks (53 percent) and whites (16 percent) (Pew Hispanic Center 2012). This is likely due to high rates of unemployment; as of December 2011, 11 percent of Hispanics were unemployed while the national average was 8.5 percent (Pew Hispanic Center 2012). Of those who are employed, Latinos make up a significant portion of workers in low paying jobs such as construction, hotels/motels, and food and drink establishments, which increases their likelihood of injury and death on the job, and often offer no health insurance benefits (National Council of La Raza [NCLR] 2010).

Nearly one-third (32.4 percent) of Hispanics in the United States are without health insurance coverage, making them more likely to be uninsured than any other minority group in the nation (Department of Health and Human Services 2011; NCLR n.d.). Castañeda (2010) utilizes Heyman et al.'s (2009) term "web of effects" to describe the multiple barriers leading to detrimental health effects for Latinos including lack of transportation, insurance, information as to where to obtain medical care, and an unfamiliarity with the U.S. health system, all of which are worsened for those with unauthorized migrant status. Although migrants have access to medical services through federally funded migrant clinics, only 10–15 percent of migrants utilize their availability (Castañeda 2010). Fear of deportation is also said to be a factor limiting use of health care services (Castañeda 2010). Taken as a whole, these multiple factors provide a setting that increases the risk of ill health among Latinos, while constraining their health care opportunities.

Syndemic theory offers an ideal lens for the examination of the social and biological aspects of co-occurring illnesses, such as those present alongside HIV/AIDS among

Latinos. Syndemic theory, developed in the early 1990s by medical anthropologist Merrill Singer, posits that co-occurring diseases/health problems are a consequence of disparate social conditions and work synergistically to increase the negative biological consequences of one another (Bulled and Singer 2011; Gonzalez-Guarda et al. 2011b; Singer and Clair 2003; Singer and Snipes 1992). Unlike comorbid diseases, which simply exist concurrently, syndemically occurring conditions actually exacerbate one another biologically by activating symptoms, accelerating detriments of disease, and/or increasing contagiousness (Mustanski et al. 2007; Singer 2010).

Central to Syndemic theory is the understanding of the actual biological interactions that can occur when infectious disease agents coexist, that is, the pathogen-to-pathogen interaction (PPI) (Singer 2010). For example, studies have demonstrated the mutually reinforcing relation between HIV and TB (Diedrich and Flynn 2011; Kwan and Ernst 2011; Singer 2010; Singer and Clair 2003; University of California San Francisco 2003; World Health Organization 2011). The immune suppression that characterizes HIV increases the risk of infection with TB. Specifically, the World Health Organization reports the likelihood of developing TB to be 20–37 times greater among HIV-positive individuals as among HIV-negative ones (World Health Organization 2011). Similarly, Family Health International estimates that an HIV-positive individual has a 50 percent lifetime risk of TB infection, as compared to a 5–10 percent risk among HIV-negative persons (University of California San Francisco 2003). In addition, progression from TB infection to full-blown disease is hastened when HIV is present.

At the global level, TB is the most common cause of death among HIV-infected individuals. Conversely, infection with TB increases the rate of HIV replication in the system, thus accelerating the progression of HIV infection. In their study of injection drug use, Singer and Clair (2003) found that 25 percent of the study participants, half of whom were Latino, were infected with HIV, with 91 percent of them having a comorbid TB or hepatitis infection. Looking specifically at TB rates among Latino Americans, the 2007 Tuberculosis Surveillance Report indicates that for four consecutive years, Latinos accounted for the largest percentage of TB cases at 29 percent (Center for Disease Control and Prevention 2008). Taking into consideration the common coinfection of TB and HIV, the high rates of infection with each illness demonstrate high risks for syndemic occurrence. Other diseases and conditions found to exist in a syndemic relation with HIV/AIDS include other STIs, mental illness, alcohol and drug addiction, hepatitis B and C, asthma, viral infections, malaria, liver disease, helminth infection, and malnutrition, among others (Himmelgreen et al. 2009; Himmelgreen and Romero-Daza 2010; Operario and Nemoto 2010; Singer 2009a; Singer et al. 2006; Singer and Clair 2003).

However, while knowledge of the biological mechanisms involved in syndemics is crucial, even more important, from an anthropological perspective, is the examination of the underlying conditions that allow such syndemics to occur. Syndemic theory provides a framework for identifying and addressing the social, economic, political, and environmental factors that impact the health and well-being of populations. Poverty is responsible for a multitude of factors including inadequate and/or unsafe housing, lack of transportation, malnutrition, and the use of illicit drugs (Singer 1996) and appears to be the common denominator in communities where syndemics thrive (Singer 2009a, 2011b; Singer and Clair 2003). Adverse social conditions most commonly cited in the development of syndemics include missing or limited resources (Singer 2010); discrimination, racism, and cultural marginalization (Bruce et al. 2011; Stall et al. 2008); interpersonal violence, substance use and abuse (Meyer et al. 2011; Operario and Nemoto 2010; Senn et al. 2010; Singer and Clair 2003; Singer and Romero-Daza 1999; Stall et al. 2008); social isolation (Egan et al. 2011; Stall et al. 2008); psychosocial stress (Stall et al. 2008; Storholm et al. 2011); poverty (Singer 1996, 2010); and structural violence, which refers to the systematic, institutionalization and delegitimization of suffering among vulnerable populations within a society (Galtung 1969).

This clustering of biological epidemics with sociocultural and economic factors is evident when examining the overall health status of underserved Latino populations. For example, Latinos experience a higher incidence of depression compared to other minority groups and often receive inadequate mental health treatment or no treatment at all (Alegría et al. 2008; Langomasino et al. 2005). Literature regarding migrants' documentation status has shown that the long-term biological stress associated with being undocumented compounds physical and mental health risks, and that the perpetual exposure to such stressful experiences is also linked with increased risks of chronic illnesses (Castañeda 2010; McGuire and Georges 2010). Additionally, injection drug use (IDU)-linked HIV/AIDS also affects Latino communities in the United States, with an IDU-linked infection rate of 19 percent among Latino men and 23 percent among Latino women (Centers for Disease Control and Prevention 2008; Gonzalez et al. 2009). Substance abuse is also connected with violence (Romero-Daza et al. 2003, 2005; Singer and Romero-Daza 1993), including both intimate partner and street violence (Gonzalez-Guarda et al. 2011a, 2011b). Although, it is hard to determine actual rates of violence, it has been suggested that Latinos experience high rates of domestic violence (Frias and Angel 2005) and low rates of utilization of violence-prevention services, often because of language barriers, fear of deportation, and social stigma (Bloom et al. 2009; Denham et al. 2010). Importantly from the syndemic perspective, studies also suggest that high rates of poverty, discrimination, racism, and overall uncertainty considerably increase stress and depression among Latinos, which in turn, contribute to higher rates of violence (Caetano and Cunradi 2003).

A clear illustration of the social and structural roots of ill health among underserved groups is the syndemic relation between HIV and malnutrition. Similar to what happens with TB, there is a clear biological interaction whereby micronutrient deficiencies compromise immune response—thus increasing the risk for HIV infection—and accelerating the progression of the infection and its consequences among already positive individuals. At the same time, HIV infection affects food intake and absorption and utilization of nutrients, exacerbating malnutrition (Himmelgreen et al. 2009). However, in order to fully understand the extent of this interaction and to address it in a meaningful way, it is necessary to go beyond the biological mechanisms, and consider the underlying factors that contribute to malnutrition. Malnutrition is often the result of food insecurity (i.e., lack of reliable access to foods of enough quantity and quality obtained in socially acceptable ways). While in some cases food scarcity is linked to factors such as famines and environmental degradation, the main contributing factors are often poverty and unequal access to resources. In areas of the world characterized by extreme poverty and food insecurity, and where limited support services exist, the practice of "survival sex" (i.e., engaging in sexual transactions in exchange for basic necessities such as food, clothing, and shelter) has become one of the main drivers of the HIV/AIDS epidemic (Himmelgreen and Romero-Daza 2010; Klein 2011). Furthermore, food insecurity also affects the progression of the disease among communities (Singer 2011) as well as individuals who are receiving treatment for HIV, as lack of access to nutritious foods affects adherence to and effectiveness of antiretroviral drug regimens (Au et al. 2006; Weiser et al. 2010).

While the syndemic interaction between food insecurity, malnutrition, and HIV/AIDS is most evident in developing areas of the world, it has also been documented in the United States (Canino et al. 2008). For example, in a comparative study of food security and nutritional status among Latino women living in Hartford, Connecticut, Himmelgreen et al. (1998) found higher levels of food insecurity (both in terms of quantity and quality of food), and worse nutritional status among drug-using individuals. Similarly, high levels of food insecurity have been documented among HIV-positive crack cocaine users, especially those who are homeless (Vogenthaler et al. 2010).

Poverty usually goes hand in hand with violence, discrimination, isolation, and lack of access to needed social and medical services, as evidenced by studies that examine the HIV epidemic among drug users (Singer 2009a). *Desperate Measures: A Syndemic Approach to the Anthropology of Health in a Violent City* (Singer 2009a) illustrates the synergistic interactions that occur between poverty, violence, drug use, and health risks, making apparent the pathways through which violence begets more violence, as victims also become perpetrators and violence and drug use serve as outlets for the anger and frustration produced by the daily indignities of life in poverty. Moreover, the institutional trivialization of these individuals' lives demonstrates the marginalized social position of those in poverty and the minimal social, economic, and health-related resources they are afforded.

In a seminal study on the relationship between substance abuse, violence, and AIDS (SAVA), Singer and Romero-Daza (1999) provide evidence of the mutually reinforcing interaction between these co-occurring epidemics in Hartford, CT. As addiction increases, the need for drugs often results in loss of employment and isolation from family and friends. Limited access to affordable housing and to drug treatment often leads drug users into homelessness. Many homeless drug-addicted individuals, especially women, find themselves involved in sex work, exchanging sex for money, drugs, or basic necessities such as food and shelter. Sex work, in turn, increases the risk of STIs, including HIV/AIDS. Life on the streets exposes individuals to many risks including drug-related violence—as both perpetrators and victims. Violence victimization leads to high levels of stress and mental problems such as anxiety and depression, and in extreme cases to post-traumatic stress disorders. In a vicious cycle, drug users, faced with limited mental health services, often increase their use of illegal drugs as a coping mechanism, which leads to increased addiction and higher risks for HIV/AIDS (Gonzalez-Guarda et al. 2011a; Romero-Daza et al. 1999, 2003, 2005). As Singer states, under these conditions, "AIDS itself emerges as an opportunistic disease, a disease of compromised health and social conditions, a disease of poverty" (Singer 1996:937). Due to these day-to-day experiences, Latinos in the United States who live in poverty are at significant risk for HIV infection.

Thus, as illustrated above, syndemic theory allows for the simultaneous examination of micro-level biological processes (i.e., the PPI), and of mid-level and macro-level social, economic, political, and behavioral conditions that provide the context for such PPI to manifest in the lived experience of individuals and populations. As Singer succinctly states, this theory focuses "simultaneously on distal and proximal causes of disease, specific mechanisms and directionalities of interaction, broader patterns and contexts of vulnerability and risk, and consequences of disease synergies that increase the overall health burden of a population" (2010:15).

As evidenced by this brief review, syndemic theory has been most commonly utilized in the study of HIV/AIDS and other infectious diseases in both domestic and international contexts. However, syndemic theory's holistic view of biosocial interactions makes it applicable in myriad disciplines. Work involving syndemics outside of HIV/AIDS and infectious diseases has focused on issues such as the prevention of mental illnesses related to violence, substance abuse, and disparities in a community setting (Embry 2006), addressing housing conditions that pose health hazards to residents (Breysse et al. 2003), and preventing, recognizing, and confronting child abuse in the State of Florida (Office of Adoption and Child Protection 2010), among many other examples. Most of these initiatives include not only research, but also the provision of educational workshops designed for various groups involved in community health, including public health practitioners, lay health workers, academics, leaders of nongovernmental organizations (NGOs), social justice organizers, and other community stakeholders.

In light of the potential for application of syndemic theory across a broad variety of health fields, it is clear that the employment of a syndemics perspective is necessary in order to reframe health and disease within a social, as well as biological, context, in which social forces such as poverty, racism, and structural violence (Galtung 1969) are embodied in illness pathologies. By utilizing a syndemics framework, researchers, clinicians, and providers of social and ancillary services can obtain a more holistic conceptualization of disease, allowing for improved understandings of etiology and pathology, as well as of the way in which ill health and disease manifest themselves in the lived, social realities of individuals and groups (Singer 2010; Singer and Clair 2003).

Accordingly, many academics and practitioners are calling for the application of a syndemics perspective within health-related research and practice (Breysse et al. 2003; Brunarski 2011; Himmelgreen and Romero-Daza 2010; Himmelgreen et al. 2009; Koblin et al. 2003; Littleton and Park 2009; Singer 2009b, 2010; Singer and Clair 2003) with the target outcome of integrated, multicomponent health interventions aimed at addressing both the social and biological aspects of disease causation and management (Littleton and

Park 2009; Operario and Nemoto 2010; Singer 2010). Unfortunately, despite significant backing from the Centers for Disease Control and Prevention and former CDC director Julie Gerberding (Gerberding 2005), a review of the syndemics literature revealed few organized efforts toward the application of syndemic theory into practice. Thus, there is clear need for the development and standardization of targeted syndemics training efforts that will familiarize a broad spectrum of both researchers and practitioners in a variety of disciplines in order to facilitate multidisciplinary collaboration to recognize and address syndemics across the nation and throughout the globe. The remainder of the article briefly discusses the current structure of health care and medical research training models, and then offers an alternative model that integrates the concepts of syndemic theory.

TRADITIONAL TRAINING MODELS

In order to understand the need and desirability for a syndemics-based training program, it is first necessary to provide a brief review of traditional training models for health practitioners and social scientists. Much of the research on health practitioner training is led by medical education institutions, following the Flexnor Report of 1910, which introduced a science-based approach to medical education and laid the foundation for the biomedical education model still utilized today. The Flexnor Report recommends that students first receive biomedical sciences training, followed by clinical training (Duffy 2011).

The biomedical model prepares practitioners to base their clinical decisions on an understanding of human biology and disease processes, assuming that decisions based on science will produce positive health outcomes. Recent developments in medical education indicate a decreased focus on the basic sciences and an increased focus on the use of evidence-based algorithms to guide clinical decision making. However, critics of the algorithm approach argue that this method dangerously moves the physician focus for clinical reasoning away from the individual patient to the population (Brass 2009). A shift away from an algorithm-based strategy is occurring with increased emphasis on humanities, ethics, and patient communication (Duffy 2011). Moreover, in 2004, the Institute of Medicine's (IOM) report titled *Improving Medical Education: Enhancing the Social and Behavioral Science Content of Medical School Curricula* proposed a movement away from an individual clinical perspective to one that includes an understanding of the social context of disease and illness (Institute of Medicine 2004). Based on the IOM recommendations, a suggested curriculum identifies key topics to incorporate in the training of future physicians, including sociocultural issues, patient behavior, and physician behavior (Satterfield et al. 2010). These additions to curriculum and clinical practice are important because while the traditional biomedical approach produces great scientific advances and improves specific health outcomes, such as life expectancy, it fails to acknowledge the nonphysiological aspects that contribute to ill health among individuals, patient concerns about not being treated as a whole person, and health disparities among different segments of a given population (Frenk et al. 2010). The utilization of syndemic theory allows for a more holistic perspective that incorporates social as well as biological influences on health.

Given that the existing health professional education system has created silos of care with little contextual and prevention focused efforts, the *Education of Health Professionals for the 21st Century: A Global Independent Commission* was formed to review the existing health education system guiding the training of future practitioners in medicine, nursing, and public health (Frenk et al. 2010). Current recommendations from the Commission are that "all health professionals in all countries should be educated to mobilize knowledge and to engage in critical reasoning and ethical conduct so that they are competent to participate in patient and population-centered health systems as members of locally responsive and globally connected teams" (Frenk et al. 2010:1924). Still, despite advances, the training of practitioners in the biomedical sciences remains, for the most part, disconnected from a true understanding of the socioeconomic, political, and ideological contexts that affect the health and well-being of individuals and populations.

In contrast to the medical model, the social sciences are based on both behavioral and social determinants of morbidity and mortality. For example, psychology considers an individual's interaction with the environment in the biopsychosocial framework (Levant and Shapiro 2002). Medical anthropology also incorporates a multilevel biocultural approach that provides a systems perspective with consideration for the ways in which health and illness are impacted by social and political environments (Whiteford and Bennett 2005). A new matrix model for clinical psychologist training, for example, assesses an individual's strengths and weaknesses in the context of their environment, viewing chronic conditions from a societal perspective to reduce stigmatization associated with illness (Snyder and Elliott 2005). Likewise, an Integrative Training Model for psychology looks at the impact of the social experience on mental and physical health outcomes (Miville et al. 2009). Finally, acknowledging the multifaceted nature of the health issues that affect populations, the field of public health requires students to receive formal training in the social and behavioral sciences, to be able to address behavior, social, and cultural considerations (Coreil 2010). Nevertheless, despite the fact that the traditional biomedical approach has begun to incorporate more content from the behavioral and social sciences to improve health outcomes, and that the social sciences are increasingly recognizing the importance of biological factors in shaping people's experiences with and responses to health and disease, there is still an urgent need for the establishment of interdisciplinary training efforts between the medical and social sciences to address systemic health issues that contribute to health disparities. This is especially important in efforts to train future generations of researchers and practitioners involved in issues such as HIV/AIDS, which are of great significance at both the individual and population levels, and which disproportionally affect ethnic minorities, including Latinos in the United States. Equally important is the recognition that ethnic minorities must be included not only as subjects, but also as agents of research (i.e., as researchers and practitioners) in social and biomedical efforts aimed at addressing health disparities. What follows is a description of a proposed model for a program designed to provide holistic and interdisciplinary training to social scientists and clinical researchers and practitioners to address HIV/AIDS among ethnic minorities utilizing a syndemic theory perspective.

USING SYNDEMIC THEORY AS AN INTERDISCIPLINARY TRAINING MODEL

Recognizing the need for a comprehensive training model that is firmly rooted in the social and medical sciences and emphasizes the syndemic nature of HIV/AIDS, an interdisciplinary group of researchers from the University of South Florida has worked to propose an innovative model of training specifically aimed at minority researchers interested in issues of HIV/AIDS among Latinos. The proposed program is unique compared to most other HIV/AIDS training programs because it is guided by the principles of syndemic theory, which will allow trainees to identify and address the social, economic, political, and environmental factors that work synergistically to increase the risk for HIV infection among Latinos. Key components of the training model include mentoring combined with methodological, cultural, and ethical training, direct work with community agencies that provide services to Latinos, and individual research with Latino groups. What follows is a description of the various training components, detailing how they specifically incorporate the tenets of syndemic theory.

Mentoring

In 2001, a National Institute of General Medical Sciences workshop was held to identify strategies for recruitment and retention of underrepresented "racial and ethnic minorities" in health and sciences research. Some of the issues identified in this workshop included a need for funding sources to encourage mentoring programs for new minority investigators (Olson and Fagen 2007). Government institutions such as the National Institute of Health (NIH) support diversity-targeted mentoring programs focused on mental health, substance abuse, and HIV/AIDS research, thus providing ideal venues for the development of innovative training efforts.

Given the growth of ethnic minority groups in the United States, a focus on increasing ethnic minority faculty to provide relevant perspectives to address health disparities is vital (Jeste et al. 2009; National Institute of Mental Health 2001). For example, minority faculty may be better able to serve the growing ethnic minority communities because they may develop better partnerships with such communities and can serve them in different ways than nonethnic minority faculty can (Yager et al. 2007). A review of existing mentoring programs suggests that programs should have a strategic plan for mentoring junior faculty utilizing evidence-based practices (Forsyth and Stoff 2009). Ethnic minority individuals need role models to encourage their involvement in the sciences and successful mentoring programs that support diversity in the sciences (Epstein 2007; Johnson 2007). Unfortunately, junior minority faculty often have few opportunities for mentoring relationships with senior faculty who are themselves of ethnic minority heritage given the limited ethnic diversity of university and institute faculties (Yager et al. 2007). The lack of available mentors from ethnic minority groups is evident given that only 10 percent of the NIH trainees are members of ethnic minority groups and they constitute only 3–4% of NIH principal investigators (Shavers et al. 2005).

Bozeman and Feeney define mentoring as "a process for the informal transmission of knowledge, social capital, and psychosocial support perceived by the recipient as relevant to work, career, or professional development." (Bozeman and Feeney 2007:731). It has been shown that mentoring reduces job anxiety and improves self-esteem and self-efficacy (Dutta et al. 2011) and that successful mentors provide career-specific guidance and increase the mentee's productivity of publications and grant funding (Cho et al. 2011). Mentoring programs such as the one run by the University of California San Francisco (UCSF), Center for AIDS Research (a joint UCSF-Gladstone Institute for Immunology and Virology, NIH-funded center), provide evidence as to the success of carefully designed training initiatives. Participants in the UCSF mentoring program, the first in the nation targeting junior faculty in HIV/AIDS research (Kahn and Greenblatt 2009), identified career guidance, networking with colleagues, and acculturation into the senior research environment as key benefits received from their mentoring experience (Kahn et al. 2008). Importantly, training on the preparation and submission of funding applications is also crucial to the success of these programs. Ongoing dialogue with mentors, immediate feedback, peer reviews, and regular group interaction were all identified as critical to UCSF trainees' successful grant application process (Zea and Belgrave 2009). An analysis of the Native Investigator Development Program found that minority junior faculty benefited from relationships with invested faculty resulting in developments of manuscript and grant applications (Buchwald and Dick 2011). In the American Dental Education Association Minority Faculty Development Program, mentoring as well as academic partnerships were vital to receiving independent funding (Sinkford et al. 2009).

As discussed earlier, the complex and multifaceted nature of the HIV/AIDS among Hispanics in the United States requires that it be approached from an interdisciplinary perspective, rather than from a single-discipline point of view. Thus, a training model based on interdisciplinary mentorship and collaboration that addresses the synergistic nature of HIV/AIDS and its antecedents, with a clear developmental approach specific to the junior researchers' needs and with measurable outcomes, is recommended (Brown et al. 2009). Such a model is already being implemented through project REIDS (Research Education Institute for Diverse Scholars), a collaborative program offered by the University of Connecticut, Yale University, and the Institute for Community Research, under the auspices of the National Institutes of Health, which aims at training ethnic and racial minority scholars to increase their representation among HIV/AIDS researchers (Center for Interdisciplinary Research on AIDS 2012).

As shown by programs described in Singer et al. (2006), interdisciplinary mentoring contributes to productive academic dialogue and fosters research efforts across disciplines, thus enriching the research and publication potential of trainees. HIV/AIDS early career investigators, in particular, need interdisciplinary mentors given a limited network of existing researchers, especially from underrepresented groups. While many mentoring programs pair mentees with more advanced researchers from their same discipline, a more innovative approach is that of "trans" mentoring, as used by the UCSF Center for AIDS Research, where the mentee and mentor are from different disciplines. The "trans" mentoring model's main benefits are the complementary use of different research perspectives and the mentee's career independence from the mentor (Kahn and Greenblatt 2009). In yet another model involving multiple mentors, mentees in the Puerto Rico Comprehensive Center for the Study of HIV Disparities (PRCCHD) and the Puerto Rico Mentoring Institute for HIV and Mental Health Research (PRMI) had a local mentor from a different field, an external institutional mentor, and a nationally recognized mentor linked with internationally based research (Rabionet et al. 2009).

The importance of mentoring goes well beyond training on specific areas of expertise, and into personal and professional development for both parties involved. This is especially so when the mentor and the mentee are from the same minority ethnic group. In such situations, the mentor becomes a role model who can guide the mentee as they deal with issues specific to minority investigators involved in research (Epstein 2007; Johnson 2007) and mentors can learn from mentees on current issues relevant to minority populations (Alegría 2009). Training programs that involve groups of mentees from minority ethnic groups also foster important support and learning from peers in a culturally specific fashion (Zea and Belgrave 2009). The Southwest Addictions Research Group (SARG) at the University of New Mexico uses a Culturally Centered Mentorship Model (CCMM) for the recruitment and retention of minority faculty. The CCMM acknowledges that, in addition to technical support, mentees need culturally based psychosocial support to address their professional challenges. This culturally centered focus provides encouragement for both academic success and success conducting community-based research (Viets et al. 2009).

Based on the principles of syndemic theory, which call for a multidimensional approach to the understanding of HIV/AIDS as a syndemic, we believe that U.S.-based training programs should incorporate dual cross-disciplinary training for the mentorship of ethnic minority researchers. Accordingly, in the model we propose to implement, each minority mentee who participates in the training program will be paired with a clinical-based mentor and a social science mentor, both of whom will work in close collaboration to provide interdisciplinary training and guidance. If at all possible, at least one of the mentors will also be a member of an ethnic minority, to provide the mentee with added support. While it would be ideal for the mentors to have had experience using syndemic theory in the conduct of their own research, this may not be possible, given the relative newness of this approach. However, at a minimum, mentors will have an appreciation for the tenets of syndemic theory, and willingness to increase their own understanding of this framework and to adopt it as they guide their mentees through the training program. Thus, it is clear that the pairing of the three researchers should enhance not only the mentees' but also the mentors' appreciation for the value of diverse perspectives in the study of HIV/AIDS, combining both biomedical and social science approaches, and specifically incorporating the multifaceted perspective espoused by syndemic theory.

Content-Specific Modules and the Mentoring Relationship

The use of a syndemic theory interdisciplinary training model will support the conduct of research addressing the complex contexts that increase Latinos' risk for HIV/AIDS. In addition to providing a solid foundation to syndemic theory, such a training program should include instruction about the methodological and ethical issues involved in the conduct of HIV/AIDS research with minority communities in general and with Latinos, specifically, and about the application of such research to collaborative initiatives that address the syndemic at the local community level. The emphasis on familiarizing mentees (and mentors, if need be) with syndemic theory and in guiding them in the use of such framework for the design and implementation of HIV/AIDS-related research makes this proposed model different from others that provide interdisciplinary training without a common underlying theoretical foundation. Based on a review of training programs funded by the NIH, we propose a two-year initiative consisting of two Training Institutes (Years I and Years II), monthly web-based training and mentorship, a research project, and development of a grant proposal. Mentees would be junior faculty and postdoctoral fellows from underrepresented minority groups, whose interests revolve around the study of HIV/AIDS among Latinos in various U.S. settings. One example of the NIH-funded training programs we reviewed that follows this structure is the above-mentioned Research Education Institute for Diverse Scholars (REIDS) program, which is a partnership of the Center for Interdisciplinary Research on AIDS (CIRA), the Yale School of Nursing (YSN), The Institute for Community Research (ICR), and the University of Connecticut's Center for Health, Intervention, and Prevention (CHIP) (Center for Interdisciplinary Research on AIDS 2012).

Drawing upon successful programs such as REIDS, we propose a program that will begin with an on-campus two-week Training Institute during the first year, during which participants will meet their mentors and start to develop relationships with them and with their fellow cohort members, as well as with local communities. In order to have a successful mentored training program centered on syndemic theory and HIV, important content-specific modules must be in place. Trainees will first be provided with a comprehensive review of HIV incidence, transmission, prevention, and treatment in the United States, with specific focus on Latinos. This will be followed by a thorough exploration of syndemic theory and its applications not only in the area of HIV/AIDS but as related to other health inequities and by an exploration of the various health conditions and social, economic, and political factors that play a role in shaping the HIV/AIDS syndemic among Latinos. A variety of topics will need to be addressed, including the history and contemporary status of different Latino groups in the United States, issues of cultural diversity among Latino subpopulations, and an overview of the health status of Latinos—especially in relation to health disparities vis-à-vis other ethnic groups. Specific modules will then be provided to address the many facets of the HIV/AIDS syndemic, including the interplay between HIV/AIDS and other STIs, hepatitis, TB, malnutrition, substance abuse, and violence. Similarly, trainees will participate in the examination of the way in which structural violence, racism, discrimination, limited educational and employment opportunities, and limited access to healthcare—including access to substance abuse treatment—exacerbate Latinos' risk of contracting HIV/AIDS. Thus, trainees will gain an understanding of the multiplicity of factors at play in shaping the daily lives of Latinos living on "the bottom rung of the ladder" (Farmer 1999:91). This background will serve as a context for the exploration of epidemiological, biosocial, and basic science research on HIV/AIDS, and will facilitate an understanding of HIV/AIDS as a syndemic condition that tends to foster and be adversely entwined with other diseases, rather than as an isolated health issue.

Other important issues, such as the ethics of research with underserved and vulnerable populations (e.g., undocumented individuals, drug users, sex workers) and the specific challenges faced in the conduct of community-based research, will also be addressed. Specific training will be provided in community-based participatory research (CBPR) to enhance mentees' ability to work with various stakeholders and gatekeepers, and to build collaborative partnerships (Baldwin et al. 2009). As part of the training program, mentees will interact closely with local organizations that provide HIV/AIDS-related and ancillary services to Latinos. Such interaction may involve frequent visits to local organizations and the shadowing of services providers, activities that will provide trainees with an opportunity to see first hand the complexities involved in HIV/AIDS risk and management.

Advanced training in research methods is needed to help mentees develop the necessary skills to research HIV syndemics from a multidisciplinary, mixed-method perspective. Training in relevant qualitative and quantitative methods for data collection and analysis, as well as in methodologies for selection and recruitment of research participants (e.g., in respondent-driven sampling approaches) should be tailored to the needs and expertise of each group of mentees.

While engaged with this Training Institute, mentees will also work with local HIV/AIDS community agencies and with their mentors to develop an HIV/AIDS research project using syndemic theory that they will conduct over a twelve-month period. Ideally, the training program will provide funds for this pilot research, which will constitute the basis for future applications for federal funding to be pursued by each participant in the second year of the program. As part of these efforts, mentees will also be trained in manuscript and grant writing. Mentees at this stage of their career will benefit greatly from group-based and individualized training in writing manuscripts and federal grant proposals. Mentors can offer mentees advice from their experiences with grant writing and allow mentees to review their previous successful and unsuccessful grant proposals (Zea and Belgrave 2009).

After the Year 1 Training Institute, mentees will return to their home institutions and receive training and interact with their mentors and other mentees via web-conferencing. To provide mentees with the maximum amount of training and support for their research projects, web-based training should optimally occur monthly. Also, to ensure mentees continue to feel engaged with their mentors, virtual meetings with mentors should also occur monthly.

As per best practices, mentees would return in Year II for another on-campus Training Institute. It is while engaged with this Training Institute that mentees will receive training on advanced data analysis and manuscript preparation. Mentees will work with their mentors and other program staff to write manuscripts derived from their pilot research projects that advance syndemic understanding and applied response, as well as begin writing a federal grant proposal (e.g., NIH, National Science Foundation [NSF]) based on syndemic research given that the program is intended to develop independent researchers. Measures of success in such training programs should include the number of manuscripts accepted and grant proposals funded, while other longer term outcomes might include promotion and tenure of mentees.

Designing and Conducting Interdisciplinary Research Projects

As noted above, as part of a training program on HIV/AIDS syndemics, junior researchers would be connected with two faculty mentors who can assist them in the design and conduct of community-based research projects. The ideal collaborative relationship should partner mentors from several different interdisciplinary backgrounds (e.g., one from the biomedical sciences and one from the social sciences) given the interdisciplinary nature of syndemic theory, as well as those from diverse backgrounds.

Faculty members who might be particularly well suited to serving as research mentors would be those who have independent research funding of their own and can provide opportunities for trainees to analyze some of the data they have gathered in their own projects and/or senior researchers who can support junior researchers through stipends or minority supplement mechanisms. These mechanisms provide trainees with the necessary experience and pilot data to begin to craft their own lines of research. In particular, the NIH's research education training grants (such as the R25 mechanism) often have a specific component of funding for pilot projects that trainees can apply for competitively. While the funds do not confer independent funding status, they do provide the resources necessary to gather appropriate pilot data that can lead to larger grant submissions and eventual large-scale funding. Since many of the successful mentors have been through the grants submission and administration process themselves, the mentorship involves not only training in designing research but also in grantsmanship.

Working With Community Agencies

Mentees in the program will also be trained in CBPR, as building trust with the community is critical to identifying strategies that will most benefit the community (Baldwin et al. 2009) and that allow them to address the multiplicity of factors involved in the HIV/AIDS syndemic. While CBPR has been commonly practiced in anthropology and other social sciences, it is more of a recent development in the health-related fields. In his 1990 report, *Scholarship Reconsidered: Priorities of the Professorate*, Ernest Boyer advocates for increased partnerships between higher education and communities (Calleson et al. 2005). Similarly, the Commission on Community-Engaged Scholarship in Health Professions (2005) encourages health professional schools to adapt their promotion and tenure policies in order to place higher value on community-engaged scholarship. In addition, it points out that diversity of faculty is also critical to develop effective community partnerships for teaching, research, and service (Commission on Community-Engaged Scholarship in the Health Professions 2005).

Community coalitions are increasingly being recognized as an effective strategy for CBPR involving ethnic minorities and addressing health disparities (Trinh-Shevrin et al. 2011). Community-based organizations provide access to "at-risk" and minority groups that may not seek medical care due to mistrust of the health care system (Walkup et al. 2008). In addition, working with community-based organizations improves awareness about cultural differences among researchers and practitioners. For example, the Latin American Cancer Research Coalition (LACRC) notes that the research participants in the program improved their cultural competence through interaction with community-based organizations (Kreling et al. 2006). For purposes of training, the inclusion of community members and representatives of community-based organizations as mentors is also critical (Norris et al. 2007).

The significance of engaging community members and community-based agencies in every aspect of HIV/AIDS research to make efforts culturally appropriate by balancing autonomy and collaboration has been noted by many (Baldwin et al. 2009; Weeks et al. 2009). The Hartford Model, developed by researchers and practitioners at the Hispanic Health Council and the Institute for Community Research used ethnography as a guiding discipline for evaluating HIV/AIDS community interventions (Singer and Weeks 2005). Further, a qualitative study interviewing health care and social service providers identified the community-based provider's perspective as crucial to understanding the syndemic relationship of HIV/AIDS and violence (Distefano and Cayetano 2011). Further, a "concept mapping" process with HIV/AIDS prevention researchers and practitioners reviewing the feasibility and impact of existing HIV/AIDS prevention efforts assessed the potential impact of several interventions ranging from taxes to medical innovation. While advances in medical interventions were identified as having the most significant impact on HIV/AIDS, there were also several community-building strategies identified including to "require all HIV prevention researchers and federal workers to complete a two-year internship in a community-based AIDS Service Organization or needle-exchange program" (Abdul-Quader and Collins 2011:782). In addition, HIV prevention initiatives of the Centers for Disease Control and Prevention (CDC), such as Replicating Effective Programs Plus (REP+), contain programs that have science-based behavioral interventions designed with and by community-based organizations (CBOs) (CDC n.d.b). In 2009, the U.S. National Institute of Mental Health and the CDC convened a meeting to review existing evidence-based efforts targeting HIV/AIDS and men who have sex with men (MSM). Participants of this meeting included researchers, advocates, community providers, and government organizations. The CDC recommends ongoing evaluation efforts of CBOs "home-grown" activities as potential evidence-based practice initiatives (Grossman et al. 2011).

Given the central role played by CBOs in efforts to address HIV/AIDS in local communities, these agencies will constitute an important resource for a training program. Representatives from local CBOs that work with Latino communities will be identified and approached to participate both as providers of training on specific issues that affect the populations with whom they work, and as informal advisors for the trainees as they develop their research projects.

CONCLUSION

Thirty years after HIV/AIDS was first identified by the scientific community and after many years of hard work in prevention practice and research, the pandemic continues to affect many vulnerable populations around the globe. As demonstrated in this article, HIV/AIDS is a complex, multifaceted phenomenon that is but one of multiple co-occurring epidemics that significantly affect the health and well-being of millions around the world. Understanding HIV/AIDS in this context is required to further increase the number of effective preventive interventions available for use in populations at risk for HIV infection. We have argued in this article that it is critical to use a syndemic theory approach to conducting HIV/AIDS research and subsequent intervention development in order to wholly examine the synergistic interactions occurring between biological and social pathologies. Training incorporating understandings of how these dynamic relationships exacerbate one another and how they influence risk is critical to the continued advancement of HIV/AIDS awareness and prevention programs. If we are to take this approach, it will be necessary for HIV/AIDS researchers to become trained in the syndemic theory training model, such as the one described in this article.

As with any training program, a significant benefit of the proposed training model is the mentorship of junior scientists by senior ones who are established and well regarded in their field of research. However, what is unique about the proposed program is its emphasis on Syndemics as an approach that provides a theoretical, methodological, and practical foundation for the conduct of HIV/AIDS-related research among Latinos. In addition to providing a comprehensive and holistic framework, such an approach truly fosters interdisciplinary dialog and collaboration not only among mentors and their mentees, but also among trainees and their peers in both social and medical sciences. Equally important, the syndemic theory mentoring approach provides a fruitful venue for collaboration between researchers and local agencies that provide services to Latinos. As stated previously, the syndemic theory model also has the potential to provide direct benefits to the mentors, by enhancing their perspectives and perhaps affecting the conduct of future research endeavors.

Another key benefit of the proposed training model is the focus on junior scientists who are members of various minority populations. Given the limited numbers of minority scientists who are involved in HIV/AIDS research, it is crucial to provide opportunities that enhance the skills of trainees from underrepresented groups, and that increase the number of minorities in academic, clinical, and community-based settings. More importantly, the adoption of a syndemic approach for training will provide minority researchers with the needed tools and perspectives to make significant contributions to the study of HIV/AIDS in their own communities. Importantly, it is also possible that minority trainees will use such training to address other health disparities that continue to figure prominently among ethnic groups in the United States (CDC 2011a, 2011b).

Given these benefits of using syndemic theory in a training program in the field of HIV/AIDS research, we encourage others to incorporate a syndemic theory approach to their current and future training programs in the various fields where syndemics have been documented to exist. Training the future cadre of independent scientists in approaching communities' greatest health concerns from a syndemic theory approach is necessary in order to have the greatest impact on improving the health and well-being of underserved groups in the United States and abroad.

REFERENCES CITED

Abdul-Quader, Abu S., and Charles Collins
  2011 Identification of Structural Interventions for HIV/AIDS Prevention: The Concept of Mapping Exercise. Public Health Reports 126(6):777–788.

Alegría, Margarita
  2009 Training for Research in Mental Health and HIV/AIDS Among Racial and Ethnic Minority Populations: Meeting the Needs of New Investigators. American Journal of Public Health 99(Suppl. 1): S26–S30.

Alegría, Margarita, Pinka Chatterji, Kenneth Wells, Zhun Cao, Chih-nan Chen, David Takeuchi, James Jackson, and Xiao-Li Meng
  2008 Disparity in Depression Treatment Among Racial and Ethnic Minority Populations in the United States. Psychiatric Services 59(11):1264–1272.

Anderson, Robert N., and Betty L. Smith
  2005 Deaths: Leading Causes for 2002. National Vital Statistics Report 53(17):1–92. National Center for Health Statistics. http://www.cdc.gov/nchs/data/nvsr53/nvsr53_17.pdf, accessed January 12, 2012.

Au, Joyce T., Kayitesi Kayitenkore, Erin Shutes, Etienne Karita, Phillip J. Peters, Amanda Tichacek, and Susan A. Allen
  2006 Access to Adequate Nutrition is a Major Potential Obstacle to Antiretroviral Adherence Among HIV-Infected Individuals in Rwanda. AIDS 20(16):2116–2118.

Baldwin, Julie A., Jeannette L. Johnson, and Christine C. Benally
  2009 Building Partnerships Between Indigenous Communities and Universities: Lessons Learned in HIV/AIDS and Substance Abuse Prevention Research. American Journal of Public Health 99(Suppl. 1):S77–S82.

Bloom, Tina, Jennifer Wagman, Rebecca Hernandez, Nan Yragui, Noelia Hernandez-Valdovinos, Marie Dahlstrom, and Nancy Glass
  2009 Partnering with Community-Based Organizations to Reduce Intimate Partner Violence. Hispanic Journal of Behavioral Sciences 31(2):244–257.

Bozeman, Barry, and Mary K. Feeney
  2007 Toward a Useful Theory of Mentoring: A Conceptual Analysis and Critique. Administration and Society 39(6):719–739.

Brass, Eric P.
  2009 Basic Biomedical Sciences and the Future of Medical Education: Implications for Internal Medicine. Journal of General Internal Medicine 24(11):1251–1254.

Breysse, Patrick N., Warren Galke, Bruce Lanphear, and Nick Farr
  2003 The Relationship Between Housing and Health: Children at Risk Workshop. National Center for Healthy Housing. http://www.nchh.org/Portals/0/Contents/Children_at_Risk_Workshop_Report.pdf, accessed January 12, 2012.

Brown, Ronald T., Brian P. Daley, and Frederick T. L. Leong
   2009 Mentoring in Research: A Developmental Approach. Professional Psychology: Research and Practice 40(3):306–313.
Bruce, Douglas, Gary W. Harper, and Adolescent Medicine Trials Network for HIV/AIDS Interventions
   2011 Operating without a Safety Net: Gay Male Adolescents and Emerging Adults' Experiences of Marginalization and Migration, and Implications for Theory of Syndemic Production of Health Disparities. Health Education and Behavior 38(4):367–378.
Brunarski, David J.
   2011 The Increasing Threat of Syndemics and the Role of Chiropractic Care. Dynamic Chiropractic 29(1):1–3.
Buchwald, Debra, and Rhonda W. Dick
   2011 Weaving the Native Web: Using Social Network Analysis to Demonstrate the Value of a Minority Career Development Program. Academic Medicine 86(6):778–786.
Bulled, Nicola, and Merrill Singer
   2011 Syringe-Medicated Syndemics. AIDS and Behavior 15(7):1539–1545.
Caetano, Raul, and Carol Cunradi
   2003 Intimate Partner Violence and Depression Among Whites, Blacks, and Hispanics. Annals of Epidemiology 13(10):661–665.
Calleson, Diane, Catherine Jordan, and Sarena Seifer
   2005 Community-Engaged Scholarship: Is Faculty Work in Communities a True Academic Enterprise? Academic Medicine 80(4):317–321.
Canino, Glorisa, William A. Vega, William M. Sribney, Lynn A. Warner, and Margarita Alegria
   2008 Social Relationships, Social Assimilation, and Substance Use Disorders Among Adult Latinos. U.S. Journal of Drug Issues 38(1):69–102.
Castañeda, Heide
   2010 Im/Migration and Health: Conceptual, Methodological, and Theoretical Propositions for Applied Anthropology. Annals of Anthropological Practice (Formerly NAPA Bulletin) 34(1):6–27.
Centers for Disease Control and Prevention
   2008 HIV/AIDS Surveillance Report, 2006. Centers for Disease Control and Prevention. http://www.cdc.gov/hiv/topics/surveillance/resources/reports/2006report/pdf/2006Surveillance-Report.pdf, accessed January 12, 2012.
   2010 Health Disparities in HIV/AIDS, Viral Hepatitis, STDs, and TB. http://www.cdc.gov/nchhstp/healthdisparities/Hispanics.html, accessed January 12, 2012.
   2011a HIV Among African Americans. National Center for HIV/AIDS, Viral Hepatitis, STD, and TB Prevention. http://cdc.gov/hiv/topics/aa/PDF/aa.pdf, accessed January 23, 2012.
   2011b HIV Among Latinos. National Center for HIV/AIDS, Viral Hepatitis, STD, and TB Prevention. http://cdc.gov/hiv/resources/factsheets/pdf/latino.pdf, accessed January 23, 2012.
   N.d.a Health Disparities Affecting Minorities Hispanic/Latino Americans. Office of Minority Health and Health Disparities. http://www.cdc.gov/minorityhealth/brochures/HL.pdf, accessed August 14, 2012.
   N.d.b Replicating Effective Programs Plus.http://www.cdc.gov/hiv/topics/prev_prog/rep/, accessed August 14, 2012.
Center for Interdisciplinary Research on AIDS (CIRA)
   2012 Research Education Institute for Diverse Scholars (REIDS). http://cira.yale.edu/training/reids/research-education-institute-diverse-scholars-reids, accessed February 14, 2012.
Cho, Christine S., Radhika A. Ramana, and Mitchell D. Feldman
   2011 Defining the Ideal Qualities of Mentorship: A Qualitative Analysis of the Characteristics of Outstanding Mentors. The American Journal of Medicine 124(5):453–458.
Commission on Community-Engaged Scholarship in the Health Professions
   2005 Linking Scholarship and Communities: Report of the Commission on Community-Engaged Scholarship in the Health Professions. Community-Campus Partnerships for Health.   http://depts.washington.edu/ccph/pdf_files/Commission%20Report%20FINAL.pdf, accessed December 22, 2011.

Coreil, Jeannine, ed.

2010 Social and Behavioral Foundations of Public Health. 2nd edition. Thousand Oaks: SAGE Publications, Inc.

Denham, Amy C., Pamela Y. Frasier, Elizabeth G. Hooten, Leigh Belton, Warren Newton, Pamela Gonzalez, Munni Begum, and Marci K. Campbell

2010 Intimate Partner Violence Among Latinas in Eastern North Carolina. Violence Against Women 13(2):123–140.

Department of Health and Human Services

2011 Overview of the Uninsured in the United States: A Summary of the 2011 Current Population Survey. http://aspe.hhs.gov/health/reports/2011/CPSHealthIns2011/ib.pdf, accessed March 8, 2012.

Diedrich, Collin R., and JoAnne L. Flynn

2011 HIV-1/Mycobacterium Tuberculosis Coinfection Immunology: How Does HIV-1 Exacerbate Tuberculosis? Infection and Immunity 79(4):1407–1417.

DiStefano, Anthony S., and Reggie T. Cayetano

2011 Health Care and Social Service Providers' Observations on the Intersection of HIV/AIDS and Violence Among Their Clients and Patients. Qualitative Health Research 21(7): 884–899.

Duffy, Thomas P.

2011 The Flexnor Report-100 Years Later. Yale Journal of Biology and Medicine 84(3):269–276.

Dutta, Rina, Sarah L. Hawkes, Elizabeth Kuipers, David Guest, Nicola T. Fear, and Amy C. Iversen

2011 One Year Outcomes of a Mentoring Scheme for Female Academics: A Pilot Study at the Institute of Psychiatry, King's College London. BMC Medical Education 11(13):1–9.

Egan, James E., Victoria Frye, Steven P. Kurtz, Carl Latkin, Minxing Chen, Karin Tobin, Yang Cui, and Beryl A. Koblin

2011 Migration, Neighborhoods, and Networks: Approaches to Understanding How Urban Environmental Conditions Affect Syndemic Adverse Health Outcomes Among Gay, Bisexual and Other Men Who Have Sex With Men. AIDS Behavior 15(Suppl. 1):S35–S50.

Embry, Dennis D.

2006 Syndemics & Simple Gifts: Silo Busting Prevention Logic for Coalitions. Paper Presented at Community Anti-Drug Coalition of America (CADCA) Mid-Year Institute, Las Vegas, June 14–17.

Epstein, Irving R.

2007 Diversity in Chemistry: Catalyzing Change. Nature Chemical Biology 3(6):299–302.

Farmer, Paul

1999 Invisible Women: Class, Gender, and HIV. *In* Infections and Inequalities: The Modern Plagues. Updated edition. Pp. 59–93. Berkeley, CA: University of California Press.

Forsyth, Andrew D., and David M. Stoff

2009 Key Issues in Mentoring in HIV Prevention and Mental Health for New Investigators From Underrepresented Racial and Ethnic Groups. American Journal of Public Health 99(Suppl. 1):S87–S91.

Frenk, Julio, Lincoln Chen, Bhutta A. Zulfiqar, Jordan Cohen, Nigel Crisp, Timothy Evans, Harvey Fineberg, Patricia Garcia, Yang Ke, Patrick Kelley, Barry Kistnasamy, Afaf Meleis, David Naylor, Ariel Pablos-Mendez, Srinath Reddy, Susan Scrimshaw, Jaime Sepulveda, David Serwadda, and Huda Zurayk

2010 Health Professional for a New Century: Transforming Education to Strengthen Health Systems in an Interdependent World. Lancet 376(9756):1923–1958.

Frias, Sonia M., and Ronald J. Angel

2005 The Risk of Partner Violence Among Low Income Hispanic Subgroups. Journal of Marriage and Family 67(3):552–564.

Galtung, Johan

1969 Violence, Peace, and Peace Research. Journal of Peace Research 6(3):167–191.

Gerberding, Julie L.

2005 Protecting Health: The New Research Imperative. Journal of American Medical Association 29(11):1403–1406.

González-Guarda, Rosa Maria, Aubrey L. Florom-Smith, and Tainayah Thomas
    2011a A Syndemic Model of Substance Abuse, Intimate Partner Violence, HIV Infection, and Mental Health Among Hispanics. Public Health Nursing 28(4):366–378.
González-Guarda, Rosa Maria, Brian E. McCabe, Aubrey L. Florom-Smith, Rosina Cianelli, and Nilda Peragallo
    2011b Substance Abuse, Violence, HIV, and Depression: An Underlying Syndemic Factor Among Latinas. Nursing Research 60(3):182–189.
González, Jeffrey S., Ellen S. Hendriksen, Erin M. Collins, Ron E. Durán, and Steven A. Safren
    2009 Latinos and HIV/AIDS: Examining Factors Related to Disparity and Identifying Opportunities for Psychosocial Intervention Research. AIDS and Behavior 13(3):582–602.
Grossman, Cynthia I., Andrew Forsyth, David W. Purcell, Susannah Allison, Carlos Toledo, and Christopher M. Gordon
    2011 Advancing Novel HIV Prevention Intervention Research With MSM-Meeting Report. Public Health Reports 126(4):472–479.
Heyman, Josiah McC., Guillermina Gina Nunez, and Victor Talavera
    2009 Health Care Access and Barriers for Unauthorized Immigrants in El Paso County, Texas. Family & Community Health 32(1):4–21.
Himmelgreen, David A., Rafael Pérez-Escamilla, Sofia Segura-Millán, Nancy Romero-Daza, Mihaela Tanasescu, and Merrill Singer
    1998 A Comparison of the Nutritional Status and Food Security of Drug-Using and Non-Drug-Using Hispanic Women in Hartford, Connecticut. American Journal of Physical Anthropology 107(3):351–361.
Himmelgreen, David A., Nancy Romero-Daza, David Turkon, Sharon Watson, Ipolto Okello-Uma, and Daniel Sellen
    2009 Addressing the HIV/AIDS-Food Insecurity Syndemic in Sub-Saharan Africa. African Journal of AIDS Research 8(4):401–412.
Himmelgreen, David A., and Nancy Romero-Daza
    2010 Bytes of Note; The Global Food Crisis, HIV/AIDS, and Home Gardens (Invited Column). Environment: Science and Policy for Sustainable Development 52(4):6–8.
Institute of Medicine
    2004 Improving Medical Education: Enhancing the Behavioral and Social Science Content of Medical School Curricula. Institute of Medicine. http://www.iom.edu/~/media/Files/Report%20Files/2004/Improving-Medical-Education-Enhancing-the-Behavioral-and-Social-Science-Content-of-Medical-School-Curricula/medschoolsfinalweb.pdf, accessed August 14, 2012.
Jeste, Dilip V., Elizabeth W. Twamley, Veronica Cardenas, Barry Lebowitz, and Charles F. Reynolds, III
    2009 A Call for Training the Trainers: Focus on Mentoring to Enhance Diversity in Mental Health Research. American Journal of Public Health 99(Suppl. 1):S31-S37.
Johnson, W. Brad
    2007 On Being a Mentor: A Guide for Higher Education Faculty. Mahwah, NJ: Lawrence Erlbaum Associates.
Kahn, James, Christine D. Des Jarlais, Loren Dobkin, Sarah French Barrs, and Ruth M. Greenblatt
    2008 Mentoring the Next Generation of HIV Prevention Researchers: A Model Mentoring Program at the University of California San Francisco and Gladstone Institute of Immunology and Virology Center for AIDS Research. Journal of Acquired Immune Deficiency Syndromes 47(1):S5–S9.
Kahn, James S., and Ruth M. Greenblatt
    2009 Mentoring Early-Career Scientists for HIV Research Careers. American Journal of Public Health 99(Suppl. 1):S37–S42.
Klein, Hugh
    2011 Using a Syndemics Theory Approach to Studying HIV Risk Taking in a Population of Men Who Use the Internet to Find Partners for Unprotected Sex. American Journal of Men's Health 5(6):466–476.

Koblin, Beryl A., Margaret A. Chesney, Marla J. Husnik, Sam Bozeman, Connie L. Celum, Susan Buchbinder, Kenneth Mayer, David McKiman, Franklyn N. Judson, Yijian Huang, Thomas J. Coates, and EXPLORE Study Team

    2003 High-Risk Behaviors Among Men Who Have Sex With Men in 6 US Cities: Baseline Data From the EXPLORE Study. American Journal of Public Health 93(6):926–932.

Kreling, Barbara A., Janet Canar, Ericson Catipon, Michelle Goodman, Nancy Pallesen, Jyl Pomeroy, Yosselyn Rodriguez, Juan Romagoza, Vanessa B. Sheppard, Jeanne Mendelblatt, and Elmer E. Huerta

    2006 Latin American Cancer Research Coalition Community Primary Care/Academic Partnership Model for Cancer Control. Cancer Supplement 107(Suppl. 8):2015–2022.

Kwan, Cadice K. and Joel D. Ernst

    2011 HIV and Tuberculosis: A Deadly Human Syndemic. Clinical Microbiology Reviews 24(2): 351–376.

Lagomasino, Isabel T., Megan Dwight-Johnon, Jeanne Miranda, Lily Zhang, Diana Liao, Naihua Duan, and Kenneth B. Wells

    2005 Disparities in Depression Treatment for Latinos and Site of Care. Psychiatric Services 56(12):1517–1523.

Levant, Ronald F., and A. Eugene Shapiro

    2002 Training Psychologists in Clinical Psychopharmacology. Journal of Clinical Psychology 58(6): 611–615.

Littleton, Judith, and Julie Park

    2009 Tuberculosis and Syndemics: Implications for Public Health in New Zealand. Social Science & Medicine 69(11):1674–1680.

McGuire, Sharon, and Jane Georges

    2010 Undocumentedness and Liminality as Health Variables. Advances in Nursing Science 26(3):185–195.

Meyer, Jamie P., Sandra A. Springer, and Frederick L. Altice

    2011 Substance Abuse, Violence, and HIV in Women: A Literature Review of the Syndemic. Journal of Women's Health 20(7):991–1006.

Miville, Marie L., Changming Duan, Roberta L. Nutt, Charles A. Waehler, Lisa Suzuki, M. Carole Pistole, Patricia Arrenondo, Michael Duffy, Brenda X. Mejia, and Melissa Corpus

    2009 Integrating Practice Guidelines into Professional Training: Implications for Diversity Competence. The Counseling Psychologist 37(4):519–563.

Mustanski, Brian, Robert Garofalo, Amy Herrick, and Geri Donenberg

    2007 Psychosocial Health Problems Increase Risk for HIV Among Urban Young Men Who Have Sex With Men: Preliminary Evidence of a Syndemic in Need of Attention. Annals of Behavioral Medicine 34(1):37–45.

National Council of La Raza.

    N.d. Twenty FAQS about Hispanics. http://www.nclr.org/index.php/about_us/faqs/most_frequently_asked_questions_about_hispanics_in_the_us/, accessed March 7, 2012.

    2010 Make the Workforce Investment Act Work for Latinos: Principles for WIA Reauthorization. http://www.nclr.org/images/uploads/publications/NCLR_WIA_Principles.pdf, accessed March 8, 2012.

National Institute of Mental Health

    2001 National Institute of Mental Health Five-Year Strategic Plan for Reducing Health Disparities. National Institute of Mental Health. http://www.nimh.nih.gov/about/strategic-planning-reports/nimh-five-year-strategic-plan-for-reducing-health-disparities.pdf, accessed August 14, 2012.

Norris, Keith C., Rebecca Brusuelas, Loretta Jones, Jeanne Miranda, Obidiugwu Kenrik Duru, and Carol M. Mangione

    2007 Partnering With Community-Based Organizations: An Academic Institution's Evolving Perspective. Ethnicity & Disease 17(1):S27–S32.

Office of Adoption and Child Protection

    2010 Florida Child Abuse Prevention and Permanency Plan: July 2010-June 2015. Office of Adoption and Child Protection. http://www.dcf.state.fl.us/programs/children/docs/5yrPrev/Five-Year%20Plan%20Section%201-%20Introduction.pdf, accessed November 30, 2011.

Olson, Steven, and Adam P. Fagen, eds.

2007 Understanding Interventions that Encourage Minorities to Pursue Research Careers: Summary of a Workshop. Washington, DC: National Academy Press.

Operario, Don, and Tooru Nemoto

2010 HIV in Transgender Communities: Syndemic Dynamics and a Need for Multicomponent Interventions. Journal of Acquired Immune Deficiency Syndrome 55(Suppl. 2):S91–S93.

Pew Hispanic Center

2011 Census 2010: 50 Million Latinos; Hispanics Account for More than Half of Nation's Growth in Past Decade. Pew Research Center. http://www.pewhispanic.org/files/reports/140.pdf, accessed August 14, 2012.

2012 Hispanics Say They Have the Worst of a Bad Economy. Pew Research Center. http://www.pewhispanic.org/files/2012/01/NSL-2011-economy-report_1_26_FINAL__.pdf, accessed March 8, 2012.

Rabionet, Silvia E., Lydia E. Santiage, and Carmen D. Zorrilla

2009 A Multifaceted Mentoring Model for Minority Researchers to Address HIV Health Disparities. American Journal of Public Health 99(Suppl. 1):S65–S70.

Romero-Daza, Nancy, Margaret Weeks, and Merrill Singer

1999 Much More Than HIV!. The Reality of Life on the Streets for Drug-Using Sex Workers in Inner City Hartford. International Quarterly of Community Health Education 18(1):107–119.

2003 "Nobody Gives a Damn if I Live or Die". Violence, Drugs, and Street-Level Prostitution in Inner City Hartford. Medical Anthropology 22(3):233–259.

2005 Conceptualizing the Impact of Indirect Violence on HIV Risk Among Women Involved in Street Level Prostitution. Aggression and Violent Behavior 10(2):153–170.

Satterfield, James. M., Shelley R. Adler. Huiju Carrie Chen, Karen Hauer, George W. Saba, and Rene Salazar, R.

2010 Creating an ideal social and behavioral sciences curriculum for medical students. Medical Education, 44: 1194–1202.

Senn, Theresa E., Michael P. Carey, and Peter A. Vanable

2010 The Intersection of Violence, Substance Use, Depression, and STDs: Testing of a Syndemic Pattern Among Patients Attending an Urban STD Clinic. Journal of the National Medical Association 102(7):614–620.

Shavers, Vickie L., Pebbles Fagan, Deidre Lawrence, Worta McCaskill-Stevens, Paige McDonald, Doris Browne, Dan McLinden, Michaele Christian, and Edward Trimble

2005 Barriers to Racial/Ethnic Minority Application and Competition for NIH Research Funding. Journal of the National Medical Association 97(8):1063–1077.

Singer, Merrill

1996 A Dose of Drugs, a Touch of Violence, a Case of AIDS: Conceptualizing the SAVA Syndemic. Free Inquiry in Creative Sociology 24(2):99–110.

2009a Desperate Measures: A Syndemic Approach to the Anthropology of Health in a Violent City. In Global Health in the Time of Violence. Barbara Rylko-Bauer, Linda Whiteford, and Paul Farmer, eds. Pp. 137–156. Sante Fe: SAR Press.

2009b Introduction to Syndemics: A Systems Approach to Public and Community Health. San Francisco: Jossey-Bass.

2010 Pathogen-Pathogen Interaction: A Syndemic Model of Complex Biosocial Processes in Disease. Virulence 1(1):10–18.

2011 Toward a Critical Biosocial Model of Ecohealth in Southern Africa: The HIV/AIDS and Nutrition Insecurity Syndemic. Annals of Anthropological Practice 35(1):8–27.

Singer, Merrill and Scott Clair

2003 Syndemics and Public Health: Reconceptualizing Disease in Bio-Social Context. Medical Anthropology Quarterly 17(4):423–441.

Singer, Merrill, Pamela I. Erickson, Louise Badiane, Rosemary Diaz, Dugeidy Ortiz, Traci Abraham, and Anna Marie Nicolaysen

2006 Syndemics, Sex and the City: Understanding Sexually Transmitted Diseases in Social and Cultural Context. Social Science and Medicine 63:2010–2021.

Singer, Merrill, and Nancy Romero-Daza

1999 A Notable Connection Between Substance Abuse, Violence, and AIDS: Initial Findings From Research in the Puerto Rican Community of Hartford. Alcohol and Drug Study Group Bulletin 34(2):9–12.

Singer, Merrill, and Charlene Snipes

1992 Generations of Suffering: Experiences of a Treatment Program for Substance Abuse During Pregnancy. Journal of Health Care for the Poor and 3(1):222–234.

Singer, Merrill and Margaret Weeks

2005 The Hartford Model of AIDS Practice/Research. *In* Community Interventions and AIDS. Edison Trickett and Willo Peguegnat, eds. Pp. 153–175. Oxford, UK: Oxford University Press.

Sinkford, Jeanne C., Joseph F. West, Richard G. Weaver, and Richard W. Valachovic

2009 Modeling Mentoring: Early Lessons From the W.K. Kellogg/ADEA Minority Dental Faculty Development Program. Journal of Dental Education 73(6):753–763.

Snyder, C.R., and Timothy R. Elliott

2005 Twenty-First Century Graduate Education in Clinical Psychology: A Four Level Matrix Model. Journal of Clinical Psychology 61(9):1033–1054.

Stall, Ron, Mark Friedman, and Joseph A. Catania

2008 Interacting Epidemic and Gay Men's Health: A Theory of Syndemic Production Among Urban Gay Men. *In* Unequal Opportunity: Health Disparities Affecting Gay and Bisexual Men in the United States. Richard J. Wolitski, Ron Stall, and Ronald O. Valdiserri, eds. Pp. 251–274. Oxford: Oxford University Press.

Storholm, Erik D., Perry N. Halkitis, Daniel E. Siconolfi, and Robert W. Moeller

2011 Cigarette Smoking as Part of a Syndemic Among Young Men Who Have Sex With Men Ages 13–29 in New York City. Journal of Urban Health: Bulletin of the New York Academy of Medicine 88(4):663–676.

Trinh-Shevrin, Chau, Henry J. Pollack, Thomas Tsang, Jihyun Park, Mary Ruchel Ramos, Nadia Islam, Su Wang, Kay Chun, Shao-Chee Sim, Perry Pong, Mariano Jose Rey, and Simona C. Kwon

2011 The Asian American Hepatitis B Program: Building a Coalition to Address Hepatitis B Health Disparities. Progress in Community Health Partnerships: Research, Education, and Action 5(3):261–271.

University of California San Francisco

2003 Tuberculosis and HIV. San Francisco, CA: University of California San Francisco. http://hivinsite.ucsf.edu/InSite?page=kb-05-01-06#S2X, accessed August 15, 2012.

Viets, Vanessa Lopez, Catherine Baca, Steven P. Verney, Kamilla Venner, Tassy Parker, and Nina Wallerstein

2009 Reducing Health Disparities through a Culturally Centered Mentorship Program for Minority Faculty: The Southwest Addictions Research Group (SARG) Experience. Academic Medicine 84(8):1118–1126.

Vogenthaler, Nicholas S., Craig Hadley, Sarah J. Lewis, Allan E. Rodriguez, Lisa R. Metsch, and Carlos del Rio

2010 Food Insufficiency Among HIV-Infected Crack-Cocaine Users in Atlanta and Miami. Public Health Nutrition 13(9):1478–1484.

Walkup, James, Michael B. Blank, Jeffrey S. Gonzalez, Steven Safren, Rebecca Schwartz, Larry Brown, Ira Wilson, Amy Knowlton, Frank Lombard, Cynthia Grossman, and Karen Lyda

2008 The Impact of Mental Health and Substance Abuse Factors on HIV Prevention and Treatment. Journal of Acquired Immune Deficiency Syndromes 47(1):S15–S19.

Weeks, Margaret, Mark Convey, Julia Dickson-Gomez, Jianghong Li, Kim Radda, Maria Martinez, and Eduardo Robles
  2009 Changing Drug Users' Risk Environments: Peer Health Advocates as Multi-level Community Change Agents. American Journal of Community Psychology 43:330–344.
Weiser, Sheri D., David M. Tuller, Edward A. Frongillo, Jude Senkungu, Nozmu Mukiibi, and David R. Bangsberg
  2010 Food Insecurity as a Barrier to Sustained Antiretroviral Therapy Adherence in Uganda. PLoS ONE 5(4):e10340.
Whiteford, Linda and Linda A. Bennett
  2005 Applied Anthropology in Health and Medicine. *In* Applied Anthropology: Domains of Application. Satish Kedia and John van Willigen, eds. Pp. 119–147. Westport, CT: Praeger.
World Health Organization
  2011 World Health Organization, HIV/TB Facts 2011. World Health Organization. http://www.who.int/hiv/topics/tb/hiv_tb_factsheet_june_2011.pdf, accessed August 15, 2012.
Yager, Joel, Howard Waitzkin, Tassy Parker, and Bonnie Duran
  2007 Educating, Training, and Mentoring Minority Faculty and Other Trainees in Mental Health Services Research. Academic Psychiatry 31(2):146–151.
Zea, Maria Cecilia, and Faye Z. Belgrave
  2009 Mentoring and Research Capacity-Building Experiences: Acculturating to Research From the Perspective of the Trainee. American Journal of Public Health 99(S1):S17–S19.

SYNDEMICS OF WAR: MALNUTRITION-INFECTIOUS DISEASE INTERACTIONS AND THE UNINTENDED HEALTH CONSEQUENCES OF INTENTIONAL WAR POLICIES

BAYLA OSTRACH
University of Connecticut

MERRILL SINGER
University of Connecticut

Syndemics play a substantial role in shaping the disease burdens of populations, especially in times of war. It is estimated that in the 20th century, sixty-two million civilians suffered war-related deaths, in addition to forty-five million combatant deaths. Many of these casualties were due to disease rather than battlefield injuries. Through a review and analysis of interdisciplinary literature on war and health, and using case studies of several wars from different periods of history, we argue that war is a disruptive biosocial process that sets in motion interactions between diseases and other conditions that increase war-related morbidity and mortality. [syndemics, malnutrition, infectious disease, war, comorbid, Iraq, Viet Nam, Spanish Civil War]

INTRODUCTION

The purpose of this article is to examine ways in which war, by causing physical and emotional trauma in populations, destroying health care systems and social infrastructures, despoiling the environment, intentionally or unintentionally causing or exacerbating food insecurity and malnutrition, creating refugee populations, and spreading infections (e.g. through the movement of troops, dislocation of civilian populations, changes in the environment) promotes the development of syndemics. Of primary focus in our discussion of this set of disruptions and traumas is the syndemic relationship between food insecurity/malnutrition and infectious disease in the context of war. Syndemics, the adverse interactions of comorbid diseases most likely to develop under conditions that promote disease clustering in communities, have been shown to be a critical feature of human health and to play a substantial role in shaping the total disease burdens of populations (Freudenberg et al. 2006; Singer 2009). We argue here that this is particularly so in times and spaces of war and armed conflict. In this article, we specifically examine a malnutrition-infectious disease syndemic that can occur in settings of war and conflict, as the nature of the health effects of malnutrition, and the ways that malnutrition contributes to the spread of infectious diseases, together demonstrate the value of

ANNALS OF ANTHROPOLOGICAL PRACTICE 36.2, pp. 257–273. ISSN: 2153-957X. © 2013 by the American Anthropological Association. DOI:10.1111/napa.12003

a syndemic analysis for developing practical approaches and applied public health and clinical practice.

It is estimated that in the 20th century alone, sixty-two million civilians suffered war-related deaths, in addition to forty-five million combatant deaths (Sivard 1996); notably, many of these civilian and military casualties were due to disease rather than battlefield injuries (Cirillo 2008). Yet, as Leaning (2000:1157) stresses, "There remain enormous gaps in our knowledge about the relationship of war and health." In this article, we raise the question—what role have deleterious disease interactions played in producing this toll? Based on a review of the literature on war and health, we argue that war is a traumatic and disruptive biosocial process that sets in motion dynamic interactions between diseases and other health conditions that significantly increase war-related morbidity and mortality. Some of the links between war-related conditions and disease interactions are clearly established in the existing literature and merely require further elucidation to reveal the nature of the syndemic relationship involved. Other connections are suggested but are less clear and warrant further study. In this article, we examine several case studies of wars fought in different regions and during different time periods in order to move toward a better understanding of the features and impacts of war-related syndemics. We explore the specific socioenvironmental pathways through which war promotes detrimental disease clustering and interaction, and consider the practical implications of applying a syndemic analysis to conflict situations. Such analysis is critical to the further development of war as a central issue in applied public health, clinical practice, and to various medical anthropology efforts in war zones, policy arenas, and clinical settings (Rylko-Bauer and Singer 2011; Levy and Sidel 2000; Singer and Hodge 2010a). Medical anthropology, in particular, can influence practical applications in war zones, all the more so by applying a syndemic analysis.

METHODS

To develop this review and our proposed model for war-related malnutrition-infectious disease syndemics, we reviewed relevant literature on known malnutrition-infectious disease interactions. The literature reviewed was identified through searches of *GoogleScholar*, *EBSCOHost*, *AnthroSource*, and *PubMed* in early 2011, using the search terms: *"malnutrition infection," "malnutrition infectious disease," "infectious disease war," "health effects war,"* and *"disease interactions war."* Relevant articles were reviewed by both authors for discussion of disease–disease interactions and apparent adverse disease synergies resulting from or exacerbated by malnutrition, as well as to identify the features of war and conflict that contribute to the resulting syndemic. The authors met frequently throughout the review process to discuss the findings of the literature reviewed, and, through an ongoing iterative process, to evaluate all of the potential relationships noted between past and current wars and risk factors for malnutrition-infectious disease synergies. We discussed the apparent interactions and intersections between biological and social risk factors for malnutrition-infectious disease syndemics and conditions that produce or contribute to them, in order to develop the theoretical model of syndemics of war presented.

After identifying the broad syndemic model of malnutrition-infectious disease synergies in situations and locations of war, we chose three wars of the 20th century to explore in detail as a way to illustrate the proposed model, and then conducted a more detailed, focused literature search to further examine syndemic conditions in the wars presented in our case studies. The wars we selected to present in the case studies were chosen based on the documented presence of external factors in each conflict; in this case the impact of sanctions, embargoes, and agricultural and infrastructure damage on conditions contributing to malnutrition, and the resulting spread of infectious diseases.

SYNDEMICS AND HISTORY

From the Civil War in the United States, in which infectious diseases arising in conditions of poor sanitation killed more people than died in battle (Civil War Society 2002) to the Influenza Pandemic of 1918 at the end of World War I that was caused by pathogenic interactions between a virus and at least one strain of bacteria (Morens et al. 2008), the idea of negative health effects caused or exacerbated by wartime conditions is well established (Cohen 2000; Mworozi 1993; Singer and Hodge 2010b). It is important to understand, however, more about the complex pathways and mechanisms through which wars produce sickness and suffering independently of direct battlefield casualties in order to guide public health interventions focused on regions of current, recent, or future violent conflict. Syndemics theory provides a framework for such work (Singer 2009). Specifically, it offers a conceptual model for focusing applied research attention on the ways social, economic, and political conditions affect the social and geographic distribution of diseases, and on the resulting ways these conditions promote new mechanisms of adverse synergistic disease interaction. Contrary to some misuses in the literature, a syndemic does not label a situation in which a social condition simply contributes to ill health or disease, but rather the term specifically defines damaging biological, biobehavioral, and/or psychobiological health-threatening interactions between two or more copresent diseases within populations that are made possible or worsened by the adverse context in which they co-occur (Bastos et al. 1999; Herring and Sattenspiel 2006; Himmelgreen et al. 2009; Stall et al. 2007).

Applying the concept of syndemics not only to current health problems but also to historical examples demonstrates the value of this model for illuminating long-range structural and biosocial factors in health and illness. By analyzing the extent to which political policies, armed organizations, and government actions create and maintain conditions that produce disease and suffering for civilians, an exploration of the syndemics of war reveals human costs of conflict that are rarely fully examined. In this light, we specifically highlight harmful interactions between malnutrition and infectious diseases given this interaction appears likely to be a component of both low intensity conflicts and full scale wars to come in the 21st century, and to demonstrate how specific situations of war and its associated policies can create and contribute to synergies that result in greater disease impacts.

The proposed interrelationship between malnutrition and infectious disease in the context of war is illustrated by the example of the civil war in Somalia in 1992. During the conflict, blocking food access was used as a weapon against civilians, leading to famine, a breakdown of public health programs, mass migration, and further exposure to food insecurity in refugee camps due to the contamination of food supplies. Resulting malnutrition among children ranged between 47 percent and 75 percent (Moore et al. 1993). The consequence was a high rate of diarrheal disease among both children and adults. Diarrheal disease, measles, and Shigella dysentery (all infectious diseases exacerbated by malnutrition) emerged as primary causes of death in refugee camps, leading to the demise of approximately 74 percent of children under 5 years in the camps (Moore et al. 1993). This is among the highest mortality rate that has been documented for a civilian population in a war zone.

With no signs of an end to human conflicts in sight, expanding our understanding of the syndemics of war has the potential to lead to an expanded awareness of war-related syndemics within medical anthropology and other disciplines, improved public health efforts for war-affected populations, and more relevant clinical practice in war zones. By examining war-related syndemic interactions in various sociocultural settings and time periods, we can better understand the implications of such syndemics for producing unmet public health needs.

INTERACTIONS BETWEEN MALNUTRITION AND INFECTIOUS DISEASES

The Geneva Declaration Secretariat (2008) reports that for each of the 600,000 people who died violently in a war between 2004 and 2007, another four died from diseases and malnutrition caused by war. Most importantly, these two common burdens of war act in cacophonous harmony, mutually enhancing their respective injurious impacts on human populations. The relationships between malnutrition and infectious diseases are expressed at both macro- and microlevels. At the microlevel of the individual, as discussed below, the immune system requires an array of macro- and micronutrients to function optimally (Bogden et al. 2000), and malnutrition results in compromised immune response (Field et al. 2002). Further, the relationship between malnutrition and infectious disease is bidirectional; malnutrition can promote infection while infection can interfere with the metabolism of nutrients.

Malnutrition can cause immune suppression similar to that seen in people infected with HIV/AIDS (Beisel 1996). As a result, malnourished individuals are not only more susceptible to contracting infection but also are less able to fight infectious diseases once acquired (Jamison et al. 1993; McDade 2005; Rice et al. 2000; Singer 2009). In addition to the myriad ways in which macronutrient protein–calorie malnutrition predisposes individuals to infectious disease, micronutrient deficiencies in particular affect metabolic processes as individuals suffering from infection have heightened nutritional needs (Guerrant et al. 2000; Semba and Tang 1999).

At the individual level, protein–caloric deficiencies affect the body's ability to produce components of the immune system needed to fight infection and repair damaged cells

(Goldenberg 2003). A common result of protein–calorie malnutrition is a significant loss of cell-mediated immunity, phagocyte function, complement system, secretory immunoglobulin A antibody concentrations, and cytokine production. Damage to these critical immune components and processes can be determinant. However, additional impairment can occur including loss of lymphoid cells at small blood vessels in the spleen and lymph nodes, resulting in the impairment of host-defense mechanism including delayed response to infection or full anergy upon exposure to various pathogens.

Deficiency of single micronutrients also results in altered immune responses: this is observed even when the deficiency state is relatively mild. Micronutrient deficiencies involving insufficient zinc, selenium, iron, copper, vitamin A, vitamin C, vitamin E, vitamin B-6; and folic acid, have significant adverse impact on immune responses (Chandra 1992). For example, a trace element like zinc plays vital roles in cellular growth, a capacity of special importance for cells (e.g., T-cells) that are rapidly turning over, like those of the immune system (Hambidge 2000).

At the societal level, malnutrition can affect an entire population (e.g., occupied territories, countries at war), or disproportionately affect a population subset within a particular setting (e.g., children, pregnant women, the elderly), and infectious diseases can likewise spread quickly through such vulnerable populations (Lonnroth et al. 2009; Tempel et al. 2006). A study in Burkina Faso (Zeba et al. 2008), for example, showed major reduction of malaria morbidity with combined vitamin A and zinc supplementation in young children, underscoring the role these micronutrients play in containing malarial infection.

Recognition of the adverse role of malnutrition, particularly in resource-deprived areas, has a long history (Cohen 2000; McDade 2005). Chandra (1992) traces this link as far back as the 12th century in England, where church records show a pattern of consecutive years of starvation and ensuing epidemic illnesses. Food deprivation and nutritional deficiencies are especially deleterious in circumstances where people are exposed to multiple disease agents (Smallman-Raynor and Cliff 2004). Malnutrition increases the likelihood of dying from a wide range of infectious diseases, including diarrheal diseases, malaria, HIV/AIDS, tuberculosis, and acute respiratory infections (Rice et al. 2000). Children are particularly vulnerable to such sequelae from malnutrition, with an estimated 54 percent of childhood deaths in developing countries attributed to the effects of malnutrition (Birn et al. 2009). Under such conditions, the potential exists for a vicious cycle of malnutrition and infection to occur among highly vulnerable populations in adverse environments (Padbidri 2002).

The interactions of malnutrition and disease have multiple expressions. Research on the effects of maternal malnutrition during pregnancy on a child's subsequent health status, for example, suggests that children who suffer from intrauterine growth retardation or low birth-weight due to maternal malnutrition during pregnancy are at greater risk for infection later in childhood, among other negative health impacts, and that such children are, "the product of both a prenatal and a postnatal environment characterized by a synergistic interaction between infection and an inadequate supply of nutrients" (Gershwin et al. 1987:1).

Multiple studies (Barker and Osmond 1986; Bryne and Phillips 2000; Chandra 1992; Gershwin et al. 1987) report that children who suffer from malnutrition as infants are likely to experience immunosuppression that may persist over time, presenting another pathway through which malnutrition in times of war can predispose people to infectious disease susceptibility, a pathway that has lasting effects far beyond the life span of any given war. Moreover, a classic study (Barker and Osmond 1986) on malnutrition at a very early age (in utero and in infancy) in Britain showed that it was linked to both earlier and more severe adult chronic disease. These researchers offer convincing evidence for an association between high rates of childhood malnutrition and corresponding high rates of ischemic heart disease later in life (Barker 1998; Barker and Osmond 1986). Research on cardiovascular disease suggests that malnutrition may elevate the risk of contracting infections associated with coronary heart disease, and "trigger the development of atherosclerotic cardiovascular disease" (Bergstrom and Lindholm 1999:310).

Further, malnutrition has been demonstrated to be a factor in tuberculosis and HIV coinfection, two diseases that frequently increase in prevalence in war-affected areas (Accorsi et al. 2005; Singer and Clair 2003). As Macallan notes, "there is good evidence, both at the population level and at the clinical level, for the effect of primary malnutrition on tuberculosis, both to increase frequency of occurrence and to exacerbate clinical manifestations." (Macallan 1999:155). Add Hogan and Burstein, "Human immunodeficiency virus (HIV) spreads faster during emergencies when conditions such as poverty, powerlessness, social instability, and violence against women are most extreme." (Hogan and Burstein 2002:41). In interaction, HIV and tuberculosis have been identified as "a deadly human syndemic" (Kwan and Ernst 2011). These examples offer but a few of the many possible scenarios in which malnutrition and infectious diseases combine in deleterious ways.

While a malnutrition/infectious disease syndemic is clearly not the only one associated with war (nor only found under conditions of war), we give it special attention here for three reasons. First, because of the multiple ways that war can interrupt food access, including causing disruptions in domestic agriculture and food production, limiting food transport, restricting access to food through embargoes and sanctions, and promoting the displacement of refugees into areas of food insecurity (Egal 2006; O'Hare and Southall 2007; Santa Barbara 2008). Second, because a population's military diminishes with infectious disease progression and pathogenic transmission, disruption of food access has become a tempting weapon of war. Finally, interactions between malnutrition and infections in the context of war can affect individuals and populations long after a war has ended with obvious public health implications. (Barker and Osmond 1986; Chandra 1992; Gershwin et al. 1987).

CASE STUDIES

The following case studies were chosen based on their known or suggested historical impacts on nutritional status and the infectious disease burden in affected populations. We also seek to explore various ways that food deprivation and resulting malnutrition are caused by war; in the following cases these include embargoes, crop destruction, infrastructure damage, and sanctions.

Spanish Civil War: Starvation and Disease

The Spanish Civil War, which lasted from 1936 to 1939, destroyed Spain's infrastructure, economy, and health care system, and divided the population between those loyal to the democratically elected Republican government, and Fascist who challenged the government and brought Franco's dictatorship to power with the support of Hitler and Mussolini (Beevor 1982, 2006). The United States, along with England, France, and Germany claimed a position of "neutrality" and refused to sell arms, supplies, or food to the Spanish Republican government, likely contributing to high rates of malnutrition suffered by soldiers and supporters on that side in the war, while apparently disregarding their own non-interventionist stance and supplying the Fascists with arms and supplies behind the scenes (Beevor 1982). After the Republicans lost their hold on Barcelona late in the war, Fascist rebels were able to cut off food supplies to retreating troops and the civilians who supported them, resulting in widespread malnutrition (Coni 2002; Beevor 1982).

It is estimated that at one point during the war, three hundred to four hundred people per day were dying from starvation in Madrid alone, where the Republicans were based, and during long sieges civilians suffered from severe malnutrition at locations around the country (Beevor 1982, 2006; Coni 2002; Garcia-Albea 1999). The widespread international "nonintervention" approach meant that in practical terms, the Republican troops and their civilian sympathizers had few sources of food aid, and depended primarily on the limited foods they could purchase from Mexico and the Soviet Union (Beevor 1982). Stories from the time, as told for example by George Orwell (who fought alongside the Republicans as part of the International Brigades), mention supplies of beans and lentils sent by Mexico that were used to feed troops and civilians alike for as long as stores lasted (Beevor 1982, 2006; Orwell 1952). At one point, Republican loyalists in Barcelona subsisted on a ration of 100 grams of lentils per day (Beevor 2006). In the mountain areas north of Madrid, the chief health official of the Republican Second Corp reported that calorie intake was severely inadequate and that soldiers lacked essential vitamins found in vegetables and fresh fruits (Seidman 1999). Highlighting the above-mentioned importance of micro-nutrients in preventing disease, Orwell also remarked on how the supply of Valencian oranges available to Republican troops during some seasons at least helped to stave off scurvy, a common result of malnutrition (Orwell 1952).

Estimates are that 165,000 people died of infectious diseases during the Spanish Civil War (Payne 1987). Malaria was a main cause of hospital admission (Coni 2002); along with typhoid fever, smallpox, diphtheria, and dysentery, malaria was an infectious disease of specific concern during the Spanish Civil War (Barona and Perdiguero-Gil 2008). Malaria has a known synergistic relationship with malnutrition (Singer 2008), while typhoid fever outbreaks are strongly associated with malnutrition (Gupta 1994). Similarly a reduced antibody response to diphtheria has been noted in malnourished children (Padbidri 2002). Additionally, dysentery was historically associated with poor hygiene and malnutrition, terms that more than adequately describe conditions during the Spanish Civil War (Padbidri 2002).

An author of several League of Nations reports on health conditions in Spain during the war emphasized the role of poor food supply in deteriorating health among civilians, particularly in Madrid (Barona and Perdiguero-Gil 2008), and health problems attributed to poor hygiene at the time are now considered to have resulted more immediately from malnutrition (Beevor 2006). Widespread malnutrition and food shortages also contributed to "deficiency illnesses" among wide sectors of the war-affected Spanish population (Barona and Perdiguero-Gil 2008). A Rockefeller Foundation investigation conducted near the end of the war acknowledged the contributions of health services organized by the Republicans, but also documented widespread outbreaks of epidemic illnesses under conditions of malnutrition (Janney 1940).

One long-term health effect of nutritional deprivation during the Spanish Civil War has been documented in the form of increased heart disease risk later in life for people born during the war, due to nutritional stress during fetal development (Gonzalez Zapata, et al. 2006). More broadly, a study of chronic diseases and disability among now-elderly Spaniards found that a higher proportion of the over 60 (at the time of the study) population was disabled than their European counterparts (Graciani et al. 2004). The difference was described as potentially attributable to this Spanish age cohort having lived through the Spanish Civil War under "harsh" conditions (Graciani et al. 2004). It should be readily apparent that many other cohorts are currently living under similar harsh conditions in present-day wars, or have lived through them during wars that have ended. Considering the impacts of conditions of conflict on human health in the form of the various syndemics of war thus offers important lessons for envisioning (and meeting) the long-term health needs of war-affected populations.

Vietnam–Agricultural Land Destruction, Malnutrition, and Disease

The American War in Vietnam was the first conflict to fully unleash the potential devastating effects of modern warfare on entire ecosystems. The widespread spraying of herbicides, including Agent Orange, by the United States military was intended to destroy food crops and forest cover used by "enemy" troops, while also contributing to losses of freshwater fish, and it has had lasting health effects with high levels of teratogenic and carcinogenic dioxin still found in Vietnamese soil and in the breast milk and tissues of affected populations (Levy et al. 2000; Quy 2005). More than eighty million liters of herbicides were sprayed over nearly 25 percent of South Vietnam, 14 percent of these herbicides were directed at agricultural lands, "primarily for the destruction of rice production . . . to expose Vietnamese people to hunger" (Quy 2005). Research suggests that targeted crop destruction in Vietnam affected 400,000 hectares of agricultural land, destroying more than 300,000 tons of food (Westing 1983).

Records of imports and exports of rice before and during the war in Vietnam indicate that crop destruction reduced Vietnamese domestic rice production by one-fifth during the war (Westing 1983). Food production increased by 18 percent in the first year after the war ended, but slowed after that, requiring food imports to avoid famine (Westing

1983). In the first few years after the end of the war, malnutrition was widespread in Vietnam, and its effects were still visible ten years later (Khan 2010; Westing 1983). While great progress has been made in the three-plus decades since the war officially ended, with fisheries in Vietnam now more plentiful, and the shrimp catch in previously polluted areas increasing yearly (Quy 2005), the lasting effects of malnutrition resulting from crop destruction during the war in Vietnam are noteworthy. Given what we have already shown about the relationships between malnutrition and infectious diseases, it is plausible that the intentional destruction of food crops in Vietnam and ensuing malnutrition may have contributed to a sudden increase in the infectious disease burden among the Vietnamese people living in heavily impacted areas.

Few sources specifically address the effects of herbicide-caused crop destruction and associated nutritional status changes on rates of infectious diseases in Vietnam. As Allukian and Atwood report, "reliable [health] data do not exist on the immediate effects of the war [in Vietnam] because of poor recordkeeping, biased perspectives, destruction of records, and massive population shifts" (Allukian and Atwood 2000:217). Additionally, during the period from 1976 to 1986, the first ten years following the reunification of Vietnam, "the massive effort required for the reconstruction of war damage and the restructuring of the former planned and centralized economy, left little room for the investigation of social issues" (Dinh 1995). However, Allukian and Atword report that in the aftermath of the war, the Vietnamese population suffered serious outbreaks of malaria, tuberculosis, leprosy, hemorrhagic fever, trachoma, cholera, plague and parasitic diseases (Allukian and Atwood 2000). A survey of tuberculosis cases found a rate that was two times that of neighboring countries (WHO 1976). The survey also found that the prevalence of trachoma reached 75 percent in Northern provinces of the country and 57 percent in the Mekong Delta. Moreover, the population of the Mekong Delta suffered a high prevalence of typhoid fever during the postwar period (Bailey 2010). Tuberculosis and typhoid, both of which interact synergistically with malnutrition as discussed earlier, were also widespread among civilians in Vietnam during the war (Vastyan 1971). Finally, studies of healthcare infrastructure damage and constraints on the medical system in Vietnam during the war documented "rampant" and "persistent" infectious diseases among a largely malnourished Vietnamese population (Goldson 1996).

In light of these suggestive data, we propose a syndemic model linking military use of herbicides, intentional and unintentional crop destruction, malnutrition, and intensified infectious disease outbreaks in postwar Vietnam. Notably, existing literature on the impact of malnutrition in war acknowledges how purposeful withholding of food during military conflicts can adversely affect vulnerable populations. As Mayer observes, "food denial in war . . . is hardest on civilians, particularly children and the elderly; where economic class distinctions are sharp, it is particularly hard on the poor" (Mayer 1967:116). A well-respected nutritional researcher and adviser to the White House, Jean Mayer argued that the use of herbicides such as Agent Orange in Vietnam led to food shortages that unavoidably had the greatest effects on children, elderly people, and pregnant and lactating women, with lesser effects on men and soldiers. This suggests that the United States military's strategic destruction of food crops in Vietnam, justified at the time as a means of disrupting combat operations by the National Front for the Liberation of Vietnam (aka VietCong), was also designed to impact the civilian population by causing food shortages. Gibson (1986:230), in fact, suggested that the "chemical destruction of Vietnamese crops . . . threaten[ed] slow starvation." As a result, there appears to have been a resulting spread of multiple infectious diseases, although there is no evidence that this was an intended outcome. In the absence of more specific literature on the relationship between malnutrition and infectious diseases that increased in prevalence during the war in Vietnam, it is difficult to do more than propose a likely role for syndemic interaction as a consequence of the war and to suggest the need for additional ethnohistorical and archival research on this issue.

Gulf War Sanctions—Infrastructure Damage, Malnutrition, and Infectious Disease in Iraq

The Persian Gulf War of 1991 and the international sanctions against Iraq that followed it resulted in widespread damage to water systems and sanitation resulting in the rapid acceleration of several epidemics: including increased incidences of cholera, typhoid, gastroenteritis, malaria, meningitis, brucellosis, measles, polio, hepatitis, and other infectious diseases, especially among children (UNCF 1993). Iraq's water treatment plants, drinking water and sewage pipes, and the sanitary functioning of flush toilets were severely affected (Siziya et al. 2009). Children living in homes affected by degraded water pipes and lacking the benefits of functional water treatment plants to process sewage were more likely to suffer from diarrheal episodes and respiratory infections—two leading causes of under-five mortality (Siziya et al. 2009).

International sanctions imposed against Iraq by the United States and its allies following the Persian Gulf War resulted in high rates of malnutrition, especially among children, likely increasing children's risk for diarrheal diseases (Siziya et al. 2009; WHO 2001). Malnutrition increased the proportion of respiratory infections that resulted in death (Hoskins 2000). Limitations on food imports under sanctions, and the decreased ability of Iraqis to produce and process their own food supplies following the war due to the lack of clean water and sanitation also contributed to the malnutrition that rapidly emerged as a threat to Iraqi health (Hoskins 2000). Public health research has repeatedly demonstrated that sanctions in Iraq had the greatest negative health effects on those "least able to bear the burden," that is, children (Birn et al. 2009). Two years after the Gulf War ended, the vast majority of the Iraqi population faced severe hunger (Birn et al. 2009). The combination of food deprivation and sanitation destruction contributed to conditions of widespread starvation that dramatically affected Iraqi children in particular. It is estimated that by 1998, 7 years into the sanctions, there were five hundred thousand "excess deaths" of Iraqi children (Arya and Zurbrigg 2007).

The strategic, targeted destruction of Iraq's water system and sanitation facilities by the U.S. military (Nagy 2001) and the introduction of U.S.-supported sanctions worsened sanitation, reduced access to clean drinking water, and contributed to widespread malnutrition (WHO 2001). Thus, the U.S. military tactics in the Persian Gulf in the 1990s and since have directly contributed to the spread of infectious diseases in Iraq

(Garfield 1999; Siziya et al. 2009). It is estimated that post-Gulf War sanctions, by affecting nutrition, access to clean water, and sanitation, as well as other health-support systems, caused the deaths of at least four civilians for every Iraqi soldier killed in battle (Garfield 1999). These deaths were not an accidental by-product. The deaths and diseases resulting from Gulf War era Iraqi water infrastructure damage, for example, were part of a deliberate plan, as admitted by the U.S. military in a declassified Defense Intelligence Agency document, in clear violation of the Geneva Conventions (Nagy 2001).

Of note, the US Veterans Affairs (USVA) provides clients and staff members with guidelines to use when screening for and treating infectious diseases among veterans who served during the Gulf War and in the region since then, including during the current, ongoing occupation of Iraq (VA 2003). The VA is concerned about the risks of exposure to malaria, tuberculosis, and other infectious diseases for service members who spent time in Iraq during and after the Persian Gulf War (VA 2003; VA 2003). The obvious implication is that these diseases posed significant health threats for civilians living there too. As the VA reports, "in areas of civil unrest... the risk of malaria increases" (VA 2003). As described earlier, malaria and tuberculosis are two infectious diseases known to interact syndemically with, respectively, malnutrition and HIV/AIDS (Singer 2008).

DISCUSSION–PATHWAYS OF INTERACTION

While the specific pathways of interaction between malnutrition and infectious diseases occurred differently in each case study discussed above, the unifying thread between them is the *intentional deprivation of food and other supplies from civilians in war zones*, and in some cases the *intentional destruction of infrastructure needed for sanitation and nutrition*. The process of reviewing articles for this article revealed gaps in the literature related to the long-term effects of herbicides used during the war in Vietnam on nutrition among civilians. We propose that one reason we found more literature about negative health effects of military tactics in the Persian Gulf War was due to increased media attention and popular demand for such information, including public struggles by veterans to obtain information from the government about their postwar health problems, following the *lack* of full disclosure about potential negative health outcomes related to military tactics in Vietnam.

In the Spanish Civil War of the 1930s, international sanctions in the form of nonintervention stances that prohibited the sale of food and other supplies to the Republicans resulted in widespread malnutrition among loyalist civilians that in turn contributed to the spread of, and civilian and military morbidity and mortality due to, infectious diseases. Depriving civilians in a war-torn country of adequate food, for political reasons, led to high rates of malnutrition-related malaria, smallpox, typhus, diphtheria, and dysentery, as well as increased risks for heart disease and disability later in life for those who survived.

During the U.S. military campaign in Vietnam, the use of herbicides for intentional, targeted, strategic crop destruction affected not only the immediate health of those sprayed with the carcinogenic and teratogenic chemicals, but also resulted in food shortages, starvation, and malnutrition among surviving civilians who were unable to grow enough food to sustain themselves after a significant number of hectares of rice fields and other crops were destroyed. A likely result was an intensification of infectious disease epidemics.

During and after the Persian Gulf War, U.S. military tactics and U.S.-supported international sanctions against Iraq caused widespread infrastructural damage, including the destruction of water sanitation plants and sewer systems, and deprived civilians of food supplies. Many of the resulting deaths, and much of the overall morbidity and mortality among children and adults during and after the Persian Gulf War resulted from diarrheal diseases and respiratory infections that were caused or worsened by the combination of conditions of malnutrition and lack of sanitation. As we have argued, these conditions occurred as the planned, strategic outcomes of *intended* destruction and deprivation. In short, in each of our cases, military and political strategies including the intended decline of food access, resulted, as well, in *unintended* (but perhaps equally damaging) infectious disease syndemics in civilian populations.

CONCLUSIONS

Beyond the immediate casualties inflicted on battlefields or in military attacks, war-related suffering takes many forms and operates at multiple and complex levels. In this article, we have examined three case studies of specific wars to propose a syndemic model that explains the impact of wartime conditions on infectious disease interactions related to malnutrition. As expressed in a widely distributed Vietnam era anti-war poster, "War is not healthy for children and other living things" (AMFP 1969). One among the many reasons this is true is because of war-related syndemics, which are particularly harsh for children given their specific dietary needs and less developed immune systems. Some of the links underlying war-related syndemics are readily apparent in the literature discussed and can be easily explored through a syndemic lens. Other connections are more suggestive of a model that deserves further study to clearly establish the pathways of interaction.

The issue of malnutrition-related infectious disease interactions is but one of many potential syndemics resulting from conditions of war. Current, ongoing military occupations in Iraq and Afghanistan undoubtedly offer more examples of such interactions (e.g., PTSD and drug addiction). The impacts of these current wars, as well as those of future military campaigns, will be inscribed in the nutritional status and disease burdens of the civilian populations in each country. Without focused research, it will remain unclear how many casualties of current and future wars involve war-related syndemic interaction and how many of these interactions are caused by sanctions or international embargoes. How many children and teens, for example, needlessly suffered from meningitis-B infections during the United States' embargo against the import of Cuba's meningitis vaccine? (BBC 1999). Did the 2011 sanctions against Libya's government result in food shortages and malnutrition for Libyans, and in turn contribute to malnutrition-related infectious disease outbreaks? Increasingly, war has been redefined as a public health issue, one that results in considerable loss of life, disability, and human suffering (Levy and Sidel 2000). Greater understanding of the syndemics of war is a needed component of emergent public health analysis and responses to the brutalities of war.

Syndemic analysis offers a useful and revealing way to expand war as a central issue in applied approaches to public health and clinical practice. Health policy-makers and providers of direct care will benefit from an improved understanding of the various ways that wars can deleteriously affect human health through syndemic interactions. At a practical level, understanding precisely how malnutrition and infectious diseases interact in war zones can (and should) inform effective approaches to treating affected populations, as well as offer information and evidence that can be used to shape political efforts to prevent or end wars; or at the very least, to reduce the harmful effects that wars have on civilian populations through sanctions, embargoes, and infrastructure damage. A syndemic analysis of the health effects of war thus is critical for further developing war as a primary focus of applied public health, and to strengthen medical anthropology efforts in war zones, policy settings, and in clinical practice.

REFERENCES CITED

Accorsi, Sandro, Massimo Fabiani, Barbara Nattabi, Bruno Corrado, Robert Iriso, Emingtone O. Ayella, Bongomin Pido, Paul A. Onek, Martin Ogwang, and Silvia Declich
    2005 The Disease Profile of Poverty: Morbidity and Mortality in Northern Uganda in the Context of War, Population Displacement and HIV/AIDS. Transactions of the Royal Society of Tropical Medicine and Hygiene 99(3):226–233.
Allukian, Myron, and Paul L. Atwood
    2000 Public Health and the Vietnam War. In War and Public Health. Barry Levy and Victor Sidel, eds. Pp. 217–237. Oxford: Oxford University Press.
Another Mother for Peace (AMFP)
    1969 "War is Not Healthy for Children and Other Living Things [poster]. Beverly Hills: AMP Press Center.
Arya, Neil, and Sheila Zurbrigg
    2007 Operation Infinite Injustice: Impact of Sanctions and Prospective War on the People of Iraq. Canadian Journal of Public Health 94(1):9–12.
Bailey, Penny
    2010 Two Decades of Research in Vietnam. August 24. http://www.wellcome.ac.uk/News/2010/Features/WTX062544.htm, accessed May 24, 2012.
Barker, David J.P.
    1998 Mothers, Babies and Health in Later Life. 2nd edition. Edinburgh: Churchill Livingstone.
Barker, David J.P., and Clive Osmond
    1986 Infant Mortality, Childhood Nutrition and Ischaemic Heart Disease in England and Wales. Lancet 327(8489):1077–1081.
Josep, Barona L., and Enrique Perdiguero-Gil
    2008 Health and the War: Changing Schemes and Health Conditions during the Spanish Civil War. Dynamis 28:103–126.
Bastos, Francisco Inacio, Christovam Barcellos, Catherine Lowndes, and Samuel R. Friedman
    1999 Co-infection with Malaria and HIV in Injecting Drug Users in Brazil: A New Challenge to Public Health? Addiction 94(8):1165–1174.
Beevor, Antony
    1982 The Spanish Civil War. London: Orbis.
    2006 The Battle for Spain: The Spanish Civil War 1936–1939. London: Weidenfeld and Nicolson.

Beisel, William R.

    1996 Nutrition in Pediatric HIV Infection: Setting the Research Agenda. Nutrition and Immune Function: Overview. Journal of Nutrition 126(10 Suppl):2611S–2615S.

Bergstrom, Jonas, and Bengt Lindholm

    1999 Malnutrition, Cardiac Disease, and Mortality. Peritoneal Dialysis International 19(Suppl 2):S309–S314.

Birn, Anne-Emanuelle, Yogan Pillat, and Timothy H. Holtz

    2009 Textbook of International Health: Global Health in a Dynamic World. 3rd edition. Oxford: Oxford University Press.

Bogden, John, Francis Kemp, Shenggao Han, Wenjie Li, Kay Bruening, Thomas Denny, James M. Oleske, Joan Lloyd, Herman Baker, George Perez, Patricia Kloser, Joan Skurnick, and Donald B. Louria

    2000 Status of Selected Nutrients and Progression of Human Immunodeficiency Virus Type 1 Infection. American Journal of Clinical Nutrition 72(3):809–815.

British Broadcasting Corporation (BBC)

    1999 Americas: Cuba Vaccine Deal Breaks Embargo. July 29, http://news.bbc.co.uk/2/hi/americas/406780.stm, accessed May 25, 2012.

Bryrne, Christopher, and David I. Phillips

    2000 Fetal Origins of Adult Disease: Epidemiology and Mechanisms. Journal of Clinical Pathology 53(11):822–828.

Chandra, Ranjit K.

    1992 Protein-Energy Malnutrition and Immunological Responses. Journal of Nutrition 122(3):597–600.

Cirillo, Vincent J.

    2008 Two Faces of Death: Fatalities from Disease and Combat in America's Principal Wars, 1775 to Present. Perspectives in Biology and Medicine 51(1):121–133.

Civil War Society

    2002 Medical Care, Battle Wounds, and Disease. http://www.civilwarhome.com/civilarmedicine.htm, accessed May 25, 2012.

Cohen, Mitchell L.

    2000 Changing Patterns of Infectious Disease. Nature 406(6797):762–767.

Coni, Nicholas

    2002 Medicine and the Spanish Civil War. Journal of the Royal Society of Medicine 95(23):147–150.

Dinh, Do Duc

    1995 The Social Impact of Economic Reconstruction in Vietnam: A Selected Review. Geneva: International Institute for Labour Studies.

Egal, Florence

    2006 Nutrition in Conflict Situations. British Journal of Nutrition 96(Suppl 1):S17–S19.

Field, Catherine, J., Ian R. Johnson, and Patricia D. Schley

    2002 Nutrients and Their Role in Host Resistance to Infection. Journal of Leukocyte Biology 71(1):16–32.

Freudenberg, Nicholas, Marianne Fahs, Sandro Galea, and Andrew Greenberg

    2006 The Impact of New York City's 1975 Fiscal Crisis on the Tuberculosis, HIV, and Homicide Syndemic. American Journal of Public Health 96(3):424–434.

García-Albea, Ristol

    1999 Deficiency Neuropathies in Madrid during the Civil War Period. Neurologia 14(3):122–129.

Garfield, Richard

    1999 The Silent, Deadly Remedy. Forum for Applied Research and Public Policy 14(2):52–58.

Geneva Declaration Secretariat

    2008 Global Burden of Armed Violence. Geneva: Geneva Declaration Secretariat.

Gershwin, M. Eric, Carl Keen, Mark Fletcher, and Lucille Hurley

    1987 Nutrition and Immunity. Proceedings of the Nutrition Society of Australia 12:1–10.

Gibson, James W.

    1986 The Perfect War: Technowar in Vietnam. New York: Atlantic Monthly Press.

Goldenberg, Robert L.

2003 The Plausibility of Micronutrient Deficiency in Relationship to Perinatal Infection. Journal of Nutrition 133(5):1645S–1648S.

Goldson, Edward

1996 The Effect of War on Children. Child Abuse and Neglect 20(9):809–819.

Gonzalez Zapata, Laura I., Carlos Avarez-Dardet, Andreu Nolasco, Nolasco Bonmati, José A. Pina Romero, and María José Medrano

2006 El Hambre en la Guerra Civil Española y la Mortalidad por Cardiopatía Isquémica: Una Perspectiva desde la Hipótesis de Barker [Famine in the Spanish Civil War and Mortality from Coronary Heart Disease: A Perspective from Barker's Hypothesis]. Gaceta Sanitaria 20(5):360–367.

Graciani, Auxiliadora, José R. Banegas, Esther López-Garcia, and Fernando Rodriguez-Artalejo.

2004 Prevalence of Disability and Associated Social and Health-related Factors among the Elderly in Spain: A Population-based Study. Maturitas 48(4):381–392.

Guerrant, Richard L., Aldo A.M. Lima, and Frances Davidson

2000 Micronutrients and Infection: Interactions and Implications with Enteric and Other Infections and Future Priorities. Journal of Infectious Diseases 182(Suppl 1):S134–S138.

Gupta, Ajay

1994 Multidrug-Resistant Typhoid Fever in Children: Epidemiology and Therapeutic Approach. Pediatric Infectious Disease Journal 13(2):134–140.

Hambidge, Michael

2000 Human Zinc Deficiency. Journal of Nutrition 130(Suppl 1):1344S–1349S.

Herring, D. Ann, and Lisa Sattenspiel

2006 Social Contexts, Syndemics, and Infectious Disease in Northern Aboriginal Populations. American Journal of Human Biology 19(2):190–202.

Himmelgreen, David, Nancy Romero-Daza, David Turkon, Sharon Watson, Ipolto Okello-Uma, and Daniel Sellen

2009 Addressing the HIV/AIDS-Food Insecurity Syndemic in Sub-Saharan Africa. African Journal of AIDS Research 8(4):401–412.

Hogan, David E., and Jonathan L. Burstein

2002 Disaster Medicine. Phildelphia: Wolters Kluwer/Lippincott Williams & Wilkins.

Hoskins, Eric

2000 Public Health and the Persian Gulf War. In War and Public Health. Barry Levy and Victor Sidel, eds. Pp. 254–278. Oxford: Oxford University Press.

Jamison, Dean, Henry Mosley, Anthony R. Measham, and Jose L. Bobadilla, eds.

1993 Disease Control Priorities in Developing Countries. New York: Oxford University Press.

Janney, John

1940 Notes on the Food Situation in Spain. Report presented to the Rockefeller Foundation, New York, October.

Khan, Nguyen Cong, Ha Huy Tue, Le Bach Mai, Le Gia Vinh, and Ha Huy Khoi

2010 Secular Trends in Growth and Nutritional Status of Vietnamese Adults in Rural Red River Delta after 30 years (1976–2006). Asia Pacific Journal of Clinical Nutrition 19(3):412–416.

Kwan, Candice K., and Joel D. Ernst

2011 HIV and Tuberculosis: A Deadly Human Syndemic. Clinical Microbiology Reviews 24(2):351–376.

Leaning, Jennifer

2000 Environment and Health: Impact of War. Canadian Medical Association Journal 163(9):1157–1161.

Levy, Barry S., and Victor W. Sidel, eds.

2000[1997] War and Public Health. Updated edition. Washington: American Public Health Association.

Levy, Barry S., Gurinder S. Shahi, and Chen Lee

2000 The Environmental Consequences of War. In War and Public Health. Barry Levy, and Victor Sidel, eds. Washington: American Public Health Association.

Lonnroth, Knut, Ernesto Jaramillo, Brian G. Williams, Christopher Dye, and Mario Raviglione

2009 Drivers of Tuberculosis Epidemics: The Role of Risk Factors and Social Determinants. Social Science and Medicine 68(12):2240–2246.

Macallan, Derek C.
  1999 Malnutrition in Tuberculosis. Diagnostic Microbiology and Infectious Disease 34(2):153–157.
Mayer, Jean
  1967 Starvation as a Weapon: Herbicides in Vietnam I. Scientist and Citizen 9(7):115–121.
McDade, Thomas W.
  2005 The Ecologies of Human Immune Function. Annual Review of Anthropology 34:495–521.
Moore, Patrick S., Anthony A. Marfin, Lynn E. Quenemoen, Bradford D. Gessner, Daniel S. Miller, Michael J. Toole, Y. S. Ayub, and Kevin M. Sullivan
  1993 Mortality Rates in Displaced and Resident Populations of Central Somalia During 1992 Famine. Lancet 341(8850):935–938.
Morens, David M., Jeffery K. Taubenberger, and Anthony S. Fauci
  2008 Predominant Role of Bacterial Pneumonia as a Cause of Death in Pandemic Influenza: Implications for Pandemic Influenza Preparedness. Journal of Infectious Diseases 198(7):962–970.
Mworozi, E.A.
  1993 AIDS and Civil War: A Devil's Alliance: Dislocation Caused by Civil Strife in Africa Provides Fertile Ground for the Spread of HIV. AIDS Analysis Africa 3(6):8–10.
Nagy, Thomas J.
  2001 The Role of Iraq Water Treatment Vulnerabilities in Halting One Genocide and Preventing Others. Paper presented to the Association of Genocide Scholars, University of Minnesota, June 12.
O'Hare, Bernadette A.M., and David P. Southall
  2007 First Do No Harm: The Impact of Recent Armed Conflict on Maternal and Child Health in Sub-Saharan Africa. Journal of the Royal Society of Medicine 100(12):564–570.
Orwell, George
  1952 Homage to Catalonia. New York: Harcourt-Brace Inc.
Padbidri, Bhaskaram
  2002 Micronutrient Malnutrition, Infection, and Immunity: An Overview. Nutrition Reviews 60(s5):S40–S45.
Payne, Stanley G.
  1987 The Franco Regime 1936–1975. Madison, WI: University of Wisconsin Press.
Quy, Vo
  2005 The Attack of Agent Orange on the Environment in Vietnam and its Consequences. Agent Orange and Dioxin in Vietnam, 35 years later, Proceedings of the Paris Conference, March 11–12.
Rice, Amy, Lisa Sacco, Adnan Hyder, and Robert E. Black
  2000 Malnutrition as an Underlying Cause of Childhood Deaths Associated with Infectious Diseases in Developing Countries. Bulletin of the World Health Organization 78(10):1207–1221.
Rylko-Bauer, Barbara, and Merrill Singer
  2011 Political Violence, War and Medical Anthropology. A Companion to Medical Anthropology. Merrill Singer and Pamela I. Erickson, eds. Pp. 219–249, San Francisco: Wiley Blackwell.
Santa Barbara, Joanna
  2008 The Impact of War on Children. In War and Public Health. 2nd edition. Barry Levy and Victor Sidel, eds. Pp. 178–192. New York: Oxford University Press.
Seidman, Michael
  1999 Quiet Fronts in the Spanish Civil War. The Historian 61(4):821–842.
Semba, Richard D., and Alice M. Tang
  1999 Micronutrients and the Pathogenesis of Human Immunodeficiency Virus Infection. British Journal of Nutrition 81(3):181–189.
Singer, Merrill
  2008 The Perfect Epidemiological Storm: Food Insecurity, HIV/AIDS, and Poverty in Southern Africa. Anthropology News 12:15.
  2009 Introduction to Syndemics: A Critical Systems Approach to Public and Community Health. San Francisco: John Wiley and Sons.
Singer, Merrill, and Scott Clair
  2003 Syndemics and Public Health: Reconceptualizing Disease in Bio-Social Context. Medical Anthropology Quarterly 17(4):423–441.

Singer, Merrill, and G. Derrick Hodge, eds.

    2010a The War Machine and Global Health: A Critical Medical Anthropological Examination of the Human Cost of Armed Conflict and the International Violence Industry. Malden, MA: AltaMira/Roman Littlefield Publishers, Inc.

Singer, Merrill, and G. Derrick Hodge

    2010b The Myriad Impacts of the War Machine on Global Health. *In* The War Machine and Global Health: A Critical Medical Anthropological Examination of the Human Cost of Armed Conflict and the International Violence Industry. Merrill Singer and G. Derrick Hodge, eds. Malden, MA: AltaMira/Roman Littlefield Publishers, Inc.

Sivard, Ruth

    1996 World Military and Social Expenditures. Washington: World Priorities.

Siziya, Seter, Adamson S. Muula, and Emmanual Rudatsikira

    2009 Diarrhoea and Acute Respiratory Infections Prevalence and Risk factors Among Under-Five Children in Iraq in 2000. Italian Journal of Pediatrics 35(8):1–9.

Smallman-Raynor, Matthew R., and Andrew D. Cliff

    2004 Impact of Infectious Diseases on War. Clinics of North America 18(2):341–368.

Stall, Ron Mark. Friedman, and Joseph A. Catania

    2007 Interacting Epidemics and Gay Men's Health: A Theory of Syndemic Production among Urban Gay Men. *In* Unequal Opportunity: Health Disparities Affecting Gay and Bisexual Men in the United States. Richard J. Wolitski, Ron Stall, and Ronald O. Valdiserri, eds. Pp. 251–274. Oxford: Oxford University Press.

Tempel, Richard A., and David E. Marcozzi

    2006 Infectious Disease in a Disaster Zone. *In* Disaster Medicine. 3rd edition. Gregory Ciottone, ed. Pp. 302–307. Philadelphia: Mosby Elsevier.

United Nations Childrens Fund (UNCF)

    1993 Children and Women in Iraq: A Situation Analysis. Baghdad: United Nations Children's Fund.

United States Department of Veterans Affairs (USVA)

    2003 Endemic Infectious Diseases of Southwest Asia. Veterans Administration: Veterans Health Initiative Independent Study Course. http://www.publichealth.va.gov/vethealthinitiative/infectious_diseases.asp, accessed May 27, 2012.

    2011 Infectious Diseases and Gulf War Veterans. www.publichealth.va.gov/exposures/gulfwar/infectious_diseases.asp, accessed May 27, 2012.

Vastyan, E. A.

    1971 Civilian War Casualties and Medical Care in South Vietnam. Annals of Internal Medicine 74(4):611–624.

Westing, Arthur H.

    1983 The Environmental Aftermath of Warfare in Viet Nam. Natural Resources Journal 23(2):365–390.

World Health Organization (WHO)

    1976 Report on the Democratic Republic of Vietnam. Geneva, Switzerland.

World Health Organization (WHO)

    2001 Health Situation in Iraq. *In* World Health Organization report presented to Iraq and the International Community Hearing of the Committee on Foreign Affairs. Brussels, Belgium: Human Rights, Common Security and Defense Policy.

Zeba, Augustin N., Hermann Sorgho, Noel Rouamba, Issiaka Zongo, Jeremie Rouamba, Robert T. Guiguemdé, Davidson H. Hamer, Najat Mokhtar, and Jean-Bosco Ouedraogo

    2008 Major Reduction of Malaria Morbidity with Combined Vitamin A and Zinc Supplementation in Young Children in Burkina Faso: A Randomized Double Blind Trial. Nutrition Journal 7:7.

HELMINTHS AND TB IN POLYNESIA:

THE IMPLICATIONS FOR HEALTH PRACTICE

JUDITH LITTLETON
University of Auckland

JULIE PARK
University of Auckland

TEKAAI NELESONE
Atiu Hospital

Tuberculosis (TB) and helminth infestation are tied in multiple ways through physiological interactions both pre- and postnatally. In the Pacific, these interactions have occurred in the context of colonial and postcolonial changes. We argue that these biocultural interactions help to explain the historical experience of TB for people in the Pacific nations of Tuvalu and the Cook Islands. Successive campaigns against specific helminths and later efforts at TB control have led to variable outcomes. In this article, we analyze the implications of controlling syndemic conditions for health practice. [syndemics, Pacific, colonialism, filariasis, geohelminths, Ellice Islands, Cook Islands]

INTRODUCTION

Tuberculosis (TB) remains one of the major causes of mortality globally, interacting with other communicable (e.g., HIV) and noncommunicable (e.g., diabetes) diseases to create nexuses of negative health conditions disproportionately experienced by people in difficult economic and social circumstances. But the interactions with HIV and diabetes are modern syndemics—the product of "new" infectious diseases or "new" environments of obesity and inequality. In this paper, we suggest that a syndemic approach to an older interaction between TB and helminth infestation may help to explain some historical patterns observed in our studies of public health in the Pacific nations of Tuvalu and the Cook Islands. This approach has implications today for the ongoing support and prioritization of public health efforts.

What it is unclear is whether TB existed in some parts of the Pacific prior to European colonialism (Miles 1997, Butterfield 2006); it certainly only occurred in epidemic form after European settlement. In colonial times it became a chronic health issue and remains at high levels among some Pacific populations today. Within the colonial records, however, TB seems to have unusual patterns of occurrence: disproportionately high levels on some islands (e.g., the southern Cooks), a signal failure of attempts at vaccination on Aitutaki (one of the Cook Islands), and absence or near absence on other islands

ANNALS OF ANTHROPOLOGICAL PRACTICE 36.2, pp. 274–294. ISSN: 2153-957X. © 2013 by the American Anthropological Association. DOI:10.1111/napa.12004

(Futter-Puati 2010). While such anomalies may be explained as the result of historical contingencies, we propose that an additional factor may be the interaction between TB and worm infestation, a long recognised problem in the Pacific and the focus of some of the first organised international public health campaigns (e.g., the Rockefeller Foundation hookworm campaign in the early 20th century).

Helminth infections are sometimes classed as a neglected tropical disease (Hotez et al. 2008). While they are remarkably widespread—one estimate is that more than a third of the world's population is infected (GAHI 2012)—it has often been assumed that their public health impact is minimal since many people appear to show few signs of disease. Yet recently new calculations have begun to point out the cost of helminths in terms of poor growth, lower productivity, poor educational outcomes and compromised immune systems (e.g., King and Dangerfield-Cha 2008). At the same time, the potential role of helminths in altering responses to vaccines for HIV, TB and malaria (Elias et al. 2007, Hatherill et al. 2009) has focussed attention on the interactions between helminths and other conditions as discussed below.

In this paper, we outline the complex and multilayered interactions between helminths and TB, examine these linkages in relation to historical accounts from the Pacific, and analyze the implications for ongoing health practice in the region.

Syndemic Interactions

Our focus on the interactions between helminths and TB is not because we think there is a single distinct syndemic involving only these two types of pathogens, but rather that a syndemic orientation forces attention on multilevel interactions. In other words, we are interested the complex relationships between helminths and TB as part of a multiplicity of ties in which both appear to be implicated in the context of colonialism. Our study focuses upon two places: Tuvalu and the Cook Islands (Figures 1 and 2), which were part of the British colonial expansion during the 19th and 20th centuries. For both island groups, TB became a major cause of mortality during this period, but it also coexisted with other conditions, such as worm infestation. What our analysis suggests is that understanding the syndemic interactions in which both TB and helminths are caught up allows us to explain some historical differences in morbidity as well as providing a model for current public health development on the islands.

Helminths

There are two major phyla of helminths: nematodes or roundworms and the platy-helminths or flat worms. The nematodes (roundworms) include the soil-transmitted helminths (e.g., hookworm) that infect the intestinal system and filarial worms that cause lymphatic filariasis (elephantiasis) and onchoceriasis. The platyhelminths include the flukes (e.g., schistosomes) and the tapeworms. It is common for infected individuals to be parasitized with more than one species of helminth and the worm burden among different individuals is heterogeneous with a small proportion of people having a heavy worm burden (Crompton 1999). Age, household clustering, and genetics have

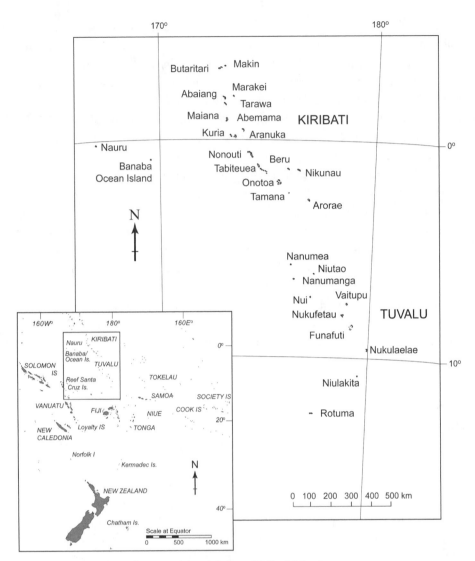

FIGURE 1. Map of the Ellice (Tuvalu) and Gilbert (Kiribati) Islands.

all been highlighted as causal in the heterogeneity of worm infestation, for example, household aggregation of lymphatic filarial infection has been described in the Cook Islands (Ottesen et al. 1981).

Infections with parasitic helminths are often asymptomatic with hosts tolerating the presence of parasites for a considerable time. If untreated, most helminth infections become chronic and it is these long-standing infections that are linked to persistent health conditions, such as anemia, fatigue, growth stunting, and poor cognitive development. These subacute conditions are much more common than advanced outcomes, such as the tissue damage of elephantiasis due to lymphatic filariasis (Hotez et al. 2008), which are often associated with heightened immune response to helminth infections.

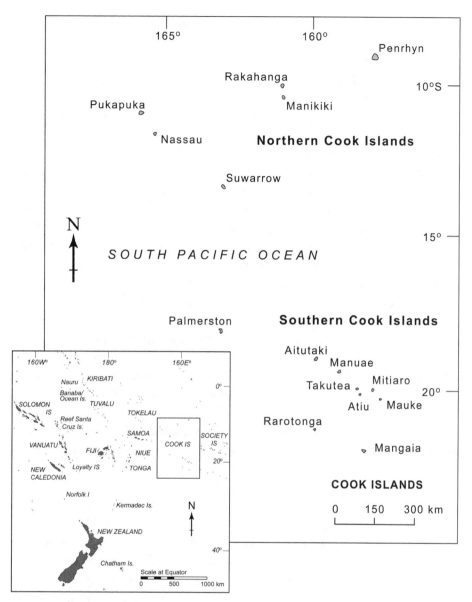

FIGURE 2. Map of the Cook Islands.

Helminths and the Immune System

Helminths have evolved to use a wide range of infection strategies and occupy a diverse range of niches within their hosts, including humans (Dunne and Cooke 2005; Hewitson et al. 2009; Maizels and Yazdanbakhsh 2003). Most helminths do not replicate in humans or other mammals so the infective stages must establish infection, grow to sexual maturity, and produce eggs or offspring for transmission to the next host. The adult parasites may live for years protected against the host's immune system.

The human immune response to different species of helminths varies and the human $CD4^+T$ cells selectively differentiate into Th1, Th2, Th17, and Tregulatory (Treg) cells in response to helminths. However, there is a stereotypical pattern of mounting what is known as the T-helper 2 (Th2) immune response that is distinct from the immune response to microbial pathogens (such as TB). The response involves cytokines (interleukin [IL]-3, IL-4, IL-5, IL-9, IL-10 and IL-13), antibody isotypes (IgG1, IgG4, and IgE), increased numbers of eosinophils, basophils, mast cells, and, alternatively, activated macrophages. The type 2 cytokines induce a range of mechanisms depending on the tissue involved. Such responses have three major roles: wound repair, control of inflammation, and resistance to the helminth. It has been hypothesized that this type 2 immunity evolved from a response to tissue injury. While a type 1 immune response may damage the parasites it can also cause collateral damage in the host tissue (e.g., lymphatic inflammation in filariasis). The Th2 cytokines modulate excessive inflammatory reactions preventing a runaway pathology, although an exaggerated Th2 response can also cause pathology, so a regulated response has to be generated—this has been called a modified Th2 cell response and is characterized by downregulation of some isotypes (Allen and Maizels 2011; Maizels and Yazdanbakhsh 2003). People responding in this way express high levels of IL-10, probably through the action of Treg cells. Those with this modified Th2 response become the main reservoir of disease transmission since they often have clinically silent infections, such as the microfilaremic carriers in filariasis pathology. It may be that this regulation of the immune response by both the host Treg cells and helminth-derived products underlies reverse correlations between helminths and allergies and some autoimmune diseases (known as the hygiene hypothesis; Carvalho et al. 2009; Liu et al. 2010; Yazdanbakhsh et al. 2002).

However, the linkage between helminths and the immune system also occurs in utero when maternal helminth infections prime the infant's immune responses. Maternal parasite infections have been argued to modulate the child's immune responses toward increased Th2 type cytokines and immune regulatory cytokines resulting in immune hyporesponsiveness to the presence of tissue-dwelling helminths (Marchant and Goldman 2005). In utero exposure is associated with greater susceptibility to filarial infection for instance, but with less filarial pathology. Animal studies confirm that prenatal exposure to helminth infection results in diminished worm burden and less pathology. These studies are ongoing, but research with mothers and children with filariasis suggests that such effects are long-lasting (Labeaud et al. 2009). As Djuardi et al. suggest, the timing of exposure to helminths, worm burdens, and other aspects of the environment could program "childhood immune responses leaving a long-term immunological footprint" (2011:1513).

Helminths and TB

Like helminth infestation, TB is also a long-standing infection involving immune responses that have become clearer with new diagnostic technologies (Dheda et al. 2010). While transmission of *Mycobacterium tuberculosis* (Mtb) is airborne and dependent largely upon close contact (although such contact is not necessarily directly person to person), not all of those exposed in high burden settings develop any overt evidence of infection. Estimates are that this may be up to 50–70 percent of close contacts (Dheda et al. 2010). Of the remaining individuals exposed to infection only a small number (5 percent) go on to develop active TB disease within five years of initial infection. The remainder develops LTBI or latent TB infection. Unless the host is immune compromised (e.g., through other infections, illness, stress or trauma) or reinfected, antigen-specific Th1 responses in the lungs and CD8+ T cells control the infection and the infected host does not develop the disease. However, a small percentage (estimated around 2–5 percent) do go on to develop disease at what may be a much later time of their life (as aging takes its toll on immunocapacity).

The first line of defense to TB is in the lungs where the alveolar macrophages amplify the innate immune response to infection. The bacteria are phagocytosed by alveolar macrophages, epithelial cells, dendritic cells, and neutrophils. The infected macrophages and dendritic cells secrete cytokines and present antigens to several T-cell populations that produce the cytokine IFN-γ that further activates macrophages in conjunction with TNF-α. These maintain the integrity of granulomae and prevent reactivation. T cells expressing IL-2 also appear important for clearing infection and resolving fibrosis. There is complex cross-regulation with Th2, Th17, and Treg cell responses and early progression to disease has been associated with alterations in the production of regulatory Th2 cytokines (e.g., IL-4 and IL-10; Dheda et al. 2010). The development of active TB then is due to the failure of immune regulation or inappropriate regulation. It is suggested that this disturbance may involve the subversion of a protective Th1 response either through downregulation of the Th1 response or a bias toward a Th2 profile and increased IL-10 producing Tregs (Elias et al. 2006; Perry et al. 2011).

Since TB resistance relies upon an active immune response, it has been suggested that helminth infections might diminish that response (Perry et al. 2011). The suggestion that helminths and TB may be linked has come from four sources of evidence: the epidemiological patterning of helminth infestation and TB; the pattern of immune response in coinfected adults; the patterning of human response to Bacillus Calmette-Guérin (BCG) vaccination; and studies within animal populations.

Globally, the coexistence of helminths and TB has been noted by multiple authors, particularly in the context of the development of new vaccines for TB, HIV, and malaria (e.g., Kaufman 2010; Labeaud et al. 2009). Similarly surveys, for example, within China (Yang et al. 2009) and South Africa (Bentwich et al. 1999), show a correlation between the two conditions. Patients with pulmonary TB in a Brazilian study (Tristão-Sá et al. 2002) had a higher rate of intestinal nematodes. Another study found a strong association between nematode infection and multibacillary leprosy (Diniz et al. 2010). In a large Ethiopian study, Elias et al. showed a greater prevalence of intestinal worm infections in patients with active TB than in their healthy household contacts (Elias et al. 2006). The prevalence increased with the number of helminth species per person.

Clinical studies are also suggestive. Two patients in China coinfected with echinococcosis (hydatids) and TB had changed immune profiles, going from a Th1 to Th2 response as the chronicity of their worm infection increased (Yang et al. 2009). In a Brazilian study, TB patients with intestinal parasites had lower IFN-γ and higher IL-10 levels compared with TB patients without helminths (Resende Co. et al. 2007). In addition, coinfected patients had more severe radiological pulmonary disease suggesting that coinfection may favor persistent infection with Mtb and a more protracted clinical course of the disease. Reduced Th1 responses have also been observed in patients with latent TB infection (Babu et al. 2009).

Studies of tuberculin skin testing (TST) and vaccination using BCG in Ethiopia have shown that deworming was associated with significant improvements in IFN-γ production following BCG vaccination (Elias et al. 2001). Coinfected individuals not treated for worms had increased production of TGF-β indicative of the Th2 phenotype (Elias et al. 2008). In Indonesia, researchers found suppressed IFN-γ responses to BCG among geohelminth-infected school children (Wammes et al. 2010). By contrast, no association between parasitism and TST was observed in a group of TB patients (some coinfected with HIV) in a Brazilian hospital although overall prevalence of enteroparasites was low (Neto et al. 2009). A similar lack of relationship between TST results and deworming was observed in an indigenous Amazon community (Zevallos et al. 2010), although it is noteworthy that the BCG vaccine was associated with significant protection against TB in this population.

Prenatal sensitization to helminth infestation also has a measurable effect on TB-related immunity. Work by Malhotra et al. (1999) in a Kenyan cross-sectional study demonstrated that children of worm-infected mothers produced less IFN-γ in response to mycobacterial purified protein derivate (PPD), while a prospective study by the same group showed that infants sensitized to filariae or schistosomes in utero also produced less IFN-γ.

In schistosome-infected mice, the protective efficacy of BCG vaccination was significantly lowered (Elias et al. 2005). A recent study by Potian et al. (2011) of mice infected with an intestinal helminth showed impairment of resistance to Mtb infection which was worsened with a second dose of helminth infection. The mice still mounted an Mtb-specific Th1 immune response, but the Th2 response to the helminths meant that alternately activated macrophages accumulated in the lungs and it appears these macrophages were less efficient in killing Mtb. Not all species of helminths seem to modify susceptibility—a study by Frantz et al. (2007) of *Toxocariasis canis* and Mtb in mice shows similar mycobacterial proliferation of Mtb among coinfected and singly infected individuals.

Studies of buffalo show similar relationships. Ezenwa et al. (2010) demonstrated that nematode infection alters immunity in buffalo. Animals more resistant to nematode infection had weaker Th1 responses, while disease modeling found that nematode-induced immune suppression could facilitate bovine TB in buffalo (Ezenwa and Jolles 2011).

As summarized by Liu et al. (2010), there is a strong correlation between intestinal helminth infection and the onset of active TB in the lungs; mycobacterial-specific immune responses improve following antihelminth therapy; helminth infection reactivates latent TB infection; and it weakens the efficacy of BCG vaccine. At the same time, there is considerable heterogeneity in response to BCG vaccines (Finan et al. 2008) and BCG and TST responses vary by helminth species (Dauby et al. 2009). This complexity is recognized by Allen and Maizels who described the web surrounding host–parasite interactions in helminth infections as "akin to a neural network, with a web of interactions and alternative pathways" (Allen and Maizels 2011:385). There is an obvious parallel with syndemic frameworks here.

The relationship between TB and helminths is complex. There are ties pre- and postnatally, ties that vary by virtue of the helminth species, by the age at which infestation occurs, and most specifically, in which environments they occur. Both conditions are associated with some of the following environmental features: poor sanitation, insufficient separation of clean and wastewater, nutritional challenges, crowding, inadequate health care, and tobacco smoking all of which are often glossed as "diseases of poverty." The genetics of host and parasites may also modulate these interactions (Allen and Maizels 2011). We are interested in whether this circuit of relationships is implicated in the distribution and colonial experience of TB and attempts to eradicate it in Tuvalu and the Cook Islands as well as whether such circuits remain salient today and hence are important in health intervention efforts.

Helminths in the Pacific

Colonial history is a vital ingredient in the helminth-TB story. The global distribution of helminths depends not just upon the physical environment (soil, climate) and the availability of vectors (e.g., Roberts 1991), but also on history—the movement of peoples and animals over time (Miles 1997). While relatively few helminth species that affect humans are endemic in the contemporary Pacific, there is even more limited evidence of their presence in precolonial times. According to Miles (1997), who undertook extensive analysis of historical sources, only filariasis due to mosquito-borne *Wucheria bancrofti* was definitely present prior to the arrival of Europeans. Filariasis was widespread in the past and is the target of elimination campaigns today (Ichimori and Crump 2005). The disease was certainly widespread (although not in every island group). Lambert (1928, 1941), for instance, referred to the disease as being widespread in Tuvalu (the Ellice Islands) but much less so in Kiribati (the Gilbert Islands). He interpreted this distribution pattern as evidence of a recent introduction into Kiribati from Tuvalu. Given that these two island groups were a joint British colony (GEIC), part of the Western Pacific High Commission, there was ample opportunity during colonialism for such exchanges. Colonial involvement included the movement of people from the Ellice Islands to the Gilberts for administrative work in addition to the movement of workers from both places to the phosphate islands, such as Ocean Island.

The most significant soil transmitted helminths today in the Pacific are hookworm, roundworm, and whipworm (*Trichiuris trichiura*). At the time of the first helminth surveys, hookworm infection was widespread and had clearly been established for a long time. Two species of hookworm were present *Necator americanus* and, less frequently, *Ankylostoma duodenale*, which was noted by Buxton in a survey of Samoa, Tonga, Tuvalu, and Vanuatu (1928) as only present where it had been introduced by Indians and Chinese. A recent survey suggests that control programs have helped to reduce the burden in many Pacific nations although up to 34 percent of schoolchildren in a Tuvalu school had light infestations (Hughes et al. 2004). Roundworm (*Ascaris lumbricoides*) was not as widespread in the 1920s, suggesting a recent introduction. Furthermore, recent surveys suggest that it is not a widespread problem in many Pacific nations, although the survey by Hughes and coworkers suggested higher rates among the Federated States of Micronesia (Hughes et al. 2004). Most prevalent in both the Cook Islands and Tuvalu currently, however, is the whipworm with prevalence rates of over 80 percent in some surveys (Hughes et al. 2004; Speare et al. 2006). Other helminths are present, but are more isolated in occurrence and the range of soil-borne (geohelminths) is generally narrow (Speare et al. 2006) although with a wide range of prevalences (Hughes et al. 2004) from less than 5 percent in Niue and Cook Islands and more than 80 percent on Kiribati and Tuvalu for soil-borne trematodes.

What is clear from the surveys is that geohelminths are a widespread problem, but that both the range of species and the prevalence can vary greatly between villages (Harmen 2009), islands (Manson-Bahr 1912), and nations (Hughes et al. 2004). So, how does TB relate to this diversity? A question that we address in our two case studies below, which are part of a wider study we are pursuing of TB and transnationalism (Littleton and Park 2009).

Tuvalu

Any interaction of helminths and TB relies upon both being introduced and brought into contact. The movement of people in colonial times provided the impetus for such connections. In particular, as in many other colonial situations, mining operations provided one (but not the only) point of contact. Phosphate mining was established on Ocean Island (Figure 1) in 1900 by the Pacific Islands Phosphate company, which was bought out in 1920 by the British Phosphate Commission. Mine labor was imported from the Gilbert and Ellice Islands (island laborers) along with workers from China and other parts of Asia. Staff from Britain, Australia, and New Zealand were involved in management. Ocean Island became a center for circulating labor between the island groups. Even in 1924 the impact of this movement for health was recognized. Writing of his visit later, Lambert, an American medical practitioner, wrote:

> From the doctor's point of view too many Chinese had been imported to Ocean Island, although the government's very good hospital was doing more than its share. The trouble was that Gilbertese and Ellice Islanders worked beside the orientals; they caught the imported diseases and carried them home. All through the twin groups I saw evidence of infections which the strangers were bringing to a lovely people. Pathologically, the march of disease was beginning to show ... Tuberculosis was working its way into handsome youths, who lack the European's immunity. Filariasis was a vexing puzzle, because it seemed impossible to control the mosquitoes that carried it. Intestinal parasites were fortunately few; the people lived near the beaches and tide-water is nature's handy sewage system. [Lambert 1942:180]

The linkage of TB and filariasis as two major health issues on Ocean Island continued over time. In 1945, Acting Resident Commissioner Wernham responding to the District Officer's description of Ellice Islander's health as "very satisfactory" wrote:

In fact, no statement regarding the health of the Ellice Islanders is complete without a reference to the high incidence of tuberculosis. With regard to filariasis, I have always understood that tests performed by the BPC on Ellice Islands labourers on Ocean Island have indicated that over 75% of the population of the Ellice Islands suffer from filariasis ... At present it would be a mistake to regard the health of the Ellice Islands as a matter for satisfaction. [WPHC 1946]

Laborers from Ocean Island were part of a continual circulation of infection around the GEIC despite efforts to control the situation. In 1946, Rose, the Senior Medical Officer for the GEIC, notes that on Ocean Island: "Clinically, there were a number of laborers with pulmonary TB. The late arrival of X-ray film has prevented the confirmation of the clinical diagnosis before the labourers were repatriated" (Rose 1946). Repatriation of course meant disease transmission back to the islands.

At the same time Ocean Island did have health services. There were three hospitals (one for Europeans, one for Asian workers, and one for native workers), filariasis testing did take place, and medical staff were present. These services were crucial in a mining environment where living conditions were poor, including periodic food shortages, drought, and crowded residences (Grimble 1952).

On the islands of the Ellice group, the most complete information deals with the prevalence of filariasis. In contrast, definitive diagnosis of TB was difficult on the outer islands away from Tarawa or Funafuti (where the hospitals and doctors were based; Resture 2010). There are occasional mentions of intestinal helminths in reports but systematic surveys were rare.

An early survey by O'Connor (1923) in 1921–22 of filariasis noted high rates of infection on the islands ranging from 38.9 percent (Nukulaelae) to 73 percent (Nui). He contrasts the distribution between the three southerly atolls (Funafuti, Nukulaelae, and Nukufetau) with the northern atolls basing the distinction on geography. In his analysis, the isolated strips of land surrounding a deep lagoon which characterized the southern atolls were less likely to harbor breeding places for mosquitoes. As part of this work he did test for intestinal helminths on Funafuti identifying *Trichuris trichuria* (pig whipworm), *N. americanus* (hookworm) and one individual with *A. lumbricoides* (roundworm). He points, however, to the extremely wide prevalence of hookworm which he identified in 85.5 percent of the people sampled on Funafuti. These high rates of infection were mirrored by TB, which was observed on every island except Nukufetau. Indeed O'Connor explicitly links hookworm and TB:

Though the hookworm here does not seem to be causative of much disastrous anaemia, its presence is obviously reflected in the general pallor and dyspepsia of the people, in their somnolence and listlessness, in their incapacity for prolonged exertion, and their want of stamina ... I think it is likely that their appalling susceptibility to tuberculosis may be due in part to the prevalence of ankylostomiasis [hookworm]. [O'Connor 1923:88–89]

More than 30 years later, surveys of filariasis show the levels of variation between the islands with rates particularly high on Vaitupu and Nanumanga where more than a third

TABLE 1. Results of a Tuberculosis (TB) Survey and Filariasis Surveys From Tuvalu in the 1950s–60s

Island	Year	Population	Percentage With Microfilaraemia (Percentage With Filarial Disease)	Year	TB Rate/10,000
Nui	1958	514	18.8% (6.4%)	1969	245
Nanumanga	1960	536	30.9% (5.5%)	1969	218
Nukufetau	1959	606	20.4% (2.4%)	1969	262
Nukulaelae	1956	258	18.9% (0.7%)	1969	63
Niutao	1959	736	15.2% (2.1%)	1969	50
Nanumea	1960	955	24.2% (2.7%)	1969	209
Funafuti	1960	564	17.7% (0.1%)	1969	157
Vaitupu	1959	788	26.0% (7.4%)	1969	85

Sources: WHPC (1961:8); Hamblett (1969)

of the population were infected (Table 1). The three southerly atolls still have lower rates but the north/south division has broken down.

Doctors also noted variation in TB. In the annual report for 1955, the senior medical officer notes:

> there is much to suggest a slowly developing resistance to disease. Nearly every child around the age of five has enlarged cervical glands.[1] It is common for these to discharge and leave chronic sinuses. Tuberculosis appears to be more prevalent in the islands where rainfall is slight, food is scarce and diet is unbalanced but this is pure conjecture at the moment as there are not as yet facilities on the outer islands for accurate diagnosis of the disease. [WPHC 1955]

As Table 1 shows there is not a neat correlation between the rate of TB and the rate of filariasis by island. The available data do not match in terms of time and by the 1950s and 1960s the distribution is affected by attempts at mosquito eradication and diagnosis issues surrounding TB (Resture 2010).

Attempts to control filariasis relied upon vector control—spraying of mosquitoes (including with dieldrin) and clearing of brush (WPHC 1956). But what runs through the health reports are the ongoing issues of sanitation, periodic food and water shortages, and interisland transport problems (as detailed by Resture 2010) which mean delays in drugs, testing, and treatment. Also, noted by Hamblett in his assessment of TB in 1969 was the impact of movement of people and TB between the islands especially the movement of contract laborers for plantation work or phosphate mining (Hamblett 1969).

Filariasis today does not occur at the levels recorded during the 1950s and 1960s, but recent reports highlight the ongoing high rates of intestinal helminths, particularly whipworm (Hughes et al. 2004; Speare et al. 2006). In a survey of schoolchildren on Nukufetau the overall prevalence of intestinal helminths was 69.9 percent, although only hookworm and trichuris were identified. Coinfection occurred in 9.7 percent of the schoolchildren tested. TB remains a major health problem for the group although it has declined since the middle of the last decade (Resture 2010). The study of intestinal helminths (Speare et al. 2006) and an analysis of skin infestations (Harmen 2009) points not only to that central role of sanitation, but also to the ongoing networks of interrelated diseases. Harmen (2009) focuses upon the relationship between skin infestations (which may result in ongoing health problems, such as valvular heart disease) and helminth infestation. She points out that such conditions become more prevalent during water shortages which are more common as the population becomes concentrated on some islands, such as Funafuti, and as climate change affects the predictability of weather patterns.

With the exception of the information from Ocean Island where workers were well aware of the co-occurrence of diseases, there is limited information on whether filariasis, other helminth infection, and TB are linked in the same individuals, but certainly these conditions flourished and were in contact in the poorly funded colonial state of the Ellice Islands and their co-occurrence was a matter of concern, particularly prior to effective drug treatment for TB. The problems of sanitation, nutrition, movement, and distance that were salient then are as crucially important postindependence.

Cook Islands

In the Cook Islands, a British protectorate annexed to New Zealand until 1965, similar diseases dominated after World War II. Romans, the Chief Medical Officer, wrote:

> without a doubt the most serious medical problem – as in so many other similar communities is the control and treatment of tuberculosis … the important diseases are leprosy, yaws and filariasis … intestinal helminthiasis is always with us. [Romans 1955:7–8]

These diseases also had an uneven distribution between the islands of the group. Intense lobbying (described by Futter-Puati 2010) meant that the Cook Islands obtained the facility for mass-miniature radiography of TB and mounted an antiTB campaign with radiography, skin testing, and BCG vaccination in 1956. This means that figures were available by island (although with difficulties of interpretation apparent). The distribution of TB as indicated by the total number of TB cases and the percent positive for the Mantoux skin test (Table 2) shows that it was more prevalent in the southern Cook Islands and in Pukapuka than in the northern Cooks.

A survey of filariasis by McCarthy (1959) presents results by island as well as a detailed discussion of each area (Table 3). The islands can be divided between those with high rates (the southern group and Pukapuka) and those with low rates (the northern atolls). He notes the high rate on Manihiki (one of the northern atolls) as anomalous and the result of recent immigration to the island from the southern Cooks of families involved in pearl shell diving. His general view is that the northern Cooks with the exception of Pukapuka had only low to moderate levels of filariasis compared to the much higher rates of the southern Cooks. Pukapuka, which is noted for its high TB and filariasis rates, is the most isolated of the Cook Islands, and lies closer to Tokelau than Rarotonga.

This coincidence of occurrence was noted by the health services. In the 1965–66 annual report, it was noted: "Many illnesses appear to be associated with filariasis and

TABLE 2. Distribution of Tuberculosis (TB) on the Cook Islands in 1956 Measured by Both Number of Diagnosed Cases and Positive Mantoux Reactions (NZDIT 1949–57; Not All Islands Surveyed)

Location	Population (1950)	Number of Known TB Cases	Rate of TB Disease/10,000	Percentage of Positive Mantoux Tests[a]
Rarotonga	6,072	123	337	48
Aitutaki	2,012	39	149	39
Mangaia	1,974	44	222	46
Pukapuka	673	16	238	37
Manihiki	864	4	50	32
Penrhyn	575	2	30	21
Total	12,775	228	178	42

[a]8,074 people Mantoux tested.

TABLE 3. Results of a 1956 Filariasis Survey Conducted by McCarthy (1959) of the Cook Islands

Island	Incidence of Filariasis (%) Male Adults	Incidence of Filariasis (%) Female Adults	Total Population
Rarotonga	44.9	33.7	7,060
Aitututaki	53.7	47.1	2,567
Atiu	54.6	26.2	1,307
Mauke	55.8	35.3	1,097
Pukapuka	56.4	29.2	660
Manihiki	59.5	26.8	651
Rakahanga	18.31	4.55	328
Penrhyn	15.5	6.0	619
Palmerston	25.0	13.3	82
Southern Cooks	49.6	36.7	
Northern Atolls	38.8	17.5	

Source: McCarthy (1959:Table V).

investigation has been commenced to attempt to classify the different manifestations of this infection" (LACI 1966:5), and in the next year: "Investigations into the clinical manifestation continued and revealed possible relationships between filarial infection and meningitis as well as pulmonary eosinophilia" (LACI 1966:6). It was found that pulmonary eosnophilia was easily confused with pulmonary TB and regimes were instituted to clarify diagnosis. In the same report it was noted that "helminthiasis was very frequent and was noted to be contributing to anaemia and respiratory infection" (LACI 1966:6).

The presence of mosquito breeding places (for filariasis), hygiene problems, and the limited availability of water and toilet facilities were all noted as major contributors. But what is also apparent is the emphasis from the mid-1950s on public health measures and campaigns. Futter-Puati (2010) has documented the level of effort in those campaigns and their early successes. One mark of success was the decline in TB rates from the 1970s onwards.

Part of these campaigns, apart from diagnosis, was vaccination with BCG. As noted earlier, BCG vaccination is associated with a wide range of efficacy particularly in relation to adult disease (Horwitz et al. 2009; Miles et al. 2008). It is, however, more successful in protecting children from disseminated TB (Finan et al. 2008; Malhotra et al. 1999). Failures in BCG vaccines have been attributed to a lack of maintenance of cold chain storage or other preexisting conditions, such as helminthiasis (Finan et al. 2008). In the 1956 TB campaign, however, there was a record of a spectacular failure of the vaccine on Aitutaki. Eighteen months after the survey, John Numa was sent to the island not only to examine leprosy, but also to check the TB status of the islanders. His team examined every person less than 30 years of age (1,809 people). The team found 83 new cases of TB (63 with contacts, 20 without). Of these 83 cases, 55 had been vaccinated 18 months previously. Many, if not most of the cases, were in children (MHO 1958).

This failure of vaccine occurred on one of the islands with a heavy filariasis load. Studies in 1974 and 1992 on the nearby island of Mauke have shown that islanders had a high level of microfilaria and circulating worm antigen plus altered immune responses, such as high levels of Ig-γ antibody. In 1974 most households had at least one member infected (Cuenco et al. 2009). More recent work has shown that in this population clearance of infection did not serve to restore normal immune responsiveness, indicative of in utero priming as well as possibly inherited responses to filarial infection (Steel and Ottesen 2001).

As in Tuvalu, the linkage between TB and helminths is suggestive: the similarity in distribution, the observations of medical professionals at the time, and, in Aitutaki, the unusual response to BCG. At the same time, there is clearly a complex of relationships—population densities, household crowding, and sanitation—which have direct linkages to either or both helminths or TB. This set of ties implicating sanitation, water availability, crowding, nutrition, and public health efforts (including mosquito control) are shown in Figure 3.

Syndemics

Why might it matter if there is a direct link between helminths and TB beyond the important finding that TB transmission may be greater and the rates of disease higher than expected? Understanding that linkage serves to shed light on issues such as the variable experience of TB within island groups and particular successes or failures of public health attempts. However, a syndemic perspective also forces us to think about the nature and directionality of ties between biological, social, and economic conditions (Singer et al. 2011). And, in this specific linkage, a syndemic framework forces attention upon children.

The impacts of helminths—anemia, stunting, respiratory infections—are disproportionately experienced by children. Infection often peaks among school age children (Awasthi 2003; Harris 2011). It is in utero that the fetus's immune system is primed by exposure to antibodies from a helminth-infected mother (Marchant and Goldman 2005). Adults may develop elephantiasis or other complications of filarial disease but these are often the long-term complications of childhood infection and then reinfection (Brooker

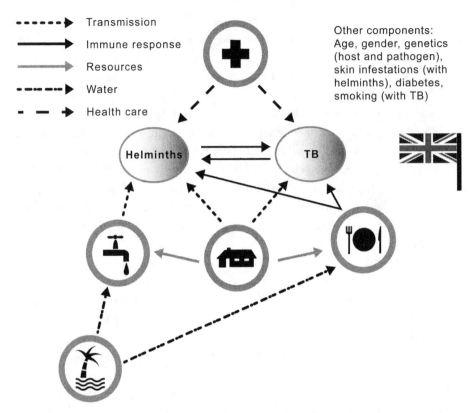

FIGURE 3. A simplified diagram of the linkages Between tuberculosis (TB) and helminths and other social and environmental conditions noted in the case of the Pacific.

et al. 2004). Helminths establish a profile of risk in children and it is the contexts of childhood (i.e., the home, the community, and the school) that are important in fostering high rates of later disease (Harmen 2009; Hughes et al. 2004).

TB affects adults and children but pediatric TB is a marker of transmission. Smaller children (who cannot maintain a productive cough) are recipients but not transmitters of infection. Children also more frequently have serious sequelae to TB disease, such as developing TB meningitis and being more susceptible to disseminated TB (Newton et al. 2008). One of today's reservoirs of TB is those adults who first became infected as children or young people in households in the 1950–70s in the Cook Islands or up to the 1990s in Tuvalu.

Conclusion

What does the evidence from Tuvalu and the Cook Islands suggest about the set of linkages between helminthiasis and TB? There is a multiplicity of ties and some ties span years or generations, such as the role of population movement in introducing infections. What is central is a set of linkages leading to the traditional foci of public health—sanitation and the availability of water, antenatal care, and household and school crowding (Figure 3). Adequate public health infrastructure in the form of clean and readily available water and adequate sewerage are crucial for not only controlling worm infestations, but also sustaining gardens and the supply of fresh food important for health immune systems, not just in homes but also in schools. Crowding at home and school promotes transmission of helminths (Hughes et al. 2004), crowding at home is linked very directly with transmission of TB (Baker et al. 2008).

While public health efforts in the past, particularly in the Cook Islands, have managed to successfully control TB and filariasis, that success was not solely through the availability of diagnostics and testing but through prevention efforts, available treatment and treaters, adequate infrastructure and community "buy-in." Furthermore, prior to the development of effective antibiotic therapy for TB, medical practitioners were alive to the potential impact of coinfection (e.g., LACI 1966; O'Connor 1923). Yet, a search for helminths or TB on research databases most frequently brings up research on drug administration or vaccine development.

The syndemic relationship of helminths and TB should alert us to the dangers of ignoring more mundane matters, such as the availability of water, food security and safety, the control of mosquito breeding areas, sewerage facilities, and adequate space for sleeping, living, and schooling. In a postcolonial Pacific, now facing increasing numbers of droughts associated with climate change, and population growth, especially in urbanizing areas, these concerns are even more important. This comprehensive approach to health is indicated by a syndemic framework addressing inequalities, resisting a focus on a single disease, and resourcing communities themselves to design and implement comprehensive health programs.

NOTES

Acknowledgments. This work is funded by a grant from the Health Research Council of New Zealand for the Transnational Pacific Health through the Lens of Tuberculosis project. We would like to acknowledge Setapu Resture and Debbie Futter-Puati whose masters' research stimulated this work. Ally Palmer has been invaluable in undertaking research assistance while Briar Sefton provided the illustrations.

1. Tuberculosis in the Ellice Islands was historically noted as resulting in very high rates of glandular TB, including TB adenitis. It is only during the 1960s that pulmonary TB becomes the predominant form of TB.

REFERENCES CITED

Allen, Judith E., and Rick M. Maizels
　2011　Diversity and Dialogue in Immunity to Helminths. Nature Reviews Immunology 11(6):375–388.
Awasthi, Shally, Donald A. P. Bundy, and Lorenzo Savioli
　2003　Helminthic Infections. British Medical Journal 327(7412):431–433.
Babu, Subash, Sajid Q. Bhat, N. Pavan Kumar, R. Anuradha, Paul Kumaran, P. G. Gopi, C. Kolappan, V. Kumaraswami, and Thomas B. Nutman
　2009　Attenuation of Toll-Like Receptor Expression and Function in Latent Tuberculosis by Coexistent Filarial Infection With Restoration Following Antifilarial Chemotherapy. PLoS Neglected Tropical Diseases 3(7):e489.
Baker, Michael, Dillip Das, Kamalesh Vengopal, and Phillipa Howden-Chapman
　2008　Tuberculosis Associated With Household Crowding in a Developed Country. Journal of Epidemiological and Community Health 62(8):715–721.

Bentwich, Zvi, Alexander Kalinkovich, Ziva Weisman, Gadi Borkow, Nulda Beyers, and Albert D. Beyers
   1999 Can Eradication of Worms Change the Face of AIDS and Tuberculosis? Immunology Today 20(11):485–487.

Brooker, Simon, Jeffrey Bethony, and Peter Hotez
   2004 Human Hookworm Infection in the 21st Century. Advances in Parasitology 58:197–288.

Butterfield, Katharine C.
   2006 Investigating Evidence of Tuberculosis in Prehistoric Polynesia: Re-evaluation and Planning Future Research. Master of Arts thesis, Department of Anthropology, University of Auckland.

Buxton, Patrick A.
   1928 Researches in Polynesia and Melanesia: An Account of Investigations in Samoa, Tonga, the Ellice Group and the New Hebrides in 1924, 1925, Parts 5–7 (Relating to Human Disease and Welfare). *In* Memoir Series of the London School of Hygiene and Tropical Medicine, 2. London: London School of Hygiene and Tropic Medicine.

Carvalho, Lucas, Jie Sun, Colleen Kane, Fraser Marshall, Connie Krawczyk, and Edward Pearce
   2009 Review Series on Helminths, Immune Modulation and the Hygiene Hypothesis: Mechanisms Underlying Helminth Modulation of Dendritic Cell Function. Immunology 126(1):28–34.

Crompton, D. W. T.
   1999 How Much Human Helminthiasis Is There in the World? The Journal of Parasitology 85(3):397–403.

Cuenco, Karen T., Eric A. Ottesen, Steven A. Williams, Thomas B. Nutman, and Cathy Steel
   2009 Heritable Factors Play a Major Role in Determining Host Responses to *Wuchereria bancrofti* Infection in an Isolated South Pacific Island Population. Journal of Infectious Diseases 200(8):1271–1278.

Dauby, Nicholas, Cristina Alonso-Vega, Eduardo Suarez, Amilcar Flores, Emmanuel Hermann, Marisol Cordova, M. Tatianna Tellez, Faustino Torrico, Carine Truyens, and Yves Carlier
   2009 Maternal Infection With *Trypanosoma cruzi* and Congenital Chagas Disease Induce a Trend to a Type 1 Polarization of Infant Immune Responses to Vaccines. PLoS Neglected Tropical Diseases 3(12):e571.

Dheda, Keertan, Stephan K. Schwander, Bingdong Zhu, Richard N. van Zyl-Smit, and Ying Zhang
   2010 The Immunology of Tuberculosis: From Bench to Bedside. Respirology 15(3):433–450.

Diniz, Lucia M., Eneida F. L. Magalhaes, Fausto E. L. Pereira, Reynaldo Dietze, and Rodrigo Ribeiro-Rodrigues
   2010 Presence of Intestinal Helminths Decreases T Helper Type 1 Responses in Tuberculoid Leprosy Patients May Increase the Risk for Multi-Bacillary Leprosy. Clinical and Experimental Immunology 161(1):142–150.

Djuardi, Yenny, Linda J. Wammes, Taniawati Supali, Erliyani Sartono, and Maria Yazdanbakhsh
   2011 Immunological Footprint: The Development of a Child's Immune System in Environments Rich in Microorganisms and Parasites. Parasitology 138(12):1508–1518.

Dunne, David W., and Anne Cooke
   2005 A Worm's Eye View of the Immune System: Consequences for Evolution of Human Autoimmune Disease. Nature Reviews Immunology 5(5):420–426.

Elias, Daniel, Hannah Akuffo, Cecilia Thors, Andrzej Pawlowski, and Sven Britton
   2005 Low Dose Chronic *Schistosoma mansoni* Infection Increases Susceptibility to *Mycobacterium bovis* BCG Infection in Mice. Clinical & Experimental Immunology 139(3):398–404.

Elias, Daniel, Sven Britton, Abraham Aseffa, Howard Engers, and Hannah Akuffo
   2008 Poor Immunogenicity of BCG in Helminth Infected Population is Associated With Increased In Vitro TGF-Beta Production. Vaccine 26(31):3897–3902.

Elias, Daniel, Sven Britton, Afework Kassu, and Hannah Akuffo
   2007 Chronic Helminth Infections May Negatively Influence Immunity Against Tuberculosis and Other Diseases of Public Health Importance. Expert Review of Anti-Infective Therapy 5(3):475–484.

Elias, Daniel, Getahun Mengistu, Hannah Akuffo, and Sven Britton
   2006 Are Intestinal Helminths Risk Factors for Developing Active Tuberculosis? Tropical Medicine & International Health 11(4):551–558.

Elias, Daniel, Dawit Wolday, Hannah Akuffo, Beyene Petros, Ulf Bronner, and Sven Britton
   2001 Effect of Deworming on Human T Cell Responses to Mycobacterial Antigens in Helminth-Exposed Individuals Before and After Bacile Calmette-Guérin Vaccination. Clinical and Experimental Immunology 123(2):219–225.

Ezenwa, Vanessa O., Rampal S. Etienne, Gordon Luikart, Albano Beja-Pereira, and Anna E. Jolles
   2010 Hidden Consequences of Living in a Wormy World: Nematode-Induced Immune Suppression Facilitates Tuberculosis Invasion in African Buffalo. American Naturalist 176(5):613–624.

Ezenwa, Vanessa O., and Anna E. Jolles
   2011 From Host Immunity to Pathogen Invasion: The Effects of Helminth Coinfection on the Dynamics of Microparasites. Internal & Comparative Biology 51(4):540–551.

Finan, Chris, Martin O. C. Ota, Anaud Marchant, and Melanie J. Newport
   2008 Natural Variation in Immune Responses to Neonatal *Mycobacterium bovis* Bacillus Calmette-Guérin (BCG) Vaccination in a Cohort of Gambian infants. PLoS One 3(10):e3485.

Frantz, Fabiani, Rogério S. Rosada, Walter M. Turato, Camila M. Peres, A.rlete M. Coelho-Castelo, Simone G. Ramos, David M. Aronoff, Célio L. Silva, and Lúcia H. Faccioli
   2007 The Immune Response to Toxocariasis Does Not Modify Susceptibility to *Mycobacterium tuberculosis* Infection in BALB/c Mice. American Journal of Tropical Medicine and Hygiene 77(4):691–698.

Futter-Puati, Debbie
   2010 Maki Maro—Tuberculosis in the Cook Islands, A Social History 1896–1975. Master of Arts thesis, Department of History, University of Auckland.

Global Atlas of Helminth Infections (GAHI)
   2012 Global Atlas of Helminth Infections. http://www.thiswormyworld.org/, accessed February 8, 2012.

Grimble, Arthur
   1952 Pattern of Islands. London: John Murray.

Hamblett, E. P.
   1969 Tuberculosis in the Gilbert and Ellice Islands Colony (1964–1968). Noumea, New Caledonia: South Pacific Commission.

Harmen, S. P.
   2009 The Prevalence and Impact of the Co-Morbidity of Scabies and Other Neglected Tropical Diseases in Two Countries in the Asia-Pacific Region. Ph.D. Thesis, Tropical Medicine and Rehabilitation Sciences, School of Public Health, James Cook University.

Harris, Nicola L.
   2011 Advances in Helminth Immunology: Optimism for Future Vaccine Design? Trends in Parasitology 27(7):288–293.

Hatherill, Mark, Vera Adams, Jane Hughes, Marwou De Kock, Wendy Mavakla, Bernadette Pienaar, Hassan Mahomed, Gregory Hussey, and Willem A. Hanekom
   2009 The Potential Impact of Helminth Infection on Trials of Novel Tuberculosis Vaccines. Vaccine 27(35):4743–4744.

Hewitson, James P., John R. Grainger, and Rick M. Maizels
   2009 Helminth Immunoregulation: The Role of Parasite Secreted Proteins in Modulating Host Immunity. Molecular and Biochemical Parasitology 167(1):1–11.

Horwitz, Marcus A., Günter Harth, Barbara J. Dillon, and Saša Maslešša Galic
   2009 Commonly Administered BCG Strains Including an Evolutionarily Early Strain and Evolutionarily Late Strains of Disparate Genealogy Induce Comparable Protective Immunity Against Tuberculosis. Vaccine 27(3):441–445.

Hotez, Peter, Paul J. Brindley, Jeffrey M. Bethony, Charles H. King, Edward J. Pearce, and Julie Jacobson
   2008 Helminth Infections: The Great Neglected Tropical Diseases. Journal of Clinical Investigation 118(4):1311–1321.

Hughes, Robert G., Donald S. Sharp, Maria C. Hughes, Siale 'Akau'ola, Paul Heinsbroek, Raman Velayudhan, Dirk Schulz, Kevin Palmer, Tommasco Cavalli-Sforza, and Gauden Galea
   2004 Environmental Influences on Helminthiasis and Nutritional Status Among Pacific Schoolchildren. International Journal of Environmental Health Research 14(3):163–177.

Ichimori, Kayuzo, and Andy Crump
  2005 Pacific Collaboration to Eliminate Lymphatic Filariasis. Trends in Parasitology 21(10):441–444.
Kaufman, Jim
  2010 Evolution and Immunity. Immunology 130(4):459–462.
King, Charles H., and Madeline Dangerfield-Cha
  2008 The Unacknowledged Impact of Chronic Schistosomiasis. Chronic Illness 4(1):65–79.
Labeaud, A. Desiree, Indu Malhotra, Maria J. King, Christopher L. King, and Charles H. King
  2009 Do Antenatal Parasite Infections Devalue Childhood Vaccination? PLoS Neglected Tropical Diseases
      3(5):e442.
Lambert, Sylvester M.
  1928 Medical Conditions in the South-Pacific. Medical Journal of Australia 2:362–378.
  1941 A Doctor in Paradise. London: J. M. Dent and Sons Ltd.
Legislative Assembly of the Cook Islands (LACI)
  1966 Report of the Health Department of the Year Ended 31 March 1966. Papers presented 1966, Vol. 1.
      Legislative Assembly Paper No. 7. Legislative Assembly of the Cook Islands, Cook Islands Parliament,
      Rarotonga. Cook Islands Archive.
Littleton, Judith, and Julie Park
  2009 Tuberculosis and Syndemics: Implications for Pacific Health in New Zealand. Social Science &
      Medicine 69(11):1674–1680.
Liu, Zhugong G., Qian Liu, David Bleich, Padimi Salgame, and William C. Gause
  2010 Regulation of Type 1 Diabetes, Tuberculosis, and Asthma by Parasites. Journal of Molecular Medicine
      88(1):27–38.
Maizels, Rick M., and Maria Yazdanbakhsh
  2003 Immune Regulation by Helminth Parasites: Cellular and Molecular Mechanisms. Nature Reviews
      Immunology 3(9):733–744.
Malhotra, Indu, Peter Mungai, Alex Wamachi, John Kioko, John H. Ouma, James W. Kazura, and Christopher
      L. King
  1999 Helminth- and Bacillus Calmette-Guérin-induced immunity in children sensitized In Utero to
      Filariasis and Schistosomiasis. Journal of Immunology 162(11):6843–6848.
Manson-Bahr, Philip H.
  1912 Filariasis and Elephantiasis in Fiji: Being a Report to the London School of Tropical Medicine.
      London: Witherby & Co.
Marchant, Arnaud, and Michel Goldman
  2005 T Cell-Mediated Immune Responses in Human Newborns: Ready to Learn? Clinical & Experimental
      Immunology 141(1):10–18.
McCarthy, D. D.
  1959 Filariasis in the Cook Islands. New Zealand Medical Journal 58(328):738–748.
Medical Health Office, Cook Islands (MHO)
  1958 CMO, 28 May 1958. In South Pacific Cook Islands Health General, 1955–66, H 333/12. Wellington:
      Archives New Zealand.
Miles, David J. C., Marianne van der Sande, Sarah Crozier, Olubukola Ojuola, Melba S. Palmero, Mariama
      Sanneh, Ebrima S. Touray, Sarah Rowland-Jones, Hilton Whittle, Martin Ota, and Arnaud Marchant
  2008 Effects of Antenatal and Postnatal Environments on CD4 T-Cell Responses to *Mycobacterium bovis*
      BCG in Healthy Infants in The Gambia. Clinical and Vaccine Immunology 15(6):995–1002.
Miles, John A. R.
  1997 Infectious Diseases: Colonising the Pacific? Dunedin, NZ: University of Otago Press.
Neto, Luanda M. S., Raquel de Vasconcellos, Carvalhaes de Oliveira, Paulo Renato Totino, Flavia Marinho
      Sant'Anna, Viviane de Oliveira Cohelho, Valeria Cavalcanti Rolla, and Graziela M. Zanini
  2009 Enteroparasitosis Prevalence and Parasitism Influence in Clinical Outcomes of Tuberculosis Patients
      With or Without HIV Co-Infection in a Reference Hospital in Rio de Janeiro (2000–2006). The
      Brazilian Journal of Infectious Diseases 13(6):427–432.

New Zealand Department of Island Territories (NZDIT)
  1949–57 Cook Islands Tuberculosis 1949–57, IT 90/10/7, Archives New Zealand, Wellington.
Newton, Sandra M., Andrew J. Brent, Susanne Anderson, Elizabeth Whittaker, and Beate Kampmann
  2008 Paediatric Tuberculosis. The Lancet Infectious Diseases 8(8):498–510.
O'Connor, Francis W.
  1923 Researches in the Western Pacific: Being a Report on the Results of the Expedition Sent From the London School of Tropical Medicine to the Ellice, Tokelau and Samoa Islands in 1921–1922. *In* Research Memoirs of the London School of Tropical Medicine, vol. 4. London: J.C. Phelp & Son.
Ottesen, Eric A., N. R. Mendell, J. M. MacQueen, P. F. Weller, D. B. Amos, and F. E. Ward
  1981 Familial Predisposition to Filarial Infection – Not Linked to HLA-A or -B Locus Specificities. Acta Tropica 38(3):205–216.
Perry, Sharon, Rabia Hussain, and Julie Parsonnet
  2011 The Impact of Mucosal Infections on Acquisition and Progression of Tuberculosis. Mucosal Immunology 4(3):246–251.
Potian, Julius A., Wasiulla Rafi, Kamlesh Bhatt, Amanda McBride, William C. Gause, and Padmini Salgame
  2011 Preexisting Helminth Infection Induces Inhibition of Innate Pulmonary Anti-Tuberculosis Defense by Engaging the IL-4 Receptor Pathway. Journal of Experimental Medicine 208(9): 1863–1874.
Resende Co, Tatianna, Cristina S. Hirsch, Zahra Toossi, Reynaldo Dietze, and Rodrigo Ribeiro-Rodrigues
  2007 Intestinal Helminth Co-Infection has a Negative Impact on Both Anti-*Mycobacterium tuberculosis* Immunity and Clinical Response to Tuberculosis Therapy. Clinical & Experimental Immunology 147(1):45–52.
Resture, Setapu A.
  2010 Te Maama Pala: Continuity and Change in Coping With Tuberculosis in Tuvalu. Master of Arts Thesis, Department of History, University of Auckland.
Roberts, Mere
  1991 The Parasites of the Polynesian Rat Within and Beyond New Zealand. International Journal for Parasitology 21(7):777–783.
Romans, T. T.
  1955 Health of My Country. *In* Medical General 6/1 1954–1956. Rarotonga: Cook Islands Archives.
Rose, M.
  1946 Medical and Sanitary Report for the Gilbert and Ellice Islands Colony. *In* Agency H, Series 1, Box 496, Record 333/3 Alternate no 32602. Wellington: Archives New Zealand.
Singer, Merrill, D. Anne Herring, Judith Littleton, and Melanie Rock
  2011 Syndemics in Global Health. *In* A Companion to Medical Anthropology. Merill Singer and Pamela Erickson, eds. Pp. 158–180. Malden, MA: Wiley-Blackwell.
Speare, Rick, Falatea Fab Latasi, Tekaai Nelesone, Sonia Harmen, Wayne Melrose, David Durrheim, and Jorg Heukelbach
  2006 Prevalence of Soil Transmitted Nematodes on Nukufetau, a Remote Pacific Island in Tuvalu. BMC Infectious Diseases 6:110.
Steel, Cathy, and Eric A. Ottesen
  2001 Evolution of Immunologic Responsiveness of Persons Living in an Area of Endemic Bancroftian Filariasis: A 17-Year Follow-Up. Journal of Infectious Diseases 184(1):73–79.
Tristão-Sá, Ricardo, Rodrigo Ribeiro-Rodrigues, Luciléia T. Johnson, Fausto E. L Pereira, and Reyanaldo Dietze
  2002 Intestinal Nematodes and Pulmonary Tuberculosis. Revista da Sociedade Brasileira de Medicina Tropical 35(5):533–535.
Wammes, Linda J., Firdaus Hamid, Aprilianto E. Wiria, Brechje de Gier, Erliyani Sartono, Rick M. Maizels, Adrian J. F. Luty, Yvonne Fillie, Gary T. Brice, Taniawati Supali, Hermelijn H. Smits, and Maria Yazdanbakhsh
  2010 Regulatory T Cells in Human Geohelminth Infection Suppress Immune Responses to BCG and *Plasmodium falciparum*. European Journal of Immunology 40(2):437–444.

Western Pacific High Commission (WPHC)

1946 Letter From Acting Resident Commissioner Wernham to Western Pacific High Commissioner, July 11, 1946. WPHC 9 1229108 10/18/4. Western Pacific Archive, University of Auckland Library, Auckland.

1955 Gilbert and Ellice Islands Medical and Sanitary Report for the Year 1955. WPHC 16 1228666 173/6/5. Western Pacific Archive, University of Auckland Library, Auckland.

1956 Gilbert and Ellice Islands Colony Medical and Sanitary Report for the Year 1956. WPHC 16 1228666 173/6/6. Western Pacific Archive, University of Auckland Library, Auckland.

1961 Gilbert and Ellice Islands Colony Medical Department: Annual Report for the Year Ending 31st December 1961. WPHC 20 1229763 207/6/9. Western Pacific Archive, University of Auckland Library, Auckland.

Yang, Yu R., Darren J. Gray, Magda K. Ellis, Shu K. Yang, Philip S. Craig, and Donald P. McManus

2009 Human Cases of Simultaneous Echinococcosis and Tuberculosis—Significance and Extent in China. Parasites & Vectors 2(1):53.

Yazdanbakhsh, Maria, Peter G. Kremsner, and Ronald van Ree

2002 Allergy, Parasites, and the Hygiene Hypothesis. Science 296(5567):490–494.

Zevallos, Karine, Katherine C. Vergara, Antonio Vergara, Carlos Vidal, Hector H. Garcia, and Carlos A. Evans

2010 Tuberculin Skin-Test Reactions Are Unaffected by the Severity of Hyperendemic Intestinal Helminth Infections and Co-Infections. American Journal of Tropical Medicine and Hygiene 83(2):319–325.

DIABETES AMONG OAXACA'S TRANSNATIONAL POPULATION: AN EMERGING SYNDEMIC

MARGARET EVERETT
Portland State University

JOSEF N. WIELAND
University of California, Irvine

Though indigenous communities have undergone rapid economic integration in the last few decades as a result of neoliberal reforms and increased migration, these communities experience a complex epidemiological profile that includes fetal and childhood undernutrition and adult obesity and diabetes. We argue here that the interaction of these burdens and the social conditions that have dismantled local food systems and propelled out-migration best explain the growing rate of diabetes in this region. We contrast this syndemic approach with the Thrifty Genotype Hypothesis, which attributes the high rate of diabetes among Native American populations to presumed genetic predisposition, triggered by lifestyle changes. We find the Thrifty Phenotype Hypothesis useful for explaining links between fetal and postnatal nutrition interruptions and chronic diseases in later life in certain populations and that a syndemics framework is useful for modeling the complex social causes of this pattern. While the syndemics model has largely been used to understand infectious diseases and addiction, social scientists have yet to use the framework to investigate the complex interactions between chronic malnutrition, metabolic syndrome, and political economy in rural Oaxacan communities. The most effective efforts to reduce diabetes will be those that address the social determinants of diabetes in this and other similar populations, rather than programs that address individual behaviors and lifestyle. [diabetes, nutrition, syndemics, indigenous populations]

INTRODUCTION

The model of the Epidemiological Transition, in which the burden of disease in a population undergoes a progressive and inevitable shift from infectious diseases to chronic diseases associated with longer lives and lifestyle changes, does not adequately characterize the indigenous populations of Oaxaca, Mexico (see Figure 1). Though indigenous communities have undergone rapid economic integration in the last few decades as a result of neoliberal reforms and increased migration, these communities experience the "dual burden" of presumably pre- and post-transition illnesses. We argue here that the interaction of these burdens (childhood undernutrition and infection, adult obesity and metabolic changes) and the social conditions that have dismantled local food

ANNALS OF ANTHROPOLOGICAL PRACTICE 36.2, pp. 295–311. ISSN: 2153-957X. © 2013 by the American Anthropological Association. DOI:10.1111/napa.12005.

FIGURE 1. Location of the state of Oaxaca

systems and propelled out-migration best explain the growing rate of diabetes in this region.

We contrast this syndemic approach with the Thrifty Genotype Hypothesis, which attributes the high rate of diabetes among Native American populations to presumed genetic predisposition, triggered by lifestyle changes. The Thrifty Phenotype Hypothesis, suggesting that interruptions in fetal growth and poor postnatal nutrition may result in a host of chronic illnesses, can be useful for understanding linkages between social conditions and increasing rates of diabetes in some communities (Hales and Barker 1992). While the syndemics model has largely been used to understand infectious diseases and addiction, social scientists have yet to use the framework to investigate the complex interactions between chronic malnutrition, metabolic syndrome, and political economy in rural Oaxacan communities. Evidence in Oaxaca supports the idea of fetal origins and social determinants of diabetes over the life course, and syndemics theory offers a way to model the synergy between social determinants and chronic disease. Drawing on secondary data on nutrition and chronic disease in Oaxaca, as well as literature on the social and economic conditions of the region, we describe how a syndemics approach could be useful in understanding and addressing the growing burden of type 2 diabetes in some populations. Finally, we discuss the policy implications of these various approaches, and argue for programs that address the social determinants of diabetes in this and other similar populations, rather than programs that address individual behaviors and lifestyle.

DIABETES AND THE EPIDEMIOLOGICAL TRANSITION IN MEXICO

Type 2 diabetes has become a significant and costly health problem in Mexico, and its prevalence has increased steadily in recent decades. Now the most common cause of death in Mexico, it is the third largest cause of death in the state of Oaxaca. The national prevalence of type 2 diabetes increased rapidly from 1993 to 2006, from 6.7 percent to 14.4 percent (Villalpando et al. 2010). The high mortality rate associated with diabetes in Mexico is also attributed to a lack of optimal care and the frequent comorbidity of hypertension and dyslipidemia (Aguilar-Salinas et al. 2003:2025).

Despite the rapid increase in chronic diseases, including diabetes mellitus in recent decades, Mexico's present profile does not entirely fit the classic model of the Epidemiological Transition. The "epidemiological transition" implies a transition in which the largest burden of disease shifts from infectious diseases to chronic and noncommunicable diseases. The model as posed in Omran's seminal 1971 article has been discussed, revised, and debated ever since but continues to shape our understanding of the interrelationship between demographic shifts, epidemiology, and health (Martínez and Gustavo 2003; Phillips 1991).

A major criticism of the model, which is relevant to the present discussion, is that it presents an overly optimistic view of the progressive direction of disease patterns. That is, implicit in the Epidemiological Transition is the expectation that a shift in mortality rates and causes would be the inevitable result of economic development, regardless of the human (policy) responses to promote health or prevent and treat disease. The model implies that the transition from infectious to chronic diseases is the "natural destiny of societies, a sort of path that sooner or later, all countries would have to follow" (Martínez and Gustavo 2003:541). More recently, scholars described a "third epidemiological transition" to refer to a new period of emerging and reemerging infectious diseases such as SARS and Avian Flu (Barrett 2010; Singer 2010). Importantly, this third transition coincides not with stages of development, but with growing levels of global inequalities. Barrett further argued that poor and wealthy countries will experience these transitions very differently, calling into question the generalizability of Epidemiological Transition theory.

A further significant limitation of the model is that it uses the nation state as a unit of analysis in describing shifts in population health, thus missing significant differences among regions (including rural and urban areas), social classes, and ethnic groups in terms of the burden of disease: "The rich and poor, urban and rural dwellers and other subgroups of populations of many countries effectively live in different 'epidemiological worlds'; a focus on national averages does a disservice to virtually all people" (Phillips 1991:viii). Finally, and particularly important for the following discussion of syndemics, the Epidemiological Transition model focuses on mortality rather than morbidity, and on the description of patterns of mortality, and not the causes of those patterns. We argue here that in order to understand those causes, a model that contemplates the interaction of adverse social conditions and illnesses, often illnesses that are associated with different "stages" of the Epidemiological Transition, is essential.

The need for such a model is evident in what Martínez and Gustavo (2003) described as Mexico's "double burden" of disease. That is, while Mexico's mortality rates have indeed declined throughout the 20th century (see Table 1), and a shift toward chronic diseases as the principal causes of mortality has occurred, the country's epidemiological profile is nonetheless quite different from that of other countries said to have undergone the Epidemiological Transition. Rather, Mexico struggles with both high rates of infectious diseases associated with the "pre-transition" stages, and high rates of chronic diseases

TABLE 1. Population, general and child deaths Mexico, 1921–95

Year	Population	General deaths	Deaths in infants under 12 months	General mortality rates per 1000 inhabitants	Child mortality rate per 1000 live births
1921	14,333,082	364,832	99,783	25.5	220.0
1930	16,552,722	441,712	107,921	26.7	131.6
1940	19,653,552	458,906	110,039	23.3	125.7
1950	25,779,254	418,430	113,032	16.2	96.2
1960	34,923,129	402,545	119,316	11.5	74.2
1970	48,225,238	485,686	146,028	10.1	68.5
1980	66,846,833	434,465	94,116	6.5	38.9
1990	81,249,645	422,803	65,428	5.2	23.9
1995	91,158,290	430,278	48,023	4.7	17.5

Source: Martinez and Leal 2003.

associated with economic development and "post-transition" stages (Frenk et al. 2006) (Table 1).

As Martínez and Gustavo explained, "Low-cost, high-yield preventive measures managed to stop many [communicable diseases] from proving fatal, yet the conditions of lack of sanitation and poverty in which large groups of population live... means that this aspect of the burden of disease is unlikely to be eliminated from the health scenario in the near future" (Martínez and Gustavo 2003:544). Perhaps not surprisingly, the poor are particularly susceptible to both noncommunicable diseases such as diabetes and hypertension, and "older" communicable diseases such as respiratory and gastrointestinal infections. Additionally, Mexico struggles with "newer" infectious diseases, including HIV/AIDS, and the persistence of infectious diseases once thought to be eradicated, including cholera, malaria, and dengue. The movement of populations, such as the flow of migrants out of Oaxacan communities to the north and back again, further complicates this epidemiological picture.

DIABETES IN OAXACA: FROM GENETICS TO SYNDEMICS

The Thrifty Gene

Research on the high rate of diabetes among indigenous populations around the world has long been linked to genetic etiologies, particularly the much-debated "thrifty genotype" hypothesis, which theorizes an evolutionary adaptation to resource scarcity predisposing some groups to diabetes in modern times, first posited by Neel in 1962. Neel argued that diabetes mellitus involved a quick insulin trigger, which evolved in hunter-gatherer ancestors in response to periodic feast-or-famine conditions. Historically recent dietary patterns made this response disadvantageous, resulting in increasing rates of diabetes among Amerindian and other populations. Though Neel later revisited his original hypothesis and acknowledged that attributing the high rate of diabetes in Amerindians to "ethnic predisposition" was unfounded (Neel 1999), the "thrifty genotype" continues to influence both lay and scientific discourses about the disease (see Diamond 2003; Martorell 2005).

The notion of genetic predisposition has been influential in scientific and policy discussions about diabetes among Mexico's indigenous population as well. The Mexican government's own analysis of its 2006 National Survey of Health and Nutrition (ENSANUT) applied the hypothesis to explain the increasing rate of chronic diseases: "Sedentary life, rapid changes in diet and lifestyle, *together with a probable genetic susceptibility in Amerindian populations*, have had an important impact on the prevalence of overweight and obesity in the Mexican population" (Instituto Nacional de Salud Pública 2007:61, emphasis added). Similarly, genetic predisposition figures in scientific research among indigenous Oaxacan populations. Escobedo et al. (2010) found particularly high prevalence of type 2 diabetes and impaired glucose tolerance in a Zapotec population in Oaxaca. While the authors cited agricultural changes and labor migration as contributing factors, they argued that "The most plausible hypothesis to explain this epidemic is Neel's thrifty genotype theory," and the authors suggested public health strategies aimed at education and lifestyle changes (Escobedo et al. 2010:412, 415). In a 1995 study in a Mixtec community, researchers found that a large portion of the study participants (42 of 101 subjects) had an impaired glucose tolerance but did not otherwise meet the criteria for type 2 diabetes (Schultz and Weidensee 1995). They therefore concluded that, "The Mixtec population may be genetically predisposed to non-insulin-dependent diabetes, although their current lifestyle provides a protective effect" (Schultz and Weidensee 1995:1274). The authors made this assertion of genetic vulnerability, despite the fact that the study population was located near a regional urban center in an area of heavy out-migration to northern Mexico and the United States. Though it is possible that the economic and social changes that had already occurred in this population, including changes in diet and activity, might explain the changes in glucose tolerance and the high risk of diabetes, the authors instead invoked the "thrifty genotype" to explain their results.

Critics of the thrifty gene hypothesis worry that the application of genetic etiologies to specific ethnic populations (American Indian, Mexican American, indigenous Mexicans) downplays the role of environmental and social conditions in producing diabetes (Benyshek et al. 2001; Cruickshank et al. 2001; McDermott 1998; Smith-Morris 2004). Chaufan, for example, argued that a focus on genes distracts from the more significant contribution of social deprivation: "Interestingly, social deprivation in an environment of relative nutritional abundance, a characteristic of contemporary poverty, rarely figures in the literature among the risk factors for type 2 diabetes" (Chaufan 2004:36). Farmer (2003) might call the attribution of diabetes among poor Mexicans to either individual biology or behavior an "immodest claim of causality," which serves to mask the social determinants that are at the root of the suffering of the poor and underserved. Ferreira and Lang charged that applying the "thrifty gene" hypothesis to indigenous populations is "a deliberate attempt to ignore the macro-social context in which diabetes originates and the political and economic aspects of its geographical distribution across so many groups of Indigenous Peoples around the world" (Ferreira and Lang 2006:8). Finally, as the nutritional research cited below demonstrates, epidemiological changes have occurred far too quickly to be explained primarily on genetic grounds (see Krieger 2006:99 for a similar point about immigrant populations). If genetic predisposition is an inadequate explanation for the changing burden of disease in this population, what alternative model can we propose?

The Syndemic Model of Disease

Thus far we have argued that etiologies such as the "thrifty genotype" fall short of explaining the high rate of diabetes in populations undergoing rapid economic, epidemiological, and nutritional changes. Medical anthropologists have long argued that a limitation of biomedicine in general is the tendency to treat diseases as discrete entities, independent both of other diseases and of the social conditions that shape the burden of disease in specific populations. The theory of syndemics offers a model for the complex interactions of health conditions and the social environment. Because diabetes in Oaxaca appears to involve the interplay between historical inequalities, nutritional deficiencies throughout the life cycle, and contemporary macroeconomic and social changes, syndemics theory offers a promising way to guide research and direct social action to improve health in this population.

The Centers for Disease Control and Prevention defines syndemics as "Two or more afflictions, interacting synergistically, contributing to excess burden of disease in a population" (CDC 2009:np). That is, the syndemics concept describes not only the coexistence of diseases or conditions in a population, but the biological interaction of those conditions and the health consequences of that interaction. But a recognition of adverse social conditions as they relate to the spread of disease and its consequences is also essential to the identification of a syndemic: "Beyond the notion of disease clustering in a location or population, and processes of biological synergism among co-dwelling pathogens, the term syndemic points to the determinant importance of social conditions in the health of individuals and populations" (Singer and Clair 2003:428). More recently, Singer has argued that, "Human social environments, including the prevailing structures of social relationships (such as social inequality and injustice) and also sociogenic environmental conditions (for example, hazards of the built environment, sales of toxic commodities, pollution, species loss, and climate change) contribute enormously to both disease clustering and interaction" (Singer 2009:21). This more comprehensive definition of syndemics best matches the scenario of chronic disease in Oaxaca, in which historical inequalities and cumulative disadvantage over the life cycle are producing high rates of chronic disease in a population that also experiences high rates of infectious disease. Singer and Clair observed, "a syndemic is a set of intertwined and mutually enhancing epidemics involving disease interactions at the biological level that develop and are sustained in a community/population because of harmful social conditions and injurious social connections" (Singer and Clair 2003:429). Harmful social conditions can include such things as inadequate housing, dangerous work environments, poverty, stigmatization, racism, and other inequalities.

The study of sexually transmitted disease has benefited from the syndemic concept, helping to bring into fuller view, for example, the way HIV/AIDS and TB interact at the biological and cellular level, and also how social conditions such as poor housing, racism, and inadequate health care contribute to the excess burden of those diseases among inner-city poor and minority populations. Singer (Singer et al. 2006) also used this framework to describe what he calls the syndemic of substance abuse, violence, and AIDS, or SAVA. Elsewhere, Singer found a synergism between food insecurity and HIV/AIDS in southern Africa (2011b), and between lead poisoning and infectious disease in children (2011a). Increasingly, syndemics theory is being applied to chronic diseases. For example, researchers have described the Chagas disease, rheumatic heart disease, and congestive heart failure syndemic in Latin America (Ventura and Mehra 2004). A study from Veracruz, Mexico found significantly higher rates of pulmonary tuberculosis among diabetic individuals than nondiabetic individuals, suggesting an increased susceptibility to TB among people with type 2 diabetes (Ponce-De-Leon et al. 2004). Osmond and Barker (2000) described the relationship between poverty, poor childhood nutrition, and adult heart disease. Singer et al. (2006) also pointed to emerging research on the relationship between type 2 diabetes and hepatitis C infections as another possible syndemic.

Among poor populations, inadequate nutrition is among the most important daily manifestations of deprivation, and it is clear that both chronic and periodic malnutrition has serious health consequences. We argue below that diabetes among Oaxaca's predominantly indigenous and significantly transnational population cannot be understood without reference to the social conditions that drive the "dual burden" of undernutrition and obesity in this population.

The Dual Burden of Growth Stunting and Obesity

As with many populations throughout Latin America, the concurrence of both growth stunting and obesity has been well documented in the state of Oaxaca. Growth stunting in a population is indicative of prenatal and early childhood undernutrition, and is increasingly part of a larger pattern: low birth weight, growth stunting, and increased risk for chronic disease in adulthood. One recent study of a Triqui community in Oaxaca was able to compare data on height, weight, and body mass index (BMI) for the same population at three different time periods (late 19th century, 1940, and 2002). The study found that while rates of stunting (low height for age) was significant in all three periods, overweight and obesity were only present in the population in 2002, with 41 percent of adult men either overweight or obese (based on BMI of > 25) and 58 percent of women overweight or obese (Ramos Rodríguez and Sandoval Mendoza 2007). Nationally, the prevalence of stunting and underweight is three times greater in indigenous populations than in nonindigenous populations (Rivera et al. 2003).

In a national study, Barquera et al. (2007) identified an association between maternal central adiposity (MCA, large waist circumference) and child stunting (CS) in Mexico through an analysis of the Mexican Nutritional Survey of 1999. That is, they found that children whose mothers carried more fat around their midsections (higher waist to hip ratios) were significantly more likely to exhibit CS. Importantly, the authors argued these conditions do not merely coexist, but rather are reinforcing: "Although MCA and CS are two conditions frequently regarded as the result of opposite determinants, our observation suggests that this is not necessarily the case, particularly in populations undergoing the nutrition transition. MCA was associated not only to chronic diseases, but also to child stunting" (Barquera et al. 2007:601). Rather than viewing the "nutrition transition" as a gradual and inevitable shift from under- to overnutrition, obesity and stunting could be the result of "the same process at different stages of the life cycle" (Barquera et al. 2007:601). The authors further hypothesized that maternal short stature and small hip circumference, combined with poor maternal nutrition, may limit in utero growth. From the perspective of syndemic theory, this "accumulated disadvantage" over generations reveals more about the causes of ill health than genetic predisposition.

Another study, which focused on young children (age 24–72 months) in rural areas of several Mexican states found that the concurrence of stunting and overweight (based on BMI for age) was surprisingly common, and that the rate of concurrent stunting and overweight for indigenous children was twice that of nonindigenous children (10 percent compared to 5 percent) (Fernald and Neufeld 2007). Rivera et al. (2004) observed that rates of CS were declining among children under 3 in Mexico, but that rates remained high in some areas and were declining slowly overall (down to 17.7 percent in 1999, compared to 22.8 percent in 1988). Similarly, studies of the Latin American region have found that low-income households often experienced the dual burden of nutritional deficits and overweight (Duran et al. 2006).

Data from rural Oaxaca demonstrated very little change in the rates of child malnutrition between 1996 and 2005 (Ávila Curiel et al. 2005:23). The same survey data showed that rural areas of Oaxaca had a prevalence of stunting of 32 percent when the home language is indigenous, compared to 22 percent when the home language was Spanish, underscoring persistent inequalities by ethnicity (Ávila Curiel et al. 2005:41). Significantly, the 2005 survey included data on labor migration, and found an elevated risk of malnutrition or stunting (30.6 percent) when a member of the family was a migrant, either within the country or abroad, compared to 26.4 percent in households with no migrants (Ávila Curiel et al. 2005:43).

While rural child malnutrition and stunting have remained fairly constant in Oaxaca, diabetes rates have increased. Barquera and colleagues found rates of type 2 diabetes increasing throughout Mexico between 1980 and 2000, but found the most dramatic rate of increase in the southern region, which includes the state of Oaxaca: "While the northern region had a relative increase of nine [percentage] points (from 1980–2000), the southern region experienced a relative increase of 92 [percentage] points" (Barquera et al. 2003:410).

Identifying both the prevalence and the causes of this "dual burden" is important because research shows that early childhood undernutrition increases the risk of both adiposity, itself a risk factor for diabetes, and increases the risk for metabolic problems independent of weight gain. Popkin et al. (1996) used data from four countries to demonstrate the association between stunting and overweight and hypothesized that nutritional deficiencies at critical growth periods (prenatal, infancy, weaning) contribute to "metabolic adaptations" that increase the risk for obesity later in life. In a Mexico

City study, Boulé et al. (2003) found that adult men with high amounts abdominal fat are more likely to have impaired glucose tolerance if they also experienced malnutrition in the first year of life. Put another way, this suggests that obesity is more detrimental to previously malnourished individuals. In a research review, Martorell et al. found more mixed evidence about the relationship between early nutrition and later adiposity (abdominal obesity), but they suggested that persons "who move across the plane of nutrition from scarcity early in life to abundance or even excess in adulthood" may be particularly susceptible to obesity and associated health problems (Martorell et al. 2001:878S–879S).

These examples support Hales and Barker's (1992) "programming hypothesis," also called the Thrifty Phenotype Hypothesis, which describes how poor fetal and early infancy nutrition during critical growth periods may have long-term consequences on pancreatic development and insulin sensitivity. Rather than thrifty genes selected during food scarcity that develop fat-storing "fast insulin triggers," Thrifty Phenotypes have been thought of as adaptive physiological responses to poor fetal environments, which in turn alter glucose-insulin metabolism in later life (Barker et al. 1993; Hales and Barker 2001). Metabolic irregularities thus become increasingly problematic in the context of changing food systems (McMillen and Robinson 2005). The evidence from Oaxaca supports a phenotypic rather than genetic explanation for the epidemiological shifts occurring in certain rural populations throughout the state.

Whatever the precise relationship between undernutrition and adult obesity, studies have identified a relationship between child nutrition and metabolic risk, which may be key to understanding the high rate of diabetes in Oaxaca. Weight at the first year of age, even independent of birth weight, has been shown to correlate with insulin sensitivity, glucose tolerance, and lipid profile in adult men (González-Barranco and Rios-Torres 2004). That is, early childhood undernutrition is predictive of metabolic problems later in life, and the risk of metabolic abnormalities increases with increases in BMI, even when BMI is within normal limits. Similarly, a study comparing stunted and nonstunted children in poor neighborhoods of São Paulo, Brazil, found that stunted children showed decreased activity in β-cell function and increased insulin sensitivity compared to nonstunted children, findings which are strongly predictive of the development of type 2 diabetes (Martins and Sawaya 2006).

Though these studies point to the interaction of nutritional experiences across the life course, and the relationship between those interactions and the burden of diabetes in certain populations, a syndemic approach requires that we further consider the social conditions in which poor nutrition (including undernutrition and obesogenic diet high in carbohydrates and fat) is common, as well as other environmental factors that might explain the complex health profile of this population.

The Social Determinants of the Dual Burden in Oaxaca

Oaxaca is one of the poorest states in Mexico, with a long history of federal neglect. The popular uprisings in the City of Oaxaca in 2006 attest to the tension between the governing elite, underpaid public employees, and the rural poor. Inequalities rooted in the colonial experience but greatly exacerbated by recent macroeconomic changes, profoundly impact the social conditions of this region. A few statistics may provide a sense of the living and social conditions of the population. For example, in 2006 the percentage of homes with dirt floors in Oaxaca was 25.9, compared to a national average of only 8.6 percent (Instituto Nacional de Salud Pública 2007:28). The percentage of homes without plumbing in Oaxaca, 19.1 percent, was also well above the national average of 7.9 percent (Instituto Nacional de Salud Pública 2007). The percentage of the population over 15 years of age that is illiterate in Oaxaca is 17.3 percent, compared to a national average of 8.7 percent (Instituto Nacional de Salud Pública 2007). Reyes Peña et al. (2010) found that measures of community well-being, such as housing conditions and education levels, were strongly correlated with children's nutritional status in Oaxaca, where communities with the lowest well-being measures had higher rates of growth stunting and underweight in children.

Oaxaca remains a predominantly rural population, and the majority of its population is indigenous. Today, 14 indigenous languages are spoken in the region, and many rural communities continue to practice traditional subsistence agriculture (*milpa*) and local governance structures (*usos y costumbres*). Community obligations in the form of *tequio* (voluntary labor for community projects) and *cargos* (community leadership positions) remain important in many communities. Deeply rooted forms of reciprocal exchange, which have been an important resource in indigenous communities (Cohen 1999), are strained by the increasing outflow of migrants (Stephen 2007).

Migration is an important aspect of the syndemic of diabetes in Oaxaca. Migration to the United States has been a significant economic strategy since the 1970s, but has increased dramatically in the past two decades as a result of neoliberal reforms and trade liberalization (Stephen 2007). Mexico's economic restructuring during the 1980s and 1990s, including the implementation of the North American Free Trade Agreement (NAFTA), opened their economy to foreign investment and imports, and brought tremendous changes to agriculture. Most notoriously, the opening of the economy made possible the import of large quantities of subsidized corn from the United States, a case of commodity dumping that has been crippling for many small-scale farmers. Regarding the impact of free trade on Mexican corn, Browning observed that "The U.S. Department of Agriculture, Foreign Agricultural Service projects Mexican Imports of U.S. corn to grow approximately 5.5 percent annually over the next five years" (Browning 2009:18), further exacerbating inequalities between the nearly 2.2 million small farmers and the few highly subsidized industrial agriculturalists. As U.S. corn imports increase, the average price that Mexican farmers received for maize dropped more than 50 percent between 1990 and 2003 (see Rossett 2006:57).

The government's current economic model abandons its support of peasant agriculture in favor of commercial agriculture for export. Government programs encourage peasants to adapt to this new environment by producing cash crops. The countryside of the Mixtec region of Oaxaca around the regional center of Tlaxiaco, for example, is dotted with greenhouses built through a government loan program to encourage tomato growing cooperatives. Migrant remittances have helped locals invest in such enterprises. So many have been built, however, that the price of tomatoes in the region plummeted. Though these programs may provide economic opportunities for some, they do not contribute to food sovereignty for the community, and rather contribute further to a loss of crop diversity and a growing dependence on pesticides and credit.

Communities closer to the city of Oaxaca experience somewhat different changes, but with similar effects on nutrition and health. The craft producing communities near the capital of Oaxaca, for example, have benefitted from tourism and the market for crafts. This craft production has allowed some to accumulate enough money to travel to the United States for work, as described by Stephen (2007) in the Zapotec community of Teotitlán del Valle. But these communities are also particularly vulnerable to changes in tourism, as with the virtual collapse of tourism during 2006–07 with the period of civil unrest. Another craft community, Atzompa, where women make the distinctive green-glazed pottery that the town is known for, has seen a significant increase in hypertension and type 2 diabetes, according to staff doctors at the community clinic (Everett 2011). In recent years Atzompa has also sold off much of its *ejido* (communal agricultural land) to peri-urban development after constitutional changes in the 1990s allowed the sale of communally held lands, thus losing their remaining connection to subsistence agriculture (Pérez 2003). These changes have sped a dietary shift associated with urbanization that has greatly contributed to the rates of diabetes in that community.

These kinds of changes in agriculture, along with the experiences of migrants themselves, increase the pace of the "nutrition transition" in Oaxaca, in which the diet of the population is increasingly one of simple carbohydrates and fats, with a declining consumption of fruits and vegetables. Economic integration has also increased the availability of cheap snack foods and sodas, both of which are ubiquitous throughout rural and urban Oaxaca. These same communities, however, continue to contend with high rates of child undernutrition, compounded by common diarrheal illnesses and respiratory infections caused by inadequate sanitation (Everett 2011). The main features of the syndemic proposed here are poor nutrition (including early undernutrition, a diet of limited variety, high in carbohydrates, sugars, and fats, and increasingly including cheap snack foods), poverty, and high rates of type 2 diabetes. Poor nutrition and social deprivation contribute to a pattern of stunting, insulin sensitivity, and adiposity gain, all of which contribute to the onset of type 2 diabetes.

Migration, leading to changes in diet and activity patterns, also contributes to this pattern. Return migrants often come home with health problems including HIV and diabetes; on a visit to a community clinic in the Mixtec region, the clinic doctor commented of migrants, "They leave skinny and they come back fat." A variety of local cultural and environmental factors may also contribute to this pattern. Among the indigenous communities of Oaxaca, gender patterns can vary considerably, but in communities where women are less valued, their nutritional status tends to be poorer than men's, leading to higher rates of growth stunting, and possibly higher risk for diabetes (Ramos Rodríguez and Sandoval Mendoza 2007). Patterns of alcohol use can also add to mortality rates for diabetes, as when binge drinking associated with reciprocal exchanges becomes an important expectation during fiestas (see Perez 2000). Other environmental factors may also come into play, such as the high lead exposure in Atzompa as a result of glazes used in pottery production. There is some evidence that lead exposure may increase the risk of developing type 2 diabetes, and that lead exposure will be particularly detrimental (especially in terms of comorbidities of hypertension and decreased kidney function) among diabetics (see Tsiah et al. 2004).

CONCLUSIONS

Why does it matter if we attribute diabetes among indigenous Oaxacans and similar populations to Thrifty Genotypes, Thrifty Phenotypes, or a syndemic rooted in structural disadvantages and historical inequalities? Social scientists have argued that how we frame the causes of disease is a question of medical ethics, especially when theories of causation contribute to a failure to identify or address the social determinants behind the excess burden of disease among poor populations (McDermott 1998). Recognizing links between social disadvantage and fetal origins of metabolic irregularities and chronic diseases in later life strengthen arguments against genetic determinism. Too easily, the burden of disease can become naturalized as an inevitable characteristic of a population, especially when notions of "genetic predisposition" are applied to imprecise racial classifications. Montoya called this process "bioethnic conscription" and argues that "ethnoracial labels do more than identify groups: the labels are used to attribute qualities to groups" (Montoya 2007:95). Holmes (2006) provided a good example of this point in his study of Oaxacan migrant farm workers in Washington State. He showed how structural inequalities, and the illness and suffering caused by poor living and working conditions, came to be naturalized as the result of presumed physical differences. Oaxacans in the northwest United States were hired to pick berries—arduous work with significant pesticide exposure—because their short stature meant that "Oaxacans like to work bent over" according to farmers and others (Holmes 2006). Assertions that diabetes among this indigenous population is attributable to genetic predisposition similarly naturalizes what is largely the result of inequality and socioeconomic change.

Understanding causation with reference to social conditions has policy implications as well. If diabetes is a result of the "detonation" of a "thrifty gene" by lifestyle changes, then programs aimed at behavior change become the policy solution. A good example of this is the Mexican government's Vamos Por Un Millon de Kilos program ("Let's Go for a Million Kilos"). The public health campaign was launched in 2007 by the Mexican Institute for Social Security (IMSS), which provides medical care to public employees, and has included health fairs and clinic programs to encourage physical activity and healthy eating. In 2008, the government launched a second phase (Let's Go for More Kilos!). At IMSS clinics, patients are encouraged to join the program, receiving cards with dietary and exercise tips, and a way to track their progress. Such efforts exemplify what Singer called "the making individual of disease, [which] involves clinical acts of privatization, with diagnosis and intervention focused at the individual level, whatever the social origin of the disease in question" (Singer 2004:15). Though some people may

FIGURE 2. Public health mural in rural Oaxaca.

benefit from these health messages, they do nothing to alter the environment in which choices are structured, nor do they acknowledge deeply rooted nutritional inequalities and their causes throughout Mexico (Figure 2).

A syndemics approach to public health policy is a shift "toward the development of a big-picture awareness of diseases, disease clustering, and disease interactions in biological, ecological, and social conditions and ultimately toward correspondingly broad-based public health initiatives" (Singer 2009:201). Using the syndemics model to understand diabetes and comorbidities in Oaxacan transnational migrant communities involves conceptualizing diabetes as part of a syndemic rooted in historical inequalities and cumulative disadvantage over the life cycle. Further research to identify the specific pathways leading to type 2 diabetes in disadvantaged populations should combine nutritional studies that demonstrate the links between undernutrition and obesity within a population with detailed accounts of the social conditions that shape nutrition and health. Addressing the problem requires efforts to improve the social and environmental conditions that shape the burden of disease in this population. This requires targeting agricultural policies on both sides of the border, international inequalities that propel migration and subject migrants to difficult and unhealthy conditions, and deep-rooted discrimination and disadvantage for Mexico's indigenous populations.

REFERENCES CITED

Aguilar-Salinas, Carlos A., Oscar Velazquez Monroy, Francisco J. Gómez-Perez, Antonio Gonzalez Chávez, Agustin L. Esqueda, Virginia M. Cuevas, Juan A. Rull-Rodrigo, and Roberto T. Conyer
  2003 Characteristics of Patients with Type 2 Diabetes in Mexico: Results From a Large Population-Based Nationwide Survey. Diabetes Care 26(7):2021–2026.

Ávila Curiel, Abelardo, Carlos Galindo Gómez, and Adolfo Chávez Villasana

    2005 Encuesta Nacional de Alimentación y Nutrición en Medio Rural (ENAL) Estado de Oaxaca. Instituto Nacional de Ciencias Médicas y Nutrición Salvador Zumbirán. http://www.nutricionenmexico.com/encuestas/enal_2005_oax.pdf, accessed January 23, 2012.

Barker, David. J. P., C. N. Hales, C. H. D. Fall, C. Osmond, K. Phipps, and P. M. S. Clark

    1993 Type 2 (Non-Insulin-Dependent) Diabetes Mellitus, Hypertension and Hyperlipidaemia (Syndrome X): Relation to Reduced Fetal Growth. Diabetologia 36(1):62–67.

Barquera, Simón, Karen E. Peterson, Aviva Must, Beatrice L. Rogers, Mario Flores, Robert Houser, Eric Monterrubio, and Juan A. Rivera-Dommarco

    2007 Coexistence of Maternal Central Adiposity and Child Stunting in Mexico. International Journal of Obesity 31:601–607.

Barquera, Simón, Victor Tovar-Guzmán, Ismael Campos-Nonato, Clicerio González-Villalpando, and Juan Rivera-Dommarco

    2003 Geography of Diabetes Mellitus Mortality in Mexico: An Epidemiologic Transition Analysis. Archives of Medical Research 34(5):407–414.

Barrett, Ron

    2010 Avian Influenza and the Third Epidemiological Transition. *In* Plagues and Epidemics: Infected Spaces Past and Present. D. Ann Herring and Alan Swedlund, eds. Pp. 81–94. Oxford: Berg.

Benyshek, Daniel C., John F. Martin, and Carol S. Johnston

    2001 A Reconsideration of the Origins of the Type 2 Diabetes Epidemic Among Native Americans and the Implications for Intervention Policy. Medical Anthropology 20(1):25–64.

Boulé, Normand G., Angelo Tremblay, J. Gonzalez-Barranco, Carlos A. Aguilar-Salinas, Juan Carlos Lopez-Alvarenga, J. P. Despres, Claude Bouchard, Francisco Javier Gomez-Perez, Lilia Castillo-Martinez, and Juan Manuel Rios-Torres

    2003 Insulin Resistance and Abdominal Adiposity in Young Men with Documented Malnutrition During the First Year of Life. International Journal of Obesity 27(5):598–604.

Browning, Anjali

    2009 South of Hope: The Impact of US-Mexican State-Level Restructuring and Faltering Corn Production on the Lives of Indigenous Zapotec Maize Farmers in Oaxaca, Mexico. Ph.D. dissertation, Department of Education, University of California, Los Angeles.

Centers for Disease Control and Prevention (CDC)

    2009 Syndemics Prevention Network. www.cdc.gov/syndemics, accessed May 15, 2009.

Chaufan, Claudia

    2004 Poverty Versus Genes: The Social Context of Type 2 Diabetes. Diabetes Voice 49(2):35–37.

Cohen, Jeffrey H.

    1999 Cooperation and Community: Economy and Society in Oaxaca. Austin: University of Texas Press.

Cruickshank, J. Kennedy, Jean C. Mbanya, Rainford Wilks, Beverley Balkau, Norma McFarlane-Anderson, and Terrence Forrester

    2001 Sick Genes, Sick Individuals or Sick Populations With Chronic Disease? The Emergence of Diabetes and High Blood Pressure in African-Origin Populations. International Journal of Epidemiology 30(1):111–117.

Diamond, Jared

    2003 The Double Puzzle of Diabetes. Nature 423(6940):599–602.

Duran, Pablo, Benjamin Caballero, and Mercedes de Onis

    2006 The Association Between Stunting and Overweight in Latin American and Caribbean Preschool Children. Food and Nutrition Bulletin 27(4):300–305.

Escobedo, Jorge, Imelda Chavira, Leticia Martínez, Xochitl Velasco, Celia Escandón, and Javier Cabral

    2010 Diabetes and Other Glucose Metabolism Abnormalities in Mexican Zapotec and Mixe Indians. Diabetic Medicine 27(4):412–416.

Everett, Margaret

    2011 They Say It Runs in the Family: Diabetes and Inheritance in Oaxaca, Mexico. Social Science & Medicine 72(11):1776–1783.

Farmer, Paul
   2003 Pathologies of Power: Health, Human Rights, and the New War on the Poor. Berkeley: University of California Press.

Fernald, Lia C., and Lynette M. Neufeld
   2007 Overweight with Concurrent Stunting in Very Young Children From Rural Mexico: Prevalence and Associated Factors. European Journal of Clinical Nutrition 61:623–632.

Ferreira, Mariana L., and Gretchen Lang
   2006 Introduction: Deconstructing Diabetes. *In* Indigenous Peoples and Diabetes: Community Empowerment and Wellness. Mariana L. Ferreira and Gretchen Lang, eds. Pp. 3–32. Durham: Carolina Academic Press.

Frenk, Julio, Eduardo González-Pier, Octavio Gómez-Dantés, Miguel Lezana, and Felicia Marie Knaul
   2006 Comprehensive Reform to Improve Health System Performance in Mexico. Lancet 368(9546):1524–1534.

González-Barranco, Jorge, and Juan M Rios-Torres
   2004 Early Malnutrition and Metabolic Abnormalities Later in Life. Nutrition Reviews 67(7):S134–S139.

Hales,C. N., and David J. P. Barker
   1992 Type 2 (Non-Insulin-Dependent) Diabetes Mellitus: The Thrifty Phenotype Hypothesis. Diabetologia 35:595–601.

Hales, C. Nicholas, and David J. P. Barker
   2001 The Thrifty Phenotype Hypothesis: Type 2 Diabetes. British Medical Bulletin 60(1):5–20.

Holmes, Seth
   2006 An Ethnographic Study of the Social Context of Migrant Health in the United States. PLoS Medicine 3(10):1776–1793.

Instituto Nacional de Salud Pública
   2007 Encuesta Nacional de Salud y Nutrición 2006. Resultados por Entidad Federativa, Oaxaca. Cuernavaca, Mexico: Instituto Nacional de Salud Pública-Secretaría de Salud.

Krieger, Nancy
   2006 If "Race" Is the Answer, What Is the Question? On "Race," Racism, and Health: A Social Epidemiologist's Perspective. Is Race Real? A Web Forum Organized by the Social Science Research Council. http://raceandgenomics.ssrc.org/Krieger/, accessed March 17, 2012.

Martínez, S. Carolina, and F. Gustavo Leal
   2003 Epidemiological Transition: Model or Illusion? A Look at the Problem of Health in Mexico. Social Science & Medicine 57(3):539–550.

Martins, Paula A., and Ana L. Sawaya
   2006 Evidence of Impaired Insulin Production and Higher Sensitivity in Stunted Children Living in Slums. British Journal of Nutrition 95(5):996–1001.

Martorell, Reynaldo
   2005 Diabetes and Mexicans: Why the Two Are Linked. Preventing Chronic Disease 2(1):1–5.

Martorell, Reynaldo, Aryeh D. Stein, and Dirk G. Schroeder
   2001 Early Nutrition and Later Adiposity. Journal of Nutrition 131(3):874S–880S.

McDermott, Robyn
   1998 Ethics, Epidemiology, and the Thrifty Gene: Biological Determinism as a Health Hazard. Social Science & Medicine 47(9):1189–1195.

McMillen, I. Caroline, and Jeffrey S. Robinson
   2005 Developmental Origins of the Metabolic Syndrome: Prediction, Plasticity, and Programming. Physiological Reviews 85(2):571–633.

Montoya, Michael J.
   2007 Bioethnic Conscription: Genes, Race, and Mexicana/o Ethnicity in Diabetes Research. Cultural Anthropology 22(1):94–128.

Neel, James V.
   1962 Diabetes Mellitus: A 'Thrifty' Genotype Rendered Detrimental by 'Progress'? American Journal of Human Genetics 14(4):353–362.

1999 The 'Thrifty Genotype' in 1998. Nutrition Reviews 57(5):S2–S9.

Omran, Abdel R.
   1971 The Epidemiological Transition. A Theory of the Epidemiology of Population Change. Milbank Memorial Fund Quarterly 4(4):509–538.

Osmond, Clive, and David J. P. Barker
   2000 Fetal, Infant, and Childhood Growth Are Predictors of Coronary Heart Disease, Diabetes, and Hypertension in Adult Men and Women. Environmental Health Perspectives 108(Suppl. 3):545–553.

Pérez, Ramona
   2000 Fiesta as Tradition, Fiesta as Change: Ritual, Alcohol and Violence in a Mexican Community. Addiction 95(3):365–373.
   2003 From Ejido to Colonia: Reforms to Article 27 and the Formation of an Urban Landscape in Oaxaca. Urban Anthropology 32(3–4):343–375.

Phillips, David R.
   1991 Problems and Potential of Researching Epidemiological Transition: Examples for Southeast Asia. Social Science & Medicine 33(4):395–404.

Ponce-de-Leon, Alfredo, Lourdes Garcia-Garcia, Cecelia Garcia-Sancho, Francisco J. Gomez-Perez, Jose L. Valdespino-Gomez, Gustavo Olaiz-Fernandez, Rosalba Rojas, Leticia Ferreyra-Reyes, Bulmaro Cano-Arellano, Miriam Bobadilla, Peter M. Small, and Jose Sifuentes-Osornio
   2004 Tuberculosis and Diabetes in Southern Mexico. Diabetes Care 27(7):1584–1590.

Popkin, Barry, Marie Richards, and Carlos Monteiro
   1996 Stunting is Associated with Overweight in Children of Four Nations That Are Undergoing the Nutrition Transition. Journal of Nutrition 126(12):3009–3016.

Ramos Rodríguez, Rosa María, and Karla Sandoval Mendoza
   2007 Estado Nutricional en la Marginacíon y la Pobreza de Adultos Triquis del Estado de Oaxaca, México. Pan American Journal of Public Health 22(4):260–267.

Reyes Peña, Maria E., Guillermo B. Chavez, Bertis B. Little, and Robert M. Malina
   2010 Community Well-Being and Growth Status of Indigenous School Children in Rural Oaxaca, Southern Mexico. Economics and Human Biology 8(2):177–187.

Rivera, Juan A., Simón Barquera, Teresa González-Cossío, Gustavo Olaiz, and Jaime Sepúlveda
   2004 Nutrition Transition in Mexico and in Other Latin American Countries. Nutrition Reviews 62(7):S149–S154.

Rivera, Juan A., Eric A. Monterrubio, Teresa González-Cossió, Raquel García-Feregrino, Armando García-Guerra, and Jaime Sepúlveda-Amor
   2003 Nutritional Status of Indigenous Children Younger Than Five Years of Age in Mexico: Results of a National Probabilistic Survey. Salud Pública de México 45(Suppl. 4):S466–S476.

Rosset, Peter
   2006 Food Is Different: Why We Must Get the WTO Out of Agriculture. Black Point, Nova Scotia: Fernwood Publishing.

Schultz, Leslie O., and Richard C. Weidensee
   1995 Glucose Tolerance and Physical Activity in a Mexican Indigenous Population. Diabetes Care 18(9):1274–1276.

Singer, Merrill
   2004 The Social Origins and Expressions of Illness. British Medical Bulletin 69:9–19.
   2009 Introduction to Syndemics: A Critical Systems Approach to Public and Community Health. San Francisco: Jossey-Bass.
   2010 Ecosyndemics: Global Warming and the Coming Plagues of the Twenty-First Century. *In* Plagues and Epidemics: Infected Spaces Past and Present. Alan Swedlund and Ann Herring, eds. Pp. 21–37. London: Berg Publishers.
   2011a Double Jeopardy: Vulnerable Children and the Possible Global Lead Poisoning/Infectious Disease Syndemic. *In* International Handbook on Global Health. Richard Parker and Marni Sommer, eds. Pp. 154–161. London: Routledge.

2011b Toward a Critical Biosocial Model of Ecohealth in Southern Africa: The HIV/AIDS and Nutritional Insecurity Syndemic. Annals of Anthropological Practice 35(1):8–27.

Singer, Merrill, and Scott Clair
2003 Syndemics and Public Health: Reconceptualizing Disease in Bio-Social Context. Medical Anthropology Quarterly 17(4):423–441.

Singer, Merrill, Pamela Erickson, Louise Badiane, Rosemary Diaz, Dugeidy Ortiz, Trazi Abraham, and Anna Marie Nicolaysen
2006 Syndemics, Sex and the City: Understanding Sexually Transmitted Diseases in Social and Cultural Context. Social Science & Medicine 63(8):2010–2021.

Smith-Morris, Carolyn M.
2004 Reducing Diabetes in Indian Country: Lessons from the Three Domains Influencing Pima Diabetes. Human Organization 63(1):34–46.

Stephen, Lynn
2007 Transborder Lives: Indigenous Oaxacans in Mexico, California and Oregon. Durham, NC: Duke University Press.

Tsaih, Shirng-Wern, Susan Korrick, Joel Schwartz, Chitra Amarasiriwardena, Antonio Aro, David Sparrow, and Howard Hu
2004 Lead, Diabetes, Hypertension, and Renal Function: The Normative Aging Study. Environmental Health Perspectives 112(11):1178–1182.

Ventura, Hector, and Mandeep Mehra
2004 The Growing Burden of Heart Failure: The 'Syndemic' Is Reaching Latin America. American Heart Journal 147(3):386–389.

Villalpando, Salvador, Teresa Shamah-Levy, Rosalba Rojas, and Carlos Aguilar-Salinas
2010 Trends for Type 2 Diabetes and Other Cardiovascular Risk Factors in Mexico From 1993–2006. Salud Pública de México 52(S1):S72–S79.

CONNECTING LIVES: REFLECTIONS ON A SYNDEMIC APPROACH TO PREVENTION INVOLVING RESEARCH ON HOW PEOPLE RELATE TO PETS

MELANIE ROCK

University of Calgary

This article elaborates on what could be meant by a syndemic approach to prevention. The main argument is that a syndemic approach to prevention comprises a set of practices intended to promote population health. These practices include research, team-building, and developing partnerships with organizations with diverse mandates. Both infectious and noninfectious diseases may be targeted, in animal as well as human populations. By way of illustration, a research program on urban pets and population health is presented. While this research program has become highly interdisciplinary, theories and practices rooted in anthropology have driven its development. [syndemic, type 2 diabetes mellitus, veterinary public health, human-animal bonds, social inequality, health inequity, community-based research, interdisciplinary research, critical theory, population health]

INTRODUCTION

Connections between animal diseases and the health of human populations are particularly visible when it comes to zoonoses (Blue and Rock 2011; Singer 2009a; Singer et al. 2011), that is, infectious diseases that are capable of jumping species boundaries. Does this situation imply that, in settings where zoonotic infections account for only a small proportion of morbidity and mortality in human populations, there is little value in adopting an approach to prevention that considers connections between people and animals? "No," is my emphatic answer.

The syndemic concept directs attention to shared causes for population health problems whose manifestations may be so dissimilar that they appear to be discrete and entirely separate, and this concept informs my conviction that human health cannot be adequately understood without reference to animals (Rock et al. 2009). These connections may be unexpected, even surprising. The incidence of HIV/AIDS, for example, has been linked to substance abuse along with violence in U.S. inner-cities. These interconnections led to the term "syndemic," which refers to synergistic interactions between health-related problems in the context of social inequality (Singer 1994; Singer and Clair 2003; Singer et al. 2011). Neither animal populations nor animal diseases were explicitly taken into account in the original conceptualization of syndemics (Singer and Clair 2003), yet inequality within as well as between human populations can reinforce deleterious effects on people, animals, and entire ecosystems (Rock et al. 2009).

ANNALS OF ANTHROPOLOGICAL PRACTICE 36.2, pp. 312–327. ISSN: 2153-957X. © 2013 by the American Anthropological Association. DOI:10.1111/napa.12006

The main argument of this article is that a syndemic approach to prevention is not the same as describing or demonstrating the existence of a syndemic. While consideration of connections between seemingly disparate problems is always necessary when characterizing syndemics, a syndemic approach to prevention entails concerted efforts to act on pathways relevant to population health. In other words, a syndemic approach to prevention is solution-focused. This practical concern with intervening along causal pathways means that available resources and the social acceptability of a given change strategy must be taken into account (Hawe and Potvin 2009). Preparedness, furthermore, can be an important dimension of a syndemic approach to prevention. While social inequality has largely been ignored in the rise of preparedness as a preoccupation in public health (Lakoff 2008), this neglect does not mean that social inequality is extraneous. In fact, as the syndemic concept highlights, social inequality has been and will remain central to people's health. The future-oriented perspective consonant with preparedness and with prevention, more generally, means that it is not necessary to prove the existence of a syndemic before taking action. Reasonable suspicion regarding the causes of harms that are potentially widespread and serious is what needs to be established (Weir et al. 2010). The potential costs and benefits of both action and inaction also warrant consideration. In particular, the potential impact of inaction should be taken into account. Put another way, "doing nothing" is tantamount to an intervention approach or political decision, and if that is the route chosen, inaction should be ethically justifiable (Nuffield Council on Bioethics 2007).

In sum, a solution-focused orientation differs from a problem-focused one *in practice*. In particular, a solution-focused orientation implies searching out ways to build on people's strengths and to channel change processes that already exist within a given context. Crucially, therefore, research to advance a syndemic approach to prevention often entails establishing rapport and building partnerships with communities and organizations that are positioned to share their knowledge and to act on the research results. A syndemic approach to prevention will, in addition, typically imply forming research teams whose members come from several different backgrounds. By way of illustration, this article outlines the genesis and development of a research program on people's pets and the public's health in an urbanized society.

GENESIS AND RATIONALE FOR A RESEARCH PROGRAM ON PEOPLE'S PETS AND THE PUBLIC'S HEALTH

A little more than ten years ago, I had no inkling of initiating a research program on pet-keeping in relation to people's health. I was in the throes of completing my Ph.D. thesis in anthropology on how diabetes had become recognized as a pressing public health problem, and on more than one occasion, diabetic cats and diabetic dogs came up in casual conversations. I heard about people's own pets, but also about diabetic pets that belonged to family members or to friends of my interlocutors. Keeping in mind that dogs, often strays sourced from local pounds, had been sacrificed as animal models in the experimental research that led up to insulin therapy (Bliss 2000[1982]), perceptions of animals and pet-keeping norms had clearly changed radically. My curiosity was piqued.

In light of debates that continue to this day about how best to define and diagnose diabetes in people (Degeling and Rock 2012a), I wondered how these people knew for certain that their own dog or their neighbor's cat had diabetes at all. How, I asked myself, did a veterinarian diagnose diabetes in a dog or cat? I also wondered about public understanding of the nature of diabetes as a disease in people being influenced by the care provided to sick pets. Up to a point, caring for sick pets resembles how animals have served as experimental models for human diseases and injuries, but only up to a point, as these animals are patients and benefit from biomedical therapies in the context of human–animal bonds (Degeling 2009; Rock et al. 2007; Schlich et al. 2009).

The very fact that a large number of people were actively involved in treating pet dogs and pet cats for diabetes was, for me, an unexpected and surprising observation. Pet-keeping was certainly something that I had never considered before as an influence on people's knowledge of diabetes. Agar (2006) calls findings like these "rich points," and suggests that ethnographic research, in particular, is often characterized by investigating what generates the unexpected in a given context and reflecting on why the researcher is surprised in the first place. In other words, "rich points" signal the importance of cultivating rather than suppressing creativity and reflexivity in the course of carrying out an ethnographic project. Stewart (1998), similarly, contends that the hallmark of ethnographic research is exploration.

To formalize the concept of "rich points," Agar turns to Peirce's formulation of abductive logic, which is as follows:

- The surprising fact, F, is observed.
- If H were true, F would be a matter of course.
- Hence, there is reason to suspect that H is true.

The "surprising fact F" echoes what I call "rich points." (Agar 2006: para. 63–64)

The unexpected and the surprising emerge, often in the form of trends (Agar 2003), from the systemic and evolving character of connections. The connections of interest apply to problems and also to potential remedies, and that is why I am arguing that "rich points" are crucially important for any syndemic approach to prevention.

Two key trends have shaped my research program. The first trend is amply reflected in epidemiological profiles. Noninfectious chronic diseases account for most morbidity and mortality in wealthy countries, and a growing portion of morbidity and mortality in low-income and middle-income countries, too. Type 2 diabetes is a prime example of these trends. The distribution of microvascular and macrovascular sequelae in cases of type 2 diabetes, known medically as "complications," should be understood as manifestations of interrelated problems. Epidemiological studies have repeatedly demonstrated that the onset of such complications tends to happen more quickly and systematically when people with type 2 diabetes come from disadvantaged populations (Degeling and Rock 2012a). Exposure to stressors also needs to be taken into account, particularly in light of the unequal and unfair distribution of type 2 diabetes and related health problems (Degeling and Rock 2012a; Rock 2003). In fact, exposure to stressors is closely associated with the distribution of blood glucose levels in entire populations (Degeling and Rock 2012a)—so much so that people diagnosed with type 2 diabetes from disadvantaged populations appear to have a better prognosis if they at least live in neighborhoods where residents perceive that people help out one another (Long et al. 2010). Inequity in the incidence of microvascular and macrovascular disease among people with type 2 diabetes is compounded when elevated blood glucose interacts deleteriously with other health problems, as has been shown for tuberculosis (Littleton and Park 2009). Put another way, type 2 diabetes in contemporary populations is a syndemic phenomenon (Ruiz and Egli 2010). What people do is key to this kind of epidemiological patterning, but so are differences in how people feel and frank inequity in how they experience the world.

The second trend underpinning my research program has to do with pet-keeping. Fully half of all households in Western industrialized countries include pets (McNicholas et al. 2005), and the popularity of pets is growing in many non-Western countries, too, such as Japan (Oka and Shibata 2009). Below, I sketch how high rates of pet ownership have become articulated to a syndemic approach to prevention.

RICH POINT #1: DIABETIC PET CARE

If *people come to understand the nature of diabetes as a disease through caring for their pets,* *then* *we might expect owners of diabetic pets to compare and contrast human health problems with their pets' health problems. And if caring for a pet's diabetes is important to people's sense of self and well-being,* *then* *we might expect the owners of sick pets to spend money on veterinary consults, to follow through on veterinary advice, and to try to promote health and quality of life for their pets.*

The unexpected phenomenon of diabetic pet care caught my attention some ten years ago because nothing that I had read about public health, urban anthropology, or medical anthropology had prepared me for imagining that pets could influence how people acquire and act on information about a disease that is neither infectious nor zoonotic. The realization that pet-keeping had something to do with what people think and do about diabetes led to a revisiting of the history of public health and of diabetes. In the early years of public health, a great deal of time and energy focused on the elimination of animal-sourced infectious diseases from urban areas through bans on keeping livestock and through food safety measures such as pasteurization of milk and inspection of meat (Hardy 2002). Yet pets have remained in cities and towns, and in fact, their numbers have swelled. An ethnographic and historical investigation of diabetic pet care connected with diabetes in people, in three main ways. First, the bodies of pet species as well as animals slaughtered for food were involved in the development and use of technologies related to insulin (Rock and Babinec 2008). Second, pet-keeping continues to influence the diffusion, interpretation, and mobilization of information about diabetes (Rock and

FIGURE 1. Walking a dog in public space can promote human health.
Source: Study participant, her Siberian Husky named Cooper, and Melanie Rock; photo credit Dwayne Brunner, Alberta Innovates—Health Solutions.

Babinec 2008, 2010). Third, many dogs, including diabetic ones, are regularly taken for walks.

For example, one man who participated in diabetic pet study described having carried his dog back home, due to hypoglycemia. As he put it:

> I had him crash on me a couple of times where his blood sugar went so low that he became very disoriented and couldn't walk. One time I had to carry him about seven, eight blocks home, and after that I started carrying something with me with glucose in it in case that ever happened again, I wasn't carrying him home. (cited in Rock and Babinec 2008:336)

In light of evidence on the preventive impact of regular physical activity (Larose et al. 2011; Sigal et al. 2007; Tuomilehto 2007), taking a diabetic dog outside for daily walks could help in preventing the onset of type 2 diabetes and preventing related complications from type 1 diabetes as well as type 2 diabetes.

The preventive potential of dog-walking was something that we emphasized in media outreach. A research participant who has type 1 diabetes agreed to be a spokesperson. She is deeply concerned about animal welfare, and she wanted to share an upbeat perspective on insulin therapy and living with diabetes. The photograph that was circulated to the media is shown in Figure 1. It is worth pausing to think about the assemblage that was keeping this duo healthy, even as they both live with chronic health conditions. Insulin is an invisible part of the picture for both of them, while access is to public space in an urbanized environment is visible in the photograph yet could be taken for granted. Here was another rich point, and that is where the research turned next.

RICH POINT #2: DOG-WALKING

If *many people get out walking out of a commitment to their dog's health, perhaps more so than to their own health,* **then** *we might expect that dog-owners will tend to walk more often than non-owners.*

Public health interest in dog-walking as physical activity has exploded in recent years, as researchers and practitioners have realized that dog-walking is a way that millions of people get out walking on a regular basis (Cutt et al. 2007; Johnson et al. 2011; Toohey and Rock 2011). In Calgary, Alberta, Canada, dog-owners were found to be more than three times more likely than non-owners to report walking year-round for recreation in their immediate neighborhoods (Lail et al. 2011). In fact, neighborhood-based walking for recreation actually increased somewhat among dog owners in winter over summer, while nonowners reported significantly less walking in winter compared to summer. Similarly, a team based in Victoria, British Columbia, Canada recently published results showing that dog owners were more likely than nonowners to visit parks and walk in inclement weather (Temple et al. 2011). As one participant . . . in a U.K. study based on focus group interviews put it, "But if you've got a dog, you've got to come out in all weathers, so it keeps you fit" (Knight and Edwards 2008:443). These studies on dog-walking stand in marked contrast with the literature on seasonal patterning of physical activity, which shows an overall decrease in physical activity during winter months (Dasgupta et al. 2010; Merchant et al. 2007; Tucker and Gilliland 2007).

RICH POINT #3: DOGS IN PUBLIC SPACE

If, *as in urbanized societies, lots of people share public space with lots of dogs,* **then** *the presence and management of dogs will influence health outcomes—positively and negatively—across entire human populations.*

When we looked at how influential newspapers and veterinary publications are portraying overweight dogs, we found that individual owners tended to be represented as wholly responsible for their dogs' health (Degeling and Rock 2012b). Remarkably little attention was paid in these texts to the social and physical dimensions of the environments that dogs share with people. Indeed, there was less concern for shared environments in the scientific literature than in the popular media (Degeling et al. 2011).

Nevertheless, dogs can contribute to the social dimension of urbanized environments by sparking positive interactions between strangers, helping people to build friendships, and promoting a sense of trust among neighbors (McNicholas and Collis 2000; Robins et al. 1991; Wells 2004; Wood et al. 2005, 2007). Yet there are also problematic aspects of dogs in public space. Dog waste left behind as litter and poorly controlled dogs may seem like mundane matters, but both emerged as surprisingly salient concerns in two literature reviews undertaken within our team. In a review of qualitative research that had been deliberately excluded from recent reviews of quantitative evidence, we identified dog litter and poorly controlled dogs as deterrents of park use in urban settings (McCormack et al. 2010). We followed up on these findings in a review of quantitative and qualitative research on dogs in public space, and we found that dogs were most likely to be associated with positive influences in more affluent neighborhoods (Toohey and Rock 2011). In neighborhoods that are disadvantaged or mixed in terms of social class and ethnicity, dogs were more likely to be associated with negative influences, and older adults, women, and children appear disproportionately affected by the negative influences associated with dogs (Toohey and Rock 2011).

With these findings in mind, we have begun to pay more attention to dog-walking patterns and to cultural norms and formal rules in Calgary on where dogs can be present, and under what conditions. City of Calgary policies that influence dog-walking include allowing dogs to be off-leash in designated areas. Our group found that proximity to a park with a designated off-leash area was positively correlated with the frequency of dog-walking (McCormack et al. 2011). Yet living near an off-leash area by no means guaranteed that dog owners would make use of this amenity. In fact, proximity to an off-leash area was negatively associated with reporting any dog-walking at all within the immediate neighborhood during a usual week. Furthermore, the middle-aged and university-educated owners in our sample were the most likely to report frequent dog-walking (McCormack et al. 2011).

WRITING GRANTS AND STRENGTHENING NETWORKS: CRUCIAL PRACTICES FOR SYNDEMIC PREVENTION

The City of Calgary is steeped in petroleum industries and is home to about one million people, many of whom are first-generation migrants from other parts of Canada or from other countries (McCoy and Masuch 2007; Smart 2001). Social inequalities and spatial patterning are manifest in Calgary's epidemiological statistics for noninfectious diseases in people, including heart disease (Bertazzon et al. 2010), which is closely tied to type 2 diabetes onset and outcomes (Degeling and Rock 2012a). Meanwhile, Calgary's dog population is large and growing. More than 120,000 dogs lived in Calgary as of 2010, which amounts to more than one dog for every ten human inhabitants (City of Calgary 2012).

According to the City of Calgary's website,

Calgary is fortunate to have 149 public off-leash areas in our multi-use parks for Calgarians and their dogs to enjoy. Calgary may have the largest number of off-leash areas and combined amount of off-leash space (more than 1,250 hectares) in North America. These off-leash designations make up for approximately 17% of the total City of Calgary Parks inventory and equate to almost 1,600 Canadian Football League fields. (City of Calgary 2011)

In 2010, the City of Calgary adopted a new policy framework for "off-leash areas," and officials carefully distinguish "off-leash areas" from "dog parks" in other jurisdictions (cf. Lee et al. 2009). In Calgary, "off-leash areas" are public spaces that are supposed to be amenable to many activities and open to all—not just to dogs and their owners. At the same time, backed by survey results showing support for additional off-leash areas among dog owners but also among nonowners, the City publicly announced plans to enter into discussions with local communities about designating additional green space as off-leash areas. I first learned about these plans in a meeting with the City of Calgary's Director of Animal and Bylaw Services. This meeting had been initiated by Alessandro Massolo, a new colleague in the Faculty of Veterinary Medicine who has become a key collaborator, as discussed in further detail below.

Upon learning about the City's plans to enter into consultations with local communities about formally redesignating public land for off-leash use, a potential fit was immediately apparent with the Population Health Intervention Research funding envelope. This operating grant competition, which is sponsored by the Canadian Institutes of Health Research—Institute of Population and Public Health, is intended to facilitate health impact assessment of policies and programs that operate outside the control of researchers. This competition facilitates rapid responses to emerging events, and our team certainly had to respond rapidly to pull together a letter of intent in time to meet the next deadline.

Fortunately, we were invited to submit a full proposal, and ultimately, our application to study of the overall health impact of the City of Calgary's plans for additional off-leash areas was funded. My coprincipal investigator, Gavin McCormack, specializes in quantitative methods to study the influence of social and physical dimensions of urban environments on walking and other forms of physical activity (e.g., McCormack and Shiell 2011; McCormack et al. 2009). Our coinvestigators are Chris Degeling, a veterinarian–philosopher (e.g., Degeling 2009; Degeling and Rock 2012a, 2012b); James Greenwood-Lee, a mathematician with a background in zoology (e.g., Greenwood-Lee and Taylor 2001; Wild et al. 2006); Alessandro Massolo, a wildlife ecologist (e.g., Massolo and Meriggi 1998; Muhly et al. 2011); and Lindsay McLaren, whose areas of expertise include survey research, health equity, and population health (e.g., McLaren et al. 2009, 2010). The organizational partners include the City of Calgary, the Calgary Humane Society for Prevention of Cruelty towards Animals, Parks Foundation Calgary and the Federation of Calgary Communities (an umbrella association for neighborhood associations). We are also working in partnership with educators in two postsecondary programs. Dawn Rault, with the Department of Justice Studies at Mount Royal University in Calgary, teaches classes and supervises field placements for students who serve as a recruitment pool for the City of Calgary and nearby municipalities (e.g., officers who enforce bylaws on pets, as well as peace officers who investigate animal neglect and abuse). Cindy Adams, a social worker—epidemiologist in the University of Calgary's Faculty of Veterinary Medicine, will be working with us to develop simulated cases derived from our research findings (as per Nogueira Borden et al. 2008), which will serve as the basis for training future veterinarians on the overall impact of social, cultural, economic, and physical dimensions of environments on both human and animal health (Adams and Kurtz 2006; Adams et al. 2006).

To write the grant, build the team, and cement relationships with organizational partners, it was necessary to marshal evidence in a persuasive manner about connections of a syndemic nature that plausibly underlie seemingly discrete problems, while emphasizing potential solutions. For this project, we are interested in people's physical activity patterns and in social interaction patterns among people, as both pertain to the prevention and control of many noninfectious diseases, including type 2 diabetes, cardiovascular disease, dementia, and depression, to name but a few. Dog-walking, we argued in the grant proposal, is a sociocultural practice that can facilitate regular physical activity and positive social interactions, but that can also give rise to tension and conflict among dog owners and with nonowners (Toohey and Rock 2011). With regard to preparedness and prevention, we are also concerned about the potential for pet-keeping to facilitate zoonotic transmission of pathogens (Gaunt and Carr 2011; Himsworth et al. 2010; Shukla et al. 2006; Westgarth et al. 2009). Throughout, we are concerned with how governance of dog populations in urbanized space impacts upon health outcomes in human populations. We are thus exploring people's diverse perceptions and relationships with animals, and we want to understand how these views and experiences may influence positively or negatively influence population health.

At the time of writing, the team is analyzing data from the fieldwork undertaken in four potential intervention sites in June and July 2010, as well as in four established off-leash areas for the purposes of comparison. The plan is to study what happens in and around the intervention sites until July 2013. After each field season, we will share our results with our partners. The case study research design is taking the form of a natural experiment (Robinson et al. 2009), and involves both quantitative and qualitative data. The final dataset will include systematic naturalistic observations of human activity in the sites (with and without dogs), information about the amount and nature of fecal contamination in the sites (from dogs as well as from coyotes and some other wildlife species), website content, questionnaires, field notes based on participant observation, face-to-face interviews, and photographs.

CONCLUSIONS

The overriding concern in our new off-leash study and the larger research program is with problem-solving. More concretely, the purpose is to seek ways to maximize the positive impact of pets while also minimizing the inevitable potential for harmful effects on animals and people. As a practicing medical anthropologist, therefore, I have invested in establishing and nourishing relationships with peers trained in other fields and disciplines, with trainees who bring a diverse range of backgrounds and insights, and with representatives of organizations whose formal mandates all touch on the management of urban environments that people share with animals. The talented students, practitioners, and researchers who have been recruited to the team effort share an interest in identifying and strengthening sustainable ways to improve and maintain the health of entire populations. A syndemic approach to prevention that encompasses animal diseases and populations (Rock et al. 2009) was integral to forming the research team and continues to underpin our work.

Both infectious and noninfectious disease in pets appear to have some of the same root causes as in human populations, due to shared environments (Degeling et al. 2011; Himsworth et al. 2010; Westgarth et al. 2008). It could be that these animal health problems interact synergistically, rather than in a strictly syndemic fashion, with problems such as type 2 diabetes in human populations (Singer 2009b:22). Yet when it comes to prevention, what matters most are root causes, and what about these root causes can be modified in a given environment. Type 2 diabetes in people, whose onset and eventual outcomes in populations are influenced by physical activity and by exposure to stressors (Degeling and Rock 2012a), has provided a touchstone for thinking about urban pets in relation to a syndemic approach to prevention. The recent surge in interest in human–animal bonds across many disciplines (Rock et al. 2007; Shapiro 2002), and, in public health more specifically, a growing body of research on dog-walking has provided crucial support for our work (Cutt et al. 2007; Toohey and Rock 2011).

The ongoing team effort catalyzed by City of Calgary policies on off-leash areas would not qualify as research oriented toward a syndemic approach to prevention, but for three things. First, the research is premised on a systems approach to conceiving of interventions and their ultimate effects (Hawe et al. 2009; Singer 2009b). Local histories and contingencies will inevitably influence the outcomes. Consequently, the causal pathways are nonlinear in nature. For example, whenever a given parcel of public land is officially converted to an off-leash area, we should not expect uniform effects. To the extent that we observe trends, we will need to look to the broader sociocultural, socioeconomic, and ecological context for clues as to why.

Second, our research on off-leash areas is about a syndemic approach to prevention because of the involvement of organizations from the outset that have a mandate and capacity to bring about change. In particular, the research stemmed from previous partnership arrangements with the City of Calgary, and developing the funding proposal helped to extend and strengthen an organizational matrix. These organizations certainly differ in capacities and in focus, but they all are clearly mandated to intervene. Research partnerships with organizations inevitably involve negotiations (Bernier et al. 2006), which are to be expected—not dreaded and certainly not avoided—in practicing anthropology in a way that is consistent with a syndemic approach to prevention. Indeed, the experience thus far has been extremely positive. The knowledge that researchers bring and distil from investigative labor can assist in instigating positive changes, but not in the absence of coherence with organizational mandates (Agar 2011).

Third, the off-leash research project is an example of syndemic prevention because it emerged from an openness to the unexpected and surprising, in keeping with abductive logic and what have been called "rich points" (Agar 2006). Investigations prompted by unexpected and surprising observations can assist in identifying and tracing trends relevant to population health. Examples from medical anthropology include an investigation of methodone as both a street drug and medical treatment in New York City during the 1970s (Agar 1977); qualitative and survey-based research showing that menopausal women tended not to report hot flashes in Japan, in marked contrast to North America (Lock 1993); and the formulation of the syndemic concept based on what could be discerned in the 1980s and 1990s, from the ground up in U.S. inner cities, about deleterious interactions between substance abuse, HIV/AIDS, and violence (Singer and Clair 2003). Unpacking the element of surprise in explorations and investigations can assist in remaining ever-mindful of the structural roots of people's daily predicaments, while also instilling health-promoting changes that build on people's strengths and existing commitments.

As illustrated by viewing type 2 diabetes through the lens of people's diverse relationships with pets, the practice of syndemic prevention entails sensitivity to how broader social, cultural, and economic trends confer structure and constraints while also giving rise to new possibilities and connections. Prevention can be based on the syndemic concept by learning about patterns and trends, and then mobilizing that knowledge to intervene in support of antisyndemic tendencies. Knowledge of patterns and trends that can help to promote population health and to redress inequity extends well beyond biomedicine and epidemiology, and certainly includes popular culture. Since health and disease emerge from relationships, anthropology's holistic perspective on society and culture remains highly relevant in adopting a syndemic approach to prevention so as to promote population health.

NOTE

Acknowledgments. During the preparation of this article, Melanie Rock held a New Investigator in Societal and Cultural Dimensions of Health Award (2007–12) from the Canadian Institutes of Health Research and a Population Health Investigator Award (2007–14) from Alberta Innovates—Health Solutions, which is funded by the Alberta Heritage Medical Research Foundation Endowment. In addition to these salary awards, her research program on people's pets and the public's health has benefited from operating funds provided by the Petro-Canada Young Innovator in Community Health Research Prize (2007), Alberta Innovates—Health Solutions (2007–14), the Social Science and Humanities Research Council of Canada (2004–09), and the Canadian Institutes of Health Research (2011–14). All team members named in this article had an opportunity to review an earlier draft and approved publication. Cindy Adams, Mike Agar, Dawn Rault, and the editors provided written comments that were helpful in revising for publication. The Calgary Humane Society's slogan, "connecting lives," inspired the title.

REFERENCES CITED

Adams, Cindy L., and Suzanne M. Kurtz
  2006 Building on Existing Models from Human Medical Education to Develop a Communication Curriculum in Veterinary Medicine. Journal of Veterinary Medical Education 33(1):28–37.
Adams, Cindy L., Debra Nestel, and Peter Wolf
  2006 Reflection: A Critical Proficiency Essential to the Effective Development of a High Competence in Communication. Journal of Veterinary Medical Education 33(1):58–64.
Agar, Michael
  1977 Going through Changes: Methadone in New York City. Human Organization 36(3):291–295.
  2003 The Story of Crack: Towards a Theory of Illicit Drug Trends. Addiction Research & Theory 11(1):3–29.
  2006 *An ethnography by any other name*. Forum: Qualitative Research [cited 28 August 2006]. Available from Available at: http://www.qualitative-research.net/fqs-texte/4-06/06-4-36-e.htm
  2011 Whose Knowledge? What Transfer? Practicing Anthropology 33(1):4–7.

Bernier, Jocelyne, Melanie Rock, Michel Roy, Renald Bujold, and Louise Potvin
  2006 Structuring an Inter-Sector Research Partnership: A Negotiated Zone. Social and Preventive Medicine 51(6):335–344.
Bertazzon, Stefania, Scott Olson, and Merril Knudtson
  2010 A Spatial Analysis of the Demographic and Socio-Economic Variables Associated with Cardiovascular Disease in Calgary (Canada). Applied Spatial Analysis and Policy. 3(1):1–23.
Bliss, Michael
  2000 [1982] The Discovery of Insulin. Toronto: University of Toronto Press.
Blue, Gwendolyn, and Melanie J. Rock
  2011 Trans-Biopolitics: Complexity in Interspecies Relations. Health: An Interdisciplinary Journal for the Social Study of Health, Illness & Medicine 15(4):353–368.
City of Calgary
  2011 *Dog Off-Leash Areas in Parks*. Parks [cited 13 December 2011]. http://www.calgary.ca/CSPS/Parks/Pages/Locations/Dog-off-leash-areas-in-parks.aspx, accessed September 21.
  2012 *Animal-Related Statistics*. [cited 2 June 2012]. Available from http://www.calgary.ca/CSPS/ABS/Pages/Animal-Services/Animal-statistics.aspx.
Cutt, Hayley E., Billie Giles-Corti, Myron Knuiman, and Valerie Burke
  2007 Dog Ownership, Health and Physical Activity: A Critical Review of the Literature. Health & Place 13(1):261–272.
Dasgupta, Kaberi, Lawrence Joseph, Louise Pilote, Ian Strachan, Ron J. Sigal, and Cathy Chan
  2010 Daily Steps Are Low Year-Round and Dip Lower in Fall/Winter: Findings from a Longitudinal Diabetes Cohort. Cardiovascular Diabetology 9:81.
Degeling, Chris
  2009 Negotiating Value: Comparing Human and Animal Fracture Care in Industrial Societies. Science, Technology and Human Values 34(1):77–101.
Degeling, Chris, and Melanie Rock
  2012a Hemoglobin A1c as a Diagnostic Tool: Public Health Implications from an Actor-Network Perspective. American Journal of Public Health 102(1):99–106. doi:10.2105/AJPH.2011.300329.
  2012b Owning the Problem: Media Portrayals of Overweight Dogs as a Window into Popular Views on the Determinants of Population Health. Anthrozoös: A Multidisciplinary Journal of the Interactions Between People and Animals 25(1):35–48.
Degeling, Chris, Melanie Rock, and Lorraine Teows
  2011 Portrayals of Canine Obesity in English-Language Newspapers and in Leading Veterinary Journals, 2000–2009: Implications for Animal Welfare Organizations and Veterinarians as Public Educators. Journal of Applied Animal Welfare Science 14(4):286–303.
Gaunt, M. Casey, and Anthony P. Carr
  2011 A Survey of Intestinal Parasites in Dogs from Saskatoon, Saskatchewan. The Canadian Veterinary Journal 52(5):497–500.
Greenwood-Lee, James M., and Peter D. Taylor
  2001 The Evolution of Dispersal in Spatially Varying Environments. Evolutionary Ecology Research 3(6):649–665.
Hardy, Anne
  2002 Pioneers in the Victorian Provinces: Veterinarians, Urban Public Health and the Urban Animal Economy. Urban History 29(3):372–387.
Hawe, Penelope, and Louise Potvin
  2009 What Is Population Health Intervention Research? Canadian Journal of Public Health 100(1):Suppl. I8–I14.
Hawe, Penelope, Alan Shiell, and Therese Riley
  2009 Theorising Interventions as Events in Systems. American Journal of Community Psychology 43(3–4):267–276.
Himsworth, Chelsea G., Stuart Skinner, Bonnie Chaban, Emily Jenkins, Brent A. Wagner, N. Jane Harms, Frederick A. Leighton, R. C. Andrew Thompson, and Janet E. Hill

2010 Multiple Zoonotic Pathogens Identified in Canine Feces Collected from a Remote Canadian Indigenous Community. The American Journal of Tropical Medicine and Hygiene 83(2):338–341.

Johnson, Rebecca A., Alan M. Beck, and Sandra McCune, eds.
2011 The Health Benefits of Dog-Walking for People and Pets. West Lafayette, IN: Purdue University Press.

Knight, Sarah, and Victoria Edwards
2008 In the Company of Wolves: The Physical, Social, and Psychological Benefits of Dog Ownership. Journal of Aging and Health 20(4):437–455.

Lail, Parabhdeep, Gavin McCormack, and Melanie Rock
2011 Does Dog-Ownership Influence Seasonal Patterns of Neighbourhood-Based Walking among Adults? A Longitudinal Study. BMC Public Health 11(1):148. doi:10.1186/1471-2458-11-148.

Lakoff, Andrew
2008 The Generic Biothreat, or, How We Became Unprepared. Cultural Anthropology 23(3):399–428.

Larose, Joanie, Ronald J. Sigal, Farah Khandwala, Denis Prud'homme, Normand Boulé, and Glen P. Kenny
2011 Associations between Physical Fitness and HbA1c in Type 2 Diabetes Mellitus. Diabetologia 54(1):93–102.

Lee, Hyung-Sook, Mardelle Shepley, and Chang-Shan Huang
2009 Evaluation of Off-Leash Dog Parks in Texas and Florida: A Study of Use Patterns, User Satisfaction, and Perception. Landscape and Urban Planning 92(3–4):314–324.

Littleton, Judith, and Julie Park
2009 Tuberculosis and Syndemics: Implications for Pacific Health in New Zealand. Social Science & Medicine 69(11):1674–1680.

Lock, Margaret
1993 Encounters with Aging: Myths of Menopause in Japan and North America. Berkeley, Los Angeles: University of California Press.

Long, J. A., Field S., Armstrong K., Chang V. W., & Metlay J. P.
2010 Social capital and glucose control. *Journal of Community Health*, 35(5), 519–526.

Massolo, Alessandro, and Alberto Meriggi
1998 Factors Affecting Habitat Occupancy by Wolves in Northern Apennines (Northern Italy): A Model of Habitat Suitability. Ecography 21(2):97–107.

McCormack, Gavin R., Melanie J. Rock, Beverley Sandalack, and Francisco A. Uribe
2011 Access to Off-Leash Parks, Street Pattern and Dog Walking among Adults. Public Health 125(8):540–546.

McCormack, Gavin R., Melanie Rock, Ann M. Toohey, and Danica Hignell
2010 Characteristics of Urban Parks Associated with Park Use and Physical Activity: A Review of Qualitative Research. Health & Place 16(4):712–726.

McCormack, Gavin R., and Alan Shiell
2011 In Search of Causality: A Systematic Review of the Relationship between the Built Environment and Physical Activity among Adults. International Journal for Behavioural Nutrition and Physical Activity 8(1):125.

McCormack, Gavin R., John C. Spence, Tanya Berry, and Patricia K. Doyle-Baker
2009 Does Perceived Behavioral Control Mediate the Association between Perceptions of Neighborhood Walkability and Moderate- and Vigorous-Intensity Leisure-Time Physical Activity? Journal of Physical Activity & Health 6(5):657–666.

McCoy, Liza, and Cristi Masuch
2007 Beyond "Entry-Level" Jobs: Immigrant Women and Non-Regulated Professional Occupations. Journal of International Migration and Integration 8(2):185–206.

McLaren, Lindsay, Jenny Godley, and Ian A. S. MacNairn
2009 Social Class, Gender, and Time Use: Implications for the Social Determinants of Body Weight? Health Reports 20(4):65–73.

McLaren, Lindsay, Lynn McIntyre, and Sharon Kirkpatrick
2010 Rose's Population Strategy of Prevention Need Not Increase Social Inequalities in Health. International Journal of Epidemiology 39(2):372–377.

McNicholas, June, and Glyn M. Collis
2000 Dogs as Catalysts for Social Interactions: Robustness of the Effect. British Journal of Psychology 91(1):61–70.

McNicholas, June, Andrew Gilbey, Ann Rennie, Sam Ahmedzai, Jo-Ann Dono, and Elizabeth Ormerod
2005 Pet Ownership and Human Health: A Brief Review of Evidence and Issues. British Medical Journal 331(7527):1252–1254.

Merchant, Anwar T., Mahshid Dehghan, and Noori Akhtar-Danesh
2007 Seasonal Variation in Leisure-Time Physical Activity among Canadians. Canadian Journal of Public Health 98(3):203–208.

Muhly, Tyler B., Christina Semeniuk, Alessandro Massolo, Laura Hickman, and Marco Musiani
2011 Human Activity Helps Prey Win the Predator-Prey Space Race. PLoS ONE 6(3):e17050.

Nogueira Borden, Leandra J., Cindy L. Adams, and Lynda D. Ladner
2008 The Use of Standardized Clients in Research in the Veterinary Clinical Setting. Journal of Veterinary Medical Education 35(3):420–430.

Nuffield Council on Bioethics
2007 Public Health: Ethical Issues [cited 19 January 2012]. Available from http://www.nuffieldbioethics.org/public-health.

Oka, Koichiro, and Ai Shibata
2009 Dog Ownership and Health-Related Physical Activity among Japanese Adults. Journal of Physical Activity & Health 6(4):412–418.

Robins, Douglas M., Clinton R. Sanders, and Spencer E. Cahill
1991 Dogs and Their People: Pet-Facilitated Interaction in a Public Setting. Journal of Contemporary Ethnography 20(1):3–25.

Robinson, Gregory, John E. McNulty, and Jonathan S. Krasno
2009 Observing the Counterfactual? The Search for Political Experiments in Nature. Political Analysis 17(4):341–357.

Rock, Melanie
2003 Sweet Blood and Social Suffering: Rethinking Cause-Effect Relationships in Diabetes, Distress and Duress. Medical Anthropology: Cross-Cultural Studies in Health and Illness 22(2):131–174.

Rock, Melanie, and Patricia Babinec
2008 Diabetes in People, Cats and Dogs: Biomedicine and Manifold Ontologies. Medical Anthropology: Cross-Cultural Studies in Health and Illness 27(4):324–252.
2010 Prototypes Connect Human Diabetes with Feline and Canine Diabetes in the Context of Animal-Human Bonds: An Anthropological Analysis. Anthrozoös: A Multidisciplinary Journal of the Interactions Between People and Animals 23(1):5–20.

Rock, Melanie, Bonnie Buntain, Jennifer Hatfield, and Benedikt Hallgrímsson
2009 Animal-Human Connections, 'One Health,' and the Syndemic Approach to Prevention. Social Science & Medicine 68(6):991–995. doi:10.1016/j.socscimed.2008.12.047.

Rock, Melanie, Eric Mykhalovskiy, and Thomas Schlich
2007 People, Other Animals and Health Knowledges: Towards a Research Agenda. Social Science & Medicine 64(9):1970–1976.

Ruiz, Juan, and Marc Egli
2010 Syndrome Métabolique, Diabète Sucré et Vulnérabilité : Une Approche ≪Syndémique≫ de la Maladie Chronique [Metabolic Syndrome, Diabetes Mellitus and Vulnerability: A Syndemic Approach of Chronic Diseases]. Revue Médicale Suisse 6(271):2205–2208.

Schlich, Thomas, Eric Mykhalovskiy, and Melanie Rock
2009 Animals in Surgery–Surgery in Animals: Nature and Culture in Animal-Human Relationship and Modern Surgery. History and Philosophy of the Life Sciences 31(3–4):321–354.

Shapiro, Kenneth
2002 The State of Human-Animal Studies: Solid, at the Margin! Society & Animals 10(4):331–337.

Shukla, Rahul, Patricia Giraldo, Andrea Kraliz, Michael Finnigan, and Ana L. Sanchez
  2006 Cryptosporidium Spp. and Other Zoonotic Enteric Parasites in a Sample of Domestic Dogs and Cats in the Niagara Region of Ontario. The Canadian Veterinary Journal. La Revue Vétérinaire Canadienne 47(12):1179–1184.

Sigal, Ronald J., Glen P. Kenny, Normand G. Boul, George A. Wells, Denis Prud'homme, Michelle Fortier, Robert D. Reid, Heather Tulloch, Douglas Coyle, Penny Phillips, Alison Jennings, and James Jaffey
  2007 Effects of Aerobic Training, Resistance Training, or Both on Glycemic Control in Type 2 Diabetes: A Randomized Trial. Annals of Internal Medicine 147(6):357–369.

Singer, Merrill C.
  1994 AIDS and the Health Crisis of the U.S. Urban Poor; the Perspective of Critical Medical Anthropology. Social Science & Medicine 39(7):931–948.

  2009a Doorways in Nature: Syndemics, Zoonotics, and Public Health. A Commentary on Rock, Buntain, Hatfield & Hallgrímsson Social Science & Medicine 68(6):996–999. doi:10.1016/j.socscimed.2008.12.041.

  2009b Introduction to Syndemics: A Critical Systems Approach to Public and Community Health. San Francisco: Jossey-Boss.

Singer, Merrill C., and Scott Clair
  2003 Syndemics and Public Health: Reconceptualizing Disease in Bio-Social Context. Medical Anthropology Quarterly 17(4):423–441.

Singer, Merrill C., Ann Herring, Judith Livingston, and Melanie Rock
  2011 Syndemics in Global Health. In Companion to Medical Anthropology. D. Ann Herring, Merrill Singer, and Pamela I. Erickson, eds. Pp. 159–179. West Sussex, UK: Blackwell Publishers.

Smart, Alan
  2001 Restructuring in a North American City: Labour Markets and Political Economy in Calgary. In Plural Globalities in Multiple Localities: New World Borders. Martha W. Rees and Josephine Smart, eds. Pp. 167–193. Lanham, MD: University Press of America.

Stewart, Alex
  1998 The Ethnographer's Method. Vol. 46. Thousand Oaks, CA: Sage.

Temple, Viviene, Ryan Rhodes, and Joan Wharf Higgins
  2011 Unleashing Physical Activity: An Observational Study of Park Use, Dog Walking, and Physical Activity. Journal of Physical Activity & Health 8(6):766–774.

Toohey, Ann M., and Melanie J. Rock
  2011 Unleashing Their Potential: A Critical Realist Scoping Review of the Influence of Dogs on Physical Activity for Dog-Owners and Non-Owners. International Journal of Behavioral Nutrition and Physical Activity 8(1):46.

Tucker, Patricia, and Jason Gilliland
  2007 The Effect of Season and Weather on Physical Activity: A Systematic Review. Public Health 121(12):909–922.

Tuomilehto, Jaakko
  2007 Evidence-Based Prevention of Type 2 Diabetes: The Power of Lifestyle Management. Diabetes Care 30(2):435–438.

Weir, Erica, Richard Schabas, Kumanan Wilson, and Chris Mackie
  2010 A Canadian Framework for Applying the Precautionary Principle to Public Health Issues. Canadian Journal of Public Health 101(5):396–398.

Wells, Deborah L.
  2004 The Facilitation of Social Interactions by Domestic Dogs. Anthrozoos: A Multidisciplinary Journal of the Interactions Between People and Animals 17(4):340–352.

Westgarth, C., Rosalind M. Gaskell, Gina L. Pinchbeck, John W. S. Bradshaw, Susan Dawson, and Robert M. Christley
  2009 Walking the Dog: Exploration of the Contact Networks between Dogs in a Community. Epidemiology and Infection 137(8):1169–1178.

Westgarth, Carri, Gina L. Pinchbeck, John W. S. Bradshaw, Susan Dawson, Rosalind M. Gaskell, and Robert M. Christley

   2008 Dog-Human and Dog-Dog Interactions of 260 Dog-Owning Households in a Community in Cheshire. The Veterinary Record 162(14):436–442.

Wild, Geoff, James Greenwood-Lee, and Peter D. Taylor

   2006 Sex Allocation and Dispersal in a Heterogeneous Two-Patch Environment. Theoretical Population Biology 70(2):225–235.

Wood, Lisa J., Billie Giles-Corti, and Max Bulsara

   2005 The Pet Connection: Pets as a Conduit for Social Capital? Social Science & Medicine 61(6):1159–1173.

Wood, Lisa J., Billie Giles-Corti, Max K. Bulsara, and Darcy A. Bosch

   2007 More Than a Furry Companion: The Ripple Effect of Companion Animals on Neighborhood Interactions and Sense of Community. Society & Animals 15(1):43–56.

INTERLOCKED INFECTIONS: THE HEALTH BURDENS OF SYNDEMICS OF NEGLECTED TROPICAL DISEASES

MERRILL SINGER
University of Connecticut

NICOLA BULLED
University of Connecticut

Tropical disease syndemics, the adverse morbidity-enhancing interaction of two or more neglected tropical diseases (NTDs), like the diseases that comprise them, have been largely unrecognized and generally neglected. However, their role in contributing to the health burden of the poor is significant. This paper presents syndemics as a new theoretical perspective with which to develop a comprehensive approach to understand and respond to the health consequences of adverse interactions among NTDS and between NTDs and other diseases. Specifically the paper examines local social factors and macro-level political economic factors that are both the ultimate source and ultimate arbiter of public and medical responses to syndemics of NTDs. [neglected tropical diseases, syndemics, diseases of poverty, social origins of disease]

INTRODUCTION

Neglected tropical diseases (NTDs) comprise a group of chronic, disabling, and often disfiguring conditions that are most commonly found among people living in extreme poverty, especially among the rural poor but among some disadvantaged urban populations as well. Although responsible for at least half a million deaths per year, almost 60 million disability adjusted life years lost annually, and impacting the lives of about one billion people worldwide (Hotez et al. 2006c), the total health burden caused by tropical diseases has been underestimated for several reasons. First, as the label NTDs indicates, despite being among the most common infections of the poorest sectors of the global population, historically many could accurately be described as the "forgotten diseases of forgotten people" (Hotez 2007a; Perera et al. 2007) even among anthropologists (Inhorn and Brown 1997). Concentrated in specific geographic and socially marginalized areas and most commonly within the range of certain environmental conditions, NTDs have not tended to spread to technologically advanced and politically powerful industrialized nations, although parallel "neglected infections of poverty" (e.g. toxocariasis, toxoplasmosis) have been identified among subordinated groups living in disadvantaged enclaves in wealthier sectors of the world system (Hotez 2007b; Hotez 2008). Second, the international health community, including health-related donors, international

ANNALS OF ANTHROPOLOGICAL PRACTICE 36.2, pp. 328–345. ISSN: 2153-957X. © 2013 by the American Anthropological Association. DOI:10.1111/napa.12007

development agencies, nongovernmental development agencies, and governments have tended to place most of their infectious disease attention and resources on combating the Big Three—HIV/AIDS, tuberculosis, and malaria—leaving comparatively limited resources for addressing NTDs (Molyneux et al. 2005). Third, significant gaps in our knowledge about many NTDs have impeded accurate calculation of their true prevalence and full health impact (Engels and Savioli 2006; Mathers et al. 2007). Fourth, the recognized clinical manifestations of many NTDs may constitute only "the tip of the disability iceberg" that they cause (Engels and Savioli 2006), as there appears to be a significant level of unrecognized and subtle morbidity associated with many of these diseases (Hotez et al. 2006a; King et al. 2005; Krishna Kumari et al. 2005). Finally, the geographic distributions of many NTDs overlap leading to unrecognized coinfections and populations burdened by two or more infectious diseases.

Like the diseases that comprise them, *tropical disease syndemics*—the adverse, morbidity-enhancing interaction of two or more NTDs—have likewise been largely unrecognized and generally neglected. Their role, however, in contributing to the health burden of the poor is significant, and, with global warming and global socioeconomic changes, are becoming an even more important contributor to the horrific health and socioeconomic status of the "bottom billion" (Hotez et al. 2009; Singer 2010a). Syndemics have dramatic effects on the health of affected populations because the adverse health outcomes they produce are greater than the sum of the negative impacts caused by copresent individual infections (Ezeamama et al. 2008; Raso et al. 2004; Singer 2009, 2010b, 2011, Singer and Clair 2003; Singer et al. 2006; Singer et al. 2011).

In light of the issues discussed above, the aims of this paper are to review existing and potential NTD syndemics in sub-Saharan Africa and the Americas and to indicate the importance of developing a comprehensive approach for understanding and responding to the health consequences of interactions among NTDs and between NTDs and other diseases (including the Big Three), as well as to NTD syndemic interactions with socioenvironmental contexts as consequences and causes of poverty, inequality, and social marginalization. The ultimate goal of this paper is to contribute to recognition of the practical utility for health improvement of the syndemics perspective.

THE WELLSPRING OF SYNDEMICS: SOCIAL CONDITIONS, NTD CLUSTERING, AND NTD EXPOSURE

A starting point for syndemic analysis is a consideration of underlying social conditions and relationships, their causes and contexts, as well as the natural and anthropogenic environmental factors that facilitate the clustering and interaction of constituent diseases. A further step in such analyses involves tracing the specific biosocial pathways that lead from social conditions to multiple disease exposures and consequent syndemic disease interactions.

Social Conditions

The ultimate cause of NTDs lies in the interface between global disparities in power, wealth, and human rights, on the one hand, and resulting less than optimal living and working conditions, access to the benefits of public health improvements, and health care, on the other. NTDs, as enduring and debilitating epidemics, are not natural in the sense that despite being biological entities they are socially produced. Their host populations, locations of concentration, and severe health and social impacts reflect the global, regional, and local structures of unequal social relationships and the benefits of inequality for dominant and powerful groups within and across nations (Baer et al. 2003; Farmer 1999; Kim et al. 2000; Whiteford and Manderson 2000). As Gill (1989) asks with reference to the place of Africa in the global system: how does the development of some countries benefit from the underdevelopment of others?; who gains advantage from indebtedness of underdeveloped nations and the structural adjustment policies of donor nations and their lender institutions?; who reaps gains from enduring conflict and instability in former colonial areas?; and, how are unequal social relationships globally and locally, both directly and as mediated by environmental conditions, expressed as health disparities? Answering these questions constitutes a critical arena of needed NTD syndemic research.

From Social Conditions to Disease Clustering

The global advancement of neoliberal policies has reduced low-income country government investment in infrastructure, including administrative planning and management, the health sector, and education (Kim et al. 2000; Smith-Nonini 2010). Disparity conditions—including increasing population size as a household survival response to limited resource access, overcrowded and stressful living conditions, exposure to public stigmatization and the internalization of oppression, food insecurity, inadequate clean water supply, limited sanitation/hygienic facilities, and lack of access to health promotion and care (de Silva et al. 2003)—are common outcomes of the channeling of primary government resources toward higher social classes. In combination with macro- and microclimates suitable for parasite and vector survival and dispersion, disparity conditions promote disease and facilitate multiple disease clustering. As Manderson et al. (2009) note, all low-income countries are affected by at least five NTDs. This suggests that disease clustering is influenced by social conditions, structures, policies, and resource distribution patterns.

From Social Conditions to Disease Exposure

Conditional impacts on disease exposure include factors at the international, national, regional, and local levels that contribute to the production and cross-generational reproduction of poverty and significant social inequality. At the international level, disease-enhancing neoliberal structural adjustment policies promoted by wealthy countries and development institutions weaken national governments while internal and international conflicts over desirable resources combine to disable health and civil infrastructures. Note Pfeiffer and Chapman, "the stories that anthropologists tell from the field overwhelmingly speak to a new intensity of emiseration produced by adjustment programs that have undermined public sector services for the poor" (Pfeiffer and Chapman 2010: 149). Further, ethnographies of the "neoliberal global health economy suggest that the violence of this inequality will continue to spiral as the exclusion of poorer societies from the global economy worsens their health" (Nguyen and Peschard 2003:447). In the context of NTDs, Franco-Paredes and Santos-Preciado argue that "poverty should be seen as the relative deprivation of freedoms and capabilities dictating a lack of opportunities and choices in life" (Franco-Paredes and Santos-Preciado 2011:1). Poverty and inequality increase the likelihood of disease exposure and cause the emergence or reemergence of infections in areas where they previously did not exist or had been successfully eliminated.

Human migration as a consequence of environmental change (often of sociogenic origin), conflict, or poverty, to increasingly overpopulated urban areas has become the most important determinant for the emergence of New World zoonotic cutaneous leishmaniasis and zoonotic visceral leishmaniasis (Alvar et al. 2006) transmitted by canine or sylvatic (e.g. opossum, sloth, anteater) reservoir hosts (Hotez et al. 2008). The reemergence of the Chickungunya virus in Delhi in 2005 is also believed to have been caused by a movement of the rural poor to high density, urban areas (Chahar et al. 2009). As both diseases are transmitted by the same vector, Dengue-Chickungunya virus coinfections have since been detected. The vector, the mosquito *Aedes aegypti*, has adapted its habits and behavior in response to human modifications in land use patterns and residence (Manderson et al. 2009).

Additionally, malnutrition, resulting from drought and lack of government assistance, increases susceptibility to infections and contributes to the progression of diseases including visceral leishmaniasis (Reithinger et al. 2007) and HIV/AIDS (Anabwani and Navario 2005; Sellen and Hadley 2011), which themselves interact, further producing serious disease and high mortality.

At the local level, limited government investment in refuse removal from low-income neighborhoods, as well as overcrowding creates ideal breeding grounds for disease vectors including mosquitoes, flies, rodents, and dogs. Suboptimal placement of low-income residences closer to open sewers and accumulated refuse that are home to disease vectors further promotes NTD transmission and the clustering of diseases. In Pau de Lima, a densely populated slum settlement on the outskirts of Salvador in Northeastern Brazil, for example, the risk of acquiring *Leptospira*, a life-threatening rat-borne zoonotic disease, was found to be inversely associated with household income as well as distance of the household from open sewers and accumulated refuse (Reis et al. 2008). Poor quality dwellings allow for living spaces with cracks in the walls and roofs for the disease vectors to enter through, such as the kissing bug that transmits Chagas (Hotez et al. 2008), a disease disproportionately represented among people living in poverty in Latin America (Franco-Paredes et al. 2007; Riley et al. 2007).

Further, limited educational achievement among the poor and refugee populations contributes to greater disease exposure as a result of poor housing quality, location, and levels of sanitation. Individuals with low socioeconomic status are more likely to obtain water from contaminated lakes, rivers, or ponds and have limited (if any) access to latrines. In Kenya, individuals living in the poorest households, without latrines, and collecting water from contaminated sources have a 3- and 2.5-fold increase of helminth infections, respectively (Walson et al. 2010). In Kenya, individuals with lower levels or no education have been found to be almost twice as likely to be infected with a helminth compared to those who completed secondary school education (Walson et al. 2010).

Lower levels of educational attainment also increase disease exposure because of the nature of the employment opportunities available. Before the invention of chewing gum synthetics, for example, traditional South American collectors of chicle—the milky sap obtained from the bark of sapodilla trees that was used in the making of chewing gum— were frequently exposed to sand flies carrying leishmaniasis (Singer 2009). Similarly, along the banks of Lake Victoria in Kenya, individuals are exposed to schistosomiasis because of their involvement in car washing and sand collecting (Black et al. 2010; Karanja et al. 2002). While sand collectors tend to be local residents, those involved in car washing include both local residents and men who have traveled from other parts of Kenya seeking employment. Despite the risks of infection posed by these occupations, without alternative means of livelihood the risk of infection, multiple concurrent infections, and repeated infections are balanced against the even greater health and social costs of no employment. Similarly, agricultural workers in tropical zones are known to be at risk for soil transmitted helminths, including trachoma, onchocerciasis, hookworm, and schistosomiasis (Benton 1998; Bethony et al. 2004; Frick et al. 2003; Perera et al. 2007). In Kenya, for example, farmers are almost twice as likely to be infected with soil-transmitted helminths than nonfarmers (Walson et al. 2010).

Notably, the relationship been poverty and both NTDs and NTD syndemics is bidirectional. Not only are disparity populations at greater risk for NTDs through disadvantaged living standards or low-status/low-income occupational exposures, NTD infections generate greater disparities among populations. Consequently, an adverse feed-back loop involving a downward spiral of interlocked poverty and disease occurs, which is accelerated by the development of multi-disease syndemics. Thus, hookworm and schis-tosomiasis infections cause anemia of chronic inflammation and iron deficiency. Anemia in children results in growth stunting and malnutrition, fatigue, diminished physical fitness, and impaired cognitive development (King and Dangerfield-Cha 2008; King et al. 2005). Helminth infections impact pediatric physical and mental development, reducing school attendance and educational performance, and thereby adversely affect future earnings (Bleakley 2007; de Silva 2003; Hotez et al. 2009; Miguel and Kremer 2004; Sakti et al. 1999). Similarly, in adults, soil-transmitted helminth infection, loss of sight from trachoma or onchocerciasis (Benton 1998; Frick et al. 2003), and chronic lymphedema and hydrocele resulting from lymphatic filariasis have been linked to re-duced productivity (Guyatt 2000; Perera et al. 2007). Moreover, treatment for NTDs, if physically available, may not be economically accessible, often costing a family's entire yearly earnings or the sale of valuable assets (Adhikari and Maskay 2003).

EXAMPLES OF NTD SYNDEMIC INTERACTIONS AND THEIR HEALTH CONSEQUENCES

The syndemic interactions among NTDs, and between NTDs and other diseases are both unidirectional (i.e., the spread of one of the diseases involved is facilitated or its impact worsened) and bidirectional (disease interaction enhances two or more comorbid diseases). In either case, significant health consequences may result.

Intra-NTD Syndemics

Helminth infections are the most common infections of humans (Bethony et al. 2006; Chan 1997; Gryseels et al. 2006), with hookworm and schistosomiasis infecting approximately 600 million people and 200 million people, respectively (Hotez et al. 2009). Individuals living in endemic areas often carry more than one species of worm infection at any given time (Brooker et al. 2000; Tchuem et al. 2003). This is possible in part because of shared transmission routes. In Brazil, for example, household crowding as well as residence in low vegetation areas, both a consequence of low socioeconomic status, are associated with *Necator americanus* and *Schistosoma mansoni* coinfection (Pullan et al. 2008). The sophisticated survival strategies of these parasites, including the secretion of immunomodulatory substances and the induction of regulatory immune responses that allow for the characteristic chronic nature of helminth infection (Maizels et al. 2004), also aid the development of concurrent infections. In addition, the intensity of helminth infections alters the risk of multiple-species infections because immunomodulatory activities modify the body's immune responsiveness to concurrent infections. Higher intensities of infection as a result of coinfection also lead to a higher risk of morbidity. For example, while anemia is the most common health consequence of single NTD infections, concomitant infection with multiple NTDs increases the odds of anemia by as much as seven times (Ezeamama et al. 2008). Researchers have speculated that concomitant helminth infections exacerbate anemia in part because two independent pathways of anemia induction occur concurrently (see Robertson et al. 1992). A recent study in Leyte, in the Philippines found that among children that were concomitantly infected by hookworm and schistosomiasis, the odds of anemia were four to seven times higher than among children infected by a single species (Ezeamama et al. 2008).

Although helminth coinfections are the most common, other NTD coinfections have been documented as well. In Nepal, for example, two patients were reported in recent years to have presented coinfected with endemic diseases leprosy and visceral leishmaniasis (Rijal et al. 2009). Physicians hypothesize that these patients may have been incubating *Mycobacterium leprae* as a result of exposure to individuals with leprosy, and manifested the disease when immunity was low as a result of visceral leishmaniasis. An exceptional triple association of American cutaneous leishmaniasis, lepromatous leprosy, and pulmonary tuberculosis was observed in a single male patient in 2002 (Delobel et al. 2003). As no underlying primary or secondary immunodeficiencies were observed in the patient, reporting physicians determined that each infection might synergistically have enhanced susceptibility to the other two pathogens.

In one further example of an intra-NTD syndemic, Gutierrez et al. (2011) recently described the large and comparatively intense dengue epidemic that occurred in Nicaragua in 2009 as possibly caused by interaction with the H1N1 influenza epidemic, with which it coincided. Although since the 1980s Nicaragua has been regularly visited by dengue outbreaks after the first rains each year, lasting typically from August to January, the outbreak of 2009 was distinctive. Not only were there more cases than in past years—about three times as many laboratory-confirmed cases than in the previous five years (with a case incidence of 4.6% compared 0.4–1.8% in 2004–09)—clinical presentation was atypical. Unique to the 2010 outbreak was the significant frequency of poor peripheral perfusion–the inadequate nutritive delivery of arterial blood to capillaries—an intensive care condition known as compensated shock. While no genetic differences were found between the strain of dengue that was most prevalent in 2010 than in the previous year, there was some laboratory support that the copresence in the population of H1N1 influenza may have been a factor in the distinctiveness of the 2010 outbreak. Gutierrez et al. (2011) suggest the possibility that H1N1 modulated the immune response of comorbid individuals, perhaps by reducing interferon levels, resulting in a more severe expression of dengue. Testing of dengue patients in 2010 found that 65.7% had been dually infected. Moreover, dengue patients with H1N1 antibodies (suggesting recent exposure) had significantly greater odds of developing compensated shock (43% vs. 28%).

Intergroup Syndemics

Coinfection with NTDs has been shown to have adverse effects on host susceptibility to non-NTDs, including HIV/AIDS, malaria, and tuberculosis, as well as on disease progression. NTDs are estimated to play a role in as much as one-half to one-third of sub-Saharan Africa's malaria and HIV/AIDS disease burden, respectively (Hotez and Kamath 2009). Studies have demonstrated that helminth regulation of cytokine responses, increases susceptibility to and severity of some malarial infections (Laranjeiras et al. 2008; Hotez et al. 2006b). Evidence of this has been found in Senegal, Malawi, and Thailand, where individuals infected with helminths had increased susceptibility to clinical malaria compared to those who were uninfected with helminths (Hotez et al. 2006b).

The ability of helminths to regulate immune responses may also increase susceptibility to HIV or exacerbating HIV progression by creating a biochemical environment that favors HIV replication. In addition, in nonhelminth infected individuals, a saturation point is eventually reached wherein the number of immune cells in the blood stream that the virus can use for replication is diminished. In helminth-infected individuals, however, the number of activated immune cells exposed to HIV infection actually increase (Singer 2009). Research in Ethiopia supports the importance of HIV and helminth interactions, as HIV viral loads there were found to be higher in coinfected individuals than in those with HIV infection alone (Bentwich et al. 2000). Effective treatment of worm infestation in this population has been shown to produce a drop in the HIV viral load (Bentwich et al. 2000). Studies also have found that schistosomiasis specifically related to *Schistosoma haematobium*, which creates genital lesions, facilitates HIV infection. A study in Zimbabwe, found that 46% of women were diagnosed with worm-induced genital lesions, and of these 41% were HIV-positive (Kjetland et al. 2006). HIV infection, in turn, promotes helminth infection. Individuals infected with schistosomiasis, who are coinfected with HIV, are more susceptible to subsequent reinfection by the parasite than are individuals who are HIV-negative (Karanja et al. 2002).

Visceral leishmaniasis (VL) also enhances HIV infection, activating HIV replication through several complex biochemical pathways. As HIV infection diminishes the immune response necessary to control leishmania infection, in HIV/leishmania interaction latent VL infection becomes active, propagates, and spreads throughout the body. In coinfected individuals, leishmaniasis has been found to "be particularly severe and unresponsive to treatment" (Olivier et al. 2003:S85). As Harms and Feldmeier observe, "Leishmania/HIV co-infection is ... an example of a deadly gridlock with detrimental interactions in both directions" (Harms and Feldmeier 2002:484). Consequently, coinfected individuals have a significantly higher mortality rate and lower mean survival time than those with parasitic infections alone (World Health Organization 1999).

Recent research that examined possible syndemic interactions between HIV and lymphatic filariasis in Tanzania suggests increases in HIV viral loads and lower CD4 immune cell counts in coinfected adults compared to individuals not infected with filariasis (Nielsen et al. 2007). Similarly, research in a small cohort of women in Kenya found lymphatic filariasis infection to be twice as likely in those who were HIV-positive compared to HIV-negative individuals (Gallagher et al. 2005). Additionally, researchers report that coinfection with one or more worm species significantly increased mother-to-child transmission of HIV compared to women without helminth infections.

Notably, it is possible that findings on the syndemic relationship between HIV and filarial worms have less to do with the worms per se, than with interactions involving a secondary bacterial infection caused by the *Wolbachia* bacterial species. *Wolbachia* may be the most common infectious bacteria on earth (Singer 2009), having a quasi-symbiotic relationship with the filarial worm that causes elephantiasis, as well as other types of roundworms and insect species. The pathogenicity of the helminths is, to a significant degree, a consequence of the intense response of the human immune system to *Wolbachia* exposure. This may explain why newcomer populations (e.g. soldiers) to a filarial endemic region have atypical reactions to infection, including hives, rashes, asthma symptoms, and other allergic reactions to an unfamiliar stimulant (Hoerauf et al. 2003). This also may account for the development of acute and severe inflammatory responses in people infected with either *Brugia malayi* or *Onchocerca volvulus* following antifilarial chemotherapy that results in the release of *Wolbachia* into the blood system (Taylor 2003).

Direct helminth interaction with bacteria also has been described. The helminth *Strongyloides stercoralis*, a parasitic roundworm that lives in the mucosa of the small intestines of infected individuals, for example, is known to interact syndemically with intestinal bacteria. This parasitic worm migrates between the intestines and the lungs, as it passes through its developmental phases, hauling with it attached intestinal bacteria that can cause significant infection in the respiratory system (Marcos et al. 2008). Despite the occurrence of strongyloidiasis/HIV coinfection, research on syndemic interaction remains inconclusive, although it appears most likely in advanced HIV infection (Feitosa et al. 2001; Pinlaor et al. 2005; Viney et al. 2004).

There is some evidence suggesting that helminth infections, especially hookworm and snail-borne flatworms, promote the activation of latent tuberculosis or adversely affect the outcome of pulmonary tuberculosis (Hotez et al. 2006b). Data in support of this process are, however, limited. Impairment of the immune system due to helminth infection is known to be associated with poor response to both tuberculosis (Elias et al. 2007) and cholera vaccines (Harris et al. 2009).

In sum, while there are areas of uncertainty and significant gaps in the available research, it is clear that NTD syndemics are multiple, varied, and in many cases significantly increase the disease burden of affected populations. In this, they enhance the challenges of prevention and intervention.

HEALTH CARE IMPLICATIONS OF SYNDEMICS: ENHANCING PREVENTION, TESTING, DIAGNOSIS, AND TREATMENT

Given the array of severe socioeconomic and health challenges faced by developing countries, NTDs do not tend to be targeted as national public health prevention priorities, and many NTDs, even in areas where they are common, are not included on public health prevention agendas (Holveck et al. 2007). Not surprisingly, the same applies to NTD syndemics, the existence of which may go unrecognized for long periods. NTD syndemic prevention can be enhanced through the development of a better understanding of overlapping geographic and seasonal ranges of interacting diseases and primary routes of cotransmission through vectors (e.g. ticks that can simultaneously transmit multiple infections), exposure to polypathogenic environments (such as soil or water), and specific behaviors (e.g. injection drug use, children's play in infected soils) (Belongia 2002; Bulled and Singer 2011; Hotez et al. 2006a; Nieto and Foley 2009).

One of the challenges of identifying NTD syndemics at an early stage is the atypical presentation produced by disease interactions (Highet 2010). Consequently, testing decisions and diagnosis must be guided by an awareness of the symptomatic manifestation, or lack of symptomatic manifestation, given the interaction of local infectious diseases. This problem is illustrated by a case report by Watt et al. (2003) of a Thai woman from a rice farming village. She presented with leptospirosis and was treated with high-dose intravenous penicillin. However, the woman did not respond well and her condition rapidly deteriorated until she died. Cause of death was determined to be infection with scrub typhus. Dual infection had not been detected given the syndemic interaction with leptospirosis had masked scrub virus symptoms. Subsequent examination of 22 adult patients diagnosed with leptospirosis revealed that almost half were coinfected with scrub typhus.

Given the limited research on NTD syndemics to date, including gaps in understanding of the biological interactions that occur among concurrent infections within the context of varying adverse socioenvironmental conditions and the potential value of particular public health therapeutic strategies, the arsenal of available approaches to primary and secondary prevention is limited (Singer 2009). There is, in particular, a need for further research on practical ways to disrupt emergent NTD syndemics, such as integrated control strategies that target multiple NTD vectors (e.g. sandflies, black flies, mosquitoes) and obstruct human-vector contact (Luckhart et al. 2010).

Progress in improving the control of NTD syndemics is influenced by recognition of the comorbid diseases present in particular populations, understanding of the pathways and manifestations of disease interactions, knowledge of the effects of pharmaceutically treating one infection on the virulence, pathogenesis, transmission of copresent diseases, and, especially, the availability of infrastructural resources for implementing an integrated multiple component treatment plan that addresses a set of potentially interactive NTDs using mass drug administration (Eigege et al. 2008; Smits 2009; Tadesse et al. 2008). Integrated treatment regimes based on combination chemotherapies that are effective with multiple conditions, administered through widespread community institutions (e.g. local schools), can be a valuable component of aggressive vertical health interventions (Molyneux et al. 2005). It has been estimated that an available four-drug rapid-impact package that could disrupt NTD syndemic interactions by controlling prevalence in disease overlap areas in Africa would only cost about US$200 million annually (US$0.40 per patient) (Hotez et al. 2006b). Comparison of the cost of stand-alone programs versus those that offer chemotherapy for multiple NTDs in sub-Saharan Africa suggests savings of 26–47% (Brady et al. 2006). Additionally, safety studies for multidrug programs targeted at multiple NTDs have produced positive findings (Horton et al. 2000; Olsen 2007). However, varied popular responses to such initiatives are understudied, an arena of potential anthropological input designed to ethnographically assess local understandings of and attitudes toward complex interventions.

With little doubt, the success of large-scale drug-based, multi-disease control programs, will be shaped by social factors, not therapeutic efficacy alone, including, as Manderson et al. (2009) emphasize—their assessment by local populations in light of cultural beliefs and practices, group history and environment, and treatment experiences. Consequently, there is a need for anthropological and other research on the acceptability of new multi-intervention drug regimes, people's experience and attitudes toward their effects and side effects, and adherence patterns across target population subgroups (e.g. by age, gender, ethnicity, health status). Similarly, there is a need for research to determine if programs include components to ensure that patients and their communities have the knowledge, motivation, skills, involvement, and resources that support adherence. As discussed below, local social factors are hardly the only issue of concern; macro-level political economic factors are both the ultimate source and ultimate arbiter of public and medical responses to syndemics.

A significant added benefit of developing large-scale treatment programs for NTDs stems from the fact that there are geographic overlaps and syndemic interactions among NTDs and the Big Three infectious diseases. As a result, control of NTDs would contribute significantly to fighting HIV/AIDS, tuberculosis, and malaria epidemics by diminishing the role NTDs play in the transmission and virulence of these most widely recognized infections (Hotez et al. 2006b; Walson and John-Steward 2008; Walson et al. 2009; Wolday 2002).

CONCLUSION

Disease has both natural and unnatural (i.e., social) causes. NTDs and the syndemics they form reflect prevailing patterns of poverty and social inequality, changing global patterns of social connection and environmental engagement, as well as national and international prioritization of resource allocation. With regard to addressing NTD syndemics and the health burdens they create at the international level, the prioritization of health within the Millennium Development Goals set by the United Nations has produced a number of positive outcomes, such as the kind of comprehensive programing seen in the Millennium Development Village (MDV) model. The village model, initiated in June 2006, involves integrated investments at the community level in agriculture, education, infrastructure, and health. Further the model provides a foundation for scaling up the control of NTDs and NTD syndemics (Hotez et al. 2006b).

Exemplary of the Millennium Village Model is Sauri, home to 65,000 people in western Kenya, and the first of over 80 millennium village projects now operating across 14 sites in ten countries in Africa (Buse et al. 2008b). Developments in Sauri include a community deworming initiative to control infection with soil helminths, a common health complaint among community members. During this activity, almost 2000 people were given anti-helminth drugs as well as hygiene education. Various hygiene and sanitation projects also were implemented in the village, along with a range of activities designed to improve the quality of life and economic status of villagers (The Millennium Development Villages Project 2009). Costs of the project have been approximately $60 per person.

A 2008 review of the MDVs by the Overseas Development Institute described a number of significant achievements, including crop yield increases between 85–350% and a 50% reduction in the incidence of malaria (Buse et al. 2008a). These gains notwithstanding, the MDV approach has its share of critics who have argued that there has been insufficient attention to the views of local people, that staff ignore local fears about criticizing the project, that there is inadequate local government support in many areas, and that there is a lack of clear plans for long-term sustainability, all issues open to ethnographic investigation. In addition, there is a need for rigorous external evaluation and long-term follow-up studies. Nevertheless, initial results suggest MDVs, with their accessible clinics, laboratory linkages, trained local personnel, and focus on sanitation and hygiene, public health education, health programing, and emphasis on community-wide participation and empowerment, provide potential platforms for the implementation of integrated NTD syndemic prevention and treatment at the local level. It remains to be seen if the MDV model can be sustained and scaled up for national and regional coverage, again issues in need of ethnographic information. Whatever the longer term assessment of MDVs, the health of the poor is dependent on incorporating a focus on NTD syndemics in global health education, prevention, and treatment initiatives (Nichter 2008).

REFERENCES CITED

Adhikari, Shiva R, and Nephi M Maskay
    2003 The Economic Burden of Kala-azar in Households of the Danusha and Mahottari Districts of Nepal. Acta Tropica 88(1):1–2.
Alvar, Jorge, Sergio Yactayo, and Caryn Bern
    2006 Leishmaniasis and Poverty. Trends in Parasitology 22(12):552–557.
Anabwani, Gabriel, and Peter Navario
    2005 Nutrition and HIV/AIDS in Sub-Saharan Africa: An Overview. Nutrition 21(1):96–99.
Baer, Hans A., Merrill Singer, and Ida Susser
    2003 Medical Anthropology and the World System. Westport, CT: Greenwood Publishing Group.
Belongia, Edward A.
    2002 Epidemiology and Impact of Co-infections Acquired from Ixodes Ticks. Vector-Borne and Zoonotic Diseases 2(4):265–273.
Benton, Bruce
    1998 Economic Impact of Onchocerciasis Control through the African Programme for Onchocerciasis Control: An Overview. Annals of Tropical Medicine and Parasitology 92(Suppl 1):S33–S39.
Bentwich, Zvi, Gary Maartens, Dina Torten, Altaf A. Lal, and Renu B. Lal
    2000 Concurrent Infections and HIV Pathogenesis. AIDS 14(14):2071–2081.
Bethony, Jeffrey, Simon Brooker, Marco Albonico, Stefan M. Geiger, Alex Loukas, David Diemert, and Peter J. Hotez
    2006 Soil-transmitted Helminth Infections: Ascariasis, Trichuriasis, and Hookworm. Lancet 367(9521):1521–1532.
Bethony, Jeffrey, Jeff T. Williams, Simon Brooker, Andrea Gazzinelli, Maria F. Gazzinelli, Philip T. LoVerde, Rodrigo Corrêa-Oliveira, and Helmut Kloos
    2004 Exposure to Schistosoma mansoni Infection in a Rural area in Brazil. Part III: Household Aggregation of Water-Contact Behavior. Tropical Medicine and International Health 9(3):381–389.
Black, Carla L., Pauline N. M. Mwinzi, Erick M. O. Muok, Bernard Abudho, Colin M. Fitzsimmons, David W. Dunne, Diana M. S. Karanja, W. Evan Secor, and Daniel G. Colley
    2010 Influence of Exposure History on the Immunology and Development of Resistance to Human Schistosomiasis Mansoni. PLoS Neglected Tropical Diseases 4(3):e637. doi:10.1371/journal.pntd.0000637
Bleakley, Hoyt
    2007 Disease and Development: Evidence from Hookworm Eradication in the American South. Quarterly Journal of Economics 122(1):73–117.
Brady, Molly A., Pamela J. Hooper, and Eric A. Ottesen
    2006 Projected Benefits from Integrating NTD Programs in Sub-Saharan Africa. Trends in Parasitology 22(7):285–291.
Brooker, Simon, Edward A. Miguel, Sylvie Moulin, Alfred I. Luoba, Donald A. P. Bundy, and Michael Kremer
    2000 Epidemiology of Single and Multiple Species of Helminth Infections among School Children in Busia District, Kenya. East African Medical Journal 77(3):157–161.
Bulled, Nicola, and Merrill Singer
    2011 Syringe-Mediated Syndemics. AIDS and Behavior 15(7):1539–1545. doi: 10.1007/s10461-009-9631-1.
Buse, Kent, Eva Ludi, and Marcella Vigneri
    2008a Beyond the Village: The Transition from Rural Investments to National Plans to Reach the MDGs. Sustaining and Scaling-up the Millennium Villages. Formative Review of the Millennium Villages Project Synthesis Report. London: Overseas Development Institute.
    2008b Can Project-Funded Investments in Rural Development Be Scaled Up? Lessons from the Millennium Villages Project. Natural Resource Perspectives #118. London: Overseas Development Institute.

Chahar, Harendra S., Preeti Bharaj, Lalit Dar, Randeep Guleria, Sushil K. Kabra, and Shobba Broor
  2009 Co-infections with Chikungunya Virus and Dengue Virus in Delhi, India. Emergent Infectious Diseases 15(7):1077–1080.

Chan, Man-Suen
  1997 The Global Burden of Intestinal Nematode Infections—50 Years On. ParasitologyToday 13(11):438–443.

Delobel, Pierre, Pascal Launois, Felix Djossou, Dominique Sainte-Marie, and Roger Pradinaud
  2003 American Cutaneous Leishmaniasis, Lepromatous Leprosy, and Pulmonary Tuberculosis Co-infection with Downregulation of the T-helper 1 Cell Response. Clinical Infection Diseases 37(5):628–633.

de Silva, Nilanthi R., Simon Brooker, Peter J. Hotez, Antonio Montresor, Dirk Engels, and Lorenzo Savioli
  2003 Soil-Transmitted Helminth Infections: Updating the Global Picture. Trends in Parasitology 19(12):547–551.

Eigege, Abel, E. Pede, Emmanuel Miri, John Umaru, Patricia Pearce, M. Y. Jinadu, and A. Ngozi Njepuome
  2008 Triple Drug Administration (TDA), with Praziquantel, Ivermectin and Albendazole, for the Prevention of Three Neglected Tropical Diseases in Nigeria. Annals of Tropical Medicine and Parasitology 102(2):177–179.

Elias, Daniel, Sven Britton, Afework Kassu, and Hannah Akuffo
  2007 Chronic Helminth Infections May Negatively Influence Immunity Against Tuberculosis and Other Disease of Public Health Importance. Expert Review on Anti-Infection Therapy 5(3):475–484.

Engels, Dirk, and Lorenzo Savioli
  2006 Reconsidering the Underestimated Burden Caused by Neglected Tropical Diseases. Trends in Parasitology 22(8):363–366.

Ezeamama, Amara E., Stephen T. McGarvey, Luz P. Acosta, Sally Zierler, Daria L. Manalo, Hai-Wei Wu, Jonathan D. Kurtis, Vincent Mor, Remigio M. Olveda, and Jennifer E. Friedman
  2008 The Synergistic Effect of Concomitant Schistosomiasis, Hookworm, and Trichuris Infections on Children's Anemia Burden. PLoS Neglected Tropical Diseases 2(6):e245. doi:10.1371/journal.pntd.0000245.

Farmer, Paul
  1999 Infections and Inequalities: The Modern Plagues. Berkeley: University of California Press.

Feitosa, Giovana, Antônio C. Bandeira, Diana P. Sampaio, Roberto Badaró, and Carlos Brites
  2001 High Prevalence of Giardiasis and Strongyloidiasis among HIV-infected Patients in Bahia, Brazil. Brazilian Journal of Infectious Diseases 5(6):339–344.

Franco-Paredes, Carlos, and Jose L. Santos-Preciado
  2011 Freedom, Justice, and Neglected Tropical Diseases. PLoS Neglected Tropical Diseases 5(8):e1235. doi:10.1371/journal.pntd.0001235.

Franco-Paredes, Carlos, Anna Von, Alicia Hidron, Alfonso J. Rodriguez-Morales, Ildefonso Tellez, Maribel Barragán, Danielle Jones, Cesar G. Naquira, and Jorge Mendez
  2007 Chagas Disease: An Impediment in Achieving the Millennium Development Goals in Latin America. BMC International Health and Human Rights 7:7.

Frick, Kevin D., Christy L. Hanson, and Gretchen A. Jacobson
  2003 Global Burden of Trachoma and Economics of Disease. American Journal of Tropical Medicine and Hygiene 69(5 Suppl 1):1–10.

Gallagher, Maureen, Indu Malhotra, Peter L. Mungai, Alex N. Wamachi, John M. Kioko, John M. Ouma, Eric Muchiri, and Christopher L. King
  2005 The Effects of Maternal Helminth and Malaria Infections on Mother-to-Child HIV Transmission. AIDS 19(16):1849–1855.

Gill, Peter
  1989 A Year in the Death of Africa: Politics, Bureaucracy and the Famine. London: Paladin Grafton Books.

Gryseels, Bruno, Katja Polman, Jan Clerinx, and Luc Kestens
  2006 Human Schistosomiasis. Lancet 368(9541):1106–1118.

Gutierrez, Gamaliel, Katherine Standish, Federico Narvaez, Maria A. Perez, Saira Saborio, Douglas Elizondo, Oscar Ortega, Andrea Nuñez, Guillermina Kuan, Angel Balmaseda, and Eva Harris

2011 Unusual Dengue Virus 3 Epidemic in Nicaragua, 2009. PLoS Neglected Tropical Diseases 5(11):e1394. doi:10.1371/journal.pntd.0001394

Guyatt, Helen

2000 Do Intestinal Nematodes Affect Productivity in Adulthood? Parasitology Today 16(4): 153–158.

Harms, Gundel, and Hermann Feldmeier

2002 HIV Infection and Tropical Parasitic Diseases: Deleterious Interactions in Both Directions? Tropical Medicine and International Health 7(6):479–488.

Harris, Jason B., Michael J. Podolsky, Taufiqur R. Bhuiyan, Fahima Chowdhury, Ashraful L. Khan, Regina C. LaRocque, Tanya Logvinenko, Jennifer Kendall, Abu S. G. Faruque, Cathryn R. Nagler, Edward T. Ryan, Firdausi Qadri, and Stephen B. Calderwood

2009 Immunologic Responses to Vibrio Cholera in Patients Co-infected with Intestinal Parasites in Bangladesh. PLoS Neglected Tropical Diseases 3(3):e403.

Highet, Megan J.

2010 "It Depends on Where You Look": The Unusual Presentation of Scurvy and Smallpox Among Klondike Gold Rushers as Revealed Through Qualitative Data Sources. Past Imperfect: The History and Classics Graduate Student Journal 16:3–34.

Hoerauf, Achim, Sabine Mand, Kerstin Fischer, Thomas Kruppa, Yeboah Marfo-Debrekyei, AlexanderYaw Debrah, Kenneth Pfarr, Ohene Adjei, and Dietrich W. Büttner

2003 Doxycycline as a Novel Strategy against Bancroftian Filariasis—Depletion of Wolbachia endosymbionts from Wuchereria bancrofti and Stop of Microfilaria Production. Medical Microbiology and Immunology 192(4):211–216.

Holveck, John C., John P. Ehrenberg, Steven K. Ault, Rocio Rojas, Javier Vasquez, Maria T. Cerqueira, Josefa Ippolito-Shepherd, Miguel A. Genovese, and Mirta R. Periago

2007 Prevention, Control, and Elimination of Neglected Diseases in the Americas: Pathways to Integrated, Inter-programmatic, Inter-sectoral Action for Health and Development. BMC Public Health 7:6. doi:10.1186/1471-2458-7-6

Horton, John, C. Witt, Eric A. Ottesen, Janis K. Lazdins, David G. Addiss, Kwablah Awadzi, Michael J. Beach, Vicente Y. Belizario, Samuel K. Dunyo, Marcos Espinel, John O. Gyapong, M. Hossain, M. M. Ismail, R. L. Jayakody, Patrick J. Lammie, William Makunde, D. Richard-Lenoble, Billy Selve, R. Krishna Shenoy, Paul E. Simonsen, C. Njeri Wamae, and Mirani V. Weerasooriya

2000 An Analysis of the Safety of the Single Dose, Two Drug Regimens used in Programmes to Eliminate Lymphatic Filariasis. Parasitology 121(Suppl 1):S147–S160.

Hotez, Peter

2007a A New Voice for the Poor. PLoS Neglected Tropical Diseases 1(1):e77. doi:10.1371/journal.pntd. 0000077

2007b Neglected Diseases and Poverty in "The Other America": The Greatest Health Disparity in the United States? PLoS Neglected Tropical Diseases 1(3):e149. doi:10.1371/journal.pntd.0000149

2008 Neglected Infections of Poverty in the United States of America. PLoS Neglected Tropical Diseases 2(6):e256. doi:10.1371/journal.pntd.0000256

Hotez, Peter, Maria E. Bottazzi, Carlos Franco-Paredes, Steven K. Ault, and Mirta R. Periago

2008 The Neglected Tropical Diseases of Latin America and the Caribbean: A Review of Disease Burden and Distribution and a Roadmap for Control and Elimination. PLoS Neglected Tropical Diseases 2(9):e300. doi:10.1371/journal.pntd.0000300

Hotez, Peter, Donald A. P. Bundy, Kathleen Beegle, Simon Brooker, Lesley Drake, Nilanthi de Silva, Antonio Montresor, Dirk Engels, Matthew Jukes, Lester Chitsulo, Jeffrey Chow, Ramanan Laxminarayan, Catherine Michaud, Jeff Bethony, Rodrigo Correa-Oliveira, Xiao Shu-Hua, Alan Fenwick, and Lorenzo Savioli

2006a Helminth Infections: Soil-transmitted Helminth Infections and Schistosomiasis. *In* Disease Control Priorities in Developing Countries. 2nd edition. Dean T. Jamison, Joel G. Breman, Anthony R. Measham, George Alleyne, Mariam Claeson, David B. Evans, Prabhat Jha, Anne Mills, and Philip Musgrove, eds. Pp. 467–482. Oxford: Oxford University Press.

Hotez, Peter, and Aruna Kamath

    2009 Neglected Tropical Diseases in Sub-Saharan Africa: Review of their Prevalence, Distribution, and Disease Burden. PLoS Neglected Tropical Diseases 3(8):e412. doi:10.1371/journal.pntd.0000412

Hotez, Peter J., Alan Fenwick, Lorenzo Savioli, and David H. Molyneux

    2009 Rescuing the Bottom Billion through Control of Neglected Tropical Diseases. Lancet 373(9674):1570–1575.

Hotez, Peter J., David H. Molyneux, Alan Fenwick, Eric Ottesen, Sonia E. Sachs and Jeffrey Sachs

    2006b Incorporating a Rapid-Impact Package for Neglected Tropical Diseases with Programs for HIV/AIDS, Tuberculosis, and Malaria. PLoS Medicine 3(5):e102. doi:10.1371/journal.pmed.0030102

Hotez, Peter J., Kari Stoever, Alan Fenwick, David H. Molyneux, and Lorenzo Savioli

    2006c The Neglected Epidemic of Chronic Diseases (Letter). Lancet 367(9510):563–564.

Inhorn, Marcia C. and Peter J. Brown

    1997 Introduction. *In* The Anthropology of Infectious Disease: International Health Perspectives. Marcia C. Inhorn and Peter J. Brown, eds. Pp. 3–30. Amsterdam, Netherlands: Gordon and Breach.

Karanja, Diana M. S., Allen W. Hightower, Daniel G. Colley, Pauline N. M. Mwinzi, Karen Galil, Julius Andove, and W. Evan Secor

    2002 Resistance to Reinfection with Schistosoma mansoni in Occupationally Exposed Adults and Effects of HIV-1 Co-infection on Susceptibility to Schistosomiasis: A Longitudinal Study. Lancet 360(9333):592–596.

Kim, Jim Yong, Joyce Millen, Alec Irwin, and John Gershman

    2000 Dying for Growth: Global Inequality and the Health of the Poor. Monroe, ME: Common Cause Press.

King, Charles H., and Madeline Dangerfield-Cha

    2008 The Unacknowledged Impact of Chronic Schistosomiasis. Chronic Illness 4(1): 65–79.

King, Charles H., Katherine Dickman, and Daniel J. Tisch

    2005 Reassessment of the Cost of Chronic Helminthic Infection: Meta-analysis of Disability-related Outcomes in Endemic Schistosomiasis. Lancet 365(9470):1561–1569.

Kjetland, Eyrun F., Patricia D. Ndhlovu, Exenevia Gomo, Takafira Mduluza, Nicholas Midzi, Lovemore Gwanzura, Peter R. Mason, Leiv Sandvik, Henrik Friis, and Svein Gunnar Gundersen

    2006 Association between Genital Schistosomiasis and HIV in Rural Zimbabwean Women. AIDS 20(4):593–600.

Krishna Kumari, A., K. Harichandrakumar, L. K. Das, and K. Krishnamoorthy

    2005 Physical and Psychosocial Burden Due to Lymphatic Filariasis as Perceived by Patients and Medical Experts. Tropical Medicine and International Health 10(6):567–573.

Laranjeiras, Ramon F., Luisa C. C. Brant, Anna C. L. Lima, Paulo M. Z. Coelho, and Erika M. Braga

    2008 Reduced Protective Effect of Plasmodium berghei Immunication by Concurrent Schistosoma mansoni Infection. Memorias do Institudo Oswaldo Cruz 103(7):674–677.

Luckhart, Shirley, Steven W. Lindsay, Anthony A. James, and Thomas W. Scott

    2010 Reframing Critical Needs in Vector Biology and Management of Vector-Borne Disease. PLoS Neglected Tropical Diseases 4(2):e566. doi:10.1371/journal.pntd.0000566

Maizels, Rick M., Adam Balic, Natalia Gomez-Escobar, Meera Nair, Matt D. Taylor, and Judith E. Allen

    2004 Helminth Parasites—Masters of Regulation. Immunological Reviews 201(1):89–116.

Manderson, Lenore, Jens Asgaard-Hansen, Pascale Allotey, Margaret Gyapong, and Johannes Sommerfeld

    2009 Social Research on Neglected Diseases of Poverty: Continuing and Emerging Themes. PLoS Neglected Tropical Diseases 3(2):e332. doi:10.1371/journal.pntd.0000332

Marcos, Luis A., Angelica Terashima, Herbert L. DuPont, and Eduardo Gotuzzo

    2008 Strongyloides Hyperinfection Syndrome: An Emerging Global Infectious Disease. Transactions of the Royal Society of Tropical Medicine and Hygiene 102(4):314–318.

Mathers, Colin, Majid Ezzati, and Alan Lopez

    2007 Measuring the Burden of Neglected Tropical Diseases: The Global Burden of Disease Framework. PLoS Neglected Tropical Diseases 1(2):e114. doi:10.1371/journal.pntd.0000114

Miguel, Edward, and Michael Kremer

2004 Worms: Identifying Impacts on Education and Health in the Presence of Treatment Externalities. Econometrica 72(1):159–217.

The Millennium Development Villages Project

2009 Sauri, Kenya, Annual Report, July 2008–June 2009. http://www.millenniumvillages. org/docs/2009_Sauri_MV1_Annual_Report.pdf, accessed March 27, 2012.

Molyneux, David H., Peter J. Hotez, and Alan Fenwick

2005 "Rapid-Impact Interventions": How a Policy of Integrated Control for Africa's Neglected Tropical Diseases could Benefit the Poor. PLoS Medicine 2(11):e336. doi:10.1371/journal.pmed.0020336

Nichter, Mark

2008 Global Health: Why Clinical Perceptions, Social Representations and Biopolitics Matter. Tucson, AZ: University of Arizona Press.

Nielsen, Nino O., Henrik Friis, Pascal Magnussen, Henrik Krarup, Stephen Magesa, and Paul E. Simonsen

2007 Co-infection with Subclinical HIV and *Wuchereria bancrofti*, and the Role of Malaria and Hookworms, in Adult Tanzanians: Infection Intensities, CD4/CD8 counts and Cytokine Responses. Transactions of the Royal Society of Tropical Medicine and Hygiene 101(6):602–612.

Nieto, Nathan C., and Janet E. Foley

2009 Meta-Analysis of Co-infection and Coexposure with *Borrelia burgdorferi* and *Anaplasma phagocytophilum* in Humans, Domestic Animals, Wildlife, and Ixodes ricinus-Complex Ticks. Vector-borne and Zoonotic Diseases 9(1):93–102.

Nguyen, Vinh-Kim, and Karine Peschard

2003 Anthropology, Inequality, and Disease: A Review. Annual Review of Anthropology 32:447–474.

Olivier, Martin, Roberto Badaro, F. Medrano, and J. Moreno

2003 The Pathogensis of Leishmania/HIV Co-infection: Cellular and Immunological Mechanisms. Annals of Tropical Medicine and Parasitology 97(Suppl 1):S79–S98.

Olsen, Annette

2007 Efficacy and Safety of Drug Combinations in the Treatment of Schistosomiasis, Soil-transmitted Helminthiasis, Lymphatic Filariasis and Onchocerciasis. Transactions of the Royal Society for Tropical Medicine and Hygiene 101(8):747–758.

Perera, Myrtle, Margaret Whitehead, David H. Molyneux, Mirani Weerasooriya, and Godfrey Gunatilleke

2007 Neglected Patients in Neglected Disease? A Qualitative Study of Lymphatic Filariasis. PLoS Neglected Tropical Diseases 1(2):e128. doi:10.1371/journal.pntd.0000128

Pfeiffer, James, and Rachel Chapman

2010 Anthropological Perspectives on Structural Adjustment. Annual Review of Anthropology 39: 149–165.

Pinlaor, Somchai, Piroon Mootsikapun, Porntip Pinlaor, Vichit Pipitgool, and Ruangsil Tuangnadee

2005 Detection of Opportunistic and Non-Opportunistic Intestinal Parasites and Liver Flukes in HIV-positive and HIV-negative subjects. Southeast Asian Journal of Tropical Medicine and Public Health 36(4):841–845.

Pullan, Rachel L., Jeffrey M. Bethony, Stefan M. Geiger, Bonnie Cundill, Rodrigo Correa-Oliveira, Rupert J. Quinnell, and Simon Brooker

2008 Human Helminth Co-Infection: Analysis of Spatial Patterns and Risk Factors in a Brazilian Community. PLoS Neglected Tropical Diseases 2(12): e352. doi:10.1371/journal.pntd.0000352

Raso, Giovanna, Anne Luginbühl, Cinthia A. Adjoua, Norbert T. Tian-Bi, Kigbafori D. Silué, Barbara Matthys, Penelope Vounatsou, Yulan Wang, Marc-Emmanuel Dumas, Elaine Holmes, Burton H. Singer, Marcel Tanner, Eliézer K. N'Goran, and Jürg Utzinger

2004 Multiple Parasite Infections and their Relationship to Self-reported Morbidity in a Community of Rural Côte d'Ivoire. International Journal of Epidemiology 33(5):1092–1102.

Reis, Renato B., Guilherme S. Ribeiro, Ridalva D. M. Felzemburgh, Felzemburgh S. Santana, Sharif Mohr, Astrid X. T. O. Melendez, Adriano Queiroz, Andréia C. Santos, Romy R. Ravines, Wagner S. Tassinari, Marília S. Carbalho, Mitermayer G. Reis, and Albert L. Ko

2008 Impact of Environment and Social Gradient on *Leptospira* Infection in Urban Slums. PLoS Neglected Tropical Diseases 2(4):e228. doi:10.1371/journal.pntd.0000228

Reithinger, Richard, Simon Brooker, and Jan Kolaczinski
  2007 Visceral Leishmaniasis in Eastern Africa—Current Status. Transactions of the Royal Society of Tropical Medicine and Hygiene 101(12):1169–1170.

Rijal, Arpana, Suman Rija, and Sanjib Bhandari
  2009 Leprosy Co-infection with Kala-azar. International Journal of Dermatology 48(7): 740–742.

Riley, Lee W., Albert L. Ko, Alon Unger, and Mitermayer G. Reis
  2007 Slum Health: Diseases of Neglected Populations. BMC International Health and Human Rights 7:2. doi:10.1186/1472-698X-7-2

Robertson, Lucy J., D. W. T. Crompton, Diva Sanjur, and Malden C. Nesheim
  1992 Haemoglobin Concentrations and Concomitant Infections of Hookworm and *Trichuris trichiura* in Panamanian Primary Schoolchildren. Transactions of the Royal Society of Tropical Medicine and Hygiene 86(6):654–656.

Sakti, Hastaning, Catherine Nokes, W. Subagio Hertanto, Sri Hendratno, Andrew Hall, Donald A. P. Bundy, and Satoto
  1999 Evidence for an Association between Hookworm Infection and Cognitive Function in Indonesia School Children. Tropical Medicine and International Health 4(5):322–334.

Sellen, Daniel W., and Craig Hadley
  2011 Food Insecurity and Maternal-to-Child Transmission of HIV and AIDS in Sub-Saharan Africa. Annals of Anthropological Practice 35(1):28–49.

Singer, Merrill
  2009 Introduction to Syndemics: A Systems Approach to Public and Community Health. San Francisco: Jossey-Bass.
  2010a Ecosyndemics: Global Warming and the Coming Plagues of the 21st. Century. *In* Plagues and Epidemics: Infected Spaces Past and Present. Alan Swedlund and Ann Herring, eds. Pp. 21–37. Oxford: Berg.
  2010b Pathogen-Pathogen Interaction: A Syndemic Model of Complex Biosocial Processes in Disease. Virulence 1(1):10–18.
  2011 Toward a Critical Biosocial Model of Ecohealth in Southern Africa: The HIV/AIDS and Nutrition Insecurity Syndemic. Annals of Anthropology Practice 35(1):8–27.

Singer, Merrill, and Scott Clair
  2003 Syndemics and Public Health: Reconceptualizing Disease in Bio-social Context. Medical Anthropology Quarterly 17(4):423–441.

Singer, Merrill, Pamela I. Erickson, Louise Badiane, Rosemary Diaz, Dugeidy Ortiz, Traci Abraham, and Anna Marie Nicolaysen
  2006 Syndemics, Sex and the City: Understanding Sexually Transmitted Disease in Social and Cultural Context. Social Science and Medicine 63(8):2010–2021.

Singer, Merrill, D. Ann Herring, Judith Littleton, and Melanie Rock
  2011 Syndemics in Public Health. *In* A Companion to Medical Anthropology. Merrill Singer and Pamela I. Erickson, eds. Pp 159–180. San Francisco: Wiley.

Smith-Nonini, Sandy
  2010 Healing the Body Politic: El Salvador's Popular Struggle for Health Rights from Civil War to Neoliberal Peace. New Brunswick: Rutgers University Press.

Smits, Henk L.
  2009 Prospects for the Control of Neglected Tropical Diseases by Mass Drug Administration. Expert Review of Anti-Infective Therapy 7(1):37–56.

Tadesse, Zerihun, Afework Hailemariam, and Jan H. Kolaczinski
  2008 Potential for Integrated Control of Neglected Tropical Diseases in Ethiopia. Transactions of the Royal Society of Tropical Medicine and Hygiene 102(3):213–214.

Taylor, Mark J.
  2003 Wolbachia in the Inflammatory Pathogenesis of Human Filariasis. Annals of the New York Academy of Sciences 990(1):444–449.

Tchuenté, L. A. Tchuem, J. M. Behnke, F. S. Gilbert, V. R. Southgate, and J. Vercruysse

    2003 Polyparasitism with *Schistosoma haematobium* and Soil-transmitted Helminth Infections among School Children in Loum, Cameroon. Tropical Medicine and International Health 8(11):975–986.

Viney, Mark E., Michael Brown, Nicholas E. Omoding, J. Wendi Bailey, Michael P. Gardner, Emily Roberts, Dilys Morgan, Alison M. Elliott, and James A. G. Whitworth

    2004 Why Does HIV Infection Not Lead to Disseminated Strongyloidiasis? The Journal of Infectious Diseases 190(12):2175–2180.

Walson, Judd, Bradley Herrin, and Grace John-Steward

    2009 Deworming Helminth Co-infected Individuals for Delaying HIV Disease Progression. Cochrane Database of Systematic Reviews 3:CD006419.

Walson, Judd L., and Grace John-Steward

    2008 Treatment of Helminth Co-infection in HIV-1 Infected Individuals in Resource-limited Settings. Cochrane Database of Systematic Reviews 1:CD006419.

Walson, Judd L., Barclay T. Stewart, Laura Sangaré, Loice W. Mbogo, Phelgona A. Otieno, Benjamin K. S. Piper, Barbra A. Richardson, and Grace John-Steward

    2010 Prevalence and Correlates of Helminth Co-infection in Kenyan HIV-1 Infected Adults. PLoS Neglected Tropical Diseases 4(3):e644. doi:10.1371/journal.pntd.0000644

Watt, George, Krisada Jongsakul, and Chuanpit Suttinont

    2003 Possible Scrub Typhus Co-infections in Thai Agricultural Workers Hospitalized with Leptospirosis. American Journal of Tropical Medicine and Hygiene 68(1):89–91.

Whiteford, Linda M., and Lenore Manderson

    2000 Global Health Policy, Local Realities: The Fallacy of the Level Playing Field. Boulder, CO: Lynne Rienner Publishers, Inc.

Wolday, Dawit, Shlomo Mayaan, Zeru G. Mariam, Nega Berhe, Teshale Seboxa, Sven Britton, Noya Galai, Alan Landay, and Zvi Bentwich

    2002 Treatment of Intestinal Worms is Associated with Decreased HIV Plasma Viral Load. Journal of Acquired Immune Deficiency Syndrome 31(1):56–62.

World Health Organization

    1999 Leishmania/HIV Co-infection, South-western Europe, 1990–1998: Retrospective Analysis of 965 Cases. Weekly Epidemiological Record 74(44):365–375. http://www.who.int/docstore/wer/pdf/1999/wer7444.pdf, accessed July 31, 2012.

TOURISM, ECONOMIC INSECURITY, AND NUTRITIONAL HEALTH IN RURAL COSTA RICA: USING SYNDEMICS THEORY TO UNDERSTAND THE IMPACT OF THE GLOBALIZING ECONOMY AT THE LOCAL LEVEL

DAVID A. HIMMELGREEN
University of South Florida

NANCY ROMERO-DAZA
University of South Florida

EDGAR AMADOR
University of South Florida

CYNTHIA PACE
University of South Florida

Rapid economic transformations have both positive and negative consequences for nutrition and health. This article presents data from an area of rural Costa Rica that has experienced a rapid economic shift from dairy farming and coffee production to a mixed economy based increasingly on tourism and to a lesser extent on agriculture. During a one-year period (2004–2005), sociodemographic, employment, dietary intake, food security, anthropometric, and ethnographic (food habits) data were collected from 148 households in two rural communities. The results show that 50 percent of the households are directly involved in the tourism industry, while many others rely on economic strategies that combine involvement in tourism with agricultural activities. Overall, high rates of food insecurity were documented (with over 70 percent of the households experiencing some level of food insecurity over the previous 12 months). The data also show high rates of caregiver and child overweight and obesity and a diet that varies according to food security status. Syndemics theory, which postulates that the dynamic interaction between co-occurring conditions magnifies the effects of each one in isolation can be used to understand how malnutrition (overnutrition) related to economic insecurity and overweight and obesity together may be contributing to the rise in chronic diet-related diseases, such as hypertension and type-2 diabetes, in the study area. The interactions between these comorbidities point to the need for the development of multidimensional public health interventions that couple individual behavior change and community-driven efforts that reduce economic insecurity and ameliorate food insecurity, resulting in more balanced diets and a reduction in overweight and obesity. [syndemic, tourism, economic insecurity, nutritional health]

ANNALS OF ANTHROPOLOGICAL PRACTICE 36.2, pp. 346–364. ISSN: 2153-957X. © 2013 by the American Anthropological Association. DOI:10.1111/napa.12008

INTRODUCTION

Syndemics Theory posits that the simultaneous presence of two or more ill-health conditions in a given population or community is not simply a matter of temporal co-occurrence, but rather implies a dynamic interaction by which each of the conditions shapes and reinforces the other, thus, magnifying their individual detrimental effects (Singer 1996; Singer and Clair 2003; Snipes 1992). Importantly, the syndemic framework brings together the biomedical realities of disease with the social (including economic and political) environment in which ill health occurs. As Singer (2009:30) states: "The syndemic perspective recognizes the fundamental importance of the biomedical construction of disease conception, is concerned with disease-host interaction in shaping disease course and expression . . . and even more important, calls attention to the often determinant socio-cultural origins of disease."

Thus, Syndemic Theory provides a useful framework to understand the dynamic interaction between food insecurity (i.e., lack of access to food of adequate quality and quantity obtained in socially acceptable ways, which often results in worry and stress) and its associated health consequences (e.g., increased risk of undernutrition and overnutrition and associated chronic and infectious diseases; Himmelgreen et al. 2009). Several studies have exemplified how food insecurity can have adverse health impacts on people infected with HIV/AIDS, such as increasing the rates of maternal-to-child transmission, creating a barrier for adhering to antiretroviral treatment, and significantly decreasing virological suppression (Anema et al. 2011; Jones 2011; Sellen and Hadley 2011). Individuals living in areas where malnutrition is endemic are at increased risk for developing diseases and coinfections. In addition, levels of distress associated with food insecurity have a disastrous effect on the immune system by reducing the development of antibodies, decreasing the amount of lymphocytes, and increasing the likelihood of infection (Singer 2011). In this article, we use the tenets of syndemics theory to examine some of the above-mentioned relations in the context of economic insecurity that results from the gradual movement away from a subsistence economy based on agriculture and dairy farming to one reliant on involvement in tourism in a rural region of Costa Rica.

STUDY SITE

The Monteverde (green mountain) zone of Costa Rica is located in the Northwestern Tilarán Highlands in the province on Puntarenas. Situated along the Continental divide at an altitude of between 1,200 and 1,400 meters above sea level, the region is characterized by weather patterns influenced by the sweeping upward warm, humid Caribbean air currents colliding with the dryer, cool winds from the Pacific. As a result, the uppermost region of the zone is often shrouded by clouds and is home to the Monteverde Cloud Forest Preserve, one of the world's most threatened ecosystems (Nardkarni and Wheelwrite 2000; Vivanco 2006). The climate is further characterized by cooler temperatures than in the surrounding lowlands and seasonal rains, which can be heavy and long-lasting.

Given the diverse topography of the region, the convergence of these climatic conditions gives rise to a large number of microecological niches, each with their own array of flora and fauna. The Monteverde zone is one of the best examples of why Costa Rica has been nicknamed "The Green Republic" (Evans 1999).

There are a over 20 towns of varying sizes and approximately 6,000 residents spread throughout the hills and highlands of the Monteverde zone including the predominantly North American Quaker community of Monteverde, which is nestled in the upper region of the zone near the Monteverde Cloud Forest Preserve (Honey 1999; Vivanco 2006). Before the arrival of the Quakers, the zone had been inhabited by Native Costa Ricans (*Ticos*) since at least the 1920s, if not earlier (Vivanco 2006). Although not fully documented or archived, there is artifactual evidence (e.g., pottery and tools) of an earlier indigenous culture that has been found by local farmers (Vargas personal communication, 2011). *Ticos* and Quakers live year-round in the zone, while increasing numbers of tourists, students, and researchers visit seasonally to vacation, study, and conduct research (Himmelgreen et al. 2006).

Because of their pacifist beliefs and the dissolution of the military in Costa Rica in 1948, several Quaker families from the United States visited the area in 1949 and eventually purchased a tract of land in the Monteverde zone and founded the town of Monteverde in 1951. During the following decades they worked together with local *Ticos* to develop an economy primarily based on dairy farming—mostly milk and cheese—coffee production, and more recently the sale of fruits and vegetables to local restaurants and hotels, and to tourists and locals (Himmelgreen et al. 2006). Historically, small family farms have been an important feature in the economy of the zone, and are organized into food cooperatives where member households and larger-scale farmers share proportionally in financial and labor investments as well as in profits (University of Georgia n.d.). The cooperatives provide mutual assistance during the agricultural cycle, and play a prominent role in the distribution and marketing of products (Alvarado et al. 1998). In one of the towns that participated in this study, the local cooperative includes more than 700 members.

During the last three decades, there has been a steady rise in the number of tourists visiting Costa Rica. For example, in 2008, over two million tourists from North America, Europe, and Central and South America visited Costa Rica (ICT 2009). Today, the Monteverde zone is considered the second most popular tourist destination in the country (ICT 2009). The 40 kilometers, a still largely dirt-covered road that goes from the Pan American Highway to the uppermost Monteverde Cloud Forest Preserve, passing through towns such as Santa Elena (a tourist hub) and Monteverde along the way, brings 250,000 tourists annually to the zone. The number of tourists visiting the zone is likely to increase substantially once the road is completely paved (Monahan 2004). The huge influx of tourists into the zone and associated economic and lifestyle changes are having a significant impact on its residents' overall well-being. An area of increasing concern is the rapidly changing diet and physical activity–related health status among inhabitants of the zone. For example, in a study of two area towns, Himmelgreen et al. (2006) found high rates of household food insecurity and obesity among women of childbearing age. Given the well-documented link between food insecurity and the resulting adult obesity on one hand, and health problems, such as type two diabetes and cardiovascular disease on the other (Dinour et al. 2007; Hanson et al. 2007; Martin and Ferris 2007), it is important to examine the multiplicity of factors that contribute to nutrition-related ill health in the Monteverde zone, especially in light of the rapidly changing social, economic, and environmental conditions brought about by tourism in particular, and globalization, in general. This article seeks to do so by using Syndemics Theory as an analytical framework, which provides the tools for the examination of the dynamic interaction between social, economic, and biological factors responsible for the observed patterns of ill health.

RESEARCH DESIGN AND METHODS

The data presented here come from a study that was conducted from September 2003 through March 2004 on a convenience sample of 148 households from two towns in the Monteverde zone: Santa Elena and San Rafael. Santa Elena is located near the Monteverde Cloud Forest Preserve and is considered the tourism hub in the zone. Here, ecotourism and adventure tourism businesses (e.g., zip-lines, horseback riding, and hiking tours), restaurants, small hotels and lodges, souvenir shops, art galleries, and food markets dot the landscape and extend out to towns further up the slope, such as Cerro Plano and Monteverde. Alternatively, the economy of San Rafael, located further down the mountain range, is characterized by an agricultural economy including coffee production. Although tourists often pass through San Rafael on their way to Arenal (where a famous volcano, lake, and hot springs are located), the town's economy is mostly geared to local residents. Nevertheless, the tentacles of tourism stretch far and wide through the Monteverde zone. The data indicate that both of these towns, which on the surface appear to have very different economic bases (see Himmelgreen et al. 2006), exhibit mixed-economy subsistence patterns, with Santa Elena showing a heavier emphasis on tourism, while San Rafael is more reliant on subsistence agriculture. Despite these differences, for the purposes of this article, the data from Santa Elena and San Rafael are combined to develop a more general understanding of the syndemic interaction between food insecurity and health in the Monteverde zone.

Data were collected from 148 women ($\geq$ 18 years) who were caregivers in households in which there was at least one child between the ages of seven and 12. Although some of these women were of mixed ethnicity (i.e., Native Costa Ricans and second generation North American Quakers), all of them self-identified as *Ticos* (Costa Ricans). Sociodemographic surveys were administered along with measures of food security, maternal-child anthropometry, and dietary intake—using a validated semiquantitative food frequency questionnaire (FFQ) (Kabagambe et al. 2001). Additionally, open-ended interviews on food access and lifestyle changes associated economic shifts were done with a subsample of 67 women. Finally, focus groups were conducted in both towns that included 13 of these study participants and focused on issues related to food access, food availability, food preparation, and decision making regarding food choices.

The level of food security was assessed using the Radimer/Cornell Scale (Frongillo et al. 1997; Radimer et al. 1990), an instrument that has been validated to screen for hunger and food insecurity (Kendall et al. 1996, 1995). The Radimer/Cornell Scale is one of the earlier tools used to measure food insecurity. While more recent scales, such as the Latin American and Caribbean Household Food Security Scale (ELCSA) and the Household Food Insecurity Access Scale (HFIAS), are more commonly used today, the research reported here was done prior to the validation of these tools. Since we have used the Radimer/Cornell Scale successfully among Latinos in the United States (Himmelgreen et al. 2000, 1998), we are confident that the results provided by this instrument are as accurate as any of these other tools.

In the conceptualization of the Radimer/Cornell Scale,

> Food insecurity is [viewed as] a managed process with a general sequence as the problem worsens. Household food insecurity is experienced first, followed by compromises in the quality and quantity of foods eaten by adults. Child hunger, characterized by decreases in the quantity of food eaten by children, is the last stage, representing the most severe problem with household food sufficiency. (Kendall et al. 1996:1020)

The Radimer/Cornell instrument includes 10 items that classify respondents into mutually exclusive groups representing increasingly severe food sufficiency problems (i.e., at the household, adult, and child levels), according to the responses provided by the interviewee. Food insecurity is examined in the context of four constructs as follows: quantity of food, quality of food, certainty of getting food, and food acceptability. As such, not only does the Radimer/Cornell Scale identify problems associated with a lack of sufficient food, but it also identifies the shortcomings of the quality of the diet from the perspective of the individual being interviewed. Therefore, the scale can be used to also examine food insecurity associated with overnutrition, where the diet is unbalanced and skewed toward calorie-dense foods that are of lower nutritional quality. Importantly, the constructs in the Radimer/Cornell scale are conceptualized to assess the negative emotions (mainly worry) experienced by participants in the face of food insecurity (with questions specifically phrased in such manner). As such, the scale allows the researcher to get an indirect measure of the emotional impact that food insecurity has on those who experience it. This is important, given the emergent literature that reports on the association between food insecurity, on one hand, and anxiety and depression, on the other (Heflin et al. 2006; Siefert et al. 2001; Whitaker et al. 2006). Although we did not specifically focus on the emotional impact of food insecurity in our sample, anecdotal evidence suggests that there is a strong association between higher levels of food insecurity and increased reports of anxiety and depression. This is an area that requires further systematic consideration.

The adult caregivers and their children in our sample were divided into a food secure group and three food insecure groups (household food insecure, adult food insecure, and child hunger), according to the Radimer/Cornell Scale. The first category refers to households where there is overall worry and uncertainty about the availability of food, but where all household members can get the basic food they need. The second category (adult food insecure) refers to households where the adults reduce the quantity of food they eat or skip meals in order to ensure that children have enough to eat. The final category (child hunger) represents the most severe form of food insecurity in which children are forced to skip meals because there is not enough food in the household. Moreover, a collapsed food insecurity group was created in which all levels of food insecurity were combined. These categories of food security/insecurity were treated as the dependent variables. Independent variables included household characteristics (e.g., employment, household goods, transportation), the frequency of food consumption for caregivers, and maternal and child anthropometric measures since we hypothesize that overweight and obesity are more likely to be found in food insecure households than in their food secure counterparts.

With a rise in social stratification in the Monteverde zone, it is assumed that increasing access to economic resources translates into a higher standard of living and a greater likelihood of household food security. For example, not having access to adequate private transportation potentially heightens the risk for food insecurity in some households, given that there are still many unpaved roads that become impassable with the daily precipitation that characterizes the higher altitude areas of the zone (the Cloud Forest). This is especially important since there are a limited number of food markets in the zone, which makes it necessary for individuals to travel great distances to purchase food. Finally, as agriculture becomes a less dominant economy strategy, some households are necessarily purchasing food from local markets that are more expensive because they, in part, must pay for the cost of shipping food to the zone, and partially because their clientele include tourists who can afford to pay more for food (Himmelgreen et al. 2006). In addition, markets usually cater to foreigners by offering foods, such as highly processed snacks, sodas, pizza, and a great many fast food items. Through their association with foreigners and with affluence, many of such items have come to be perceived as highly desirable, and as "status" food by locals, who prefer them to more traditional foods.

The data for this project were collected by Native Spanish-speaking researchers, one a Costa Rican from the Monteverde zone and the other a Colombian national. Data on household and caregiver characteristics, household food security status, caregiver and child anthropometry (e.g., body weight, height, body mass index or BMI), and the frequency of food consumption along with some observational and open-ended interview data will be presented here.

Descriptive statistics were used to capture individual and household characteristics, household food security status, caregiver frequency of food consumption, and caregiver and child anthropometry. To control for age and gender differences in child anthropometry, z-scores were used to report child weight, height, and BMI. While BMI does not measure body fat directly, it is correlated with direct measures of body fat (Garrow and Webster 1985; Mei et al. 2002). Moreover, BMI is considered an excellent measure for screening for weight categories that are associated with morbidity and mortality (WHO 1995, 2006). The four BMI cutoffs used for the caregivers in this study were as follows: underweight status (BMI < 18.5), normal weight status (BMI 18.5–24.9), overweight status (BMI 25.0–29.9), and obese status (BMI ≥ 30; CDC 2011a). For children, BMI-for-age percentiles were used to control for maturational differences by age and gender (CDC 2011b; WHO 2006). The categories used were as follows: underweight status (less than 5th percentile of reference), healthy weight (5th to < 85th percentile of reference), overweight (85th to less than 95th percentile of reference), and obese (≥ 95th percentile of reference). Finally, given that the standard deviations for some of food variables and food groups were large, the Kruskal–Wallis H statistic was used to compare caregiver daily food intake, which was rank-ordered and compared across food security categories.

Student t-tests were used to compare participants by sex and household food security status. Explanatory variables involved in bivariate associations with a p-value of ≤ .1 were selected for inclusion in the multivariate models where food security variables (i.e., the food secure, household food insecure, adult food insecure, child hunger, and food insecure collapsed—a combined variable of the previous three) were the outcome variables.

Multivariate analyses were conducted using forward stepwise conditional multiple logistic regression. This method builds an explanatory model in which variables are sequentially added to the model based on their effect on food insecurity. As a result, the model with the greatest explanatory power and parsimony is chosen. Beta values, odds ratios, and p values are presented for each independent variable that predicts food insecurity. Positive beta values are associated with food insecurity and negative ones are associated with food security. Analysis of the data was conducted using SPSS (Version 17.0).

RESULTS

Household Characteristics

Data were collected for 148 Costa Rican women (≥ 18 years) who were caregivers in households in which there was at least one child (7–12 years). The mean age for the caregivers was 36.6 years (SD = 8.2) and 9.1 years (SD = 2.0) for the children (N = 146). Table 1 shows that the mean number of household members was 4.8 (SD = 1.4) and that each house had about three rooms. Nearly half of households had one or more household members working in tourism, either part- or full-time. Over 40 percent of the women reported that their households grew their own food or raised animals; more than 20 percent reported participating in a food cooperative; and four in ten indicated that their households exchanged goods with other households, a practice that was more widespread in the past according to several key informants. Finally, a little more than half of the households had working transportation.

Food Security Status

Results from the Radimer/Cornell Scale on food insecurity and hunger are presented in Table 2 for 145 households (three missing cases). As shown, about 27 percent of households were classified as being food secure. That is, the caregivers did not report problems

TABLE 1. Demographic and Socioeconomic Characteristics of Households in Two Communities in the Monteverde Zone

Characteristics of Household	N	Total Sample Mean	SD
Number of household members	148	4.82	1.38
Number of rooms in house	147	2.73	.86
Number of household members who work (contribute income)	148	1.37	.61

	N	Frequency	Percentage
Involved in tourism	143	70	49.0
Member of a cooperative	146	34	23.3
Grow food or raise animals	147	62	42.2
Own home	148	119	80.4
Have bank account	148	73	49.3
Buy food on credit	148	74	50.0
Working microwave	148	66	44.6
Working transport	148	82	55.4
Receive government aid	147	28	19.0
Participate in exchange of goods	147	61	41.5
Have telephone service	148	120	81.1

TABLE 2. Radimer/Cornell Measures of Food Security in Two Communities in the Monteverde Zone

Variables	Total Sample, $n = 145$ Number	Percentage
Food-secure	39	26.9
Food insecure[a]	106	73.1
Household food insecure	15	10.3
Adult food insecure	61	42.1
Child hunger	30	20.7

[a]Food insecure includes household food insecure, adult food insecure, and child hunger. Differences between the two communities not significant on a chi-square ($p = .152$).

with the quality or quantity of food consumed in their households or concerns about running out of food or money to buy food during the previous 12 months. Conversely, more than seven in ten households experienced some level of food insecurity. The term food insecurity is used here as a general category that includes three levels: household food insecurity (least severe), adult food insecurity, and child hunger (most severe). Food insecurity was related to one or more of the following factors: anxiety over the household not having enough food (household food insecurity), adults eating less or skipping meals (adult food insecurity), or children sometimes going hungry (child hunger). The results in Table 2 show that over 40 percent of adults were reported to have skipped meals or to have eaten less during the previous 12 months and that one in five children had actually gone hungry on one or more days during the same period of time. These results make sense in a cultural milieu in which children are buffered against hunger at the expense of adults.

Caregiver and Child Anthropometry

Mean body weight, height, and BMI for the caregivers ($N = 145$) were 66.6 kilograms (SD = 12.5), 155.3 cm (SD = 5.4), and 27.5 (SD = 5), respectively. For children ($N = 146$), the mean z-score for body weight was 0.04 (SD = 1.1) and for height it was −0.26 (SD = 1.1). Table 3 shows the number and percentage of caregivers and children by BMI categories. More than two-thirds of caregivers were classified as overweight (37.3 percent) or obese (29.6 percent). Using BMI-for-age percentiles, approximately 5 percent of children were underweight, while 12 percent were overweight, and 10 percent were obese. There were no significant differences in weight categories by sex among the children. About 10 percent of the children were growth stunted (height-for-age less than 5th percentile) and the difference in this index was not statistically significant by sex.

Caregiver and Child Anthropometry and Food Security Status

The association between mean caregiver BMI and household food security status is presented in Figure 1. As shown, mean BMI increases with increasing food insecurity. This is significant ($p = .034$) when comparing caregivers in food secure households to their food insecure counterparts in the catchall food insecurity category (i.e., household food insecure, adult food insecure, and child hunger groups). There was no statistically significant difference ($p = .16$) in caregiver age by household food security status, thereby ruling out the potential influence of increasing age on BMI. Among children, there is a statistically significant decrease in the z-score for mean height when comparing those living on food secure households ($z = +0.06$) with their counterparts living in the combined food insecure group ($z = −0.40$; $p = .018$). This association is even more significant when comparing food secure children ($z = +0.06$) with those living in child hungry households—the most severe level of food insufficiency ($z = −0.82$; $p = .05$).

Frequency of Food Consumption and Food Security Status

A validated FFQ (Kabagambe et al. 2001) was administered to the caregivers but this was not feasible to do with the children. Being that caregivers in the zone are the primary gatekeepers when it comes to food acquisition and preparation, the data presented here reflect direct and indirect measures of household food intake and food sufficiency. Figure 2 shows the mean daily frequency of consumption of desserts according to food security status. As shown, there is a statistically significant reduction in the frequency of desserts consumed on a daily basis as household food insecurity worsens ($p = .000$). The frequency of desserts consumed was lowest in child hungry households. While the nutritional value of desserts is variable (and sometimes questionable), these data suggest that the ability to purchase desserts—which are usually considered a luxury—is inversely associated with food security, pointing to the role of economic factors in food security status in this population.

The same trend is seen in Figure 3 which shows a lower daily frequency of vegetable consumption as the household food insecurity gets worse. However, in this case, this

TABLE 3. Caregiver's and Study Child's BMI Weight Categories

	Caregiver's BMI, $n = 142$		Study child's BMI, $n = 145$		Boys, $n = 69$		Girls, $n = 76$	
	Number	Percentage	Number	Percentage	Number	Percentage	Number	Percentage
Underweight	1	0.7	17	4.8	4	5.8	3	3.9
Normal	46	32.4	105	72.4	50	72.5	55	72.4
Overweight	53	37.3	18	12.4	8	11.6	10	13.2
Obese	42	29.6	15	10.3	7	10.1	8	10.5

Differences between boys and girls not significant on a chi-square ($p = .954$).

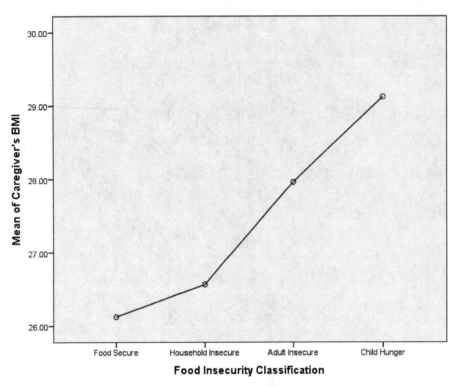

FIGURE 1. Mean caregiver body mass index (BMI) according to food security status.

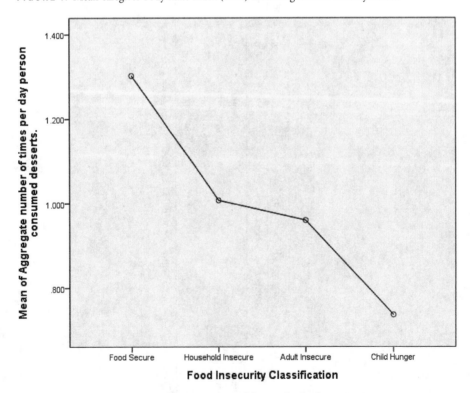

FIGURE 2. Caregiver frequency of consumption of desserts by food security status.

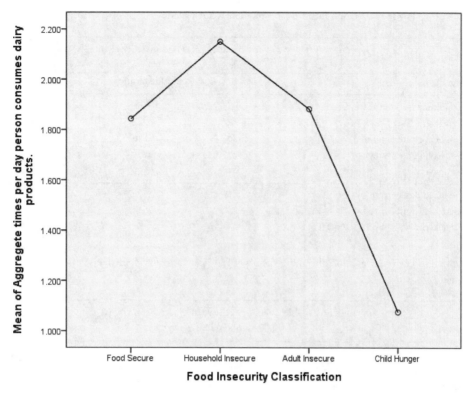

FIGURE 3. Caregiver frequency of consumption of dairy products by food security status.

is only statistically significant when comparing caregivers from food secure households with those from child hungry households ($p = .027$). Other FFQ data show a lower frequency of consumption for dairy products ($p = .016$), fruits ($p = .018$), and animal protein (i.e., meat, fish, and eggs; $p = .012$) as food security worsens especially in child hungry households.

Multivariate Findings: Predictors of Food Security Status

The multivariate findings are presented in Tables 4 and 5 and only include those cases in which there were no missing data ($N = 108$ and $N = 102$, respectively). A forward conditional stepwise logistic regression was used to determine if food insecurity could be predicted using household sociodemographic data, caregiver and child anthropometry, and caregiver frequency of food consumption. Since food security is coded as zero and food insecurity is coded as one, negative beta values (slope of the relationship) are associated with an inverse relationship with food insecurity and positive beta values are associated with a positive relationship with food insecurity. The model shows that the limited availability of condiments—again, a relatively expensive item—(odds ratio = 0.36), higher caregiver BMI (odds ratio = 1.32), not having a working microwave (odds ratio = 4.38), not being a member of a local food cooperative (odds ratio = 4.86), and not having a working stove (odds ratio = 6.28) predict food insecurity. The model predicted 81.5 percent of the cases correctly (see Himmelgreen et al. 2006).

TABLE 4. Logistic Regression for Predictors of Food Security Status

	Dependent Variable = Food Security (0), Food Insecurity (1) Total Sample, $n = 108$		
Variables	B	Odds Ratio	Significance
Condiments added at the table	− 1.013	.363	.000
Caregiver's BMI	.295	1.342	.000
Not being a member of a coop	1.580	4.856	.023
Not having a working stove	1.837	6.275	.007
Not having a working microwave	1.476	4.377	.020

Predicted 81.5 percent of cases:
Model chi-square = 43.114, $p = .000$.
Nagelkerke $R^2 = 0.487$.

TABLE 5. Logistic Regression of Food Predictors of Food Insecurity for Households in Both Communities

	Dependent Variable = Food Security (0), Food Insecurity (1) Total Sample, $n = 102$		
Variables	B	Odds Ratio	Significance
Aggregate per day consumption of legumes	− 0.157	0.855	.038
Aggregate per day consumption of carbohydrates	0.386	1.471	.017
Aggregate per day consumption of desserts and condiments	− 0.449	0.638	.001
Aggregate per day consumption of milk products	0.321	1.379	.127

Predicted 80.4% of cases:
Model chi-square = 23.290, $p = .000$.
Nagelkerke $R^2 = 0.304$.
Model was better at predicting food insecure (94.8%).

Data from a FFQ was collapsed into general food categories where the units represent servings per day. It is important to note that this does not reflect caloric intake in any way. It is, however, a way to try to determine if households that are food insecure are eating different types of foods more or less frequently. A forward conditional stepwise logistic regression was used to determine if food insecurity could be predicted based on daily consumption of servings of the different food categories. Because some observations had missing data, they had to be excluded from this analysis; the resulting subsample of usable observations was 102. The results show that decreased consumption of legumes and desserts and increased consumption of carbohydrates and dairy products predicts food insecurity. The finding regarding dairy consumption makes sense given that many less well-off households in the study produced their own dairy products. Although dairy consumption by itself only approached significance, it was added to the model because it significantly increased the model's overall accuracy; the model predicted 80.4 percent of the cases correctly. What the model suggests is that different patterns of food consumption predict food security and food insecurity.

Many countries in Latin America are increasingly relying on tourism to generate foreign capital to spur economic development (Leatherman and Goodman 2005). And there have been a number of studies that have focused on the impact of tourism on lifestyle and health among residents in such communities (Anderson-Fye 2004; Daltabuit and Leatherman 1998; Gurri et al. 2001; Himmelgreen et al. 2006; Leatherman and Goodman 2005; Whiteford 1992). In particular, Leatherman and coworkers have spent more than 20 years studying Mayan communities in the Yucatan looking at the impact of tourism-led social, economic, and cultural change on nutrition, and on other indicators of well-being (Leatherman and Goodman 2005). Some studies have shown that as income and economic resources have increased, diets have become more diverse and have improved over time (Daltabuit and Leatherman 1998; Leatherman and Goodman 2005). Others have reported significant declines in agricultural output and in the availability of locally produced food, which have been translated into in diminished dietary diversity, poorer nutritional status, and poorer health. The emphasis on tourism has resulted in dietary delocalization, whereby local communities rely more on imported foods as local production diminished through time (Leatherman and Goodman 2005). Daltabuit (1988) has documented this phenomenon in the Yucatan where there was a shift away from locally produced foods, such as honey, tubers, and wild meat, toward commercially produced rice, pasta, and government subsidized staples (e.g., rice, beans, and pasta). Himmelgreen et al. (2006) reported a similar trend in the Monteverde zone where there was an increased reliance on processed foods, including condiments, such as ketchup and packaged salsa.

The results presented here show that about 50 percent of households are involved in the tourism economy. With the rapid increase of tourism in the global economy, residents, such as those in Monteverde, find ample employment opportunities within this field. The need to contribute to the family's economic security motivates many individuals to seek jobs in this high employment arena (Elijah-Mensah 2009; Ladkin 2011; Veijola 2009). Furthermore, many households are engaged in a mixed economy where income is derived from tourism and agriculture. Inadequate transportation, poor roads, being off the beaten track, and nonparticipation in food cooperatives pose potential barriers in terms of achieving food security. The data also show high rates of caregiver and child overweight and obesity and a diet that varies according to food security status. For example, there is a lower daily frequency consumption of vegetables, dairy, animal protein, and desserts with worsening food insecurity, especially when looking at child hungry households. On one hand, predictors of food insecurity included lower frequency of consumption of legumes and desserts, which might be explained by limited availability and high cost. On the other hand, higher consumption of carbohydrates and dairy also predict food insecurity. As expected, carbohydrates are widely available in the zone and are inexpensive (some are government subsidized). Although the price of dairy products is increasing, they are readily available and there are still a significant number of households in the zone that produce milk and make cheese. Therefore, the consumption of these foods might reflect an adaptive strategy to stretch food money as far as possible.

As documented in the literature, the high rates of overweight and obesity along with the consumption of a carbohydrate-dense diet have important implications for the development of chronic diseases, such as hypertension and type 2 diabetes (Hu et al. 2001). Personal conversations with medical staff at one of the major health clinics in the area indicate that, indeed, these problems are on the rise, and pose major concerns for the future well-being of adults and children in the zone (personal communication, 2011). According to the most current health report from Monteverde (Acevedo and Mario 2010), the highest incidence of chronic diseases in the area is represented by hypertension, asthma, and diabetes, all of which are most commonly found among obese and overweight individuals. Moreover, the report describes the typical diet as very high in fat and carbohydrates, which contribute to the rising rates of obesity. In response to this situation, local health and community organizations are developing initiatives, such as nutrition education activities and weight loss programs for obese individuals, in efforts to combat chronic disease in the area (Acevedo and Mario 2010).

Syndemics Theory provides an appropriate framework to interpret these results in the context of the rapidly changing economy of the Monteverde zone. With increased reliance on the tourism industry, there has been a movement away from local food production, which once was the main source of subsistence and income generation for both households and communities. The decrease in locally produced crops has resulted in the need to bring food into the area from other parts of the country and elsewhere, increasing cost, which in turn affects the ability of households to access foods of enough quantity and quality. In addition, while economically favorable, involvement in the tourism industry is highly seasonal and sporadic, thus, making the financial well-being of tourism-dependent households fluctuate considerably through the year (Acevedo and Mario 2010). Our previous research demonstrates that households that are solely—or mainly—involved in tourism have higher overall rates of food insecurity than those with mixed economic strategies or who rely solely on agriculture (Himmelgreen et al. 2006). To make matters worse, since local businesses cater to tourists, who have more economic resources, the price of food in the zone is very high when compared to other areas of the country with fewer tourists. This price inflation affects the food security of households throughout the year, and especially during the low-tourism season when jobs are drastically reduced while the cost of living remains high (Himmelgreen et al. 2006). Taken together, these factors increase the risk for food insecurity for individuals and households, as described in this article. In an effort to deal with food insecurity, households increase their consumption of less expensive carbohydrate-laded, such as pasta, rice, and white bread. While these food staples provide enough energy, they have limited nutritional value, especially in terms of micronutrients, vitamins, and proteins. In addition, overconsumption of foods high in sugars and carbohydrates often leads to overweight and obesity (as reported in this article), which in turn increase the risk for hypertension and type 2 diabetes. Anecdotal evidence provided by local medical personnel indicates that these two medical problems are on the rise in the Monteverde zone. While the effects of food insecurity on physical health have been extensively documented, equally important is the impact such condition has on mental health and well-being (Stuff et al. 2004; Weaver and Hadley 2009). Studies currently being conducted by our research group examine the association between food insecurity and anxiety and depression, with preliminary findings pointing to a positive association among the two. Therefore, as demonstrated here, Syndemics Theory is appropriate for understanding how multiple health-related issues interact and amplify each other, which over time will change the health profile and health care needs in the Monteverde zone.

The results of this study point to the need for the development of multidimensional public health interventions that couple individual behavior change and education with community-driven efforts that reduce economic insecurity and increase food security. Involvement with local communities and stakeholders can result in tangible solutions, such as the reestablishment of local food cooperatives that provide a safety net for participating households, as well as the creation of initiatives such as shared gardens in settings such as community centers and schools. Such efforts can improve access to nutritionally rich locally produced foods, which will result in more balanced diets and a reduction in overweight and obesity among adults and children. Importantly, our conversations with residents of the Monteverde zone indicate that such efforts can also contribute to the social well-being of local communities, by fostering social interaction, and the transmission of agricultural based knowledge from one generation to the next. Based on the results of our longitudinal studies, our local partners are already undertaking some of these initiatives, along with efforts to increase physical activity (which is surprisingly low among youth) among residents of the Monteverde zone. Future programming led by local stakeholders will also address the creation of income-generating initiatives that increase economic security for individuals and households, thus, addressing some of the main contributors to food insecurity and the resulting ill health in the Monteverde zone.

REFERENCES CITED

Alvarado, Alfredo, Frank J. Smith, and T. Jot Smith
   1998 Baseline Study of Land Use Management and Decision Making Processes With a Focus on Non-Traditional Crops, Small Farmers, Agro-Industry, and Development Policy in Costa Rica. Collaborative Research Support Program, U.S. Agency for International Development. http://intdss.soil.ncsu.edu/download/documents/CRica_Baseline.pdf, accessed May 24, 2012.
Anderson-Fye, Eileen P.
   2004 A "Coca-Cola" Shape: Cultural Change, Body Image, and Eating Disorders in San Andres, Belize. Culture, Medicine, and Psychiatry 28(4):561–595.
Anema, Aranka, Sheri D. Weiser, Kimberly A. Fernandes, Erin Ding, Eirikka K. Brandson, Alexis Palmer, Julio S.G. Montaner, and Robert S. Hogg
   2011 High Prevalence of Food Insecurity Among HIV-Infected Individuals Receiving HAART in a Resource-Rich Setting. AIDS Care 23(2):221–230.
Centers for Disease Control and Prevention (CDC)
   2011a About BMI for Adults. http://www.cdc.gov/healthyweight/assessing/bmi/adult_bmi/index.html, accessed by May 24, 2012.

2011b About BMI for Children and Teens. http://www.cdc.gov/healthyweight/assessing/bmi/childrens_bmi/about.html, accessed by May 24, 2012.

Daltabuit, Magalí D.
1988 Ecologia Humana en una Comunidad de Morelos. Mexico, DF: Universidad Nacional Autonoma de Mexico.

Daltabuit, Magalí and Thomas L. Leatherman
1998 The Biocultural Impact of Tourism on Mayan Communities. *In* Building a New Biocultural Synthesis: Political-economic Perspectives on Human Biology. Alan H. Goodman and Thomas L. Leatherman, eds. Pp. 317–338. Ann Arbor, MI: University of Michigan Press.

Dinour, Lauren M., Dara Bergen, and Ming-Chin Yeh
2007 The Food Insecurity-Obesity Paradox: A Review of the Literature and the Role Food Stamps May Play. Journal of the American Dietetic Association 107(11):1952–1961.

Elijah-Mensah, Angela
2009 Motivation and Age: An Empirical Study of Women-Owners of Tourism Ventures in Ghana. Journal of Travel and Tourism Research 9(2):139–153.

Evans, Sterling
1999 The Green Republic: A Conservation History of Costa Rica. Austin, TX: University of Texas Press.

Frongillo, Edward A., Jr., Barbara S. Rauschenbach, Christine M. Olson, Anne Kendall, and Ana G. Colmenares
1997 Questionnaire-Based Measures are Valid for the Identification of Rural Households with Hunger and Food Insecurity. Journal of Nutrition 127(5):669–705.

Garrow, John S., and Joan D., Webster
1985 Quetelet's Index (W/H2) as a Measure of Fatness. International Journal of Obesity 9(2):147–153.

Gurri, Francisco D., Gilberto Balam Pereira, and Emilio F. Moran
2001 Well-Being Changes in Response to 30 Years of Regional Integration in Maya Populations from Yucatan, Mexico. American Journal of Human Biology 13(5):590–602.

Hanson, Karla L., Jeffery Sobal, and Edward A. Frongillo
2007 Gender and Marital Status Clarify Associations Between Food Insecurity and Body Weight. The Journal of Nutrition 137(6):1460–1465.

Heflin, Colleen M., Kristine Siefert, and David R. Williams
2006 Food Insufficiency and Women's Mental Health: Findings From a 3-year panel of Welfare Recipients. Social Science & Medicine 61(9):1971–1982.

Himmelgreen, David A., Rafael Pérez-Escamilla, Sofia Segura-Millán, Yu-Kuei Peng, Anir Gonzalez, Merrill Singer, and Ann Ferris
2000 Food Insecurity Among Low-Income Hispanics in Hartford, Connecticut: Implications for Public Health Policy. Human Organization 59(3):334–342.

Himmelgreen, David A., Rafael Pérez-Escamilla, Sofia Segura-Millán, Nancy Romero-Daza, Mihaela Tanasescu, and Merrill Singer
1998 A Comparison of the Nutritional Status and Food Security of Drug-Using and Non-Drug-Using Hispanic Women in Hartford, Connecticut. American Journal of Physical Anthropology 107(3): 351–361.

Himmelgreen, David A, Nancy Romero-Daza, David Turkon, Ipolto Okello-Uma, and Daniel Sellen
2009 Addressing the HIV/AIDS—Food Insecurity Syndemic in Sub-Saharan Africa. African Journal of AIDS Research 8(4):401–412.

Himmelgreen, David A, Nancy Romero-Daza, Maribel Vega, Humberto Brenes Cambronero, and Edgar Amador
2006 "The Tourist Season Goes Down but Not the Prices." Tourism and Food Insecurity in Rural Costa Rica. Ecology of Food and Nutrition 45(4):295–321.

Honey, Martha
1999 Ecotourism and Sustainable Development: Who Owns Paradise? Washington, DC: Island Press.

Hu, Frank B., JoAnn E. Manson, Meir J. Stampfer, Graham Colditz, Simin Liu, Caren G. Solomon, and Walter C. Willett

2001 Diet, Lifestyle, and the Risk of Type 2 Diabetes Mellitus in Women. The New England Journal of Medicine 345(11):790–797.

Instituto Costarricense de Turismo (ICT)

2009 Anuario Estadístico de Turismo [Annual Tourism Statistics]. San José, Costa Rica. http://unpan1.un.org/intradoc/groups/public/documents/icap/unpan044099.pdf, accessed November 26, 2012.

Jones, Chaunetta

2011 "If I Take My Pills I'll Go Hungry": The Choice Between Economic Security and HIV/AIDS Treatment in Grahamstown, South Africa. Annals of Anthropological Practice 35(1):67–80.

Kabagambe, Edmond K., Ana Baylin, Damon A. Allan, Xinia Siles, Donna Spiegelman, and Hannia Campos

2001 Application of the Method of Triads to Evaluate the Performance of Food Frequency Questionnaires and Biomarkers as Indicators of Long-Term Dietary Intake. American Journal of Epidemiology 154(12);1126–1135.

Kendall, Anne, Christine M. Olson, and Edward A. Frongillo, Jr.

1995 Validation of the Radimer/Cornell Hunger and Food Insecurity Measures. Journal of Nutrition 80(5):2793–2801.

1996 Relationship of Hunger and Food Security to Food Availability and Consumption. Journal of the American Dietetic Association 96(10):1019–1024.

Ladkin, Adele

2011 Exploring Tourism Labor. Annals of Tourism Research 38(3):1135–1155.

Leatherman, Thomas L., and Alan H. Goodman

2005 Coca-Colonization of Diets in the Yucatan. Social Science & Medicine 61(4):833–846.

Ledezma, Acevedo, and Oscar Mario

2010 Analisis de Situacion Integral en Salud [Comprehensive Health Situation Analysis]. Unpublished report. Monteverde, Costa Rica: Caja Costarricense de Seguro Social.

Martin, Katie S., and Ann M. Ferris

2007 Food Insecurity and Gender are Risk Factors for Obesity. Journal of Nutrition Education 39(1):31–36

Mei, Zuguo, Laurence M. Grummer-Strawn, Angelo Pietrobelli, Ailsa Goulding, Michael I. Goran, and William H. Dietz

2002 Validity of Body Mass Index Compared With Other Body-Composition Screening Index for the Assessment of Body Fatness in Children and Adolescents. American Journal of Clinical Nutrition 75(6): 978–985.

Monahan, Jane

2004 Unique Costa Rica Rainforest at Risk. BBC News World Edition. http://news.bbc.co.uk/2/hi/americas/4061833.stm, accessed May 24, 2012.

Nadkarni, Nalini M., and Nathaniel T. Wheelwright

2000 Monteverde: Ecology and Conservation of a Tropical Cloud Forest. New York: Oxford University Press.

Radimer, Kathy L., Christine M. Olson, and Cathy C. Campbell

1990 Development of Indicators to Assess Hunger. Journal of Nutrition 120(Suppl. 11):1544–1548.

Sellen, Daniel and Craig Hadley

2011 Food Insecurity and Maternal-to-Child Transmission of HIV and AIDS in Sub-Saharan Africa. Annals of Anthropological Practice 35(1):28–49.

Siefert, Kristine, Colleen M. Heflin, Mary E. Corcoran, and David R. Williams

2001 Food Insufficiency and the Physical and Mental Health of Low-Income Women. Women & Health 32(1–2):159–177.

Singer, Merrill

1996 A Dose of Drugs, A Touch of Violence, A Case of AIDS: Conceptualizing the SAVA Syndemic. Free Inquiry in Creative Sociology 24(2):99–110.

2009 Introduction to Syndemics: A Critical Systems Approach to Public and Community Health. San Francisco, CA: Jossey-Bass.

2011 Toward a Critical Biosocial Model of Ecohealth in Southern Africa: The HIV/AIDS and Nutrition Insecurity Syndemic. Annals of Anthropological Practice 35(1):8–27.

Singer, Merrill, and Scott Clair

2003 Syndemics and Public Health: Reconceptualizing Disease in Bio-Social Context. Medical Anthropology Quarterly 17(4):423–441.

Singer, Merrill, and Charlene Snipes

1992 Generations of Suffering: Experiences of a Treatment Program for Substance Abuse During Pregnancy. Journal of Health Care for the Poor and Underserved 3(1):222–234.

Stuff, Janice E., Patrick H. Casey, Kitty L. Szeto, Jeffery M. Gossett, James M. Robbins, Pippa M. Simpson, Carol Connell, and Margaret L. Bogle

2004 Household Food Insecurity is Associated With Adult Health Status. The Journal of Nutrition 134(9):2330–2335.

University of Georgia, Ecolodge San Luis, and Research Station

N.D. San Luis Community. http://www.externalaffairs.uga.edu/costa_rica/index.php/tourists/san_luis_community, accessed November 26, 2012.

Veijola, Soile

2009 Gender as Work in the Tourism Industry. Tourist Studies 9(2):109–126.

Vivanco, Luis A.

2006 Green Encounters: Shaping and Contesting Environmentalism in Rural Costa Rica. New York: Berghahn Books.

Weaver, Lesley Jo, and Craig Hadley

2009 Moving Beyond Hunger and Nutrition: A Systematic Review of the Evidence Linking Food Insecurity and Mental Health in Developing Countries. Ecology of Food and Nutrition 48(4):263–284.

Whitaker, Robert C., Shannon M. Phillips, and Sean Orzol

2006 Food Insecurity and the Risks of Depression and Anxiety in Mothers and Behavior Problems in their Preschool-Aged Children. Pediatrics 118(3):859–868.

Whiteford, Michael B.

1992 From Gallo Pinto to Jack's Snacks: Observations on Dietary Change in a Rural Costa Rican Village. Ecology of Food and Nutrition 27(3–4):207–218.

World Health Organization (WHO)

1995 World Health Report 1995: Bridging the Gaps. http://www.who.int/whr/1995/en/index.html, accessed November 26, 2012.

2006 BMI Classification. http://apps.who.int/bmi/index.jsp?introPage=into_3.html, accessed May 24, 2012.

EVIDENCE FOR A SYNDEMIC IN AGING HIV-POSITIVE GAY, BISEXUAL, AND OTHER MSM: IMPLICATIONS FOR A HOLISTIC APPROACH TO PREVENTION AND HEALTH CARE

Perry N. Halkitis
New York University

Sandra A. Kupprat
New York University

Melvin B. Hampton
New York University

Rafael Perez-Figueroa
New York University

Molly Kingdon
New York University

Jessica A. Eddy
New York University

Danielle C. Ompad
New York University

The theory of syndemics has been widely applied in HIV-prevention studies of gay, bisexual, and other MSM (men who have sex with men) over the last decade. Our investigation is the first to consider the applicability of the theory in a sample of aging (ages 50 and over) HIV-positive MSM, which is a growing population in the United States. A sample of 199 men were actively recruited and assessed in terms of mental health and drug-use burden, as well as sexual risk behaviors. Bivariate and multivariable analyses indicate a high level of association between psychosocial burdens (i.e., drug use and mental health) and same-sex unprotected sexual behaviors, providing initial support for the applicability of the theory of syndemics to this population. Further support can be seen in participants' narratives. Findings suggest the mutually reinforcing nature of drug use, psychiatric disorders, and unprotected sexual behavior in older, HIV-positive, gay, bisexual, and other MSM, highlighting the need for holistic strategies to prevention and care among this population of older and sexually active individuals. In short, the generation of gay men who came of age in the late 1970s and 1980s, "the AIDS Generation," are continuing to mature such that further efforts must be enacted to meet the multidimensional nature of these men's physical, mental, and sexual health needs. [HIV-positive men, gay, bisexual and other MSM, aging, syndemic, sexual risk-taking, drug use, mental health]

ANNALS OF ANTHROPOLOGICAL PRACTICE 36.2, pp. 365–386. ISSN: 2153-957X. © 2013 by the American Anthropological Association. DOI:10.1111/napa.12009

Current predictions in the United States indicate that by 2015 approximately 50 percent of persons living with HIV will be over 50 years old (Luther and Wilkin 2007). This represents a dramatic increase, given that in 2005 people age 50 and older represented approximately 24 percent of those living with HIV (Centers for Disease Control and Prevention [CDC] 2008). Furthermore, men who have sex with men (MSM) are disproportionally impacted by the HIV/AIDS epidemic. Although MSM represent 2–10 percent of the population in the United States, more than 50 percent of those living with HIV are MSM (CDC 2011). Evidence shows that the alarming trend of HIV rates among individuals age 50 and older is present even among, gay, bisexual, and other MSM (Luther and Wilkin 2007). These reasons underscore the need to study this population.

The increasing prevalence of HIV among older adults is due, in part, to improvements in antiretroviral therapies (ART), which have resulted in decreased morbidity and mortality among HIV-positive individuals (Manfredi 2004; Palella et al. 1998), as well as due to the reality that older individuals continue to seroconvert, including at age 50 and later (CDC 2011; Shah and Mildvan 2006). Thus, the population of aging HIV-positive gay, bisexual, and other MSM in the United States includes both long-term survivors, diagnosed prior to the advent of ART in 1996 (Palella et al. 1998, 2006), and more recent seroconverts diagnosed after 1996. Those infected and diagnosed before 1996, received treatment after years of ill health and of witnessing large numbers of friends or partners dying. This delineation between the experiences of long-term survivors and recent seroconverts is important due to the very different personal histories whose effects on physical health, mental health, substance use, and sexual behaviors remain understudied.

Although sexual activity may decrease with age, older adults continue to be sexually active well into the later decades of life (Lindau et al. 2007). Furthermore, although people may decrease their sexual risk-taking upon learning of an HIV-positive diagnosis (Marks et al. 2005), HIV-positive MSM continue to engage in sexual risk-taking and substance use after their seroconversion (Purcell et al. 2001; van Kesteren et al. 2007). For example, Lovejoy et al. (2008), in exploring the sexual-risk behaviors of HIV-positive individuals over 50, found that MSM reported more inconsistencies in their condom use than their heterosexual peers. Pappas and Halkitis (2011), studying club drugs use in a sample of HIV-positive MSM in New York City, found that men who had been living with HIV for a longer period of time were more likely to report seroconcordant unprotected anal intercourse (UAI). Further literature supports that HIV-positive MSM continue to engage in sexual risk-taking into older adulthood, with an HIV-positive serostatus being related to a greater likelihood of engaging in unprotected receptive and unprotected insertive anal intercourse (Jacobs et al. 2010).

Similar to sexual activity and unprotected sexual behaviors, in particular, the presence of substance abuse or dependence has been documented in the literature on aging HIV-positive MSM. Specifically, it is important to note that substance use may be related to HIV status, with HIV-positive individuals reporting increased rates of substance use as compared to HIV-negative individuals (Justice et al. 2004). In addition, in a recent investigation of HIV-positive gay and bisexual men in New York City, Pappas and Halkitis (2011) found that older participants reported different patterns of substance use and sexual-risk behaviors than younger participants. Overall drug use was prevalent across all age groups in this study. Furthermore, younger men in New York City were more likely to report unprotected sex with serodiscordant partners than older men in the sample.

Gay, bisexual, and other MSM, in general and across the lifespan, also demonstrate elevated rates of depression and other mental health problems (Cochran and Mays 2008; Mills et al. 2004). For aging HIV-positive gay, bisexual, and other MSM, these psychiatric conditions may be explained and exacerbated by the synergistic effects of stigma related to age and aging, sexual orientation, race/ethnicity, and HIV (David and Knight 2008; Diaz et al. 2001; Emlet 2006; Jerome and Halkitis 2009; Parker and Aggleton 2002).

Furthermore, the extant literature points to the presence of drug use and sexual risk-taking behaviors in conjunction with elevated mental health burdens among aging HIV-positive MSM (Halkitis 2010). These findings support the importance of exploring the impact and interplay of HIV, sexual risk-taking, substance use, and mental health in MSM over 50 in the United States as informed by a model of syndemics. Such a holistic understanding of health disparities aligns with the recommendations of the Institute of Medicine (2011) to reduce the health disparities faced by the LGBT population.

Syndemics theory, as initially proposed by Merrill Singer (1994, 1996), and later extended to gay men by Singer (2006) and Stall et al. (2008), holds that within certain communities there exists a dynamic and complicated synergy between multiple epidemics and endemics that decrease the overall health and well-being of both entire communities as well as of individual people. Thus far, syndemics theory, as it has been applied and extended within the fields of public health and psychology, has only focused on younger (Mustanski et al. 2007; Storholm et al. 2011) or middle-aged MSM (Moeller et al. 2011; Stall et al. 2003). However, given the above noted literature and epidemiological evidence in support of overlapping and reinforcing health problems among older HIV-positive individuals, especially among older gay, bisexual, and other MSM, we believe that syndemics theory has the potential to frame the complicated interplay of multiple epidemics and endemics over the entire course of an individual's life.

In line with this, the overarching goal of our analyses for this article was to examine the extent to which a theory of syndemics is applicable to explaining unprotected sexual behaviors in HIV-positive gay, bisexual, and other MSM ages 50 and over. Specifically, we aimed (1) to describe the current drug use and mental health burdens among 199 HIV-positive gay, bisexual, and other MSM ages 50 and over; (2) to determine the association between these current psychosocial burdens; (3) to examine the combined effects of the current psychosocial burdens in explaining unprotected sexual behavior; (4) to delineate the individual burdens that most contribute to our explanation of unprotected sexual behaviors; and (5) to discuss the prevention/intervention implications of our findings.

METHODS

Study Design

Data for this study, locally named Project GOLD, were collected in two phases: (1) from May 2010 through August 2010 and (2) March 2011 through August 2011. Trained researchers recruited 200 HIV-positive gay, bisexual, and other MSM (100 men in each phase), who were aged 50 and older, through a variety of in-person and online outreach methods. Using a targeted sampling strategy, we oversampled MSM of color, given the prevalence of HIV in this segment of the population (CDC 2011).

Eligible participants were required to (1) be 50 years or older, (2) be HIV-positive, (3) be born biologically male, (4) still identify as male, and (5) have had sex with a man in the past six months. Sex was defined as any physical contact that could lead to an orgasm, not including cyber or phone sex. Of the 200 men assessed, 199 were included in the final analytic sample. One participant's data were expunged because he did not have sex with men, making him ineligible for the study, despite information provided in his screener materials. Additionally, standard data cleaning procedures were implemented to ensure data integrity in the study.

Our recruitment efforts included partnering with local community-based organizations. These collaborative outreach efforts and activities included presenting the goals of the study to agency staff and distributing study flyers/palm cards to potential participants. Palm cards were also utilized to recruit participants in gay neighborhoods, clubs, bars, gay pride, organizational fundraisers, and other events/venues that attracted older gay male community members. Lastly, online recruitment efforts included placing ads on online dating and sex websites, as well as on popular online posting databases.

After completing an initial phone screening, eligible participants were scheduled for a three-hour survey and interview at our research center in downtown Manhattan. All interviewers were trained in human subjects' protocols, with firm confidentiality requirements to ensure participants' privacy. Researchers read the consent form aloud to all participants to ensure understanding, regardless of reading ability. Once written consent was obtained, the interviewer commenced survey administration. Taking part in the survey involved minimal risks and every step was taken to minimize the discomfort participants may have felt in answering questions. A total of 262 men were screened in phase 1 and an additional 247 men were screened in phase 2. In terms of the final analytic sample of 199 men, the majority of the sample was recruited through active methods: 30 percent ($n = 59$) from efforts at community-based agencies, 22 percent ($n = 44$) from Internet-based recruitment, and 12 percent ($n = 24$) from the distribution of palm cards and other advertisements. An additional 32 percent ($n = 64$) entered the study via referral from a friend.

Participants in phase 1 completed a computer administered survey and a Timeline Followback (TLFB; Sobell and Sobell 1996). In addition, phase 1 participants were engaged in an in-depth discovery interview. Phase 2 participants completed the survey, a TLFB, and underwent testing for oral, penile, and rectal gonorrhea, as well as penile and rectal Chlamydia.

The computer survey utilized *Audio Computer Assisted Self-Interview* (ACASI) software, which allows participants to listen to questions read aloud through headphones. Using *ACASI* has been found to eliminate the effects that low literacy rates have on internal validity and can be used with people from diverse ethnic backgrounds (Gribble et al. 1999). The TLFB was researcher-administered. The protocol was approved by the IRB of New York University and included written consent from all participants. Participants received a $50 incentive for their participation in the study.

MEASURES

Quantitative Survey

This cross-sectional assessment gathered information pertaining to a range of personal factors, mental health burdens, substance use behaviors, and unprotected sexual behaviors.

Personal factors

Sociodemographic data included information on age, race/ethnicity (black, white, Latino, and other), sexual orientation (gay/homosexual, bisexual, straight/heterosexual, and other), and year of HIV diagnosis. Employment status was based on participants' reports of whether they were currently working full-time, part-time, or not working. Furthermore, participants were asked to indicate their level of educational attainment (less than high school, high school graduate/graduate equivalency diploma (GED), associate's degree, bachelor's degree, or graduate degree).

Mental health burdens

Posttraumatic stress disorder (PTSD) was assessed using the Trauma Awareness and Treatment Center (TATC) scale, which is informed by the PCL-C (Weathers et al. 1993; Weathers and Ford 1996). This measure uses ten Likert-type items to assess participants' levels of PTSD symptomatology. Typical items examine how often in the last week an individual has experienced upsetting memories or flashbacks, avoided specific places or things, or had upsetting thoughts associated with a trauma. Answer options for frequency ranged from 0 "Not all " through 5 "Extremely." Summed scores of the ten items were calculated and the measure demonstrated high internal consistency ($\alpha = .94$). Scores were dichotomized as having symptoms of PTSD (≥ 6) or not having symptoms of PTSD (< 6 or no trauma history). Levels of depression in the past two weeks were assessed using the Beck Depression Inventory-Version II (BDI; Beck et al. 1988), which consists of 21 Likert-type items. Items assess for indicators of depression including experiences of loss of pleasure, feelings of worthlessness, and experiences of loss of energy. Answer options ranged from 0 "None" through 3 "Very much." This measure has been shown to have high internal consistency and test–retest reliability, as well as convergent and construct validity (Beck et al. 1988). In our study, sum scores of the 21 items were calculated and the measure demonstrated high internal consistency ($\alpha = .93$). Scores were dichotomized as depressed (≥ 16) and not depressed (< 16). Cut scores for this measure reflect the mean cut scores from multiple studies (Sherr et al. 2011).

Substance use behaviors

With the assistance of the interviewer, participants completed a 30-day calendar of their alcohol and illicit drug use using the TLFB method (Sobell and Sobell 1996), which has been noted as a highly effective method for capturing reliable drug-use behavior data (Halkitis et al. 2009). We assessed the number of days of use for alcohol to intoxication, marijuana, inhalant nitrates (poppers), powder cocaine, crack cocaine, ecstasy, gamma-hydroxybutyric acid (GHB), ketamine, heroin, methamphetamine, and rohypnol. For analytic purposes, the days of use were recoded to create the following dichotomous variables of drug use in the period of assessment: alcohol until intoxication, marijuana, inhalant nitrates (poppers), and all other illicit drugs.

Unprotected sexual behaviors

Utilizing the same TLFB method noted above (Sobell and Sobell 1996), participants completed a 30-day calendar of their sexual behaviors prior to the day of assessment. This is a recommended method for capturing data on sexual risk behaviors (Parsons et al. 2005). Data were collected on the number of episodes of unprotected insertive and receptive anal intercourse with HIV-positive, as well as HIV-negative or status-unknown men. For analytic purposes, the following dichotomous variables of sexual risk were created: unprotected insertive anal intercourse with HIV-positive men, unprotected insertive anal intercourse with HIV-negative/status-unknown men, unprotected receptive anal intercourse with HIV-positive men, and unprotected receptive anal intercourse with HIV-negative/status-unknown men. In addition, two more variables, any UAI with HIV-positive men and any UAI with HIV-negative/status-unknown men, were calculated.

Discovery-Based Interview

The discovery-based interview was guided by *The Listening Guide Method of Psychological Inquiry*, which enabled researchers to explore the psychological logic of participants (Gilligan et al. 2003). This method stresses the importance of understanding a person's conception of the world and requires careful attention to be paid to the cultural and relational aspects of a person's experience. To adhere to the tenets of the Listening Guide methodology, the interview protocol comprised broad-based domains rather than individual questions so as to mimic the flexibility of a natural conversation or inquiry, rather than a regimented structural interview. The domains explored in the interviews included the relational, physical, and psychosocial aspects of living with HIV as a man age 50 and older. Interview lengths ranged from 30 minutes to 1 hour and were captured using a digital recorder. The interviews were then transcribed and reviewed for quality assurance purposes. Quotes from these interviews have been included in this manuscript to both contextualize the study findings and give voice to a population that is seldom heard in the discourse on HIV in the United States.

Analytic Plan

We undertook a descriptive analysis of our sample characteristics. Then we created dichotomous variables for each of the six current psychosocial burdens, which we defined as usage in the previous 30 days of four drug-related categories (alcohol to intoxication, marijuana, inhalant nitrates, and other illicit drugs), as well as two mental health burdens, depression and PTSD. The depression and PTSD dichotomies were based on the cut scores determined in the literature. Levels of association, in the form of unadjusted odd ratios, were subsequently calculated for these six psychosocial burden variables. At this point, a total current psychosocial burden score was computed via summation of these variables. We then assessed burden score associations with participants' demographic characteristics using ANOVA, as well as in relation to each of the six UAI variables (any unprotected anal, insertive anal, or receptive anal intercourse with an HIV-positive partner, and any unprotected anal, insertive anal, or receptive anal intercourse with an HIV-negative/status-unknown partner in the 30 days prior to assessment) using both odds ratios (ORs) and Spearman rank correlations. Binary logistic regression models were then constructed to assess the extent to which total current psychosocial burden scores explained the likelihood of engaging in any UAI with an HIV-positive partner or any UAI with an HIV-negative/status-unknown partner, while controlling for the potentially confounding effects of age, years living with HIV, and race/ethnicity. Finally, each individual psychosocial burden was then assessed in relation to these two unprotected sexual risk behaviors to determine the unadjusted impact of each burden on UAI. Throughout the reporting of our results, data were drawn from the qualitative interviews described above in order to clarify and contextualize our quantitative findings.

RESULTS

Sample

The mean age of the 199 participants was 55.49 (SD = 4.54, Md = 55, range 50–69), and participants had been living with HIV an average of 18.14 years (SD = 6.31, Md = 20, range 1–27), first becoming aware of their HIV status on average in 1992, when they were in their 30s. The introduction of highly active ART in 1996 was a turning point in the HIV epidemic, which led to decreases in AIDS mortality (Palella et al. 1998, 2006). Therefore, we dichotomized the sample based upon this historical cutoff. Those diagnosed before 1996 comprised 70 percent (n = 140) of the sample. Moreover, 44 percent (n = 67) of our sample was diagnosed as seropositive in the first decade of the epidemic in the 1980s. Participants were racially and ethnically diverse with 76 percent (n = 150) of the men being men of color. Regarding sexual orientation, approximately 75 percent (n = 149) of the sample was gay-identified. Educational attainment in our sample varied, with 47 percent having a high school education or less and 53 percent having an associate's degree or higher. A majority of the men, 77 percent (n = 153), were not currently working. Of those not working, reasons for nonwork varied: 35 percent (n = 53) were either looking for work or unable to find work, 13 percent (n = 20) were retired, 46 percent (n = 70) were on disability, and 2 percent (n = 3) were enrolled in school full-time. Participant characteristics are shown in Table 1. Significant differences in educational attainment based on race/ethnicity were detected ($\chi^2(12) = 26.18$, $p = .01$), as were differences in employment status by race/ethnicity ($\chi^2 (6) = 15.86$, $p < .05$). In particular, white men (65 percent, n = 30) in our sample were less likely to

TABLE 1. Demographic Characteristics of HIV-Positive MSM Ages 50 and Older, New York City 2010–11, $N = 199$

	% (n)
Race	
Black	47.4 (93)
White	23.5 (46)
Latino	14.3 (28)
Mixed race/other	14.6 (29)
Missing	1.5 (3)
Sexual orientation	
Gay/homosexual	74.9 (149)
Bisexual	18.1 (36)
Straight/heterosexual	2.0 (4)
Other	5.0 (10)
Date of diagnosis	
Pre-HAART (prior to 1996)	70.4 (140)
Post-HAART (1996 or later)	29.6 (59)
Education	
Less than HS	11.6 (23)
High School/GED	35.7 (71)
Associate's degree	18.6 (37)
Bachelor's degree or higher	23.6 (47)
Graduate degree	10.6 (21)
Employment status	
Employed full-time	9.0 (18)
Employed part-time	14.1 (28)
Not currently working	76.9 (153)

report not currently working than black (74 percent, $n = 69$) or Latino (93 percent, $n = 26$) men. Black (31 percent, $n = 29$) and Latino (21 percent, $n = 6$) men were less likely to have a bachelor's degree or higher than their white counterparts (54 percent, $n = 25$).

Current Psychosocial Burdens

Approximately one-fifth of the men reported symptoms consistent with both PTSD and depression. Furthermore, although 13 percent ($n = 25$) of the men reported drinking to intoxication in the month prior to assessment, marijuana was the substance that participants most frequently reported using (38 percent, $n = 75$). In addition, 14 percent ($n = 27$) reported using inhalant nitrates (poppers) and 26 percent ($n = 52$) reported using any other illicit drugs. The rates of occurrence of the psychosocial burdens in our sample are further described in Table 2.

Table 3 provides a summary of the unadjusted ORs for the associations across six psychosocial burdens. The data indicate a high level of association between the drug-use variables, in particular between alcohol to intoxication, marijuana (OR = 2.85, 95 percent CI = 1.21, 6.73), and other illicit drugs (OR = 4.56, 95 percent CI = 1.91, 10.85) in the previous 30 days. Similarly, recent use of marijuana and other illicit drugs in the previous

TABLE 2. Psychosocial Burdens and Unprotected Anal Intercourse Among MSM Ages 50 and Older, New York City 2010–11, $N = 199$

	% (n)
Current mental health burden	
Depression	20.1 (40)
PTSD	20.6 (41)
Drug-use burden, past 30 days	
Alcohol to intoxication	12.6 (25)
Inhalant nitrates (poppers)	13.6 (27)
Marijuana	37.7 (75)
Other drugs[a]	26.1 (52)
Unprotected sex, past 30 days	
HIV-positive partners	
Unprotected anal insertive	12.6 (25)
Unprotected anal receptive	13.1 (26)
Any unprotected anal	19.6 (39)
HIV-negative or status-unknown partners	
Unprotected anal insertive	6.0 (12)
Unprotected anal receptive	8.0 (16)
Any unprotected anal	10.1 (20)

[a]Other drugs include club drugs, cocaine, crack, heroin, and methamphetamine.

30 days were found to be associated (OR $= 3.46$, 95 percent CI $= 1.79$, 6.67). A very high level of association was further found between recent depression and PSTD symptoms (OR $= 9.01$, 95 percent CI $= 4.10$, 19.76).

A total current psychosocial burden score was created by adding the drug-use and mental health variables, suggesting a theoretical range from 0 to 6. Among the 199 participants, the mean psychosocial burden score was computed at 1.31 (SD $= 1.15$, Md $= 1$, range 0–5). Although the number of years a participant had been living with HIV and his age were significantly related ($r = .16$, $p < .05$), the total psychosocial burden score was only related to age ($r = -.20$, $p < .01$). This relation was negative, indicating that older participants would be assumed to have lower total psychosocial burden scores than younger participants. In addition, differences in the total current psychosocial burden score emerged in relation to race/ethnicity ($F (3, 192) = 3.65$, $p = .01$). Post hoc analyses indicated that black men in our sample had higher total burden scores than Latino men (1.45 vs. 0.96, $p < .05$) and white men (1.45 vs. 1.00, $p < .05$). Similarly, participants who indicated that their race/ethnicity was mixed/other reported higher burden scores than both Latino (1.69 vs. 0.96, $p < .05$) and white men in our study (1.72 vs. 1.00, $p = .01$).

From a qualitative perspective, the men described their experiences of these burdens in ways that lend support to our quantitative findings. For example, one participant articulates his experience with substance use in this statement:

> I've had a lot of bad experiences. Yeah, I'm still frightened. People still scare me. I done put down a lot of my old ways, but I haven't put down the lifestyle . . . Cause certain things

TABLE 3. Association (OR, 95% CI) Between Psychosocial Burdens and Unprotected Anal Intercourse among MSM Ages 50 and Older, New York City 2010–11, $N = 199$

	(1) Alcohol to Intoxication	(2) Inhalant Nitrates	(3) Marijuana	(4) Other Illicit Drugs	(5) Depression	(6) PTSD	(7) Any UAI HIV+ Partners	(8) Any UAI HIV−/ UNK Partners
1		1.73	2.85**	4.56***	1.30	0.71	3.33**	3.61**
		(0.59, 5.07)	(1.21, 6.73)	(1.91, 10.85)	(0.48, 3.50)	(0.23, 2.18)	(1.36, 8.15)	(1.24, 10.50)
2			1.65	0.99	0.46	0.44	1.92	7.32***
			(0.73, 3.73)	(0.39, 2.49)	(0.13, 1.60)	(0.13, 1.54)	(0.77, 4.77)	(2.67, 20.03)
3				3.46***	0.99	0.46	1.76	1.40
				(1.79, 6.67)	(0.48, 2.03)	(0.21, 1.01)	(0.87, 3.57)	(0.55, 3.56)
4					1.28	1.05	2.40*	2.05
					(0.59, 2.74)	(0.48, 2.28)	(1.15, 5.01)	(0.78, 5.33)
5						9.01***	0.39	0.68
						(4.10, 19.76)	(0.13, 1.18)	(0.19, 2.44)
6							1.20	0.40
							(0.52, 2.78)	(0.90, 1.79)

$^*p \leq .05;\ ^{**}p \leq .01;\ ^{***}p \leq .001.$

still excite me. X-rated tapes excite me . . . Drugs still excite me and I wish it wasn't that way . . . Everything don't change overnight. It took me 22 years to get this addiction, it took me 8 years to get well. I done had the virus 8 years. But, I didn't just get it over night. It built up. It built up. See what I'm saying? So, I have to get my force up. You know, my tools . . . To fight my addiction as well as my HIV and it's not easy. [Black, age 57, living with HIV 8 years]

The burden created by illicit drug use can further be seen in these men's lives when one participant stated:

I was smoking $600 a day. That's my minimum, 600 . . . Yes, crack cocaine. Right now, to tell you the truth, crystal meth costs more than crack. Cause for $120 you only get this, this amount. $120 in crack will get you something bigger . . . I'm not real proud of my drug use. It cost me a lot. Cost me my family. I am distanced from my family. [Black, age 57, living with HIV 8 years]

Another participant spoke about how his social environment at work influenced/reinforced his drug use, impacting his entire life:

I was working for [a fashion magazine] . . . my clients were just all high end, whether it was editorial or commercial, they were high-end people. I woke up one day and realized that I had done cocaine every day for two years. Because of being involved with all these different people. And that wasn't a good thing, and I needed to stop. Because it wasn't really being fun anymore, although I never felt like I was addicted. It was more like I was expected. [White, age 57, living with HIV 25 years]

Furthermore, a participant described his experiences with multiple psychosocial burdens in his life, including his HIV status, when he said:

> It was just five years of denial, and denying everything. It was not a good time to be HIV-positive. Even the gay community was not very kind. I didn't want to tell them [parents] because, um . . . . When I was, well, there's another traumatic event I—I totally left out—when I was 19, my brother died, he was hit by a car. Ugh, that was terrible. I didn't want them [parents] to have to go through that again, so, I didn't want to tell them. I didn't want to do anything about it but drink and drugs. [White, age 53, living with HIV 23 years]

While other participant described how after being diagnosed with HIV his cocaine use led to a dramatic shift in his life.

> I had three cars and it's just it, was just crazy, I had a nice place out in Queens and there was a very lovely life for a minute. But then as the stress came in and I was losing money. That's when more cocaine came in, snorting cocaine. I needed to work long hours so I used the excuse that I needed cocaine just to keep me up. And then finally it just all crumbled and lost it and that kind of shifted my mind, it just shifted me. I was such a go-getter and then I was kind of happy being homeless and I always say I was happy being homeless cause I had no responsibilities. [Latino, age 52, living with HIV 12 years]

Unprotected Sexual Behavior

In our exploration of unprotected insertive and receptive anal intercourse, we distinguished between unprotected sexual behaviors with seroconcordant (HIV-positive) and serodiscordant (HIV-negative or status-unknown) men. The percentage of men in our study who engaged in UAI ranged from 6 percent ($n = 12$) for unprotected insertive anal intercourse with an HIV-negative/status-unknown partner to 13 percent ($n = 26$) for unprotected receptive anal intercourse with an HIV-positive partner. Table 2 summarizes these results. We found a significant association between the likelihood of engaging in unprotected insertive and unprotected receptive anal intercourse with an HIV-positive partner (OR = 10.55, 95 percent CI = 4.06, 27.44). Specifically, 48 percent ($n = 12$) of the men who engaged in unprotected insertive anal intercourse also reported engaging in receptive intercourse with a seroconcordant partner. The same pattern emerged when we examined UAI with an HIV-negative/status-unknown partner (OR = 44.75, 95 percent CI = 11.11, 180.32). In particular, 67 percent ($n = 8$) of those who engaged in unprotected insertive anal intercourse engaged in unprotected receptive behaviors with a serodiscordant partners. Given these associations, we created a new variable for both HIV-positive and HIV-negative/status-unknown partners, titled "any unprotected anal intercourse." We then test the association of this variable with the total current psychosocial burden. Accordingly, 20 percent ($n = 39$) of our sample reported UAI with an HIV-positive partner and 10 percent ($n = 20$) reported UAI with an HIV-negative/status-unknown partner. We further found that there was no association between any UAI with an HIV-positive partner and any UAI with an HIV-negative partner (OR = 1.42, 95 percent CI = 0.48, 4.18).

The men in our study asserted that despite getting older, they still are sexually active:

I know the brain is the largest sex organ and I-mine's really active regardless of whether I'm physically being active or not. [White, age 57, living with HIV 25 years]

Another participant spoke about the way in which sexual interactions allowed him to manage/escape the burdens in his life.

I've been a sex addict for like my whole life. I'm like a casual sex friend. I definitely have an issue with that. I definitely can go online and just have sex with someone. So, I think it made me. I never was very inclined to relationships. I was always very inclined to like fool around and have casual sex and then after he passed [boyfriend/partner] it was kind of an easy way to not, you know, kind of deal with anything. It's kind of like a way that I sometimes medicate myself to kind of forget about things. [White, age 52, living with HIV 17 years]

Meanwhile, another participant reveled in his continued sexual prowess as he grew older, tallying his sexual encounters.

Yeah you're a sex addict you're a real slut. How? I want, I want quantification. I want to know how many times did I suck a dick? How many times did I get it up the ass? How many hands did I have up my hole? And so on. So I made up my own damn spreadsheet, I have kept it up since that day. [White, age 59, living with HIV 21 years]

Psychosocial Burden in Relation to Unprotected Sexual Behavior

We next considered the relations between our total current psychosocial burden score and UAI among the men in our sample. We found that there was a high level of association (unadjusted ORs) between the total burden score and unprotected sexual behaviors. In particular, any unprotected anal sex with an HIV-positive partner (OR = 1.38, 95 percent CI = 1.00, 1.91) and any unprotected anal sex with an HIV-negative/status-unknown partner (OR = 1.61, 95 percent CI = 1.05, 2.46) were both significantly related to the total burden score.

To examine the association between psychosocial burdens and UAI, while controlling for the potential confounding effects of age, years living with HIV, and race/ethnicity, we tested two binary logistic regression models using any UAI with an HIV-positive partner and any UAI with an HIV-negative/status-unknown partner as the criterion variables. In each case we constructed hierarchical models using two blocks, with our demographic variables in the first block and the total current psychosocial burden score in the second block. The results of these models are shown in Table 4.

The model for UAI with an HIV-negative/status-unknown partner fit in two steps (χ^2 (6) = 12.65, $p < .05$), with the addition of the burden score in step 2 improving the fit over the first model, which only included the demographic variables (χ^2 (1) = 4.88, $p < .05$). Years living with HIV and total burden score were both positively associated with the odds of engaging in UAI with an HIV-negative/status-unknown partner. The model for UAI with an HIV-positive partner also fit in two steps (χ^2 (6) = 12.11, $p < .05$), with

TABLE 4. Binary Logistic Regressions Explaining Unprotected Anal Intercourse Among MSM Ages 50 and Older, New York City 2010–11, $N = 199$

	Unprotected Anal Intercourse		Unprotected Anal Intercourse	
	HIV-Positive Partners		HIV-Negative/ Status-Unknown Partners	
	OR (95% CI)	p	OR (95% CI)	p
Age	0.95 (0.86, 1.04)	.26	0.92 (0.81, 1.05)	.20
Years living with HIV	1.00 (0.94, 1.06)	.94	1.12 (1.01, 1.23)	.03
Race/ethnicity	N/A	.08	N/A	.75
Total current psychosocial burden	1.38 (1.00, 1.91)	.05	1.61 (1.05, 2.46)	.03
Final model fit	$\chi^2 (6) = 12.11, p < .05$		$\chi^2 (6) = 12.65, p < .05$	
Pseudo-R^2 (Nagelkerke)	9.5%		13.1%	

psychosocial burden again improving the fit of the model over the demographic variables alone ($\chi^2 (1) = 3.80, p < .05$). In this model, the total current psychosocial burden alone was positively associated with the odds of engaging in UAI with an HIV-positive partner.

Finally, we further examined the association between UAI with an HIV-positive or an HIV-negative/status-unknown partner and each of the six psychosocial burden variables, to determine the most salient burdens (see Table 3). UAI with an HIV-negative/unknown status partner in the past 30 days was significantly associated with alcohol to intoxication (OR = 3.61, 95 percent CI = 1.24, 10.50) and using inhalant nitrates (OR = 7.32, 95 percent CI = 2.67, 20.03) in the same period. Additionally, UAI with an HIV-positive partner was associated with drinking to intoxication (OR = 3.37, 95 percent CI = 1.36, 8.15) and the use of other illicit drugs in the previous 30 days (2.40, 95 percent CI = 1.15, 5.01). Lastly, UAI with either partner type was not associated with the use of marijuana, depression, or PTSD.

Transactional sex emerged in our qualitative assessment as a factor connecting substance use and unprotected sexual behaviors:

> Cause a lot of times it's just been sex for drugs. It's really not sex for money. It's really sex for drugs. I want drugs from them. I been receiving oral sex for the drugs. The guy would give me a blow job and sex. I would do the drugs while he's giving me the oral sex. [Black, age 57, living with HIV 8 years]

Meanwhile, another participant described how his life unraveled after the death of his partner, focusing on how his substance use and sexual behaviors fueled each other, eventually leading to his seroconversion:

> From that point on, I was still drinking every night, got drunk, got drunk, got drunk. I was trying to drown the sorrows and the pain cause I was angry- plus I was pissed at [my partner] for dying. But anyway that's how I got into cocaine that's how I really got into drugs. After he was dead and we had him cremated I said maybe I should test myself. I did get tested and I was negative. So I was like oh great you know . . . Phew. But my addictions

were getting deeper and deeper and deeper and at least my addiction circle, we got into a circle of people, we would get a motel room for a weekend and everybody would pool their money and we would just do drugs the whole weekend. Drugs and sex, and that's how I got it. And I know how I got it. [Black, age 58, living with HIV 16 years]

DISCUSSION

The findings of our investigation of HIV-positive gay, bisexual, and other MSM ages 50 and over indicate a high prevalence of psychosocial burdens, including psychiatric disorders and substance use among the men sampled. These burdens also are evidenced in the stories relayed by the study participants. Approximately 20 percent of the men in our sample were classified as currently being depressed, with a similar proportion demonstrating symptoms of PTSD. Because national epidemiological studies to date do not include assessments of sexual orientation (Institute of Medicine 2011), we are not able to make comparisons of this sample to larger gay population estimates. However, previous literature has highlighted that gay and bisexual men experience elevated health disparities in the form of depression and other mental illnesses as compared to their heterosexual peers (Cochran and Mays 2008). Moreover, in the National Comorbidity Study, individuals who suffered from chronic physical illnesses, defined as hypertension, arthritis, asthma, and ulcers, demonstrated a lower prevalence of current depression (10 percent) than our cohort of older men living with HIV (Kessler et al. 2003).

Similarly, rates of PTSD in our sample of seropositive gay, bisexual, and other MSM are on par with prevalence estimates of PTSD among those who have experienced traumatic events, 15–24 percent of whom develop symptoms of PTSD after exposure to the event (Breslau 2001). This comparability in prevalence may be explained by the fact that gay men as a whole have experienced an ongoing traumatic event in the form of the HIV epidemic. This trauma may be even more pronounced among those who were diagnosed with HIV prior to the implementation of highly effective antiviral therapies in 1996 (Palella et al. 1998, 2006), when the mortality rate for those diagnosed with HIV was astronomical (Callen 1990). In our sample, the majority of men (70 percent) were diagnosed prior to 1996 and would be classified as long-term survivors. It may be suggested that this set of men constitute "The AIDS Generation," (Halkitis, 2013) a group that, by all accounts, should have died but somehow have managed to survive into older adulthood, living with the posttraumatic stress of the HIV epidemic. At the same time, it is important to note that this generation offers researchers and clinicians valuable life experiences that could inform future models of resiliency and survival (Emlet et al. 2011). This reality is important to explore in that HIV-positive gay, bisexual, and other MSM continue to survive, while their individual and community-level resiliencies remain relatively unexplored and untapped in designing behavioral interventions for the larger community (Herrick et al. 2011). Overall, our findings regarding mental health in aging seropositive MSM align with the elevated rates of psychiatric disorders among HIV-positive individuals reported elsewhere, including depression, anxiety, and severe mental illness (Chander et al. 2006). Moreover, these results complement previous studies in which psychosocial burdens, including depression, have been shown to be related to an HIV-positive serostatus in MSM (Stall et al. 2003).

Compared to other samples of MSM and older adults, this sample had a lower prevalence of problem drinking. Approximately 12.6 percent reported drinking alcohol to intoxication at least once in the last month. We compared this to estimates from the 2008 National HIV Behavioral Surveillance System (NHBSS), where 35 percent of MSM aged 50 and older reported binge drinking (Finlayson et al. 2011). This is also lower than estimates from younger MSM populations (Finlayson et al. 2011) and gay men in the Behavioral Risk Factor Surveillance System (BRFSS) (Conron et al. 2010). The difference between these estimates may be due to differences in the variable definitions. We also found that using alcohol to intoxication was associated with increased odds of unprotected anal sex. Mustanski (2008) has demonstrated that age moderates the relationship between daily alcohol use and risky sexual behavior and reports that there is a growing body of evidence suggesting that alcohol has a stronger influence on risk behavior among older MSM as compared to younger MSM.

This sample of older HIV-positive MSM had relatively high rates of drug use. For example, we found that 37.7 percent of the men in our study used marijuana in the past month. In the 2008 NHBSS (Finlayson et al. 2011), 25 percent of MSM aged 50 and older reported marijuana use. Furthermore, in our sample just over a quarter of the men (26.1 percent) reported other illicit substance use in the past month, which included such substances as cocaine, crack, ecstasy, GHB, ketamine, and methamphetamine. Additionally, 13.6 percent of our sample reported using poppers (i.e., amyl nitrite). Our estimate of popper use is similar to that of the NHBSS, in which 13 percent of MSM aged 50 and older reported using poppers (Finlayson et al. 2011). However, NHBSS found less illicit drug use among older men. Specifically, they found that 9 percent used cocaine, 3 percent used methamphetamine, and 3 percent used ecstasy (Finlayson et al. 2011). These differences could be due to regional differences, as NHBSS collects data from 22 metropolitan statistical areas, while our sample comes from only one. In the New York City NHBSS subsample, 26 percent of all MSM used cocaine (Finlayson et al. 2011).

We did not observe a significant relation between UAI and marijuana use, regardless of partner serostatus. These results contradict findings among recently infected MSM, which showed that marijuana use was associated with UAI (Drumright et al. 2006). Similarly, Bedoya et al. (2012) have shown marijuana use to be associated with serodiscordant UAI among Latino MSM. However, these samples included broad age range as young as 16 (Bedoya et al. 2012) and 18 (Drumright et al. 2006). No studies to our knowledge have addressed this relation among older MSM exclusively.

With regard to sexual behaviors, our results support the notion that HIV-positive MSM ages 50 and older do engage in unprotected anal sex. These findings concur with previous research (Lovejoy et al. 2008; Pappas and Halkitis 2011). In our sample we found that within partner serostatus, engaging in unprotected insertive anal intercourse and unprotected receptive anal intercourse were related. However, no relations were observed for UAI across partner HIV status (i.e., UAI with an HIV-positive partner was not found to be related to UAI with an HIV-negative/status-unknown partner). Approximately 19 percent of our sample reported any UAI with an HIV-positive partner, while roughly ten percent reported any UAI with an HIV-negative/status-unknown partner. Other studies on HIV-positive MSM with more general samples have reported a prevalence of sexual-risk behaviors that ranged from 8 to 46 percent (Van Kesteren et al. 2007).

This manuscript presents findings from one of the first research studies to test a theory of syndemics in aging HIV-positive gay, bisexual, and other MSM. Although previous studies have highlighted the strong relations between psychosocial burdens and sexual risk-taking in age-diverse samples of MSM (Egan et al. 2011; Moeller et al. 2011; Stall et al. 2003), much of the focus of this research has been on the applicability of syndemics theory to understanding sexual risk-taking in adolescent, emerging, and young adult gay, bisexual, and other MSM (Halkitis et al. 2013; Mustanski et al. 2007; Solomon et al. 2011; Storhlom et al. 2011). Like these previous investigations, we demonstrate a high level of association between psychosocial burdens and UAI, with the men who possessed higher overall burden scores also indicating a higher likelihood of engaging in UAI. This relation holds true for UAI with both HIV-positive and HIV-negative/status-unknown partners.

Like each of the above noted studies of syndemics among gay, bisexual, and other MSM, we applied an additive model of psychosocial burdens to test for association and provide support for the model. However, we also have been able to provide support for a theory of syndemics in young gay and bisexual men using more elaborate models in the form of structural equation modeling (Halkitis et al. 2013), that we hope to apply to future studies of syndemics in aging MSM.

Limitations

There are several limitations to this study. First, this is a self-selected sample of older HIV-positive, gay, bisexual, and other MSM from one geographic context, New York City. Second, because all the measures are self-reported, we cannot rule out the possibility of participants answering in a socially desirable manner. For our most critical data, drug use and unprotected sex, we utilized the TLFB method, which captures the previous month's sexual and substance use behaviors and has been shown to have good test–retest reliability and convergent validity (Fals-Stewart et al. 2000; Halkitis et al. 2009). However, it is important to note that since the researchers and participants completed this measure face-to-face, it is possible that participants responded differently across researchers, possibly depending on perceptions of age, race, gender, or sexual orientation. Third, this study employed a cross-sectional design and, as is the case with such designs, associations are subject to spuriousness. Also a larger sample size would have increased statistical power and allowed for more sophisticated statistical analyses in the form of possible measurement model construction, lending more support to the theory. Since this was a study of aging HIV-positive men, cognitive deficits or early dementia due to age, HIV, long-term ART, or any combination thereof, may have impacted one's recollection of time, persons, or events.

The men in this sample survived through the early AIDS epidemic, when transmission and mortality rates were high. As a result, another potential limitation of this study is survivor bias, which occurs when a disease results in high mortality rates, leaving one to conduct studies with only the survivors of the disease (Schlesselman 1982). It is likely that the outcomes (i.e., UAI) and exposures (i.e., depression, PTSD, and substance use) are associated with mortality in this population, and thus by studying these survivors the observed associations between the syndemic effects and UAI are biased. However, we believe that the estimates would be biased away from the null (i.e., underestimated).

CONCLUSIONS

As the HIV-positive population of gay, bisexual, and other MSM continue to age, these men will undoubtedly confront many of the complications faced by older adults in general, although, perhaps, in an even more pronounced way given their HIV infection. Still, as has been evidenced across the population "50 is the new 40," and adults continue to remain vibrant and active as they mature. For gay, bisexual, and other MSM, this may include active sexual lives and alcohol and illicit drug use. The findings of our analysis highlight the presence of both sexual and drug risk-taking behaviors in older men and that syndemics theory has as much relevance in understanding these behaviors in older HIV-positive MSM as it does in younger MSM, where the theory has been predominantly applied. We believe future research will elucidate the relevance of syndemics theory in studies of older MSM regardless of serostatus, given the ongoing interplay of various epidemics and endemics beyond HIV, which affect MSM across the lifespan.

The graying of AIDS, as well as the graying of the U.S. populous in general, will be fueled by the baby-boomer generation. This group of individuals is radically different than previous generations, calling for innovative and dynamic research approaches, which can then aid us in reconsidering the manner in which we will deliver services and fashion prevention strategies for this growing population of older adults. Given evidence for a syndemic in this segment of the population and the evidence of risk behaviors that extend into older adulthood, strategies for prevention and care will need to be holistic and multidimensional in nature. Taken together, these findings indicate that policies and programming must be developed to consider the needs and behaviors of this growing population of gay men, recognizing that strategies that work for 20-year-olds may not be effective for 50-, 60-, or even 70-year-olds.

For health practitioners serving this population, it is imperative that the delivery of care simultaneously consider the impacts of living with HIV, the process of aging, and the ongoing syndemic factors evidenced in these men's lives. Especially important in a holistic approach to care will be attention to the psychosocial stressors that function as catalysts to a syndemic and which may have as much power to influence/create syndemic conditions in the lives of older HIV-positive men as they do in creating risk states in younger gay men. For mental health practitioners, therapeutic approaches also must recognize that among older HIV-positive men there is likely a lifelong pattern of a syndemic to which they must attend. An important part of this work will be contextualizing various health burdens in older adulthood, which is already fraught with its own medical and psychiatric complications even without a diagnosis of HIV.

For those developing prevention strategies, it will be critical to attend to the active sexual lives of older HIV-positive MSM, to recognize that both illicit substance and alcohol use are occurring among these men, and that similar risk factors that predispose younger men to risk-taking also likely will predispose older HIV-positive men to congruent risk behaviors. While addressing the underlying stressors that lead to a syndemic is likely the most effective approach to ameliorating risk, the manner in which these stressors are addressed must be tailored to the differing developmental contexts that exist for older gay men as compared to younger gay men.

A final and critical concern in addressing the possible syndemic in older HIV-positive gay, bisexual, and other MSM noted in this manuscript is the recognition that a substantial portion of these men are long-term survivors of HIV. They have witnessed and survived the devastation inflicted upon the gay community within the first two decades of the epidemic, back when AIDS was "a gay plague." Thus these men also possess emotional and physical fortitudes, as well as demonstrate high levels of resiliency. It is important that such resiliency be understood and harnessed to both serve these men individually, as they enter into the later stages of life, and the gay community as a whole, which continues to be disproportionately affected by HIV over time. The stories of survival of "the AIDS generation" should serve as a model of resiliency to assist in informing HIV prevention and care moving forward, as well as possibly prevention and care for other demanding medical conditions.

NOTE

Acknowledgments. This study was funded, in part, by a pilot grant (Halkitis, PI) from the National Institute on Drug Abuse parent grant 3P30DA011041–20S1.

REFERENCES CITED

Beck, Aaron T., Robert A. Steer, and Margery G. Carbin
   1988 Psychometric Properties of the Beck Depression Inventory: Twenty-Five Years of Evaluation. Clinical Psychology Review 8(1):77–100.
Bedoya, Andres C., Matthew J. Mimiaga, Geetha Beauchamp, Deborah Donnell, Keneth H. Mayer, and Steven A. Safren
   2012 Predictors of HIV Transmission Risk Behavior and Seroconversion Among Latino Men Who Have Sex With Men in Project EXPLORE. AIDS and Behavior 16(3):608–617.
Breslau, Naomi
   2001 The Epidemiology of Posttraumatic Stress Disorder: What is the Extent of the Problem? Journal of Clinical Psychiatry 62(Suppl 17):16–22.
Callen, Michael
   1990 Surviving AIDS. New York: Harper Collins Publishers.
Chander, Geetanjali, Seth Himelhoch, and Richard D. Moore
   2006 Substance Abuse and Psychiatric Disorders in HIV-Positive Patients: Epidemiology and Impact on Antiretroviral Therapy. Drugs 66(6):769–789.

Center for Disease Control and Prevention

2008 HIV/AIDS Among Persons Aged 50 and Older. http://www.cdc.gov/hiv/topics/over50/resources/factsheets/pdf/over50.pdf, accessed November 1, 2011.

2011 HIV Surveillance Report, 2009, Vol. 21. http://www.cdc.gov/hiv/topics/surveillance/resources/reports/. Published February 2011. Accessed November 1, 2011.

Cochran, Susan D., and Vicki M. Mays

2008 Prevalence of Primary Mental Health Morbidity and Suicide Symptoms Among Gay and Bisexual Men. *In* Unequal Opportunity: Health Disparities Affecting Gay and Bisexual Men in the United States. Richard Wolitski, Ron Stall and Ronald O. Valdiserri, eds. Pp. 97–120. Oxford: Oxford University Press.

Conron, Kerith J., Matthew Mimiaga, and Stewart J. Landers

2010 A Population-Based Study of Sexual Orientation Identity and Gender Differences in Adult Health. American Journal of Public Health 100(10):1953–1960.

David, Steven, and Bob G. Knight

2008 Stress and Coping Among Gay Men: Age and Ethnic Differences. Psychology and Aging 23(1):62–69.

Diaz, Rafael M., George Ayala, Edward Bein, Jeff Henne, and Barbara V. Marin

2001 The Impact of Homophobia, Poverty, and Racism on Mental Health of Gay and Bisexual Latino Men: Findings From 3 US Cities. American Journal of Public Health 91(6):927–932.

Drumright, Lydia N., Susan J. Little, Steffanie A. Strathdee, Donald J. Slymen, Maria Rosario G. Araneta, Vanessa L. Malcarne, Eric S. Daar, and Pamina M. Gorbach

2006 Unprotected Anal Intercourse and Substance Use Among Men Who Have Sex With Men With Recent HIV Infection. Journal of Acquired Immune Deficiency Syndromes 43(3):344–350.

Egan, James E., Victoria Frye, Steven P. Kurtz, Carl Latkin, Minxing Chen, Karin Tobin, Cui Yang, and Beryl A. Koblin

2011 Migration, Neighborhoods, and Networks: Approaches to Understanding How Urban Environmental Conditions Affect Syndemic Adverse Health Outcomes Among Gay, Bisexual, and Other Men Who Have Sex With Men. AIDS and Behavior 15(Suppl 1):35–50.

Emlet, Charles A., Shakima, T., and Victoria, H. Raveis

2006 You're Awfully Old to Have This Disease: Experiences of Stigma and Ageism in Adults 50 Years and Older Living With HIV/AIDS. The Gerontologist 46(6):781–790.

2011 "I'm not going to die From the AIDS": Resilience in Aging With HIV Disease. The Gerontologist 51(1):101–111.

Fals-Stewart, William, Timothy J. O'Farrell, Timothy T. Freitas, Susan K. McFarlin, and Peter Rutigliano

2000 The Timeline Follow Back Reports of Psychoactive Substance Use by Drug-Abusing Patients: Psychometric Properties. Journal of Consulting and Clinical Psychology 68(1):134–144.

Finlayson, Teresa, J., Binh Le, Amanda Smith, Kristina Bowles, Melissa Cribbin, Isa Miles, Alexandra M. Oster, Tricia Martin, Alicia Edwards, and Elizabeth DiNenno

2011 HIV Risk, Prevention, and Testing Behaviors Among Men Who Have Sex With Men—National HIV Behavioral Surveillance System, 21 U.S. Cities, United States, 2008. Morbidity and Mortality Weekly Report: Surveillance Summaries 60(SS14):1–34.

Gilligan, Carol, Renee Spencer, Katherine Weinberg, and Tatiana Bertsch

2003 On the Listening Guide: A Voice-Centered Relational Model. *In* Qualitative Research in Psychology: Expanding Perspectives in Methodology and Design. Paul M. Camic, Jean E. Rhodes and Lucy Yardley, eds. Pp. 157–172. Washington, DC: American Psychological Association.

Gribble, James N., Heather G. Miller, Susan M. Rogers, and Charles F. Turner

1999 Interview Mode and Measurement of Sexual Behaviors: Methodological Issues. Journal of Sex Research 36(1):16–24.

Halkitis, Perry N.

2010 Reframing HIV Prevention for Gay Men in the United States. American Psychologist 65(8): 752–763.

2013 The AIDS Generation: Stories of Survival and Resilience. New York: Oxford University Press.

Halkitis, Perry N., Robert W. Moeller, Daniel E. Siconolfi, Erik D. Storholm, Todd M. Solomon, and Kristen L. Bub

   2013 Measurement Model Exploring a Syndemic in Emerging Adult Gay and Bisexual Men. AIDS and Behavior 172:662–673.

Halkitis, Perry N., Todd M. Solomon, Robert W. Moeller, Stephanie A. R. Doig, Lindsay S. Espinosa, Daniel Siconolfi, and Bruce D. Homer

   2009 Methamphetamine Use Among Gay, Bisexual and Non-Identified Men-Who-Have-Sex-With-Men: An Analysis of Daily Patterns. Journal of Health Psychology 14(2):222–231.

Herrick, Amy L. Sin How Lim, Chongyi Wei, Helen Smith, Thomas Guadamuz, Mark S. Friedman, and Ron Stall

   2011 Resilience as an Untapped Resource in Behavioral Intervention Design for Gay Men. AIDS and Behavior 15(Suppl 1): 25–29.

Institute of Medicine

   2011 The Health of Lesbian, Gay, Bisexual, and Transgender People: Building a Foundation for Better Understanding. http://www.iom.edu/Reports/2011/The-Health-of-Lesbian-Gay-Bisexual-and-Transgender-People.aspx, accessed November 1, 2011.

Jacobs, Robins J., M. Isabel Fernandez, Raymond L. Ownby, G. Stephen Bowen, Patrick C. Hardigan, and Michael N. Kane

   2010 Factors Associated With Risk for Unprotected Receptive and Insertive Anal Intercourse in Men Aged 40 and Older Who Have Sex With Men. AIDS Care 22(10):1204–1211.

Jerome, Roy C., and Perry N. Halkitis

   2009 Stigmatization, Stress and the Search for Belonging in Black Men Who Have Sex With Men and Who Use Methamphetamine. Journal of Black Psychology 35(3):343–365.

Justice, Amy C., Kathleen A. McGinnis, J. Hampton Atkinson, Robert K. Heaton, Corrina Young, Joseph Sadek, Tamra Madenwald, James T. Becker, Joseph Conigliaro, Sheldon T. Brown, David Rimland, Steve Crystal, Michael Simberkoff, for the VACS 5 Project Team

   2004 Psychiatric and Neurocognitive Disorders Among HIV-Positive and Negative Veterans in Care: Veterans Aging Cohort Five-Site Study. AIDS 18(Suppl. 1):49–59.

Kessler, Ronald C., Johan Ormel, Olga Demler, and Paul E. Stang

   2003 Comorbid Mental Disorders Account for the Role Impairment of Commonly Occurring Chronic Physical Disorders: Results From the National Comorbidity Survey. Journal of Occupational and Environmental Medicine 45(12):1257–1266.

Lindau, Stacy T., L. Philip Schumm, Edward O. Laumann, Wendy Levinson, Colm A. O'Muircheartaigh, and Linda J. Waite

   2007 A Study of Sexuality and Health Among Older Adults in the United States. New England Journal of Medicine 357(8):762–774.

Lovejoy, Travis I., Timothy G. Heckman, Kathleen J. Sikkema, Nathan B. Hansen, Arlene Kochman, Julie A. Suhr, John P. Garske, and Christopher J. Johnson

   2008 Patterns and Correlates of Sexual Activity and Condom Use Behavior in Persons 50-Plus Years of Age Living With HIV/AIDS. AIDS and Behavior 12(6):943–956.

Luther, Vera P., and Aimee M. Wilkin

   2007 HIV Infection in Older Adults. Clinics in Geriatric Medicine 23(3):567–583.

Manfredi, Roberto

   2004 Impact of HIV Infection and Antiretroviral Therapy in the Older Patient. Expert Review of Anti-infective Therapy 2(6):821–824.

Marks, Gary, Nicole Crepaz, J. Walton Senterfitt, and Robert S. Janssen

   2005 Meta-Analysis of High-Risk Sexual Behavior in Persons Aware and Unaware They Are Infected With HIV in the United States: Implications for HIV Prevention Programs. Journal of Acquired Immune Deficiency Syndrome 39(4):446–453.

Mills, Thomas C., Jay Paul, Ron Stall, Lance Pollack, Jesse Canchola, Y. Jason Chang, Judith Moskowitz, and Joseph A. Catania

2004 Distress and Depression in Men Who Have Sex With Men: The Urban Men's Health Study. American Journal of Psychiatry 161(2):278–285.

Moeller, Robert W., Perry N. Halkitis, and Katie Surrence
2011 The Interplay of Syndemic Production and Serosorting in Drug-Using Gay and Bisexual Men. Journal of Gay and Lesbian Social Services 23(1):89–106.

Mustanski, Brian S.
2008 Moderating Effects of Age on the Alcohol and Sexual Risk Taking Association: An Online Daily Diary Study of Men Who Have Sex With Men. AIDS and Behavior 12(1):118–126.

Mustanski, Brian S., Robert Garofalo, Amy Herrick, and Geri Donenberg
2007 Psychosocial Health Problems Increase Risk for HIV Among Urban Young Men Who Have Sex With Men: Preliminary Evidence of a Syndemic in Need of Attention. Annals of Behavioral Medicine 34(1):37–45.

Palella, Frank J. Jr., Rose K. Baker, Anne C. Moorman, Joan S. Chmiel, Kathleen C. Wood, John T. Brooks, and Scott D. Holmberg, and HIV Outpatient Study investigators
2006 Mortality in the Highly Active Antiretroviral Therapy Era: Changing Causes of Death and Disease in the HIV Outpatient Study. Journal of Immune Deficiency Syndromes 43(1):27–34.

Palella, Frank J. Jr., Kathleen M. Delaney, Anne C. Moorman, Mark O. Loveless, Jack Fuhrer, Glen A. Satten, Diane J. Aschman, J. Diane, Scott D. Holmberg, and HIV Outpatient Study Investigators
1998 Declining Morbidity and Mortality Among Patients With Advanced Human Immunodeficiency Virus Infection. The New England Journal of Medicine 338(13):853–860.

Pappas, Molly K., and Perry N. Halkitis
2011 Sexual Risk Taking and Club Drug Use Across Three Age Cohorts of HIV-Positive Gay and Bisexual Men in New York City. AIDS Care 23(11):1410–1416.

Parker, Richard and Peter Aggleton
2002 HIV/AIDS-Related Stigma and Discrimination: A Conceptual Framework and an Agenda for Action. New York: The Population Council, Inc. http://www.popcouncil.org/pdfs/horizons/sdcncptlfrmwrk.pdf, accessed August 21, 2012.

Parsons, Jeffrey T., Eric W. Schrimshaw, Richard J. Wolitski, Perry N. Halkitis, David W. Purcell, Colleen C. Hoff, and Cynthia Gomez.
2005 Sexual Harm Reduction Practices of HIV Seropositive Gay and Bisexual Men: Serosorting, Strategic Positioning, and Withdraw Before Ejaculation. AIDS 19(Suppl. 1):S13–S25.

Purcell, David W., Jeffry T. Parsons, Perry N. Halkitis, Yuko Mizuno, and William J. Woods
2001 Substance Use and Sexual Transmission Risk Behavior of HIV-Positive Men Who Have Sex With Men. Journal of Substance Abuse 13(1–2):185–200.

Schlesselman, James J.
1982 Case-Control Studies: Design, Conduct, and Analysis. New York: Oxford University Press.

Shah, Sanjiv, and Donna Mildvan
2006 HIV and Aging. Current Infectious Disease Reports 8(3):241–247.

Sherr, Lorraine, Claudine Clucas, Richard Harding, Elissa Sibley, and Jose Catalan
2011 HIV and Depression—A Systematic Review of Interventions. Psychology, Health, and Medicine 16(5):493–527.

Singer, Merrill
1994 AIDS and the Health Crisis of the U.S. Urban Poor: The Perspective of Critical Medical Anthropology. Social Science & Medicine 39(7):931–948.
1996 A Dose of Drugs, a Touch of Violence, A Case of AIDS: Conceptualizing the SAVA Syndemic. Free Inquiry in Creative Sociology 24(2):99–110.
2006 A Dose of Drugs, A Touch of Violence, A Case of AIDS, Part 2: Further Conceptualizing the SAVA Syndemic. Free Inquiry in Creative Sociology 34(1):39–51.

Sobell, Linda C., and Mark B. Sobell
1996 Timeline Followback User's Guide: A Calendar Method for Assessing Alcohol and Drug Use. Toronto: Addiction Research Foundation.

Solomon, Todd M., Perry N. Halkitis, Robert W. Moeller, Daniel E. Siconolfi, Matthew V. Kiang, and Staci B. Barton

    2011 Sex Parties Among Young Gay, and Bisexual, and Other Men Who Have Sex With Men in New York City: Attendance and Behavior. Journal of Urban Health 88(6):1063–1075.

Stall, Ron, Mark Friedman, and Joseph A. Catania

    2008 Interacting Epidemics and Gay Men's Health: A Theory of Syndemic Production Among Urban Gay Men. *In* Unequal Opportunity: Health Disparities Affecting Gay and Bisexual Men in the United States. Richard J. Wolitski, Ron Stall, and Ronald O. Valdiserri, eds. Pp. 251–274. Oxford: Oxford University Press.

Stall, Ron, Thomas C. Mills, John Williamson, Trevor Hart, Greg Greenwood, Jay Paul, Lance Pollack, Diane Binson, Dennis Osmond, and Joseph A. Catania

    2003 Association of Co-Occurring Psychosocial Health Problems and Increased Vulnerability to HIV/AIDS Among Urban Men Who Have Sex With Men. American Journal of Public Health 93(6):939–42.

Storholm, Erik D., Perry N. Halkitis, Daniel E. Siconolfi, and Robert W. Moeller

    2011 Cigarette Smoking as Part of a Syndemic Among Young Men Who Have Sex With Men Ages 13–29 in New York City. Journal of Urban Health 88(4):663–676.

Van Kesteren, Nicole M. C., Harm J. Hospers, and Gerjo Kok

    2007 Sexual Risk Behavior Among HIV-Positive Men Who Have Sex With Men: A Literature Review. Patient Education and Counseling 65(1):5–20.

Weathers, Frank W., and Julian D. Ford

    1996 Psychometric Properties of the PTSD Checklist (PCL-C, PCL-S. PCL-M, PCL-PR). *In* Measurement of Stress, Trauma, and Adaptation. B. Hudnall Stamm, eds. Pp. 250 – 252. Lutherville, MD: Sidran Press.

Weathers, Frank W., Brett T. Litz, Debra S. Herman, Jennifer A. Huska, and Terence M. Keane

    1993 The PCL-C Checklist (PCL): Reliability, Validity, and Diagnostic Utility. Paper presented at the Annual Meeting of the International Society for Traumatic Stress Studies, San Antonio, TX, October 24–27, 1993.

"THERE'S NOWHERE I CAN GO TO GET HELP, AND I HAVE TOOTH PAIN RIGHT NOW": THE ORAL HEALTH SYNDEMIC AMONG MIGRANT FARMWORKERS IN FLORIDA

NOLAN KLINE
The University of South Florida

This article explores the syndemic interaction between poverty, food insecurity, and limited access to dental care among migrant farm laborers in Central Florida. Although a great deal of syndemic research examines the role of pathogen–pathogen interaction (PPI; Singer 2010; Ventura and Mehra 2004), social factors, such as poverty, may be of greater importance than the pathogens that infect the body (Singer and Clair 2003) and demand increased research and policy attention. The data presented in this article show how poverty, food insecurity, and limited access to dental care work synergistically to exacerbate poor health conditions, presenting a syndemic that necessitates increased attention to mitigate poverty circumstances and promote what I call "oral health security" in an effort to advocate for vulnerable populations. [oral health, migrant health, syndemics, farmworkers, Latinos, health disparities, food insecurity]

INTRODUCTION

Xiomara trembled as she led me outside the clinic to begin our interview about access to dental services.

"Thank you for doing this study," she said, "it's so important because no one knows how hard it is to see a dentist."

Like many of the Mexican-origin farmworkers I interviewed at the faith-based clinic in central Florida, Xiomara talked about not being able to access dental care because she could not afford the cost of a dental visit. She further explained that she had trouble finding work, and without work, she could not afford to put food on her table, let alone visit the dentist.

"There's just not a lot of work here. When there's no work, there's no money; when there's no money, there's no food. Of course I have to skip meals! I go to bed and I'm hungry . . . but there's no work."

Xiomara's labor-related hardships prevent her from accessing dental care and from providing food for her family. Her story is common among Mexican-born migrant farm laborers in Central Florida: low wages concomitant with agricultural labor and precarious

ANNALS OF ANTHROPOLOGICAL PRACTICE 36.2, pp. 387–401. ISSN: 2153-957X. © 2013 by the American Anthropological Association. DOI:10.1111/napa.12010

growing seasons hinder migrants' access to basic necessities, revealing the role poverty plays in producing a syndemic—"a set of enmeshed and mutually enhancing health problems that, *working together* in a context of deleterious social and physical conditions that increase vulnerability, significantly affect the overall disease status of a population" (Singer 2010). Although a great deal of syndemic research examines the role of pathogen–pathogen interaction (PPI; Singer 2010), social factors, such as poverty, may be of greater importance than the specific pathogens that infect the body (Singer and Clair 2003) and demand increased research and policy attention.

Syndemic approaches to understanding health concerns have examined specific populations' incurrence of diseases, such as men who have sex with men (Bruce et al. 2011; Egan et al. 2011; Herrick et al. 2011; Kurtz 2008; Mustanski et al. 2007; Safren et al. 2010; Stall et al. 2003; Storholm et al. 2011) or one specific disease's interaction with other illnesses, such as diabetes mellitus (Ruiz and Egli 2010), obesity (Candib 2007; Myslobodsky and Eldan 2010), sexually transmitted diseases/infections (Senn et al. 2010; Singer et al. 2006), drug use (Kurtz 2008; Romero-Daza et al. 2003), psychosocial health concerns (Mustanski et al. 2007; Stall et al. 2003), and heart failure (Ventura and Mehra 2004). HIV, in particular, has been given a great deal of attention in an effort to understand how the virus interacts with other health concerns (Cain et al. 2007; Diedrich and Flynn 2011; Freudenberg et al. 2006; Gielen et al. 2007; González-Guarda et al. 2011; Mustanski et al. 2007; Operario and Nemoto 2010; Safren et al. 2010; Van Tieu and Koblin 2009). Moreover, syndemic understandings of health can offer suggestions on how to effectively treat concurrent illnesses, such as HIV and tuberculosis (Kwan and Ernst 2011), and inform behavioral health interventions, such as population-specific smoking cessation programs (Storholm et al. 2011).

Research emphasizing the role of socioeconomic status (SES) on syndemic health conditions has shown how mutually reinforcing epidemics, such as substance use and AIDS, relate to cycles of violence and labor-related vulnerability, such as prostitution (Romero-Daza et al. 2003). Vulnerability may play a role in excessive burdens of disease, but the clustering of health disparities among some vulnerable populations, such as immigrants and refugees, remains understudied (Edberg et al. 2011; Singer 1994; Starfield 2007). Existing work on immigrants' syndemic health concerns has focused on structural vulnerabilities and legal statuses that produce the harmful context in which a syndemic is created (Cartwright 2011). Research presented in this article applies the syndemic concept to immigrants' structural hardships and examines two poverty-related health constraints that mediate poor health outcomes among Mexican-born migrant laborers in Central Florida: malnutrition and oral health concerns.

In this article, I demonstrate how poverty, the excess burden of food insecurity, and limited access to oral health care among Latino migrant farm laborers in Central Florida intertwine to impact oral health and have systemic health implications. I further underscore the social determinants that provide the foundation for health disparities and disproportionate access to health services. Ultimately, I argue that the concurrence of poverty, food insecurity, and limited access to dental care constitute a syndemic, working synergistically to exacerbate social and biological conditions. The oral health syndemic requires increased policy and biosocial research attention to mitigate poverty circumstances and promote what I refer to as "oral health security."

BACKGROUND

Food insecurity and access to dental services are a significant concern for Latino migrant laborers and for Hispanic populations in general. In 2009, 85.3 percent of households in the United States were food secure and nearly 15 percent of households experienced some level of food insecurity; 9.0 percent experienced low food security, and 5.7 percent experienced very low food security (Nord et al. 2010). At a rate of at 26.9 percent, Hispanic households experienced higher rates of food insecurity than any other ethnic group. Similarly, in 2009, approximately 62 percent of U.S. residents ages 18–64 had visited the dentist in the past year, but only 37.6 percent of Hispanic or Latino populations 100 percent of the poverty line had visited the dentist in the past year (National Center for Health Statistics 2011:316). These data highlight the disparities in food security and access to oral health care among Latino migrant laborers, and the data presented in this article focus on Latino migrant laborers who may experience higher barriers to care because of the low wages associated with their labor and migratory lifestyle.

This article reports findings that contribute to the understudied clustering of health concerns among immigrant populations, specifically examining the synergistic relationship between poverty, malnutrition, oral health problems, and limited access to dental care among migrant farm laborers in Central Florida. It further contributes to a growing body of scholarship about migrant oral health (Barker and Horton 2008; Castañeda et al. 2010; Horton and Barker 2008, 2010) and the impacts of socioeconomic variables on access to care (Castañeda et al. 2010). While a great deal of migrant health literature points to cultural beliefs as barriers to care, new research has shown that socioeconomic variables play a greater role in hindering access to dental care (Castañeda et al. 2010). Moreover, oral health disparities are comparatively underresearched among public health researchers and medical anthropologists, and a syndemic understanding of oral health disparities is absent from the migrant health literature. A syndemic approach to understanding migrant oral health disparities allows for examining social variables, such as poverty, not just as risk factors, but instead as part of synergistic system that influences and is influenced by biology.

Migrants in the United States are excluded from several avenues of the formal health sector because of their documentation status, low wages associated with their labor, and geographic isolation from dental services. Some employers also arrange systems of indebtedness among laborers by restricting where employees can purchase goods, setting up "company stores," and selling commodities at inflated prices to ensure laborers owe employers future work (Bletzer 2004). For undocumented migrants specifically, legal status serves as a barrier for being eligible for public assistance programs, such as Medicare or Medicaid, and migrants' low wages from working piecework farm jobs or other migratory labor hinder their ability to pay for private health services. As a result of being excluded from the formal health sector, many migrants rely on charitable services for health care that can only provide short-term solutions (Castañeda et al. 2010) and are not always capable of meeting all of the populations' health needs (Kline 2010).

Migrant farm laborers, in particular, are at high risk for developing chronic communicable diseases (Bechtel et al. 1995) and face numerous occupational health hazards related to pesticide exposure, injury, eye trauma, skin disorders, and harmful environmental conditions (Arcury and Quandt 2007; Arcury et al. 2001, 2003, 2005). HIV/AIDS and drug use have also been significant concerns in agricultural communities (Bletzer 2003). Several studies have demonstrated that oral health is one of the top health concerns for migrant farmworkers, yet there are few oral health resources available for migrant populations (Call et al. 1987; Chaffin et al. 2003; Lukes and Simon 2005; Nurko et al. 1998; Quandt et al. 2007; Woolfolk et al. 1984). Research on migrants' access to oral health care highlights the complexity of the problem and the potential barriers to care, including beliefs about primary teeth not being important (Hilton et al. 2007), education (Quandt et al. 2007), and broader structural factors, such as lack of dental providers, and market conditions, such as low reimbursement rates for Medicaid providers who see Medicaid-eligible patients (Castañeda et al. 2010).

Oral health is an important aspect of overall health because research has indicated connections between dental disease and systemic health, especially inflammatory diseases, such as diabetes (Hein and Small 2006; Iacopino 2009), cardiovascular disease (Beck et al. 1996; Loesche et al. 1998), and pancreatic cancer (Michaud et al. 2007). Among women, poor oral health can also result in adverse pregnancy outcomes (Pitiphat et al. 2008). Moreover, oral health has a reciprocal relationship with nutrition. Poor nutrition can harm teeth, and poor oral health can lead to nutritional deficiencies. Research on oral health and nutrition has demonstrated that oral health problems can contribute to nutritional deficiencies and low body mass index (Mojon et al. 1999), and some scholars have specifically stated there should be an emphasis on understanding how oral health mediates nutrition and nutrient intake (Ritchie et al. 2002). Furthermore, research on endentulism (tooth loss) has shown that poor oral health impacts an individual's nutrition and can lead to avoiding nutritious foods (Medina-Solís et al. 2006a; Sheiham et al. 1999). Poor nutrition, and protein-energy malnutrition, specifically, has been linked to oral health concerns, such as dental caries (Alvarez 1995), enamel hypoplasia (missing enamel), salivary gland hypofunction, and altered tooth eruption timing (Psoter et al. 2005).

Modified social behaviors, such as limiting smiling or talking have also been linked to poor oral health (Quandt et al. 2007), and recent research has shown a relationship between poor oral health, low SES, and increased salivary cortisol production as a result of stress (Boyce et al. 2010). In addition to the deleterious consequences of poor oral health, teeth carry a social significance as they are a component of the mouth and the "means by which we express ourselves" (Exley 2009). The mouth and teeth, highly visible in social situations, are important in social interactions and can influence perceptions of self and how others respond to an individual (Exley 2009). Teeth are also a "marker of social vulnerability," and demonstrate ways in which people embody social inequalities (Horton and Barker 2010). Even though some migrant laborers can access healthcare through charitable providers, this research highlights that dental care and nutritious foods are not always available for migrants in Florida.

METHODS

The data collected for this research expand upon existing efforts to better understand how socioeconomic factors constrain access to dental care among migrant families in Central Florida (Carrion et al. 2011; Castañeda et al. 2010). To better understand limited access to dental care among migrant farmworkers in Central Florida, I conducted 40 ethnographic surveys (theoretically grounded surveys informed by other data sources [Schensul et al. 1999]) measuring ideas about oral health, medical care, dental care, access to care, perceptions about care, and food security among migrants seeking services from a faith-based organization's (FBO) medical clinic. The clinic provides basic health screenings and OB/GYN care to migrants, but does not provide dental care because of limited access to equipment and providers in the area. A physician assistant oversees the clinic and the staff of two nurses, one intake specialist, and one volunteer physician.

The ethnographic survey was designed after six months of participant-observation at the FBO clinic, interviews with the clinic director, and exploratory interviews with FBO patients. The participant-observation and preliminary interviews guided the development of survey questions. The survey was pilot tested among members of the research population, and pilot-test participants provided input about how to best word the survey questions to ensure clarity. All surveys were conducted in Spanish. Survey participants were recruited in the waiting room of the clinic and informed that their medical care was not contingent on participation. All participants in the waiting room were asked to participate and then screened for eligibility. To be eligible, participants had to have engaged in farmwork in the past two years and moved season to season.

To collect food security data, the survey included the *U.S. Household Food Security Survey Module: Six-Item Short Form* available through the United States Department of Agriculture (USDA Economic Research Service 2012). The six-item short form of the food security module was used to limit the burden of time on participants; the entire survey with the six-item food security module typically took 20–25 minutes to complete. Food security questions focused on whether or not participants had enough money to purchase food, skipped meals because they could not afford food, and went hungry because they did not have enough money to purchase food or they ran out of food. The scores for each participant are not reported here; percentages of food-secure and food-insecure participants are reported.

To explore participants' access to dental care, all participants were asked when they last visited the dentist, the purpose of their visit, and what they believed to be the biggest barrier to obtaining dental care. Participants also were asked if they believed dental care was more, less, or equally important as medical care, to test assumptions regarding the populations' attitudes about the importance of oral health. In addition to gathering data related to food security and dental services, I asked participants to assess the condition of their teeth. I considered this to be a feasible way to obtain biologically relevant oral health data since a dental provider was not available on site to assess the populations' oral health condition, and access to dental records would be nearly impossible due to participants' migratory lifestyle. All participants' identities were kept confidential, and names reported in this article are pseudonyms. The University of South Florida institutional review board (IRB) approved this research.

FINDINGS

The food security data shed light on how labor-related poverty circumstances constrain access to adequate amounts of nutritious food. Food security survey results revealed an overwhelming number of participants, 82.5 percent ($n = 33$), were food insecure. Ethnographic data collected with the surveys reveal how participants connected food insecurity to their wages and limited access to health services. Rosalva, 32 years old, explained that she prioritizes food and shelter over all other needs, especially when food is inconsistently available. "Food first," she exclaimed, "then we worry about doctors, or not having glasses, or not going to the dentist." Similarly, another participant explained that the amount of food she can purchase is dependent on how much she works: "When there isn't any work it's difficult, and I only work 2–3 hours a day, 2–3 days a week, so you can't always buy all the food that you want."

In addition to discussing the role of poverty in accessing food, participants also discussed the way poverty impacted their ability to access dental care. Participants were asked to report their last dental visit to measure accessibility of dentists and provide a way to compare access to dental care to the broader U.S. population. When asked about their last dental visit, 35 percent ($n = 14$) of migrants reported visiting the dentist in the past year. Another 14 participants (35 percent) had been to the dentist between one and five years, and the remaining participants (30 percent) had either never been to the dentist ($n = 7$), could not remember their last visit ($n = 4$), or had been to the dentist more than five years ago ($n = 1$).

Possible reasons for not visiting the dentist could be less emphasis on the importance of dental care, and therefore all participants were asked how important they believed dental care to be. When asked if dental care was more important, less important, or as important as medical care, the majority of participants, 92.5 percent ($n = 37$), answered that dental care is either *as important* as or *more important* than medical care. One participant stated, "They're both important. Good teeth are part of being healthy."

In general, participants did not prioritize medical care over dental care, and all participants were given the opportunity to freely list what they felt were the biggest barriers to care. The majority of respondents ($n = 34$; 85 percent) listed economic factors as a barrier. Other barriers listed included the length of time needed to obtain an appointment ($n = 5$), a shortage of dentists ($n = 3$), language barriers ($n = 3$), and transportation ($n = 2$; some respondents listed more than one barrier, therefore the total responses is not equal to the number of participants). Some participants discussed their difficulty accessing care relative to their low wages.

Juan Carlos, a 39-year-old man from Guerrero, believed dental care is extremely important—"you should go to the dentist every month if you can," Juan Carlos asserted, "just to make sure everything is okay." Juan Carlos works on strawberry farms and lives in a house with his wife, child, and two other family members with whom he splits the rent. When I asked Juan Carlos about the difficulties in accessing care, his response was immediately related to labor: "There's just not enough work to be able to miss a day. I'm only earning $30, $40, $60 a week and rent is $200–$300 (a week). And right now there is less work because of the ice and a lot of strawberries have grown small and not really round, so people won't buy them because they don't like the ones that aren't perfectly round."

Another example highlights both the individual labor and structural constraints to obtaining care: Esme, for example, worked on the farms last year but now runs a daycare in her home. Esme believes that dental care is even more important than medical care, and says that the costs and her personal financial situation prohibit her from going the three to four times a year she would like to go (even though American Dental Association recommendations are every six months). "The cost is very high and I don't have a lot of money. If I had more money and I could afford it, I would go to the dentist. Imagine paying $100 for a dentist. If I earn $200 a week and then spend $100 on the dentist, how will I pay rent? If it were only $20 for a cleaning and $30 for a filling, I could do it." The responses demonstrate how the problem of accessing dental care is both a macro- and microlevel concern tied to larger labor-related hardships. Labor-related poverty produces the economic constraints that prevent this population from accessing dental care.

To capture data on the state of their teeth, participants were asked to self-report the condition of their teeth using categories of excellent, very good, good, fair, or bad. More than half of the participants ($n = 21$) answered that their teeth were fair or bad. Although some respondents answered that their teeth were in good ($n = 12$) or very good ($n = 5$) condition, some of these respondents also claimed to have previously been in pain and recently had pain-causing teeth removed, or received medication for pain. One respondent specifically explained: "I went to the emergency room because my teeth were decayed and I was in pain. They gave me pills to help with the pain and now [my teeth are] okay." Another participant shared a similar response: "I take a pill for the [tooth] infection and the pain goes away."

One in four participants ($n = 10$) reporting feeling constant dental pain at the time of the interview and none of them knew of a nearby low-cost dental clinic to treat their condition. As one participant stated, "There's nowhere I can go to get help, and I have tooth pain right now."

DISCUSSION

In a position statement about oral health and nutrition, The American Dietetic Association writes that "Scientific and epidemiological data show a lifelong synergy between nutrition and the integrity of the oral cavity in health and disease," calling for professional partnerships between dental professionals, dieticians, and other health professionals (American Dietetic Association 2007:1418). While connections between malnutrition and oral health may be recognized, vulnerable populations, such as the migrant farmworkers discussed in this article, are without access to dental services and are susceptible to malnutrition, as demonstrated by food insecurity scores.

Food security data demonstrate the population's poverty circumstances and the excess burden of food insecurity. At rates of 82.5 percent, migrants in Central Florida experience much higher rates of food insecurity than the national average or the average Hispanic household 100 percent below the poverty line. These data underscore what many participants, such as Mariana, a young mother of three, stated: "we just don't have enough food; there's not enough money to buy it."

Economic disparities hinder access to nutritious foods, such as fresh fruits and vegetables, lean meats, and whole grains (Drewnowski and Darmon 2005). Furthermore, cost is a significant factor in individual food choices (Glanz et al. 1998), and nutrient poor foods with added sugars and fats are attractive options to consumers because they cost less than more nutritious foods (Drewnowski and Specter 2004). Not having enough money for nutritious food and having greater access to nutrient-poor food poses considerable oral and systemic health risks. Potential pathways of interaction between malnutrition and poor oral health include developing diabetes as a result of purchasing low-cost, energy-dense foods composed of fats and sugars (Drewnowski and Specter 2004). Diabetes is a significant risk factor for developing periodontitis, an oral inflammatory infection attacking supporting structures of the teeth. If left untreated, periodontitis can result in tooth loss (Hirsch 2004). Similarly, tooth status and endentulism may lead to avoiding less nutritious foods because of changed tastes or difficulties chewing (Medina-Solís et al. 2006b; Sheiham et al. 1999), highlighting reciprocal oral and systemic health links between malnutrition and oral health.

Moreover, diet variables play a role in developing dental caries: consumption of fermentable carbohydrates and less nutritious foods with higher levels of sucrose increase the risk of developing dental caries (Kandelman 1997). High sucrose foods and fermentable carbohydrates further harm teeth by interacting with cariogenic bacteria, such as *Streptococcus mufans*, which produce lactic acids and slowly erode tooth enamel (Kandelman 1997). Preventative oral health care and behaviors can help reduce the risk of tooth decay and gum disease that can lead to endentulism and altered eating habits. Food insecurity and poor nutrition are therefore risk factors for oral health conditions that may require more than preventive dental care, but as demonstrated by participants' responses, dental care is not always regularly accessible.

Although the responses about dental visits were fairly evenly distributed, when compared to the broader U.S. resident population, the data reveal an increased burden in limited access to dental care. Participants in my study were nearly 50 percent less likely than the general U.S. population to have visited the dentist in the past year. Only 35 percent of migrants in this study had been to the dentist in the past year, a notably low percentage when compared to the national averages (National Center for Health Statistics 2011). Moreover, the data in this study are consistent with larger studies that report Hispanic or Latino populations having limited access to dental care (National Center for

Health Statistics 2011), and pose questions regarding access to oral health service among Latino populations in general.

When asked about limited access to care, participants identified economic barriers to be the most significant and discussed economic barriers on both macro- and microlevels. On a microlevel, participants referred only to the high cost of care, and on the macrolevel, participants noted that their wages prevented them accessing care, directly linking their labor to the inability to purchase care. Labor inequity that produces poverty was therefore the most significant barrier to care, exceeding other barriers, such as transportation or language.

Poverty was therefore a barrier to accessing nutritious foods and a barrier to accessing oral health care, further suggesting oral and systemic health implications. Lack of access to a dental provider can exacerbate poor oral health conditions, and poor dental status can led to a two- to threefold increase in stroke, and a threefold increase in risk of death from coronary heart disease (Slavkin and Baum 2000).

Although the malnutiriton and oral health syndemic has biological impacts, measuring the biological condition of migrants' teeth was not feasible, and accurately capturing the biological data proved to be a shortcoming in this research. Tooth decay is often present without symptoms, therefore self-reporting tooth condition was problematic because participants may not have been aware of oral health problems. Future research examining the biological condition of teeth could focus on measuring prevalence of decay-causing bacteria, *Lactobacilli* and *Mutans Streptococci* and relating these measurements to food security data to assess relationships between tooth condition and nutrition.

In addition to not incorporating any biological data, this research is further limited by its small sample size and sampling technique. Participants were recruited from one clinic offering free medical services, and any migrant farm laborer seeking services at the clinic over the age of 18 was eligible and recruited to participate. The purposive sampling technique therefore could be related to the results of the food insecurity data, since it is possible that lower income populations are more likely to be food insecure and seek health services at a free clinic.

DEVELOPING ORAL HEALTH SECURITY

For migrants, such as Xiomara, who stressed to me the importance of gathering data on her oral health and food security hardships, there is a need to specifically note how the bodies of the marginalized incorporate social conditions in an effort to advance advocacy endeavors and counter health disparities. Oral health security research must use a biosocial approach to examine access-related needs, structural influents, and biological impacts of limited dental care among any population. Access-related needs include the ability to visit dentists for preventative and restorative care, secure plentiful amounts of nutritious food and clean water, and the ability to obtain a toothbrush and floss. Related structural factors include job security, transportation, overcoming language barriers, and the availability of dental providers in a specific area. Lastly, biological data that highlight the presence of cariogenic bacteria are needed to specifically link social factors to biological realities.

Through a biosocial approach, the concept of oral health security advances a syndemic approach to understanding social determinants of health that create lasting biological impacts. This type of work ultimately connects macrolevel social factors with microlevel biological realities, showing how the bodies of the vulnerable suffer due to disparate social conditions.

CONCLUSION

Migrants in central Florida are unable to secure dental care services and experience high rates of food insecurity as a result of their labor-related poverty; the interaction of these social factors increases risks for both oral and systemic health concerns. This article highlights the synergistic interaction between poverty, food insecurity, and limited access to oral health care providers to shed light on how this syndemic works to further exacerbate poor health and poverty conditions. Migrants' poverty circumstances prevent them from accessing dental services and securing plentiful amounts of nutritious food. Without nutritious food, migrants are at risk for developing acute chronic diseases that would not only negatively impact quality of life, but also impact their ability to work. Poverty, food insecurity, and limited access to dental providers therefore interact synergistically to negatively affect migrants biologically and socially. Limited access to oral health providers, specifically, is the result of inequality that permanently marks the bodies of the poor and vulnerable. Oral health disparities become embodied evidence of inequality (Horton and Barker 2010) as teeth display the signs of irregular or unavailable dental care and poor nutrition. Although teeth may demonstrate social inequality, gathering biological data on the condition of teeth can be difficult, especially among migrant populations whose transient labor makes accessing dental records challenging. Advanced methodologies for gathering this data must be used to further demonstrate on how social factors become an enduring biological reality manifested by poor oral health. While some studies have shown relationships between oral health and psychosocial factors, such as stress and SES (Boyce et al. 2010), these studies limit SES to variables, such as education, and do not account for how health inequity is related to labor or inability to access health services in a market-based medical system.

Social conditions, in addition to the biological data, are of significant importance, and as the data provided in this article highlight, poverty is a significant barrier to dental care. The data presented in this article further demonstrate a need to raise the level of awareness about oral health's syndemic impacts. Oral health is not given the same level of importance as overall health (Castañeda et al. 2010) and when examined in a syndemic context, the way oral health interacts with other concerns such as nutrition, and labor-related social conditions such as poverty, becomes increasingly clear. The importance of oral health and its syndemic connections necessitate increased research and policy attention to address socioeconomic inequalities in an effort to reduce oral health disparities. Behavioral interventions alone are not necessarily effective since some populations, such as migrants in Central Florida, may be aware of good oral hygiene habits. Examining oral health disparities therefore requires an approach that addresses a population's broader structural hindrances in accessing dental care, such as availability of dentists and cost of care (Castañeda et al. 2010), and also necessitates a methodology that conceptualizes dental care and access to dentists as a type of health insecurity. Research on "oral health security" among vulnerable populations is therefore needed to inform policy makers and advocacy groups about how social conditions work synergistically to impact oral health.

NOTE

Acknowledgments. The author thanks Heide Castañeda and Rachel Newcomb for their feedback on this article, and the Institute for the Study of Latin America and the Caribbean (ISLAC) at the University of South Florida for funding a portion of this research.

REFERENCES CITED

Alvarez, José O.
   1995 Nutrition, Tooth Development, and Dental Caries. The American Journal of Clinical Nutrition 61(2):410S–416S.
American Dietetic Association
   2007 Position of the American Dietetic Association: Oral Health and Nutrition. Journal of the American Dietetic Association 107(8):1418–1428.
Arcury, Thomas A., and Sara A. Quandt
   2007 Delivery of Health Services to Migrant and Seasonal Farmworkers. Annual Review of Public Health 28(1):345–363.
Arcury, Thomas A., Sara A. Quandt, Altha J. Cravey, Rebecca C. Elmore, and Gregory B. Russell
   2001 Farmworker Reports of Pesticide Safety and Sanitation in the Work Environment. American Journal of Industrial Medicine 39(5):487–498.
Arcury, Thomas A., Sara A. Quandt, and Beverly G. Mellen
   2003 An Exploratory Analysis of Occupational Skin Disease Among Latino Migrant and Seasonal Workers in North Carolina, U.S.A. Journal of Agricultural Safety and Health 9(3):221–232.
Arcury, Thomas A., Sara A. Quandt, Pamela Rao, Alicia M. Doran, Beverly M. Snively, Dana B. Barr, Jane A. Hoppin, and Stephen W. Davis
   2005 Organophosphate Pesticide Exposure in Farmworker Family Members in Western North Carolina and Virginia: Case Comparisons. Human Organization 64(1):40–51.
Barker, Judith C., and Sarah B. Horton
   2008 An Ethnographic Study of Latino Preschool Children's Oral Health in Rural California: Intersections Among Family, Community, Provider and Regulatory Sectors. BMC Oral Health 8(1):8.
Bechtel, Gregory A., Mary Anne Shepherd, and Phyllis W. Rogers
   1995 Family, Culture, and Health Practices Among Migrant Farmworkers. Journal of Community Health and Nursing 12(1):15–22.
Beck, James, Raul Garcia, Gerardo Heiss, Pantel S. Vokonas, and Steven Offenbacher
   1996 Periodontal Disease and Cardiovascular Disease. Journal of Periodontology 67(Suppl. 10):1123–1137.
Bletzer, Keith V.
   2003 Risk and Danger Among Women-Who-Prostitute in Areas where Farmworkers Predominate. Medical Anthropology Quarterly 17(2):251–278.
   2004 Open Towns and Manipulated Indebtedness Among Agricultural Workers in the New South. American Ethnologist 31(4):530–551.
Boyce, W. Thomas, Pamela K. Den Besten, Juliet Stamperdahl, Ling Zhan, Yebin Jiang, Nancy E. Adler, and John D. Featherstone
   2010 Social Inequalities in Childhood Dental Caries: The Convergent Roles of Stress, Bacteria and Disadvantage. Social Science & Medicine 71(9):1644–1652.

Bruce, Douglas, Gary W. Harper, and The Adolescent Medicine Trials Network for HIV/AIDS Interventions

    2011   Operating Without a Safety Net: Gay Male Adolescents and Emerging Adults' Experiences of Marginalization and Migration, and Implications for Theory of Syndemic Production of Health Disparities. Health Education & Behavior 38(4):367–378.

Cain, Kevin P., Nong Kanara, Kayla F. Laserson, Chhum Vannarith, Keo Sameourn, K. Samnang, M. L. Qualls, Charles D. Wells, and Jay K. Varma

    2007   The Epidemiology of HIV-Associated Tuberculosis in Rural Cambodia. The International Journal of Tuberculosis and Lung Disease 11(9):1008–1013.

Call, Richard L., Beverly Entwistle, and Terri Swanson

    1987   Dental Caries in Permanent Teeth in Children of Migrant Farm Workers. American Journal of Public Health 77(8):1002–1003.

Candib, Lucy M.

    2007   Obesity and Diabetes in Vulnerable Populations: Reflection on Proximal and Distal Causes. Annals of Family Medicine 5(6):547–556.

Carrion, Iraida V., Heide Castañeda, Dinorah Martinez–Tyson, and Nolan Kline

    2011   Barriers Impeding Access to Primary Oral Health Care Among Farmworker Families in Central Florida. Social Work in Health Care 50(10):828–844.

Cartwright, Elizabeth

    2011   Immigrant Dreams: Legal Pathologies and Structural Vulnerabilities along the Immigration Continuum. Medical Anthropology 30(5):475–495.

Castañeda, Heide, Iraida V. Carrion, Nolan Kline, and Dinorah Tyson-Martinez

    2010   False Hope: Effects of Social Class and Health Policy on Oral Health Inequalities for Migrant Farmworker Families. Social Science & Medicine 71(11):2028–2037.

Chaffin, Jeffrey G., Satish Chandra, S. Pai, and Robert A. Bagramian

    2003   Caries Prevalence in Northwest Michigan Migrant Children. Journal of Dentistry for Children 70(2):124–129.

Diedrich, Collin R., and JoAnne L. Flynn

    2011   HIV-1/Mycobacterium Tuberculosis Coinfection Immunology: How Does HIV-1 Exacerbate Tuberculosis? Infection and Immunology 79(4):1407–1417.

Drewnowski, Adam, and Nicole Darmon

    2005   Food Choices and Diet Costs: An Economic Analysis. Journal of Nutrition 135(4):900–904.

Drewnowski, Adam, and S. E. Specter

    2004   Poverty and Obesity: The Role of Energy Density and Energy Costs. The American Journal of Clinical Nutrition 79(1):6–16.

Edberg, Mark, Sean Cleary, and Amita Vyas

    2011   A Trajectory Model for Understanding and Assessing Health Disparities in Immigrant/Refugee Communities. Journal of Immigrant and Minority Health 13(3):576–584.

Egan, James E., Victoria Frye, Steven P. Kurtz, Carl Latkin, Minxing Chen, Karin Tobin, Cui Yang, and Beryl A. Koblin

    2011   Migration, Neighborhoods, and Networks: Approaches to Understanding how Urban Environmental Conditions Affect Syndemic Adverse Health Outcomes Among Gay, Bisexual and Other Men Who Have Sex With Men. AIDS and Behavior 15(Suppl. 1):S35–50.

Exley, Catherine

    2009   Bridging a Gap: The (Lack of a) Sociology of Oral Health and Healthcare. Sociology of Health & Illness 31(7):1093–1108.

Freudenberg, Nicholas, Marianne Fahs, Sandro Galea, and Andrew Greenberg

    2006   The Impact of New York City's 1975 Fiscal Crisis on the Tuberculosis, HIV, and Homicide Syndemic. American Journal of Public Health 96(3):424–434.

Gielen, Andrea C., Reem M. Ghandour, Jessica G. Burke, Patrick Mahoney, Karen A. McDonnell, and Patricia O'Campo

    2007   HIV/AIDS and Intimate Partner Violence: Intersecting Women's Health Issues in the United States. Trauma, Violence, & Abuse 8(2):178–198.

Glanz, Karen, Michael Basil, Edward Maibach, Jeanne Goldberg, and Dan Snyder
   1998   Why Americans Eat What They Do: Taste, Nutrition, Cost, Convenience, and Weight Control Concerns as Influences on Food Consumption. Journal of the American Dietetic Association 98(10):1118–1126.

González-Guarda, Rosa M., Brian E. McCabe, Aubrey Florom-Smith, Rosina Cianelli, and Nilda Peragallo
   2011   Substance Abuse, Violence, HIV, and Depression: An Underlying Syndemic Factor Among Latinas. Nursing Research 60(3):182–189.

Hein, Casey, and Doreen Small
   2006   Combating Diabetes, Obesity, Periodontal Disease and Interrelated Inflammatory Conditions with a Syndemic Approach. Grand Rounds in Oral-Systematic Medicine 2:36–47.

Herrick, Amy L., Sin How Lim, Chongyi Wei, Helen Smith, Thomas Guadamuz, Mark S. Friedman, and Ron Stall
   2011   Resilience as an Untapped Resource in Behavioral Intervention Design for Gay Men. AIDS Behavior 15 (Suppl. 1):S25–S29.

Hilton, Irene V., Samantha Stephen, Judith C. Barker, and Jane A. Weintraub
   2007   Cultural Factors and Children's Oral Health Care: A Qualitative Study of Carers of Young Children. Community Dentistry and Oral Epidemiology 35(6):429–438.

Hirsch, Robert Steven
   2004   Diabetes and Periodontitis. Australian Prescriber 27(2):36–38.

Horton, Sarah, and Judith C. Barker
   2008   Rural Latino Immigrant Caregivers' Conceptions of Their Children's Oral Disease. Journal of Public Health Dentistry 68(1):22–29.
   2010   Stigmatized Biologies: Examining Oral Health Disparities for Mexican American Farmworker Children and their Cumulative Effects. Medical Anthropology Quarterly 24(2):199–219.

Iacopino, Anthony M.
   2009   Surveillance Spotlight: New "Syndemic" Paradigm for Interprofessional Management of Chronic Inflammatory Disease. Journal of the Canadian Dental Association 75(9):632–633.

Kandelman, Daniel
   1997   Sugar, Alternative Sweeteners and Meal Frequency in Relation to Caries Prevention: New Perspectives. British Journal of Nutrition 77(Suppl. 1):S121–S128.

Kline, Nolan
   2010   Disparate Power and Disparate Resources: Collaboration Between Faith-based and Activist Organizations for Central Florida Farmworkers. NAPA Bulletin 33(1):126–142.

Kurtz, Steven P.
   2008   Arrest Histories of High-Risk Gay and Bisexual Men in Miami: Unexpected Additional Evidence for Syndemic Theory. Journal of Psychoactive Drugs 40(4):513–521.

Kwan, Candice K., and Joel D. Ernst
   2011   HIV and Tuberculosis: A Deadly Human Syndemic. Clinical Microbiology Reviews 24(2):351–376.

Loesche, Walter J., Anthony Schork, Margaret S. Terpenning, Yin-Miao Chen, B. Lisa Dominguez, and Natalie Grossman
   1998   Assessing the Relationship Between Dental Disease and Coronary Heart Disease in Elderly U.S. Veterans. Journal of the American Dental Association 129(3):301–311.

Lukes, Sherri M., and Bret Simon
   2005   Dental Decay in Southern Illinois Migrant and Seasonal Farmworkers: An Analysis of Clinical Data. Journal of Rural Health 21(3):254–258.

Medina-Solís, Carlo E., Ricardo Pérez-Núñez, Gerardo Maupomé, and Juan F. Casanova-Rosado
   2006a   Edentulism Among Mexican Adults Aged 35 Years and Older and Associated Factors. American Journal of Public Health 96(6):1578–1581.

Medina-Solís, Carlo E., América Segovia-Villanueva, Ricardo Estrella-Rodríguez, Gerardo Maupomé, Leticia Ávila-Burgos, and Ricardo Pérez-Núñez

2006b Association Between Socioeconomic Status and Oral Hygiene Among Preschoolers Enrolled in the IMSS Preventive Dental Program in Campeche. Gaceta medica de Mexico 142(5):363–368.

Michaud, Dominique S., Kamundi Joshipura, Edward Giovannucci, and Charles S. Fuchs
2007 A Prospective Study of Periodontal Disease and Pancreatic Cancer in US Male Health Professionals. Journal of the National Cancer Institute 99(2):171–175.

Mojon, Philippe, Ejvind Budtz-Jorgensen, and Charles Henri Rapin
1999 Relationship Between Oral Health and Nutrition in Very Old People. Age and Ageing 28(5):463–468.

Mustanski, Brian, Robert Garofalo, Amy Herrick, and Geri Donenberg
2007 Psychosocial Health Problems Increase Risk for HIV Among Urban Young Men Who Have Sex With Men: Preliminary Evidence of a Syndemic in Need of Attention. Annals of Behavioral Medicine 34(1):37–45.

Myslobodsky, Michael, and Anya Eldan
2010 Winning a Won Game: Caffeine Panacea for Obesity Syndemic. Current Neuropharmacology 8(2):149–160.

National Center for Health Statistics
2011 With Special Feature on Death and Dying. Table 93: Dental Visits in the Past Year, by Selected Characteristics: United States, Selected Years 1997–2009. Pp. 316. Hyattsville, MD: U.S. Department of Health and Human Services, Centers for Disease Control and Prevention.

Nord, Mark, Alisha Coleman-Jensen, Margaret Andrews, and Steven Carlson
2010 Household Food Security in the United States, 2009. ERR-108. U.S. Department of Agriculture, Economic Research Service.

Nurko, Carlos, Luis Aponte-Merced, Edwin L. Bradley, and Liesl Fox
1998 Dental Caries Prevalence and Dental Health Care of Mexican-American Workers' Children. ASDC Journal of Dentistry for Children 65(1):65–72.

Operario, Don, and Tooru Nemoto
2010 HIV in Transgender Communities: Syndemic Dynamics and a Need for Multicomponent Interventions. Journal of Acquired Immune Deficiency Syndromes 5(Suppl. 2):S91–S93

Pitiphat, Waranuch, Kaumudi J. Joshipura, Matthew W. Gillman, Paige L. Williams, Chester W. Douglass, and Janet W. Rich-Edwards
2008 Maternal Periodontitis and Adverse Pregnancy Outcomes. Community Dentistry and Oral Epidemiology 36(1):3–11.

Psoter, Walter J., Britt C. Reid, and Ralph V. Katz
2005 Malnutrition and Dental Caries: A Review of the Literature. Caries Research 39(6):441–447.

Quandt, Sara A., Heather M. Clark, Pamela Rao, and Thomas A. Arcury
2007 Oral Health of Children and Adults in Latino Migrant and Seasonal Farmworker Families. Journal of Immigrant and Minority Health 9(3):229–235.

Ritchie, Christine S., Kaumundi Joshipura, Hsin-Chia Hung, and Chester W. Douglass
2002 Nutrition as Mediator in the Relation Between Oral and Systemic Disease: Associations Between Specific Measures of Adult Oral Health and Nutrition Outcomes. Critical Reviews in Oral Biology and Medicine 13(3):291–300.

Romero-Daza, Nancy, Margaret Weeks, and Merrill Singer
2003 "Nobody Gives a Damn if I Live or Die": Violence, Drugs, and Street Level Prostitution in Inner-City Hartford, Connecticut. Medical Anthropology 22(3):233–259.

Ruiz, Juan, and Marc Egli
2010 Metabolic Syndrome, Diabetes Mellitus and Vulnerability: A Syndemic Approach of Chronic Diseases. Revue Médicale de la Suisse Romande 6(271):2205–2208.

Safren, Steven A., Sari L. Reisner, Amy Herrick, Matthew J. Mimiaga, and Ronald D. Stall
2010 Mental Health and HIV Risk in Men Who Have Sex With Men. Journal of Acquired Immune Deficiency Syndromes 55(Suppl. 2):S74–S77.

Schensul, Stephen L., Jean J. Schensul, and Margaret D. LeCompte
1999 Essential Ethnographic Methods, Book 2. Walnut Creek, CA: Altamira Press.

Senn, Theresa E., Michael P. Carey, and Peter A. Vanable

    2010 The Intersection of Violence, Substance Use, Depression, and STDs: Testing of a Syndemic Pattern Among Patients Attending an Urban STD Clinic. Journal of the National Medical Association 102(7):614–620.

Sheiham, Aubrey, Jimmy G. Steele, Wagner Marcenes, Stephen Finch, and Angus W.G. Walls

    1999 The Impact of Oral Health on Stated Ability to Eat Certain Foods; Findings From the National Diet and Nutrition Survey of Older People in Great Britain. Gerodentology 16(1):11–20.

Singer, Merrill

    1994 AIDS and the Health Crisis of the Urban Poor: The Perspective of Critical Medical Anthropology. Social Science & Medicine 39(7):931–948.

    2010 Pathogen-Pathogen Interaction: A Syndemic Model of Complex Biosocial Processes in Disease. Virulence 1(1):10–18.

Singer, Merrill, and Scott Clair

    2003 Syndemics and Public Health: Reconceptualizing Disease in Bio-Social Context. Medical Anthropology Quarterly 17(4):423–441.

Singer, Merrill, Pamela I. Erickson, Louise Badiane, Rosemary Diaz, Dugeidy Ortiz, Traci Abraham, and Anna M. Nicolaysen

    2006 Syndemics, Sex and the City: Understanding Sexually Transmitted Diseases in Social and Cultural Context. Social Science & Medicine 63(8):2010–2021.

Slavkin, Harold C., and Bruce J. Baum

    2000 Relationship of Dental and Oral Pathology to Systemic Illness. Journal of the American Medical Association 284(10):1215–1217.

Stall, Ron, Thomas C. Mills, John Williamson, Trevor Hart, Greg Greenwood, Jay Paul, Lance Pollack, Diane Binson, Dennis Osmond, and Joseph A. Catania

    2003 Association of Co-Occurring Psychosocial Health Problems and Increased Vulnerability to HIV/AIDS Among Urban Men Who Have Sex With Men. American Journal of Public Health 93(6):939–942.

Starfield, Barbara

    2007 Pathways of Influence on Equity in Health. Social Science & Medicine 64(7):1355–1362.

Storholm, Erik D., Perry N. Halkitis, Daniel E. Siconolfi, and Robert W. Moeller

    2011 Cigarette Smoking as Part of a Syndemic Among Young Men Who Have Sex With Men Ages 13–29 in New York City. Journal of Urban Health 88(4):663–676.

USDA Economic Research Service

    2012 Food Security in the U.S.: Survey Tools. http://www.ers.usda.gov/topics/food-nutrition-assistance/food-security-in-the-us/survey-tools.aspx#six, accessed November 27, 2012.

Van Tieu, Hong, and Beryl A. Koblin

    2009 HIV, Alcohol, and Noninjection Drug Use. Current Opinion in HIV AIDS 4(4):314–318.

Ventura, Hector O., and Mandeep R. Mehra

    2004 The Growing Burden of Heart Failure: The "Syndemic" is Reaching Latin America. American Heart Journal 147(3):386–389.

Woolfolk, Marilyn, Margot Hamard, Robert A. Bagramian, and Harold Sgan-Cohen

    1984 Oral Health of Children of Migrant Farm Workers in Northwest Michigan. Journal of Public Health Dentistry 44(3):101–105.

COCIRCULATING EPIDEMICS, CHRONIC HEALTH PROBLEMS, AND SOCIAL CONDITIONS IN EARLY 20TH CENTURY LABRADOR AND ALASKA

LISA SATTENSPIEL
University of Missouri-Columbia

SVENN-ERIK MAMELUND
Work Research Institute, Oslo

Analyses of mortality in Alaska and Labrador during the 1918 influenza pandemic indicate that influenza itself was only one of several factors influencing mortality in different communities. We discuss the added impact of exposure to influenza prior to the major waves of the pandemic in 1918 and cocirculation of other acute infectious diseases, including pneumonia, smallpox, and measles; chronic conditions such as nutritional deficiencies and tuberculosis; and social and cultural factors such as the economic climate, ethnicity, official responses, and access to health care. The emphasis is on potential explanations for differential mortality in these regions and on how the experiences of Labradoreans and Alaskans can help to inform us about the multitude of interrelated factors influencing modern health issues. [1918 influenza pandemic; syndemics; mortality; Alaska; Labrador; pandemic preparedness planning]

INTRODUCTION

The epidemiological and popular literatures are filled with tales of particular infectious disease epidemics through human history. For example, innumerable studies and novels have centered on the Black Death in 14th century Europe, cholera in 19th century Britain and France, or malaria in Africa and Southeast Asia. All too often, however, these studies have treated the diseases of interest as if they were the only unusual circumstance facing the affected populations. Even when bringing in other issues such as socioeconomic differences, the influence of political structures, or the impact of nutritional status, discussion of the morbidity and mortality experiences of epidemics is often limited to one or two broader issues. In recent years, however, there has been a growing interest in embracing the complexity of real-world situations in attempts to evaluate how different influences may interact to determine how and why human populations experience infectious disease epidemics in the ways that they do.

Perhaps the biggest push toward developing this more encompassing approach to the study of health and disease in human groups has been the work of Merrill Singer et al., who have promoted the need to use a syndemic approach. This approach explicitly considers how two or more diseases or health conditions may interact within the broad social,

ANNALS OF ANTHROPOLOGICAL PRACTICE 36.2, pp. 402–421. ISSN: 2153-957X. © 2013 by the American Anthropological Association. DOI:10.1111/napa.12011

economic, and political arenas that make up the environment in which we live (Singer and Clair 2003; Singer 2009). It is probably impossible to consider simultaneously all the various dimensions of society and how they may influence health, but there are a growing number of studies that attempt to situate the experience of disease within a wider context, and these studies consider an interesting array of dimensions. For example, Singer et al. (2006) related high rates of sexually transmitted diseases in young African American and Puerto Rican adults living in Hartford, CT to a number of social factors, including socioeconomic conditions, stability of their homes, availability of positive role models, and prevalence of domestic violence. Herring and Sattenspiel (2007) stressed the importance of social, historical, and economic factors such as inadequate housing and diet, poverty, and political marginalization in determining the impact of infectious diseases on North American aboriginal communities. Littleton and Park (2009) looked at how tuberculosis and diabetes are linked in Pacific populations resident in New Zealand, especially in relation to smoking, adequacy of housing, and nutritional factors. In studies of infectious disease, there is also growing recognition of the need to consider the prevalence of other pathogens in addition to the primary pathogen of interest (see Singer 2010 for a recent discussion). For example, researchers have considered interactions between HIV and a variety of pathogens, including measles, malaria, leishmania, helminths, tuberculosis, and smallpox (e.g., Desjeux and Alvar 2003; Hartgers et al. 2008; Korenromp et al. 2005; Nilsson and Chiodi 2011; Sánchez et al. 2009; Weinstein et al. 2010). Studies have also looked at the interactions between influenza and tuberculosis (Noymer 2009, 2011), *Streptococcus pneumoniae* (McCullers and Rehg 2002; McCullers 2006) and bacterial pneumonia (pneumococci, streptococci, and staphylococci) (Morens et al. 2008).

In this article, we look at a prominent historical event, the 1918 influenza pandemic, in two regions, Labrador and Alaska, which are widely separated in space, yet have similar geographic and environmental constraints and overlap ethnically. In spite of these broad similarities, the pandemic impact and the specific factors influencing that impact were highly heterogeneous both within and between the two regions. These factors encompass not only cultural, social, and political factors, such as differences in daily and seasonal activity patterns or implementation of quarantine, but also biological factors such as other circulating pathogens, exposure to influenza prior to the major waves in 1918, and prevalence of chronic health conditions. These two regions thus provide an interesting illustration of how myriad factors interact with one another and influence the variation among populations' experiences in relation to specific health conditions, such as an influenza epidemic.

We begin with a brief overview of the 1918 influenza pandemic in both Labrador and Alaska. Following this, we discuss different dimensions of the local and regional contexts within which the pandemic spread and how those contexts may have influenced the observed patterns of disease spread and mortality. Finally, we discuss what we have learned overall from our study and how those insights, including research on the 2009 pandemic, may improve planning for the next influenza pandemic.

Both Labrador and Alaska were devastated by the 1918 influenza pandemic and experienced mortality much higher than most other parts of the world. Average mortality among all Labrador communities with information on the number of deaths was 34%; average mortality across communities reporting deaths in Alaska was 8% (Mamelund et al. 2013). Both of these averages are well above the estimated global mortality of 2.5–5.0% (Johnson and Mueller 2002; Mamelund 2011). Yet there is significant heterogeneity in mortality within each region as well, and up to one fifth in each region escaped the pandemic altogether.

Labrador experienced two waves of the pandemic, the first in the summer of 1918 and the second in October and November that same year. These two waves correspond to the first two waves noted by Crosby (1989) and observed in many places throughout the world. As was the case elsewhere, the first wave was mild with widespread sickness, but little mortality; the second wave was severe with high mortality in many locations. The summer wave affected only Southeastern Labrador; the fall wave affected all of Central Labrador and the central third of Northern Labrador. Communities in both the northern and southern thirds of Northern Labrador were unaffected by either wave of the pandemic.

In Southeastern Labrador, mortality averaged about 1% among communities reporting the epidemic, and all deaths occurred during the summer wave (Mamelund et al. 2013). The average mortality in Central Labrador was about 13%, but the majority of the deaths occurred in the communities surrounding the Sandwich Bay in the southern half of this region. Mortality in these communities ranged from 12–82%, with all but one community experiencing over 35% mortality. The range of mortality in communities around the Hamilton Inlet in the northern part of Central Labrador ranged from 0–17%, with most well under 10%. Mortality among all Central Labrador communities south of the Hamilton Inlet (including the Sandwich Bay communities) ranged from 8–82%. The average mortality in Northern Labrador was around 34%, but this average is highly misleading. Deaths were reported from five of the northernmost communities, but base population estimates needed to calculate the percentage dying were available for only four of these communities; their mortality ranged from 68–89%. Southern communities in Northern Labrador with reports of the pandemic appear to have escaped it altogether (Mamelund et al. 2013).

The geographic patterning within Alaska was equally heterogeneous (Mamelund et al. 2013). The region also experienced two major waves, but the timing was different. Alaska's first wave coincided with and was as severe as the second (fall) wave in Labrador and elsewhere, but the second Alaskan wave did not occur until May–June 1919. The first wave affected mostly coastal villages, although the western Aleutian Islands, communities along Bristol Bay in the southern part of the region, and communities along the northwestern and northern coasts were unaffected. Inland communities were affected in the Seward Peninsula and Yukon Delta, but central Alaska was not significantly affected. The second

Alaskan wave was limited to communities in the Aleutian Islands and Bristol Bay that had escaped the first wave. Some island communities in the Bering Sea and some interior river communities escaped both waves.

In general, mortality was low in Southeastern and Central Alaska (Mamelund et al. 2013). Average mortality in the former region was slightly under 1% and ranged from 0–3%. Average mortality in the latter region was slightly over 1%, with most communities experiencing mortality well under 1%, although 11% died in one Central Alaskan community and 18% died in another. Average mortality was much higher in other regions. In Northwestern and Northern Alaska, average mortality was around 15% when all communities were included, but the average mortality in Inupiaq native villages was almost 55%. The range among all Northwestern and Northern Alaskan communities reporting deaths was 19–90%, with most around 50% (although many communities in the region reported no deaths). Mortality in the Yukon Delta averaged near 4%, with most communities experiencing well under 10% mortality, but one with 32% mortality. In the Bristol Bay region, which was hit during the second wave, mortality in affected communities ranged from 0–67%, with most above 30%. The average mortality among all communities in this region was over 30%. The average mortality in the Aleutian Islands was nearly 7%, although the heterogeneity was marked. Most communities had rates below 15%, but the range was 0–79% among all communities.

FACTORS INFLUENCING THE 1918 PANDEMIC EXPERIENCE IN LABRADOR AND ALASKA

Given the extreme heterogeneity in mortality estimated across both Labrador and Alaska, it is clear that explanations for the patterning of the pandemic cannot be simplistic and unifactorial. Rather, explanations may be more credible if based on a syndemic approach that considers the joint influence of multiple factors that include both other pathogens and social variables. However, the extreme heterogeneity also suggests that the influence of different possible cofactors varied by location.

A number of potential influences are clearly important across both regions. Most of our study communities were small, fragmented, remote, and physically isolated. In addition, unlike more developed regions of North America, at the time of the pandemic they also had not completed either the demographic or epidemiological transitions, meaning that they had high fertility rates, high infant mortality, and a high prevalence and mortality from a number of infectious diseases. Risk factors for severe outcomes from influenza, such as poor underlying health and a high number of pregnancies, were thus highly prevalent in the people living in these areas. In spite of these broad similarities, there were also significant differences across communities (elaborated below), and the suite of variables that determined epidemic outcomes in different regions overlapped but were not uniform in space. In the following sections, we describe many of these variables and the influences they appear to have had on the pandemic in both regions.

Cocirculation of Other Pathogens and Prior Exposure to Influenza

Archival materials from Labrador and Alaska clearly illustrate the effects of other circulating pathogens on patterns of spread and mortality from influenza. The most important of these other diseases are pneumonia and tuberculosis, but several others may also have had an impact. Pneumonia of all types always accompanies influenza epidemics (Morens et al. 2008), to such a degree that even today the WHO *International Classification of Diseases* (ICD) groups the two diseases within the same major category, and usually they are reported together in official health data as pneumonia/influenza (P&I). Pulmonary tuberculosis was the leading cause of death in Newfoundland and Labrador until the 1920s; from 1920 on only old age killed more residents than tuberculosis. Furthermore, the number of tuberculosis deaths was consistently two or more times higher than the number of influenza and pneumonia deaths, even during epidemic years (Newfoundland House of Assembly 1910–1912, 1915–1924).

Cocirculation of other pathogens may have played a large role in the patterning of the 1918 pandemic in Northern Labrador, which was quite different from that observed in Southeastern and Central Labrador, in spite of similar general environmental conditions. Northern Labrador experienced the greatest heterogeneity in mortality (and presumably morbidity) of all of Labrador. As mentioned above, five communities in Northern Labrador reported deaths during the pandemic; these communities were all located in the central third of that region. The few communities to the north of this area (the northern third of Northern Labrador) and all communities in the southern third of the region apparently escaped the pandemic completely (both summer and fall waves).

The few northernmost communities in Northern Labrador appear to have missed the pandemic because of geographic and social isolation, but this does not seem to have been the case for the communities in the southern third of Northern Labrador. Widespread epidemics of measles and/or a mild form of smallpox (occasionally attributed to chickenpox) were reported in all of the communities in this latter area; these communities were unaffected by influenza when the pandemic was raging in adjoining communities in the central third of Northern Labrador and in Central Labrador to the south (Hettasch 1986[1918]; Leacock and Rothschild 1994; Paddon 2003; Perrett 1986a[1918], 1986b[1919]). Leacock and Rothschild (1994) present the personal diary of William Duncan Strong, an ethnographer working in Central Labrador during the pandemic years. Strong, Hettasch, and Perrett, who were Moravian missionaries in Northern Labrador, and Paddon, the resident doctor in Central Labrador, all suggested at the time that these other epidemics may have protected people when they were exposed to influenza. It is important to note, however, that there are other possible explanations, including potential social and biological factors linked to ethnicity. This possibility is discussed further below.

The idea that other epidemics could somehow protect individuals from a different disease, termed a countersyndemic in the syndemic literature (Singer 2009), is not one that is commonly proposed by scientists today. However, the impact of exposure to multiple pathogens, which is central to a syndemic approach, has been examined by a few researchers. For example, Aaby et al. (Aaby et al. 1995, 2003, 2010; Kristensen et al. 2000) studied the impact of measles vaccination in Guinea-Bissau and Bangladesh and suggested that vaccination may have resulted in nonspecific effects that reduced overall mortality among children, especially females. Furthermore, they showed that the diphtheria-pertussis-tetanus (DPT) and polio vaccines were not associated with similar reductions in mortality, but that use of the tuberculosis BCG vaccine was. In another study, Sørup et al. (2011) showed that live virus smallpox vaccination reduced overall childhood morbidity and mortality. It may be that exposure to natural cases of a disease confers a similar sort of protection against other pathogens circulating in a population at about the same time. If this is confirmed in additional studies, it could explain the lack of influenza in the southern communities of Northern Labrador.

Measles and the mild smallpox apparently did not reach the communities in the central third of Northern Labrador that were totally devastated by influenza (all experienced over 65% mortality, far worse than other regions). It is not clear why they were hit so hard, however. Communities throughout the entire Northern Labrador region were under the influence of the Moravian missionaries, almost all communities were composed almost totally of fully indigenous nomadic peoples, and all were under substantial nutritional stress due to a lack of prey animals as well as long-term cultural changes in diet (Hanrahan 2008). Besides the presence of other circulating pathogens in the communities unaffected by the flu pandemic, what is different in the southern and central thirds of Northern Labrador is the timing of the last supply boat before winter freeze-up. In most years this boat would travel up the coast from central Labrador, but it was delayed in the fall of 1918 and so it went first to the central third of the region before heading south to slightly warmer waters (Budgell 1994). By the time the boat reached the southern third of the region, little if any infection may have been present among its crew and passengers, and that, combined with the presence of other cocirculating pathogens may explain the absence of the flu in these communities in spite of its presence both to the north (the central third of Northern Labrador) and to the south (Central Labrador).

Like the communities in the southern third of Northern Labrador, Southeastern Labrador was barely affected by the 1918 influenza pandemic. Only two deaths from influenza and/or pneumonia are reported in the Labrador Death Registers during 1918–1919; both of these deaths occurred in the summer of 1918 (Newfoundland and Labrador Death Records 1918–1919). It appears that the summer outbreak was widespread in the region; furthermore, several sources indicate that the region was largely unaffected during the major pandemic wave in the fall of 1918 (e.g., Brewer 1919; Johnson 1919; Muir 1918; Paddon 1919a; Parsons 1919). This also seems to have been the situation in the Northern Peninsula of Newfoundland, the part of that island closest to Labrador (Palmer et al. 2007; Sattenspiel 2011). Worldwide the spring/summer wave of the influenza pandemic was mild with low mortality; Labrador and the Northern Peninsula of Newfoundland fit this picture. Opinion is divided on whether exposure to this mild wave conferred immunity to affected individuals that protected them from death in the later, deadly wave, however (e.g., Andreasen et al. 2008; Barry et al. 2009; Fraser et al. 2011; Herring and Padiak 2008; Mamelund 2003; Mathews et al. 2010; Shanks et al. 2010). Because the pandemic occurred nearly 100 years ago, data on the immune status of individuals are usually not readily available, even in the most developed parts of the world at the time. Nonetheless, Southeastern Labrador and the Northern Peninsula of Newfoundland provide another example of a situation where widespread exposure to the summer 1918 wave was associated with very low mortality (but not necessarily low risk of infection) during the subsequent fall wave, even though neighboring regions were severely affected in terms of mortality during the second wave.

Lack of exposure to the 1918 strain of influenza may also explain some of the heterogeneity in regional patterns of morbidity and mortality during the pandemic. In remote regions such as Alaska and Labrador, with sparse, dispersed, and isolated populations, it is common for communities to escape even widespread, severe epidemics. The nomadic lifestyle of some of the indigenous groups reinforced this isolation at the time of the annual influenza epidemics. During the winter, many of these groups lived in remote inland areas, thus lowering the risk of being exposed to influenza, but they aggregated in less isolated villages by the coast during the summer. Data from Alaska clearly indicate the lack of exposure for some communities. For example, serological data collected in the 1950s show that people living in several Northern mainland and Bering Sea island villages had no antibodies to the 1918 influenza strain (A/H1N1) (Philip and Lackman 1962), supporting historical sources from 1918 stating that these communities escaped the two waves of pandemic influenza in Alaska in 1918 and 1919.

Little or no exposure to a genetic ancestor or closely related strain to the H1N1 1918 influenza virus circulating in the 19th century (i.e., a lack of immunological memory [Ahmed et al. 2007]) may also be important in explaining the generally high mortality in Alaska and Labrador in 1918–19. Mamelund (2011) used demographic data (including previously unused church books) to test the immunological memory hypothesis in explaining the large mortality differences between several remote and urban areas within the Nordic countries, USA (including Hawaii and Alaska), Canada (including Labrador), Australia, New Zealand, and seven Pacific Islands. He found that persons over age 60 living in well-connected urban societies had lower than expected mortality, partly explaining the relatively low overall mortality rates (< 1%) observed in these places. This is most likely a consequence of previous exposure to similar influenza viruses. However, the remotely living elderly did not have lower than expected mortality, which suggests that they had less prior exposure to influenza than their urban counterparts (Mamelund 2011).

To what extent the level of immunological memory was unequally distributed within Alaska and Labrador remains a question open to speculation. However, it is tempting to suggest that nomadic people living in the central third of Northern Labrador had less prior exposure to influenza than people living in the southern third of Northern Labrador, a small but larger number of whom were of European decent living in permanent villages by the coast. These people may have enjoyed some protection to fight the 1918 pandemic because of more prior exposure to influenza epidemics in the 19th century (at their place of residence or in Europe).

Environmental Influences

The environment affected all Labrador and Alaskan populations in a fairly similar way. The climate throughout the region was and is harsh, especially during the winter. Many of Labrador's residents in all regions engaged in a practice known as seasonal transhumance, where they would live in coastal communities during the summer and then move inland to more sheltered environments during the winter (Kennedy 1996). Yet life during the winter was stressful even with the move to these more sheltered winter communities—the shelter did not remove the bitter cold and snow that was omnipresent in Labrador and Alaskan winters. In addition, travel on the landscape was difficult and dangerous due to cold, snow, and ice. These conditions likely increased the risks of severe disease relative to people living in more temperate climates. In addition, as noted by Herring (1994) and Wolfe (1982), harsh winter conditions in conjunction with high influenza mortality of providers significantly increased the rate of secondary mortality from starvation or freezing in children and the elderly.

Nutritional Factors

Most regions of Labrador experienced chronic nutritional stress, especially at the time of the flu pandemic when major prey animals were also in short supply due to environmental circumstances (Hanrahan 2008; Paddon 2003). The health of some Alaskan groups may also have been compromised due to nutritional inadequacies. At the time of the pandemic, depletion of traditional resources of the Inupiaq resulted in changes in their subsistence strategy (Schaaf and Smith 1996). In addition, all Alaskan groups experienced various levels of acculturation in terms of their diet due to contact with European, Russian, and other populations. This usually meant a decrease in traditional food and an increase in processed, purchased food. Such changes have been associated with conditions such as obesity, diabetes, and hypertension (Draper 1977), and may have impacted pregnant females even more significantly due to their increased caloric needs.

Clearly, early 20th century Labrador and Alaska can be considered populations in transition with regard to nutrition. This transitional status and the high impact of infectious diseases in these preepidemiological transition regions undoubtedly played major roles in accounting for the poorer health, higher mortality, and shorter lifespans of residents of Labrador and Alaska. Furthermore, although in contemporary populations the predominant diseases are more likely to be chronic in nature rather than acute infections, similar interactions between poor nutrition and disease-related health conditions continue to compromise the health of aboriginal populations throughout the world (see, e.g., Littleton and Park 2009).

The Economic and Business Climate

The economic situation in different regions of Labrador and Alaska was another important factor influencing the severity of the pandemic. The degree of acculturation of local communities was heavily influenced by the business interests of other countries. For example, Alutiiq communities in the Pribolof Islands, Alaska were influenced first by

Russian hunters and fur traders, and subsequently by commercial fishing and canneries owned by European-derived populations, which have dominated the economy since the late 19th century (Pritzker 2000). Employees of these businesses brought with them wood-framed houses and a hospital that provided free medical care. These changes also resulted in substantial Westernization of the indigenous groups (Corbett and Swibold 2000; Wolfe 1982).

In Southeastern and Central Labrador, large companies such as the Hudson's Bay Company or (mostly) absentee owners of land and fishing boats affected many aspects of life. These regions were centers of the lucrative cod fishing trade until the fisheries collapsed in the 1970s. During the late 19th and early 20th centuries, up to 25,000 men and their families came to the Labrador shores during the summer fishing season (Grenfell 1895). The influx of these fishermen is probably a major reason for the wide extent of the summer influenza epidemic in Southeastern Labrador. The economy of Central Labrador was based more on fur trapping than fishing, and the activities of the Hudson's Bay Company played a significant role in the health and well being of this region's residents. The nature of fur trapping activities and other issues in Central Labrador are addressed further in the section on integrated factors below.

Access to Health Care

Inadequate access to health care in the majority of Labrador and Alaskan communities, which ranged from minimal to nonexistent, helps to explain why the two regions were generally affected more severely than other parts of the world. The Grenfell Mission, a medical mission started by Wilfred Grenfell and based in St. Anthony on the tip of the Northern Peninsula of Newfoundland, was founded in order to provide basic health services to the large summer population of fishermen off the coast of Labrador, but once the weather turned cold and the seas began to freeze up in the early fall, the visiting fishermen as well as Grenfell and his associates returned home, leaving the small and dispersed resident population of mostly European-derived fishermen and their families without ready access to medical care. Similarly, Moravian missionaries provided some health care to the indigenous peoples in Northern Labrador, but at most times, including during the 1918 influenza pandemic, trained physicians were not available; rather, the only care was provided by the missionaries themselves, who had little formal medical training (Paddon 1919b).

The lowest mortality in Alaska occurred in the Southeast region, the area where people were best able to care for the ill. This area had the highest concentration of preexisting hospitals and doctors in Alaska. In addition, at the peak of Alaska's first wave in November 1918, Governor Riggs hired doctors and nurses from the San Francisco and Seattle areas and dispatched them to the region (Crosby 1989). Moreover, the Southeast also had good transportation systems in open coastal waters, and the supplies, skills, and political and health institutions capable of utilizing these advantages (Crosby 1989). However, most of Alaska generally had great shortages of hospitals and trained health care personnel.

Institutional Responses to the Pandemic

Institutional responses to the pandemic, especially the implementation of quarantines, were observed in both Alaska and Labrador, but their extent and success varied markedly and help to explain some of the differences between the two regions. In Alaska, ample warning was given about the risk of importation of the virus to the territory. After severe outbreaks of influenza in Seattle, Washington in early October 1918, Governor Riggs ordered all steamship companies to check all passengers bound north and prevent the embarkation of any sick person. Persons with symptoms of influenza were required to be isolated at the port of debarkation, along with all direct contacts. Moreover, Governor Riggs halted all travel to the interior and ordered all villages to establish quarantines and create a *cordon sanitaire* on all trailheads and along rivers (Crosby 1989; Ganley 1998; Lautaret 1986; Philip and Lackman 1962). Although the maritime quarantine did not hinder the pandemic from entering the ports of Alaska, there are indications that inland quarantine helped to prevent widespread dissemination of the disease to central Alaskan communities (Crosby 1989; Ganley 1998; Mamelund et al. 2013; Philip and Lackman 1962). In St. John's, Newfoundland, ships with sick sailors on board were quarantined, but there was no official action taken that would interfere with the regular shipping schedule covering the Northeast coast of Labrador. Thus, quarantine appeared to have little impact in Labrador.

Ethnicity

Ethnicity seems to be associated at least somewhat with pandemic severity across communities in both Labrador and Alaska. For example, most of the unaffected communities in the southern third of Northern Labrador consisted of higher numbers of people of pure European or mixed European-indigenous ancestries than did the severely affected communities in the central third of the region, which consisted largely of fully indigenous people (Mamelund 2011). The extent of admixture with indigenous peoples in Southeastern Labrador was minimal (Cuff 1994), and this region also largely escaped the severe effects of the pandemic.

A similar association has been observed in an analysis of mortality among the Sami in Norway during the 1918 influenza pandemic (Mamelund 2003) and in an analysis of the impact of ethnicity in multiple influenza pandemics over the last century in New Zealand (Wilson et al. 2012). Although it is not clear why the degree of indigenous ancestry may be important, rates of mortality overall in both Labrador and Alaska appear to correlate with the extent of European-indigenous admixture (Mamelund 2011; Mamelund et al. 2013).

Teasing apart the relative contributions of genetic differences and socioeconomic and other social factors is a challenging task. The cross-sectional and/or individual-level data needed to do multivariate analyses for Alaska and Labrador are not yet available or ready for analysis. Although the effect of Sami origin on 1918 influenza-pneumonia mortality in Norwegian medical districts was reduced after controlling for wealth, poverty, crowding, occupational structure, and exposure to the summer wave, it was still significantly higher than that of Caucasians (Mamelund 2003). The reduction in the effect of Sami origin on mortality suggests that the Sami had a lower socioeconomic status than Caucasians, which was important to control for in the analysis. The independent effect of Sami origin on cross-sectional mortality may be accounted for by poorer immunological memory and genetic factors, but it could also be due to poorly specified control variables or socioeconomic confounders not controlled for (e.g., education) (Mamelund 2003).

Considering Integrated Factors: The Case of Central Labrador

The preceding discussion highlights the variety of factors that can impact infectious disease patterns in various places. A primary advantage of a truly syndemic approach, however, is to move away from the consideration of single factors toward a more unified view that jointly considers a cluster of factors. The 1918 pandemic in Central Labrador provides an excellent illustration of how such an approach can aid in understanding the underlying reasons for observed disease patterns.

The people of Central Labrador were primarily of mixed indigenous-European ancestry (called Settlers), the product of unions between European fishermen and fur trappers and indigenous women (Kennedy 1995). The region can be divided into two subregions: a southern half centered around Sandwich Bay and including towns to the south, and a northern half centered around the Hamilton Inlet. Residents of both subregions engaged in a mixed economy based on cod and/or salmon fishing in the summer and trapping in the winter, although communities to the south of Sandwich Bay depended more heavily on fishing than those in Sandwich Bay and the Hamilton Inlet (Kennedy 1995) and the people living near the Hamilton Inlet depended more heavily on trapping than did the Sandwich Bay residents (Tanner 1944). The Grenfell Mission provided health care throughout the region, though most of the care was seasonal (summer only) for the Sandwich Bay region, while the Hamilton Inlet area had a summer hospital near the coast and an inland winter hospital, along with a physician and nurses who were resident year-round. Communities to the south of Sandwich Bay experienced the summer wave of influenza rather than the severe fall wave; the rest of Central Labrador missed the summer wave. The Sandwich Bay region itself was devastated in the fall wave, while the Hamilton Inlet experienced widespread illness but limited mortality during that wave.

The economic set-up of both the Hudson's Bay Company and the fishing industry was based on credit or barter rather than cash exchange between the Settlers and the merchants (Kennedy 1995). The situation was generally one of exploitation of the Settlers (Kennedy 1995; Moody 1905), leading to constant attempts by the Settlers to do business with traders other than their suppliers (Kennedy 1995). The result of this was that nearly all permanent residents of Central and Southeastern Labrador, regardless of their ethnicity, were economically disadvantaged and suffered chronic nutritional stress, especially during the winter (Hanrahan 2008; Kennedy 1995). Furthermore, according to Kennedy (1995), the predominantly fishing communities south of the Sandwich Bay experienced greater poverty than the mixed economy residents of more northern Central Labrador communities, yet these fishing communities missed the major pandemic wave altogether. It is not clear how far north the mild summer wave extended, and so it is possible that the most economically disadvantaged communities south of the Sandwich Bay missed the major wave because of this prior exposure. Nonetheless, the general similarity in economic status throughout most of Central Labrador suggests that economic differences are probably not the most important factor influencing the differential mortality between the southern half of the region near Sandwich Bay and the northern half surrounding the Hamilton Inlet.

It is not clear what the significant factors were, however. The availability of health care, which was much greater in the Hamilton Inlet region than in the Sandwich Bay region or communities to the south, was certainly a difference between the subregions. Local variability in fur trapping activities may also have been important. In general, during the winter men traveled to inland fur trapping camps, leaving their wives and children behind in much smaller settlements. Harry Paddon, the resident doctor in the Hamilton Inlet region, noted that all of the long-distance trappers in North West River, the major town in that region, had left for their trapping grounds by the time of the pandemic (Paddon 2003). These territories were at some distance from the village and so the men would normally be away from their families from October until January (Tanner 1944). The small size of the remaining settlement, 75 persons, combined with the immediate presence of high quality medical care, was likely a major factor explaining the fact that 67 of the 75 individuals became sick but only two died (Paddon 2003). Like the Hamilton Inlet trappers, the Sandwich Bay men also tended to be at their trapping lines beginning in October, but their territories were close enough to the settlements to allow regular visits with their wives and children (Tanner 1944). This ability to maintain contact throughout the winter and the poorer health care than that available in the Hamilton Inlet communities are likely major reasons for the more severe flu mortality in the Sandwich Bay region.

LESSONS FOR THE FUTURE

Mortality from the 1918–19 influenza was extremely high in many but not all indigenous populations throughout Alaska and Labrador. Data also indicate that one-fifth of the population in both regions escaped the pandemic altogether. We have argued that part of the explanation for the high mortality in some areas was that, in general, neither Labrador nor Alaska had completed the epidemiological and demographic transitions observed elsewhere in North America. Because they were in a pretransition state, residents of these regions, and especially indigenous populations, had high levels of risk for severe outcomes from influenza, such as chronic underlying health conditions, infectious diseases, pregnancy, inadequate access to health care, and perhaps delayed seeking of care.

American Indian and Alaskan native people living in Alaska, First Nations people in Canada, Aboriginals in Australia, Torre Strait Islanders, Maori on New Zealand, and native people on several Pacific islands also suffered disproportionally from severe disease, hospitalization, and death during the 2009 influenza pandemic (CDC 2009a; Helferty et al. 2010; La Ruche et al. 2009; Wenger et al. 2011).Many contemporary indigenous populations still suffer from "historical" or present-day "developing country" infectious diseases and risk factors (including a higher number of pregnancies at a young age), while at the same time, they also suffer severely from "modern" or present-day "developed country" diseases/risk factors such as diabetes mellitus, asthma, smoking, chronic obstructive pulmonary disease, and obesity. After controlling for several of the "old" and "new" risk factors one multivariate study of the 2009 pandemic found no difference in the risk of hospitalization between indigenous and nonindigenous Western Australians (Goggin et al. 2011). Moreover, only the presence of two or more comorbid conditions was an independent predictor of hospitalization. This indicates that the higher hospitalization rates among the indigenous people were attributable to a higher prevalence of underlying chronic disease, and not due to any genetic predisposition or vulnerability (Goggin et al. 2011).

In a study from Manitoba, Canada, however, Zarychanski et al. (2010), found that First Nations status was independently associated with increasing severity of disease during the 2009 pandemic (patients admitted to intensive care unit vs. patients cared for in community, and patients admitted to intensive care unit vs. patients admitted to hospital but not to an intensive care unit). They suggested that the increased risk was associated with uncontrolled factors, including genetics, housing or living conditions, income adequacy, additional underlying comorbidities or access to health care resources (Zarychanski et al. 2010). The conflicting findings from Australia and Canada suggest that the causes and outcomes of 2009 pandemic influenza may be context specific, and are complex and interrelated. The same can also be concluded when the possible causes of mortality differences in Alaska and Labrador in 1918 are reviewed. More research is therefore needed in order to understand and explain the ethnic differences in severe outcomes from historical and recent influenza pandemics.

Indigenous peoples were at high risk for early and substantial morbidity and mortality from the 2009 pandemic (CDC 2009a; La Ruche et al. 2009; Helferty et al. 2010; Wenger et al. 2011), and they remain at a higher risk for seasonal influenza as well (Wenger et al. 2011). One crucial factor in explaining the ethnic differences is the geographic remoteness and extreme isolation that still is characteristic of many indigenous communities in both Alaska and Labrador. As discussed above, better access to health care and excellent transportation networks in open coastal waters (which could ship crisis help from the San Francisco and Seattle areas) in the less remote Southeastern region of Alaska is probably important in explaining the low mortality from the 1918 pandemic there. Northwest, North and Interior Alaska were less fortunate in terms of the level of health care and mortality. For example, there was only one physician at Nulaka on the Yukon; the only one for 500 miles in either direction along that river (Crosby 1989). Air travel was not introduced into Alaska before the late 1920s and in the following decade it was expanded to include even the most remote villages (Philp and Lackman 1962). However, the continued remoteness and extreme isolation of many indigenous communities, a significant number of which continue to be accessible only by plane year-round, is still a barrier to recruiting and retaining nurses and trained health care professionals and complicates access to advanced medical care (Charania and Tsuji 2011a).

The overall mortality rates for most countries in the world were lower in the 2009 pandemic than during normal seasonal influenza. This may be partly due to similar mechanisms that were at work in 1918 (and described above) also being in operation in 2009. Those who are older than 65 years usually have the highest mortality associated with seasonal influenza, but because of preexisting immunity, stemming from exposure to the H1N1 1918 virus and subsequent 1918-like viruses, few elderly people became ill and died in 2009. Serological studies from Europe, Japan, and the USA have shown that preexisting immunity was highest among those born before 1918, but also those born later had some protection. Those born after 1949 had little or no immunity against the A (H1N1) virus in 2009 (CDC 2009b; Fraser et al. 2009; Hancock et al. 2009; Ikonen et al. 2010; Itoh et al. 2009; Miller et al. 2010).

It is reasonable to assume that the level of preexisting immunity in remote and isolated populations in 2009 was lower than in their urban counterparts due to less frequent exposure to influenza in the remote than in the urban populations. A lower level of prepandemic immunity would therefore also be one of the factors in explaining the severe outcomes of 2009 influenza in remotely living indigenous people. However, few immune status studies have been carried out specifically for remote populations. In one exception, Trauer et al. (2011) analyzed the prepandemic immunity in remote and indigenous groups in Northern Territory, Australia. The prevalence of preexisting immunity was lowest in those born after 1980 and nonexistent in children. The level of preexisting immunity was highest in those born before 1950, but lower than that observed in data from North America (CDC 2009b; Hancock et al. 2009). This may reflect regional and/or ethnic differences or be the result of the 1976 mass-vaccination campaign against swine-origin H1N1 virus in the United States (Trauer et al. 2011). More research on the prepandemic immune status of remotely living populations is needed to determine the extent of differences in immunity compared with urban populations.

The findings we have presented for the 1918 pandemic in Labrador and Alaska and those of others for the 2009 H1N1 influenza pandemic have clear implications for infectious disease planning, including distributions of economic (e.g. housing) and human resources (nurses and other trained health care professionals), and stockpiling and distribution plans for vaccines and antivirals (Charania and Tsuji 2011a; Wenger et al. 2011). Programs to improve housing conditions and crowding, for example, may help reduce disease transmission in climates where a higher proportion of daily life is conducted indoors because of colder and harsher climates than elsewhere. Contingency plans must also take into account the remoteness, distance to population centers, including health care centers and hospitals, and other logistic issues that may complicate assistance efforts, including dispatching of health care resources and health care professionals (Wenger et al. 2011). Public health planners also need to assume that preexisting immunity may increase with age in their future pandemic morbidity and mortality models, but they should make the additional assumption that such immunity may be lower in populations living in remote and isolated areas.

In the almost certain event of a new pandemic, decision-makers also need to include vulnerable persons in discussions designed to build informed policy and practice decisions that are sensitive to ethnic and contextual factors (Silva 2010). Qualitative research in Canada's remote and isolated First Nation communities concluded after the 2009 pandemic that increased formal communication and collaboration between responsible government bodies will assist in clarifying roles and responsibilities and improve the next pandemic response (Charania and Tsuji 2011b).

Results from our study also highlight the complex interactions between different social and biological factors that are all known to affect disease patterns individually. These interactions ensure that epidemic experiences will continue to vary across space and time, which complicates the task of developing general strategies for epidemic control. As illustrated in our study, this variability can be extreme even when the distances between locations are relatively small; the degree of variability highlights the dangers of treating human populations as culturally and biologically homogeneous. It is also clear from the analysis of the Labrador and Alaska experiences during the 1918 influenza pandemic that the nature of available resources, especially medical care and adequate food and housing, strongly influences the severity of diseases. The lessons from early 20th century Labrador and Alaska clearly illustrate how important it is to take a syndemic approach if we are to improve our understanding of the forces that determine the potential impact of future infectious disease epidemics in today's world.

REFERENCES CITED

Aaby, Peter, Abbas Bhuiya, Lutfun Nahar, Kim Knudsen, Andres de Francisco, and Michael Strong
    2003 The Survival Benefit of Measles Immunization May Not Be Explained Entirely by the Prevention of Measles Disease: A Community Study from Rural Bangladesh. International Journal of Epidemiology 32(1):106–115.
Aaby, Peter, Cesário L Martins, May-Lill Garly, Carlito Balé, Andreas Andersen, Amabelia Rodrigues, Henrik Ravn, Ida M Lisse, Christine S Benn, and Hilton C Whittle
    2010 Non-specific Effects of Standard Measles Vaccine at 4.5 and 9 Months of Age on Childhood Mortality: Randomised Controlled Trial. BMJ 341:c6495.
Aaby, Peter, Badara Samb, Francois Simondon, Awa M. C. Seck, Kim Knudsen, and Hilton Whittle
    1995 Non-specific Beneficial Effects of Measles Immunisation: Analysis of Mortality Studies from Developing Countries. BMJ 311(7003):481–485.
Ahmed, Rafi, Michael B. A. Oldstone, and Peter Palese
    2007 Protective Immunity and Susceptibility to Infectious Diseases: Lessons from the 1918 Influenza Pandemic. Nature Immunology 8(11):1188–1193.
Andreasen, Viggo, Cécile Viboud, and Lone Simonsen
    2008 Epidemiological Characterization of the 1918 Influenza Pandemic Summer Wave in Copenhagen: Implications for Pandemic Control. Journal of Infectious Diseases 197(2):270–278.
Barry, John M., Cécile Viboud, and Lone Simonsen
    2009 Cross-Protection Between Successive Waves of the 1918–1919 Influenza Pandemic: Epidemiological Evidence from US Army Camps and from Britain. Journal of Infectious Diseases 198(10): 1427–1434.
Brewer, Francis
    1919 Spotted Islands—Summer, 1918. Among the Deep Sea Fishers 16(4):171–172.
Budgell, Anne
    1994 The Spanish Influenza of 1918 in Okak and Hebron, Labrador. Archived manuscript, Center for Newfoundland Studies, Memorial University of Newfoundland, St. John's, NL.
Centers for Disease Control and Prevention (CDC)
    2009a Deaths Related to 2009 Pandemic Influenza A (H1N1) among American Indian/Alaska Natives— 12 States. Morbidity and Mortality Weekly Report 58(48):1341–1344.

2009b Serum Cross-Reactive Antibody Response to a Novel Influenza A (H1N1) Virus After Vaccination with Seasonal Influenza Vaccine. Morbidity and Mortality Weekly Report 58(19):521–524.

Charania, Nadia A., and Leonard J. S. Tsuji

2011a The 2009 H1N1 Pandemic Response in Remote First Nation Communities of Subarctic Ontario: Barriers and Improvements from a Health Care Service Perspective. International Journal of Circumpolar Health 70(5):564–575.

2011b Government Bodies and Their Influence on the 2009 H1N1 Health Sector Pandemic Response in Remote and Isolated First Nation Communities of Sub-Arctic Ontario, Canada. Rural and Remote Health 11(3):1781. http://www.rrh.org.au/articles/subviewnthamer.asp?ArticleID=1781, accessed June 1, 2013.

Corbett, Helen D., and Susanne M. Swibold

2000 The Aleuts of the Pribilof Islands, Alaska. *In* Endangered Peoples of the Arctic: Struggles to Survive and Thrive. Milton M. R. Freeman, ed. Pp. 1–16. Westport, CT: Greenwood Press.

Crosby, Alfred W.

1989 America's Forgotten Pandemic: The Influenza of 1918. Cambridge: Cambridge University Press.

Cuff, Robert H.

1994 Settlers. *In* Encyclopedia of Newfoundland and Labrador, Volume 5. Cyril F. Poole, ed. Pp. 142–143. St. John's, NL: Harry Cuff Publications Limited.

Desjeux, Phillipe, and Jorge Alvar

2003 *Leishmania*/HIV Co-infections: Epidemiology in Europe. Annals of Tropical Medicine and Parasitology 97(Suppl. 1):S3–S15.

Draper, Harold H.

1977 The Aboriginal Eskimo Diet in Modern Perspective. American Anthropologist 79(2):309–316.

Fraser, Christophe, Christl A. Donnelly, Simon Cauchemez, William P. Hanage, Maria D. Van Kerkhove, T. Déirdre Hollingsworth, Jamie Griffin, Rebecca F. Baggaley, Helen E. Jenkins, Emily J. Lyons, Thibaut Jombart, Wes R. Hinsley, Nicholas C. Grassly, Francois Balloux, Azra C. Ghani, Neil M Ferguson, Andrew Rambaut, Oliver G. Pybus, Hugo Lopez-Gatell, Celia M Alpuche-Aranda, Ietza Bojorquez Chapela, Ethel Palacios Zavala, Dulce Ma. Espejo Guevara, Francesco Checchi, Erika Garcia, Stephane Hugonnet, Cathy Roth, and The WHO Rapid Pandemic Assessment Collaboration

2009 Pandemic Potential of a Strain of Influenza A (H1N1): Early Findings. Science 324(5934):1557–1561.

Fraser, Cristophe, Derek A. T. Cummings, Don Klinkenberg, Donald S. Burke, and Neil M. Ferguson

2011 Influenza Transmission in Households During the 1918 Pandemic. American Journal of Epidemiology 174(5):505–514.

Ganley, Matt L.

1998 The Dispersal of the 1918 Influenza Virus on the Seward Peninsula, Alaska: An Ethnohistoric Reconstruction. International Journal of Circumpolar Health 57(Suppl. 1):247–251.

Goggin, Leigh S., Dale Caricone, Donna B. Mak, Gary K. Dowse, Carolien M. Giele, David W. Smith, and Paul V. Effer

2011 Chronic Disease and Hospitalisation For Pandemic (H1N1) 2009 Influenza in Indigenous and Non-Indigenous Western Australians. Communicable Diseases Intelligence 35(2):172–176.

Grenfell, Wilfred T.

1895 Vikings of To-day. Or Life and Medical Work among the Fishermen of Labrador. London: Marshall Brothers.

Hancock, Kathy, Vic Veguilla, Xiuhua Lu, Weimin Zhong, Eboneé N. Butler, Hong Sun, Feng Liu, Libo Dong, Joshua R. DeVos, Paul M. Gargiullo, T. Lynnette Brammer, Nancy J. Cox, Terrence M. Tumpey, and Jacqueline M. Katz

2009 Cross-Reactive Antibody Responses to the 2009 Pandemic H1N1 Influenza Virus. New England Journal of Medicine 361(20):1945–1952.

Hanrahan, Maura

2008 Tracing Social Change among the Labrador Inuit and Inuit-Métis: What Does the Nutrition Literature Tell Us? Food, Culture and Society: An International Journal of Multidisciplinary Research 11(3):315–333.

Hartgers, Franca C., Benedicta B. Obeng, Daniel Boakye, and Maria Yazdanbakhsh

    2008 Immune Responses During Helminth-Malaria Co-infection: A Pilot Study in Ghanaian Schoolchildren. Parasitology 135(Special Issue 07):855–860.

Helferty, Melissa, Julie Vachon, Jill Tarasuk, Rachel Rodin, John Spika, and Louise Pelletier

    2010 Incidence of Hospital Admission and Severe Outcomes During the First and Second Waves of Pandemic (H1N1) 2009. CMAJ 182(18):1981–1987.

Herring, D. Ann

    1994 "There Were Young People and Old People and Babies Dying Every Week": The 1918–1919 Influenza Pandemic at Norway House. Ethnohistory 41(1):73–105.

Herring, D. Ann, and Janet Padiak

    2008 The Geographical Epicentre of the 1918 Influenza Pandemic. In Proceedings of the Eighth Annual Conference of the British Association for Biological Anthropology and Osteoarchaeology. Megan Brickley and Martin Smith, eds. Pp. 1–8. BAR International Series, 1743. London: Archaeopress.

Herring, D. Ann, and Lisa Sattenspiel

    2007 Social Context, Syndemics, and Infectious Diseases in Northern Aboriginal Populations. American Journal of Human Biology 19(2):190–202.

Hettasch, Paul

    1986 [1918] Letter to the British Mission Board, November 15, 1918. Them Days 11(3):34.

Ikonen, Niina, Mari Strengell, Leena Kinnunen, Pamela Österlund, Jaana Pirhonen, Mia Broman, Irja Davidkin, Thedi Ziegler, and Ilkka Julkunen

    2010 High Frequency of Cross-reacting Antibodies Against 2009 Pandemic Influenza A(H1N1) Virus Among the Elderly in Finland. Eurosurveillance 15(5):pii=19478. http://www.eurosurveillance.org/ViewArticle.aspx?ArticleId=19478, accessed June 1, 2013.

Itoh, Yasushi, Kyoko Shinya, Maki Kiso, Tokiko Watanabe, Yoshihiro Sakoda, Masato Hatta, Yukiko Muramoto, Daisuke Tamura, Yuko Sakai-Tagawa, Takeshi Noda, Saori Sakabe, Masaki Imai, Yasuko Hatta, Shinji Watanabe, Chengjun Li, Shinya Yamada, Ken Fujii, Shin Murakami, Hirotaka Imai, Satoshi Kakugawa, Mutsumi Ito, Ryo Takano, Kiyoko Iwatsuki-Horimoto, Masayuki Shimojima, Taisuke Horimoto, Hideo Goto, Kei Takahashi, Akiko Makino, Hirohito Ishigaki, Misako Nakayama, Masatoshi Okamatsu, Kazuo Takahashi, David Warshauer, Peter A. Shult, Reiko Saito, Hiroshi Suzuki, Yousuke Furuta, Makoto Yamashita, Keiko Mitamura, Kunio Nakano, Morio Nakamura, Rebecca Brockman-Schneider, Hiroshi Mitamura, Masahiko Yamazaki, Norio Sugaya, M. Suresh, Makoto Ozawa, Gabriele Neumann, James Gern, Hiroshi Kida, Kazumasa Ogasawara, and Yoshihiro Kawaoka

    2009 In Vitro and In Vivo Characterization of the New Swine-Origin H1N1 Influenza Viruses. Nature 460(7258):1021–1025.

Johnson, Frank C.

    1919 Spotted Islands Station, 1919. Among the Deep Sea Fishers 17(3):83–85.

Johnson, Niall P. A. S., and Juergen Mueller

    2002 Updating the Accounts: Global Mortality of the 1918–1920 "Spanish" Influenza Pandemic. Bulletin of the History of Medicine 76(1):105–115.

Kennedy, John C.

    1995 People of the Bays and Headlands: Anthropological History and the Fate of Communities in Unknown Labrador. Toronto: University of Toronto Press.

    1996 Labrador Village. Prospect Heights, IL: Waveland.

Korenromp, Eline L., Brian G. Williams, Sake J. de Vlas, Eleanor Gouws, Charles F. Gilks, Peter D. Ghys, and Bernard L. Nahlen

    2005 Malaria Attributable to the HIV-1 Epidemic, Sub-Saharan Africa. Emerging Infectious Diseases 11(9):1410–1419.

Kristensen, Ines, Peter Aaby, and Henrik Jensen

    2000 Routine Vaccinations and Child Survival: Follow Up Study in Guinea-Bissau, West Africa. BMJ 321(7274):1435–1438.

La Ruche, Guy, Arnaud Tarantola, Philippe Barboza, Laëtitia Vaillant, Juliette Gueguen, and Marc Gastellu-Etchegorry

    2009 The 2009 Pandemic H1N1 Influenza and Indigenous Populations of the Americas and the Pacific. Eurosurveillance 14(42):pii=19366. http://www.eurosurveillance.org/ViewArticle.aspx?ArticleId=19366, accessed June 1, 2013.

Lautaret, Ronald L.

    1986 Alaska's Greatest Disaster. The 1918 Spanish Influenza Epidemic. The Alaska Journal. History and Arts of the North 16:238–243. Anchorage, Alaska: Alaska Northwest Publishing Company.

Leacock, Eleanor B., and Nan A. Rothschild, eds.

    1994 Labrador Winter: The Ethnographic Journals of William Duncan Strong, 1927–1928. Washington, DC: Smithsonian Institution Press.

Littleton, Judith, and Julie Park

    2009 Tuberculosis and Syndemics: Implications for Pacific Health in New Zealand. Social Science and Medicine 69(11):1674–1680.

Mamelund, Svenn-Erik

    2003 Spanish Influenza Mortality of Ethnic Minorities in Norway 1918–1919. European Journal of Population 19(1):83–102.

    2011 Geography May Explain Adult Mortality from the 1918–20 Influenza Pandemic. Epidemics 3(1):46–60.

Mamelund, Svenn-Erik, Lisa Sattenspiel, and Jessica Dimka

    2013 Influenza-associated Mortality During the 1918–19 Influenza Pandemic in Alaska and Labrador: A Comparison. Social Science History37(2): 177–229.

Mathews, John D., Emma S. McBryde, Jodie McVernon, Paul K. Pallaghy, and James M. McCaw

    2010 Prior Immunity Helps to Explain Wave-like Behaviour of Pandemic Influenza in 1918–19. BMC Infectious Diseases 10:128.

McCullers, Jonathan A.

    2006 Insights into the Interaction Between Influenza Virus and Pneumococcus. Clinical Microbiology Reviews 19(3):571–582.

McCullers, Jonathan A., and Jerold E. Rehg

    2002 Lethal Synergism between Influenza Virus and *Streptococcus pneumoniae*: Characterization of a Mouse Model and the Role of Platelet-Activating Factor Receptor. Journal of Infectious Diseases 186(3):341–350.

Miller, Elizabeth, Katja Hoschler, Pia Hardelid, Elaine Stanford, Nick Andrews, and Maira Zambon

    2010 Incidence of 2009 Pandemic Influenza A H1N1 Infection in England: A Cross-sectional Serological Study. Lancet 375(9720):1100–1108.

Moody, William R.

    1905 With Dr. Grenfell on the Labrador. Record of Christian Work 24(12):985–994.

Morens, David M., Jeffery K. Taubenberger, and Anthony S. Fauci.

    2008 Predominant Role of Bacterial Pneumonia as a Cause of Death in Pandemic Influenza: Implications for Pandemic Influenza Preparedness. Journal of Infectious Diseases 198(7):962–970.

Muir, Ethel Gordon

    1918 "The Diana" and Battle Harbor Hospital. Among the Deep Sea Fishers 16(3):103–105.

Newfoundland. House of Assembly

    1910 Report of the Registrar General of Births Marriages and Deaths for the Year Ended December 31st, 1909. Journal of the House of Assembly of Newfoundland 1910:475–486.

    1911 Annual Report of the Registrar General of Births Marriages and Deaths for the Year Ended December 31st, 1910. Journal of the House of Assembly of Newfoundland 1911:567–578.

    1912 Annual Report of the Registrar General of Births Marriages and Deaths for the Year Ended December 31st, 1911. Journal of the House of Assembly of Newfoundland 1912:559–570.

    1915 Annual Report of the Registrar General of Births Marriages and Deaths for the Year Ended December 31st, 1914. Journal of the House of Assembly of Newfoundland 1915:813–825.

    1916 Annual Report of the Registrar General of Births Marriages and Deaths for the Year Ended December 31st, 1915. Journal of the House of Assembly of Newfoundland 1916:659–671.

1917 Annual Report of the Registrar General of Births Marriages and Deaths for the Year Ended December 31st, 1916. Journal of the House of Assembly of Newfoundland 1917:485–497.

1918 Annual Report of the Registrar General of Births Marriages and Deaths for the Year Ended December 31st, 1917. Journal of the House of Assembly of Newfoundland 1918:633–646.

1919 Annual Report of the Registrar General of Births Marriages and Deaths for the Year Ended December 31st, 1918. Journal of the House of Assembly of Newfoundland 1919:759–771.

1920 Annual Report of the Registrar General of Births Marriages and Deaths for the Year Ended Dec. 31st, 1919. Journal of the House of Assembly of Newfoundland 1920:677–695.

1921 Annual Report of the Registrar General of Births Marriages and Deaths for the Year Ended December 31st, 1920. Journal of the House of Assembly of Newfoundland 1921:585–597.

1922 Annual Report of the Registrar General of Births Marriages and Deaths for the Year Ended Dec. 31st, 1921. Journal of the House of Assembly of Newfoundland 1922:179–191.

1923 Annual Report of the Registrar General of Births Marriages and Deaths for the Year Ended Dec. 31st, 1922. Journal of the House of Assembly of Newfoundland 1923:269–281.

1924 Annual Report of the Registrar General of Births Marriages and Deaths for the Year Ended Dec. 31st, 1923. Journal of the House of Assembly of Newfoundland 1924:497–511.

Newfoundland and Labrador Death Records
1918–1919 Death Records, Reels 32 and 33. Provincial Archives of Newfoundland and Labrador, St. John's, NL.

Nilsson, Anna, and Francesca Chiodi
2011 Measles Outbreak in Africa—Is There a Link to the HIV-1 Epidemic? PLoS Pathogens 7(2):e1001241.

Noymer, Andrew
2009 Testing the Influenza–Tuberculosis Selective Mortality Hypothesis with Union Army Data. Social Science & Medicine 68(9):1599–1608.

2011 The 1918 Influenza Pandemic Hastened the Decline of Tuberculosis in the United States: An Age, Period, Cohort Analysis. Vaccine 29(Suppl. 2):B38-B41.

Paddon, Harry L.
1919a Emily Beaver Chamberlin Hospital: Winter 1918–19. Among the Deep Sea Fishers 17(3):80–83.

1919b The Orphaned Children of Labrador and Their Prospects. Among the Deep Sea Fishers 17(3): 94–95.

Ronald, Rompkey, ed.
2003 The Labrador Memoir of Dr. Harry Paddon, 1912–1938. Montreal: McGill-Queen's University Press.

Palmer, Craig T., Lisa Sattenspiel, and Chris Cassidy
2007 Boats, Trains, and Immunity: The Spread of the Spanish Influenza on the Island of Newfoundland. Newfoundland and Labrador Studies 22(2):473–504.

Parsons, Charles E.
1919 Battle Harbor Hospital. Summer, 1918. Among the Deep Sea Fishers 17(1):10–12.

Perrett, Walter W.
1986a [1918] Letter to the British Mission Board, November 22, 1918. Them Days 11(3):35–36.

1986b [1919] The Superintendent's Report to the S. F. G. Them Days 11(3):38–42.

Philip, R. N., and D. B. Lackman
1962 Observations on the Present Distributions of Influenza A/Swine Antibodies Among Alaskan Natives Relative to the Occurrence of Influenza 1918–1919. American Journal of Hygiene 75(3):322–334.

Pritzker, Barry M.
2000 A Native American Encyclopedia: History, Culture, and Peoples. Oxford: Oxford University Press.

Sánchez, María S., James O. Lloyd-Smith, Brian G. Williams, Travis C. Porco, Sadie J. Ryan, Martien W. Borgdorff, John Mansoer, Christopher Dye, and Wayne M. Getz
2009 Incongruent HIV and Tuberculosis Co-dynamics in Kenya: Interacting Epidemics Monitor Each Other. Epidemics 1(1):14–20.

Sattenspiel, Lisa
2011 Regional Patterns of Mortality During the 1918 Influenza Pandemic in Newfoundland. Vaccine 29(Suppl. 2):B33–B37.

Schaaf, Jeanne, and Thetus Smith, eds.

    1996 Ublasaun, First Light: Inupiaq Hunters and Herders in the Early Twentieth Century, Northern Seward Peninsula, Alaska. Anchorage, AK: Interior Department, National Park Service, Alaska Support Office, Alaska Region, Shared Beringian Heritage Program.

Shanks, G. Dennis, Alison MacKenzie, Ruth Mclaughlin, Michael Waller, Peter Dennis, Seung-eun Lee, and John F. Brundage

    2010 Mortality Risk Factors During the 1918–1919 Influenza Pandemic in the Australian Army. Journal of Infectious Diseases 201(12):1880–1889.

Silva, Diego S.

    2010 H1N1 Influenza: Global Pandemic, Global Vulnerabilities. Health Science Inquiry 1(1):31–32.

Singer, Merrill

    2009 Introduction to Syndemics: A Critical Systems Approach to Public and Community Health. San Francisco: Jossey-Bass.

    2010 Pathogen-Pathogen Interaction: A Syndemic Model of Complex Biosocial Processes in Disease. Virulence 1(1):10–18.

Singer, Merrill, and Scott Clair

    2003 Syndemics and Public Health: Reconceptualizing Disease in Bio-social Context. Medical Anthropology Quarterly 17(4):423–441.

Singer, Merrill C., Pamela I. Erickson, Louise Badiane, Rosemary Diaz, Dugeidy Ortiz, Traci Abraham, and Anna Marie Nicolaysen

    2006 Syndemics, Sex and the City: Understanding Sexually Transmitted Diseases in Social and Cultural Context. Social Science and Medicine 63(8):2010–2021.

Sørup, Signe, Marie Villumsen, Henrik Ravn, Christine Stabell Benn, Thorkild I. A. Sørensen, Peter Aaby, Tine Jess, and Adam Roth

    2011 Smallpox Vaccination and All-Cause Infectious Disease Hospitalization: A Danish Register-based Cohort Study. International Journal of Epidemiology 40(4):955–963.

Tanner, Vaino A.

    1944 Outlines of the Geography, Life, and Customs of Newfoundland-Labrador. (the Eastern Part of the Labrador Peninsula). Cambridge: Cambridge University Press.

Trauer, James M., Karen L. Laurie, Joseph McDonnell, Anne Kelso, and Peter G. Markey.

    2011 Differential Effects of Pandemic (H1N1) 2009 on Remote and Indigenous Groups, Northern Territory, Australia, 2009. Emerging Infectious Diseases 17(9):1615–1623.

Weinstein, Raymond S., Michael M. Weinstein, Kenneth Alibek, Michael I. Bukrinsky, and Beda Brichacek

    2010 Significantly Reduced CCR5-tropic HIV-1 Replication in vitro in Cells from Subjects Previously Immunized with Vaccinia Virus. BMC Immunology 11:23.

Wenger, Jay D., Louisa J. Castrodale, Dana L. Bruden, James W. Keck, Tammy Zulu, Michael G. Bruce, Donna A. Feary, Joe McLaughlin, Debby Hurlburt, Kim Boyd Hummel, Sassa Kitka, Steve Bently, Timothy K. Thomas, Rosalyn Singleton, John T. Redd, Larry Lane, James E. Cheek, and Thomas W. Hennessy

    2011 2009 Pandemic Influenza A H1N1 in Alaska: Temporal and Geographic Characteristics of Spread and Increased Risk of Hospitalization among Alaska Native and Asian/Pacific Islander People. Clinical Infectious Diseases 52(Suppl. 1):S189–S197.

Wilson, Nick, Lucy T. Barnard, Jennifer A. Summers, G. Dennis Shanks, and Michael G. Baker

    2012 Differential Mortality Rates by Ethnicity in 3 Influenza Pandemics Over a Century, New Zealand. Emerging Infectious Diseases 18(1):71–77.

Wolfe, Robert J.

    1982 Alaska's Great Sickness, 1900: An Epidemic of Measles and Influenza in a Virgin Soil Population. Proceedings of the American Philosophical Society 126(2):91–121.

Zarychanski, Ryan, Tammy L. Stuart, Anand Kumar, Steve Doucette, Lawrence Elliott, Joel Kettner, and Frank Plummer

    2010 Correlates of Severe Disease in Patients with 2009 Pandemic Influenza (H1N1) Virus Infection. CMAJ 182(3):257–264.

AUTHORS' BIOSKETCHES

Edgar A. Amador, M.A., is a Ph.D. candidate at the University of South Florida. He is a biocultural anthropologist with research interests in biocultural adaptability, psychosocial stress, poverty, nutrition, food security, acculturation, immigration, globalization, and economic anthropology. He has conducted research on community development, education reform, the effectiveness of health interventions, and economic change in the United States and Costa Rica. He is currently working on his dissertation on human adaptability to urban poverty and food insecurity in Tampa, Florida.

Julie A. Baldwin, Ph.D., is a Professor in the Department of Community and Family Health in the USF College of Public Health. Her areas of specialization include HIV/AIDS prevention and Native American populations.

Nicola Bulled, Ph.D., M.P.H., is a Lecturer in Anthropology at Tufts University. Previously, she served as an epidemiologist with the Massachusetts Department of Public Health. Dr. Bulled has recently completed a study of biocommunicability and the political economy of HIV/AIDS risk among emergent adults in Lesotho in southern Africa. Her work on syndemics includes publication of an analysis of the role of syringes in dual disease transmission. Her broader interests include health and the internet, HIV prevention, and critical medical anthropology.

Isabella Chan is a Master student in the Dual Medical Anthropology/Public Health program at USF.

Rosina Cianelli, Ph.D., M.P.H., R.N., F.A.A.N., a nurse midwife with over 20 years' experience working with Chilean women and their families, is currently an Associate Professor at the University of Miami School of Nursing and Health Studies. Dr. Cianelli completed a Ph.D. in Nursing at the University of Illinois at Chicago. She also studied at Pontificia Universidad Catolica de Chile, earning a BSN in nurse midwifery and later serving as a professor in the Escuela de Enfermería. Dr. Cianelli completed a Master of Public Health at the Universidad de Chile. Her clinical specialty is midwifery. She teaches and conducts research in women's health, health disparities, and international health. Dr. Cianelli also studies HIV prevention and was the recipient of a Fogarty AIDS International Training and Research traineeship at the University of Illinois, Chicago.

Jessica Eddy is a researcher at Center for Health, Identity, Behavior and Prevention Studies (CHIBPS).

Margaret Everett, Ph.D., is Dean of Graduate Studies and Professor of Sociology at Portland State University. A medical anthropologist, her research interests include health promotion, nutrition and chronic disease prevention in Mexico and among Latino communities in Oregon. Recent projects include a diabetes study in Oaxaca, Mexico, community-based participatory research with Latinos in Oregon, and a study of urban Pentecostal groups in Mexico.

ANNALS OF ANTHROPOLOGICAL PRACTICE 36.2, pp. 422–427. ISSN: 2153-957X. © 2013 by the American Anthropological Association. DOI:10.1111/napa.12012

Rafael Perez Figueroa is a post-doctoral fellow at CHIBPS.

Aubrey L. Florom-Smith, Ph.D.(c), R.N., is a doctoral student, NIH/NINR Predoctoral Fellow, and a Jonas Nurse Leader Scholar at the University of Miami School of Nursing and Health Studies. Ms. Florom-Smith's research interests include the prevention of HIV/AIDS and intertwined conditions such as stigma, mental health, and risk behaviors, the development of culturally tailored interventions, and the elimination of health disparities among marginalized groups. Ms. Florom-Smith is a member of Sigma Theta Tau International and the Association of Nurses in AIDS Care.

Rosa M. Gonzalez-Guarda, Ph.D., M.P.H., R.N., C.P.H., is an Assistant Professor at the University of Miami School of Nursing and Health Studies and the codirector of the Research Training and Education Core of the Center of Excellence for Health Disparities Research: El Centro which is funded through the National Institute of Minority Health and Health Disparities. Dr. Gonzalez-Guarda has worked on community health nursing and public health programs and research targeting Hispanics and other health disparity populations in the United States, Latin America, the Caribbean, and Europe. Her current research focuses on the intersection of substance abuse, intimate partner violence, and risky sexual behaviors among Hispanics and the development of culturally tailored interventions to address these. She is currently the principal investigator of a community-based participatory research study funded by the Robert Wood Johnson Foundation Nurse Faculty Scholars Program that aims to develop and pilot test a teen dating violence prevention program for Hispanic families.

Perry N. Halkitis is Professor of Applied Psychology and Public Health (Steinhardt School), and Population Health (Langone School of Medicine), Director of the CHIBPS, and Associate Dean at New York University. The team at CHIBPS envisions, develops, and enacts research with and for the communities we study.

Melvin Hampton is a Counseling Psychology doctoral student and Research Assistants at CHIBPS.

David A. Himmelgreen, Ph.D., is a Professor in Anthropology at the University of South Florida. He is a biocultural anthropologist with expertise in maternal and child health focusing on nutrition, growth and development, food insecurity, HIV/AIDS prevention, the nutrition transition, and migrant health. Himmelgreen has conducted research in Lesotho, Costa Rica, the United States, and India. He recently completed a three-year NSF supported longitudinal project on tourism and changes in lifestyle, diet, and nutritional health in the Monteverde zone of Costa Rica. He is the codirector of an NSF REU field school for training students in community health in the same region, and is the coeditor of the Annals of Anthropological Practice and an associate editor of Ecology of Food and Nutrition.

Nolan Kline, M.A., is completing his doctoral research in the Department of Anthropology, University of South Florida. His research interests include migrant health, social inequalities and healthcare disparities, political economy of health, structural violence and health, social determinants of health, health syndemics, biopower and technologies of biological governance, critical medical anthropology, faith-based organizations as healthcare providers, and Moroccan and Latin American immigration to Spain.

Sandra Kupprat is a Counseling Psychology doctoral students and Research Assistants at CHIBPS.

Celia Lescano, Ph.D., is a Research Associate Professor in the Department of Mental Health Law and Policy at USF. Her research focuses on health disparities and HIV among Latino families.

Judith Littleton is Associate Professor of Biological Anthropology in the Department of Anthropology, The University of Auckland. Her areas of research include biocultural perspectives on health, political ecology, and human osteology. She has worked with Julie Park since 2002 on the study of tuberculosis in contemporary New Zealand using TB as a lens into local ecological networks of infectious disease. Their current project is Transnational Pacific Health through the lens of tuberculosis and diabetes and encompasses both historical and contemporary studies. Her other main research project involves collaboration with Aboriginal communities from South Australia on the analysis of prehistoric health and diet.

Svenn-Erik Mamelund holds a Ph.D. in demography and is a Senior Advisor at the Norwegian Institute of Public Health. His areas of research include the impact of seasonal and pandemic influenza on health, mortality, and fertility, as well as the effect of attitudes and demographic predictors on influenza vaccine use. Recent articles include "Geography May Explain Adult Mortality from the 1918–20 Influenza Pandemic" (*Epidemics* 3(1):46–60; 2011) and "Vaccine history, gender and influenza vaccination in a household context" (*Vaccine* 29(51): 9441–9450; 2011).

Brian McCabe, Ph.D., is a Research Assistant Professor at the School of Nursing and Health Studies at the University of Miami. He received his Ph.D. in Counseling Psychology from the University of Miami Department of Education and Psychological Studies in 2011. He has an M.S. in Community Counseling and an Ed.S. in Mental Health Counseling from Indiana University, and completed a Psychology Internship at the VA Ann Arbor HealthCare System/University of Michigan. He teaches courses on statistical analysis for the health care and the social and behavioral sciences. His research focuses on the etiology and treatment of mental health and substance use disorders, health disparities in substance use, and mental health disorder incidence and interventions, longitudinal analysis methods for randomized clinical trials, and the influence of culture on psychological measurement.

Tekaai Nelesone is a Medical Officer working for the Ministry of Health of the Government of Cook Islands since mid–2008. He is currently managing a peripheral hospital in one of the outer islands called Atiu with the support of nine other health care providers. He has a background in clinical health and public health, and was involved in TB clinical work and helminth research in Tuvalu from 2001 to 2005. His interests include determining whether or not a reliable followup system in a small health setting can produce good health outcomes with the delayed onset of diabetic complications such as retinopathy and neuropathy.

Danielle Ompad is Research Associate Professor in the Department of Nutrition, Food Studies and Public Health and a research affiliate at CHIBPS. CHIBPS advances research and knowledge to improve the lives of those affected with or by HIV, substance abuse and mental health burden through the rigorous application of social science and public health research paradigms.

Bayla Ostrach, M.A., is a doctoral student and founding member of the Medical Anthropology Forum at the University of Connecticut and a Society of Family Planning Junior Fellow. Ms. Ostrach's research interests include obstacles to reproductive healthcare, health policy, Medicaid, and other health systems, Critical Medical Anthropology, syndemics, health disparities, and applied advocacy work using research findings to improve healthcare accessibility. Ms. Ostrach is currently completing her doctoral fieldwork in Catalunya, investigating access to publicly funded abortion in the wake of recent policy changes.

Cynthia Pace, M.P.H., has conducted research in Brazil and Costa Rica on topics of child nutrition, public health, and physical activity in elderly populations. She is pursuing her Ph.D. in the applied anthropology program at the University of South Florida. Pace will be conducting doctoral research to examine the direct and indirect health impacts of the Belo Monte Dam construction upon ribeirinho communities along the Xingu River in the Brazilian Amazon.

Wilson Palacios, Ph.D., is an Associate Professor in the Department of Criminology at USF, and a visiting Associate Researcher Scientist at the Center for Interdisciplinary Research on AIDS at Yale University.

Julie Park is a Professor of Social Anthropology in the Department of Anthropology, The University of Auckland. She has research interests in New Zealand society, Polynesia, and health and illness. In addition to her work with the Transnational Pacific Health project she is in the final stages of a book based on long-term research with people with hemophilia in New Zealand. She collaborates on a project with Otago University colleagues and students investigating moral reasoning at the intersection of genetic difference and reproductive technologies, and is a coeditor with S. Trnka and C. Dureau of Senses and Citizenships: Embodying Political Life (Routledge 2013).

Nilda (Nena) P. Peragallo, Dr. P.H., R.N., F.A.A.N., is Professor and Dean at the University of Miami's School of Nursing and Health Studies. She has an extensive background in health promotion, health disparities research, and the development and testing of interventions to reduce HIV sexual risk among Latino women. Dr. Peragallo has been the Principal Investigator in several NIH-, CDC- and OAS-funded studies. She is currently the PI of the National Institute of Minority Health and Health Disparities Center of Excellence for Hispanic Health Disparities Research (El Centro) and Director of the Pan American Health Organization/World Health Organization Collaborating Center for Nursing Human Resources.

Melanie Rock, Ph.D., is Associate Professor and Alberta Innovates—Population Health Investigator Director, Population Health Intervention Research Centre, Institute for Public Health, University of Calgary. Her research interests include medical anthropology, ethnographic research, science and technology studies, health promotion, diabetes, and animal–human studies.

Nancy Romero-Daza, Ph.D., is an Associate Professor in the Department of Anthropology at the University of South Florida. She is a medical anthropologist with specialization in HIV/AIDS research among minority populations. Romero-Daza has conducted research in Lesotho, the United States, and Costa Rica, and also has experience in the delivery and evaluation of HIV-related interventions. Along with David Himmelgreen (USF) Romero-Daza has recently received funding through the National Science Foundation Research Experience for Undergraduates to train anthropology and environmental engineering students in the use of cross disciplinary methods for the conduct of community-based health-related research in rural Costa Rica.

Lisa Sattenspiel is a Professor of Anthropology at the University of Missouri. Recent research involves collection of archival data and computer simulation of the 1918–19 influenza pandemic in Newfoundland and Labrador. She published *The Geographic Spread of Infectious Diseases: Models and Applications* in 2009. Her articles include "Boats, trains, and immunity: the spread of the Spanish influenza on the island of Newfoundland" (*Newfoundland and Labrador Studies* 22(2):473–504; 2007) and "Regional patterns of mortality during the 1918 influenza pandemic in Newfoundland" (*Vaccine* 29S:B33-B37; 2011).

Merrill Singer, Ph.D., is a Professor in the Departments of Anthropology and Community Medicine, and a Senior Research Scientist at Center for Health, Intervention and Prevention at the University of Connecticut. Over his career, his research and writing have focused on HIV/AIDS in highly vulnerable and disadvantaged populations, illicit drug use and drinking behavior, community and structural violence, health disparities, and the political ecology of health. Dr. Singer has published over 250 articles and book chapters and has authored or edited 24 books. He is a recipient of the Rudolph Virchow Prize, the George Foster Memorial Award for Practicing Anthropology, the AIDS and Anthropology Paper Prize, the Prize for Distinguished Achievement in the Critical Study of North America, and the Solon T. Kimball Award for Public and Applied Anthropology from the American Anthropological Association.

Mackenzie Tewell is a recent graduate from the dual Master degree program in Anthropology and Public Health at USF.

David Tilley is a doctorate student in the College of Public Health.

Amber L. Vermeesch, Ph.D., M.S.N., F.N.P.C., R.N., is an Assistant Professor at Michigan State University College of Nursing. She was a Research Assistant of SEPA II, an HIV risk reduction efficacy trial for Hispanic women, which provided the baseline data for this study. Her research focuses on identifying exercise motivators and barriers among Latinas and the development of culturally tailored programs to increase their exercise rates. She is interested in the use of participatory photography and the role of acculturation and exercise. Her current research focuses on determining the generalizability of exercise motivators and barriers identified in South Florida among Latinas living in Michigan.

Josef N. Wieland is a Ph.D. student in Anthropology at the University of California, Irvine specializing Anthropologies of Medicine, Science, and Technology. He has worked with food sovereignty programs in Oaxaca, Mexico, and on projects addressing the social determinants of Latino health in Portland, Oregon, and Santa Ana, California. Josef's present work focuses on knowledge and value transformation by looking simultaneously at semiprecious gemstone mining in Brazil and crystal healing practices in the western United States.

Heather J. Williamson is a doctoral student in the College of Public Health, University of South Florida.